The Uncertain Promise of Law
Lessons from Bhopal

With the possible exception of the Chernobyl nuclear accident, the world's worst industrial disaster occurred in December 1984, when a massive explosion and discharge of poisonous gas from Union Carbide's pesticide factory in Bhopal, India, killed over 2,500 people. Hundreds more have since died and many thousands were injured. In this book Jamie Cassels traces the origins of the Bhopal tragedy and examines the legal aftermath and global implications. The inability of the law to prevent or cope with such a catastrophe is exposed in the story of how the victims struggled for compensation and justice and how the lawsuit they initiated turned out to be a second tragedy. In addition, Cassels illustrates how dangers are posed by hazardous substances and facilities because of the kind of decision-making prevalent in the political and economic context of industrial production in the developing world.

The disaster gave rise to the world's largest lawsuit, one that wound its way half-way around the globe and dragged on for more than seven years. Although the final settlement satisfied the imperatives of the company and the Government of India, it was condemned by the victims. Cassels concludes, with the Supreme Court of India, that in a time of exploding technology we cannot be satisfied entirely with the 'uncertain promises of law.' He suggests a number of fundamental reforms that must be forged if future Bhopals are to be prevented.

JAMIE CASSELS is Professor of Law, University of Victoria.

JAMIE CASSELS

The Uncertain
Promise of Law:
Lessons
from Bhopal

UNIVERSITY OF TORONTO PRESS
Toronto Buffalo London

© University of Toronto Press Incorporated 1993
Toronto Buffalo London
Printed in Canada

Reprinted 1996

ISBN 0-8020-2841-1 (cloth)
ISBN 0-8020-7722-6 (paper)

Printed on acid-free paper

Canadian Cataloguing in Publication Data

Cassels, Jamie
  The uncertain promise of law: lessons from Bhopal

  Includes index.
  ISBN 0-8020-2841-1 (bound) ISBN 0-8020-7722-6 (pbk.)

  1. Union Carbide Ltd. (India) – Trials, litigation, etc.
  2. Union Carbide Corporation – Trials, litigation, etc.
  3. India – trials, litigation, etc.
  4. Liability for hazardous substances pollution damages.
  5. Liability for industrial accidents – India.
  6. Disaster victims – India – Bhopal.
  7. Bhopal Union Carbide Plant Disaster, Bhopal, India, 1984.   I. Title.

  KF228.I53C38 1993   346.54038   C92-095656-4

This book has been published with the help of a grant from the
Social Science Federation of Canada, using funds provided by the
Social Sciences and Humanities Research Council of Canada.

To my parents, Marion and Walter

Contents

viii Contents

Preface

In December 1984, a massive explosion and discharge of lethal gas from the Union Carbide factory in Bhopal, India, killed more than 2,500 people. In the intervening years hundreds more have died, and many thousands remain injured or affected. With the possible exception of the Chernobyl nuclear explosion (the long-term effects of which are still unknown) the Bhopal disaster was the worst single-incident industrial catastrophe in history.

While the international memory of Bhopal faded in the intervening years, the suffering of the victims continued practically unabated. This suffering, and the victims' quest for justice, gave rise to the world's largest single lawsuit. This lawsuit turned out to be a second catastrophe for the victims. It wound its way halfway around the globe and dragged on for more than eight years. The complex legal issues were debated in courts at two levels in the United States, and then began a treacherous course through the Indian courts, proceeding from the District Court in Bhopal eventually to the Supreme Court of India. It resulted in a final settlement which, while satisfying the imperatives of the Union Carbide Corporation and the Government of India, was roundly condemned by the victims themselves.

This book describes the course of the Bhopal litigation. It examines the promises made by law to the victims of hazardous technologies and 'social progress,' and attempts to gauge the ability of the legal process to prevent such disasters or to repair the harm done. It concludes, as did the Supreme Court of India, that in an era of exploding technology we cannot yet be satisfied with the 'uncertain promises of law.'

Three questions organize the book's focus and format. The first is, how did Bhopal happen? What was the combination of human, technological, and legal failures that set the wheels in motion, leading almost inevitably to this catastrophe? Chapters 1 and 2 both analyse the specific conditions present at the Bhopal facility and locate these within the wider legal, political, and economic context of hazardous industrial production in the developing world.

The second question is, what is, and what should be, the response of law to the victims of the disaster? How does law set about controlling risks to human health and the environment and repairing the damage from 'mass-exposure torts'? Chapters 3 and 4 describe the challenges presented by a disaster of such proportions and suggest a number of relatively modest criteria against which the legal response can be measured. They draw on developments in England and North America to provide the legal background to the issues thrown up by the Bhopal case. These chapters describe existing approaches to toxic hazards and examine other examples of such litigation in order to illustrate how, even in the developed countries, the law frequently falters when confronted with the complex problems posed by modern forms of industrial and environmental harm.

Chapters 5–10 return to the story of the Bhopal litigation itself, describing the unique problems confronted by the victims and relating the story of their quest for justice over an eight-year period.

The final question is, of course, what can be learned from the Bhopal tragedy? Throughout the narrative, I seek to highlight the problems posed by a catastrophe of such magnitude, and to analyse both the successes and the failures of the Bhopal litigation itself. Significant among these (often representing both success and failure at the same time) were the consolidation of the claims by the Indian government; the attempt to pursue the action in the courts of the United States; the formulation of a principle of absolute liability for industrial hazards; the effort to develop a scheme for interim compensation for the victims; and, finally, the suggestion of a theory of enterprise liability by which a multinational corporation might be liable for the defaults of its subsidiaries. The concluding chapter summarizes the lessons to be learned, argues for the need to reorient our thinking about environmental and industrial hazards, and suggests some new directions.

I should admit from the outset that the analysis offered is couched in the context of considerable scepticism about the ability of both traditional litigative responses and the private law of tort to play a serious role in preventing such a tragedy, or to repair the human consequences once one has occurred. One might object, therefore, that, because of the disaster's magnitude and its unique political, economic, and cultural context, the Bhopal case too easily illustrates a preconceived conclusion. What I hope to demonstrate is that, while the Bhopal case may be a *vivid* illustration of the problem, it is neither unique nor peculiar. While the Bhopal disaster must be understood in the context of the relationship between multinationals and developing countries, it cannot be confined to that context. Toxic harm is not limited to countries of the developing world, and even the most developed legal systems have a long way to go before they can be said to have dealt with the problems. The problems faced by the Bhopal victims in their quest for justice were certainly magnified by reason of their socio-economic position and the limitations of Indian law. Yet these factors provide only a very partial explanation for what went wrong. Indeed, in many ways, the response of the Indian legal system to the plight of the Bhopal victims went well beyond what might have been expected in any other country. A foreign observer cannot help but be impressed by the dynamism of Indian law, and occasionally be excited by its promises. Yet, in the end, the Bhopal story is about the limitations of law; and, while the Indian legal system differs in important ways from Western systems, this story holds lessons for us all.

Acknowledgments

I owe numerous debts of gratitude to people in India, Canada, and the United States. Much of the research for this book was conducted in India, during a visit in 1985 and a four-month sabbatical leave in 1988, and on two subsequent occasions. This research was supported and aided by the Faculty of Law and the University of Victoria, and by the Social Sciences and Humanities Research Council. Among the many individuals and organizations in India who supplied me with valuable information, I owe special thanks to the Indian Law Institute in New Delhi, and to its staff, for providing me with research facilities on these occasions. Upendra Baxi has performed an invaluable public service by collecting much of the Bhopal documentation in three volumes published by the Institute. And, in Bhopal, I also owe a real debt to the chief and staff of the Bhopal Gas Tragedy Relief and Rehabilitation Department for their gracious on-site assistance. I hope that the critical analysis of the relief effort will not be read as a criticism of their personal effort and commitment.

I am also grateful to Dr David Dembo, of the Council on International and Public Affairs in New York, who generously and speedily provided me with many documents that could not easily be obtained elsewhere. Alison Brewin and Claire Tollefson afforded me valuable research assistance in Victoria, and Rosemary Garton the very best secretarial support. Judi Hoffman and Kim Hart Wensley helped greatly with final editing and proof-reading. Finally, numerous colleagues have read the manuscript at various times, offering their advice and assistance. Their greater expertise in many of the areas over which the manuscript ranges saved me from errors. Special thanks in this regard go to John McLaren,

Mark Gillen, Ted McDorman, Murray Rankin, and Maureen Maloney of the Faculty of Law, University of Victoria; and to Jim Irwin, Department of Economics, Central Michigan University. From Maureen Maloney especially I received the intellectual and personal support that made it possible to carry out this project.

THE UNCERTAIN PROMISE OF LAW:
LESSONS FROM BHOPAL

1

The Anatomy of a Disaster

A Night of Terror

Bhopal is the capital city of the state of Madhya Pradesh ('Middle Province') in central India. An ancient town, revitalized in the eighteenth century by an Afghan soldier of fortune, Bhopal now has a population of about 900,000 people. The city is dominated on two sides by the Shamla and Idgah hills. On the slope of the western hills stands the Taj-ul-Masjid, said to be one of the largest mosques in India, and to the south the 'Upper' and 'Lower' lakes border the newer part of the city. The new city contains modern government buildings and commercial establishments, green parkland, and the homes of the more affluent citizens of Bhopal. Beginning on the slope of the hills and extending northwards over a broad plane is the old city. Criss-crossed by dusty laneways lined with small shops and bursting with activity, the old town just barely contains its teeming market-places, mosques and temples, and burlap-covered shanty-town dwellings. Bordering the old city to the north is an industrial area, containing the bus station, the Straw Products factory, the hutment dwellings of thousands of poor daily-wage labourers, and the Union Carbide plant.

At about midnight on Sunday, 2 December 1984, there was a massive leak of toxic gas from storage tank number 610 of the Union Carbide plant. The lethal white vapour poured out of the tank for over two hours, blanketing the city for miles with a deadly fog. Thousands of people were killed in their sleep or as they fled in terror, and hundreds of thousands remain injured or affected to this day. This was the worst single-incident industrial accident in history. A respected Indian magazine described the scene:

An entire settlement was scampering out of their homes running southwest, towards the city centre without really knowing where to go or what to do. Many collapsed on the way, some for ever. Children vomited blood. Pregnant women stumbled and fell on the ground crying in pain and bleeding profusely. With the grey clouds of death chasing them their fear turned into panic. Relatives did not wait to pick up the bodies of those they loved and were alive only moments ago. Children got separated from their parents, husbands from their wives and brothers from their sisters, in the mad rush to run away from the clouds. Many were trampled to death. As a terrified and sick population moved forward, more people – the residents of neighbouring Chola Road, Tilla Jampalpura, Sindhi colony, Railway colony and Chandbad settlements – joined them. The resourceful and the affluent had already fled in whatever transport they could manage to secure. Only the poor were left behind.[1]

The Union Carbide plant in Bhopal manufactured pesticides and insecticides, including Sevin, which in turn is compounded from methyl isocyanate (MIC). The unit from which the gas escaped had been in operation for only four years. This chemical is known to be very dangerous; it is extremely volatile and highly toxic. It reacts easily and violently when contaminated or subjected to temperature variations. When inhaled in its gaseous form, it has horribly diverse effects on human beings, including pulmonary oedema, vomiting, nausea, blindness, and numerous forms of respiratory disease. The long-term consequences of exposure to MIC are not fully known, but are likely to include permanent damage to the tissues of the lungs, kidney, and liver; nervous illnesses; and gynaecological disorders.

The leak was initially noticed at 12:20 a.m. by workers at the plant. It continued for at least two hours. The explosion was caused by the introduction of water into MIC storage tank number 610. Forty tonnes of the liquid chemical went through an exothermic reaction and vaporized into a white cloud. The reaction was so 'hot' that the storage tank was cauterized and forced into a caterpillar shape; and though the incident occurred in the middle of winter, the ambient air temperature in Bhopal was raised to 34 degrees Celsius (from a low of 13 degrees) during the day following the explosion.[2]

The gas spread sufficiently far to seriously injure people within eight kilometres downwind. Most of the victims, fleeing in panic, ran with the wind rather than against it. The most seriously affected areas were the densely populated shanty towns immediately surrounding the plant – Jayaprakash Nagar, Kazi Camp, Chola Kenchi – and the Railway

Colony. Having no means of transportation, the terrified masses were forced to flee on foot through the narrow laneways that wind between the hutments. Many were trampled as they tried to make their way through these crowded and unlit streets. In the days following the panic, many of these people were taken for dead, mistakenly loaded onto funeral trucks destined for the cremation piles. The victims were almost entirely the poorest members of the population. One doctor remembers arranging the bodies into Hindu and Muslim groups on the first night and noticing 'the one body I did not find was that of a sardar [a business, community, or police leader]. There was not one sardar.'[3]

Estimates of the number of dead and injured vary widely. Poor documentation, mass burials and cremations, and conflicting medical opinions ensure that the precise number of victims will never be known. The interests of the parties making the estimates guarantee that the gaps between their figures will remain large. The original (and conservative) count was more than 2,000 dead. It is likely that, owing to informal burials and cremations, the actual immediate death toll was higher. In addition, death records may not include homeless and transient individuals who perished. The mortality figures have increased as more victims have succumbed to their injuries (at the rate of about one death per day in the first three years following the disaster). By 1987 the official death toll stood at about 3,500, and by 1992 it was over 4,000. Victims' organizations placed the figure many thousands higher. In addition, 30,000 to 40,000 people were maimed and seriously injured,[4] and 200,000 were otherwise affected through minor injury, death of a family member, and economic and social dislocation.

Twenty-four different research projects, coordinated by the Indian Council of Medical Research, struggled for years to determine the long-term effects of the disaster. Those who inhaled the gas now experience breathlessness and fatigue resulting from damaged lung tissue. Many continue to cough blood and to suffer from continuous pain, weakness, and vertigo. Thousands of the victims are no longer able to do even light work. The gas blinded many victims, and thousands must now wear the spectacles provided for them by the government. Hundreds of children were orphaned. Women continue to suffer from a number of gynaecological illnesses. Since the disaster, health workers have reported unusually high numbers of miscarriages, premature births, and birth defects. A study prepared by the Indian Council of Medical Research has found that the spontaneous abortion rate following the gas leak was 24.2 per cent, about three times the national average. The stillbirth rate was 26.1 per 1,000 deliveries, compared with a national figure of 7.9 per 1,000. A year after the disaster, the infant mortality rate in Bhopal was 110 per 1,000 births, compared with a national average of 65.2 per thousand.[5]

The longer-term health effects of the gas poisoning remain uncertain. Damage to the lungs of the survivors would result in increased susceptibility to respiratory ailments such as emphysema, bronchitis, and infection. Studies are under way to determine whether the gas is carcinogenic and whether it will cause genetic damage, birth defects, and further eye damage. Dr Heeresh Chandra, the head of the department of forensic medicine at Bhopal's Gandhi Medical College, has suggested that one result of exposure is serious damage to the victim's immune system, resulting from the way in which the gas reduces the capacity of the blood to carry oxygen. If so, many will succumb more easily to the natural illnesses prevalent in an Indian city. All of the victims continue to suffer from the resulting psychological trauma, which manifested itself in the increasing incidence of depression, suicide, and family violence.

The disaster caused a massive disruption in the city. Tens of thousands migrated out of Bhopal, and the economic life of the city was virtually paralysed for months. Daily-wage labourers were left without work, and therefore without the means even to subsist. Hundreds of businesses were disrupted and many never reopened. Fears were that environmental and property damage were widespread. At least 2,000 commercial animals were killed at the time of the reaction, crops were destroyed, and there was considerable anxiety over soil and water contamination.

In the days immediately following the disaster, the response was disorganized and disappointing. Few realized the extent of the horror that had befallen the city. The local medical community made heroic efforts but was entirely overwhelmed by the magnitude of the disaster and the complete lack of knowledge about the nature of the poisoning. The army loaded bodies on trucks and took them away to be disposed of in mass burials and cremations. The federal government sent medical teams to the city to treat the victims and to study the medical consequences of the gas leak. Voluntary organizations, including the Red Cross and numerous social-action groups, entered the city to provide what assistance they could. A food-distribution system was organized and operated for a short period. Subsistence level cash payments were made to some of the population who had escaped immediate death from the poison but were now facing starvation. The U.S. embassy donated $25,000 towards the relief effort. Union Carbide also sent a team of experts to render the plant safe and to assist the victims. Not unexpectedly, their presence during this exercise, dubbed 'operation faith,' was not universally welcomed.

A Litany of Neglect

The Bhopal incident, unique in the extent of its consequences, was not a freak occurrence or an isolated event. It was the result of a combination of legal, technological, organizational, and human errors. The immediate cause of the chemical reaction was the seepage of water into the MIC storage tank. The results of this reaction were exacerbated by the failure of containment and safety systems, and the human consequences were magnified by a complete absence of community information and emergency preparation. The long-term effects were made worse by the absence of systems to care for and compensate the victims. A detailed investigation of the causes of the Bhopal incident may therefore help us to reduce the risk of such a disaster occurring in the future, and to minimize the harm caused by those hazards that do materialize.

In Search of an Immediate Explanation

In the days and weeks following the disaster, the government, Union Carbide, and the press began frantically to search for its immediate causes. This search was given added urgency by the fact that another storage tank (number 611) still contained 18 tonnes of MIC, and the populace was terrified by the possibility of a repeat of the disaster. The Indian Central Bureau of Investigation sealed the factory and seized thousands of pages of plant records, and both the Government of India and Union Carbide sent technical investigation teams to determine what had happened on the night of 2 December.

The tank from which the gas escaped was one of three intermediate chemical-storage units. MIC, which is a component of the pesticides manufactured at the plant, was stored in these tanks, awaiting transfer to the 'charge pot' where it would be processed into Sevin, the final product. Both the government and Union Carbide eventually came to the conclusion that the reaction had been caused by the introduction of water into tank number 610. But from this point on, their theories diverged radically. Union Carbide initially claimed that the accident was caused by a group of Sikh extremists known as 'Black June,'[6] and later charged that it was the work of a disgruntled employee. These allegations, formulated initially without any corroborating evidence, were maintained consistently by Union Carbide officials in the years following the disaster.

The more widely accepted theory of the immediate technical cause of the leak was based on reports prepared for the Indian government by scientist Srinivas Vardharajan and the Indian Council of Scientific and Industrial Research.[7] These reports indicated that everything had been normal at the plant until about midnight. The chemical in tank number 610 was not being used at this time, and the logs showed that, at 10:20 p.m., several hours before the leak, the pressure in this tank was noted to be normal, at 2 pounds per square inch. The Sevin facility was drawing MIC from tank number 611, and the logs showed that the last transfer from this tank to the Sevin 'charge pot' took place at 11:30 p.m. A shift change had taken place at about 10:45 p.m., and no problems were noticed until 11:30 p.m., when a small MIC leak was reported to the MIC supervisor. The supervisor, however, did not look into the problem until after a tea break between 12:15 and 12:40 a.m. Just after this break, an operator noticed a sudden pressure rise in tank number 610, which sent the gauge off the scale. A visual inspection of the site revealed that the tank was rumbling and the concrete above it was cracking. Within minutes, the exothermic reaction ruptured the safety valve of the tank and released the gas.

The Indian reports suggest that the reaction must have been caused by the introduction of some 500 litres of water into the MIC tank and the 'water-washing theory' was advanced to explain how this happened. On the night of 2 December the plant superintendent ordered an employee to wash a series of pipes in the MIC filtration unit. These pipes were connected to the relief-valve vent header, routing gas from the MIC tank to the vent-gas scrubber. Both employees were relatively new to the MIC operation, and the pipes were part of a complicated network that they may not have fully understood. The cleaning operation involved flushing the lines with water, which would drain out through a series of bleeder valves. These valves, however, were clogged, and water may have built up in the line. During the flushing process, the valves connecting the pipes to a further series of lines that lead ultimately to the MIC tank are closed and further sealed by inserting a slip blind (a metal disk) into the valve. This disk was found not to be in place when the site was inspected after the accident, and the valve alone was probably insufficient to close the connection. The water, which was not draining properly through the bleeder valves, may have built up in the pipe, rising high enough to pour back down through another series of lines into the MIC storage tank. Alternatively, the water may have been routed through another stand-by 'jumper line' that had only recently been connected to the system.[8] Indian scientists suggested that additional water may have been introduced as 'back-flow' from the defectively designed vent-gas scrubber. Later analysis revealed the presence of sodium in tank number 610, indicating ingress from the scrubber, which uses caustic soda.[9]

Union Carbide vigorously disputed this theory. It claimed that the water-washing scenario was developed largely by reporters in search of a 'scoop,' by government officials seeking to blame Union Carbide, and by employees seeking to escape responsibility for their part in the disaster. The company hired Arthur Little Associates, a firm of technical consultants, to undertake an 'independent investigation.'[10] This firm concluded, first, that the water-washing theory was physically impossible and could not withstand 'even minimal scientific scrutiny.' In the first place, in order for the water to reach the MIC tank during a washing, it would have had to travel through dozens of metres of piping, pass through several valves, and finally climb 3.5 metres to reach the tank opening. The team estimated that even if all the valves had, indeed, failed to function on the night of the incident, the introduction of water through the lines would have required some 2000 litres of water at considerable pressure. The team denied that more than one of the bleeder valves was malfunctioning and also asserted that at least one of the intermediate sealing valves was closed. Finally, if the water-washing theory was correct, it would be expected that there would be water left in the lines after the event. Yet, two months later, when a hole was drilled in the lowest point of the piping, no water was found, or so these investigators alleged. The team concluded that the washing theory was simply untenable (though, as Indian technicians pointed out, most of the water was forced out of the lines by the explosion and the remainder had been drained the day following the disaster).

In place of the water-washing theory, the Union Carbide team asserted that the water must have been introduced directly into the MIC tank. Its final report, completed on 10 May 1988, elaborated upon this theory. In the first place, it asserted that the reaction had been noticed earlier but that the logs had been altered by employees to cover this up. A sample of the MIC in the line leading to the Sevin facility (the 'charge pot') seemed to be chemically similar to the MIC stored in tank number 610 rather than that in tank number 611. Yet the latter was the tank from which the chemical was being withdrawn at the time for pesticide formulation. The team concluded that the last transfer of chemical from the MIC storage area to the Sevin facility must therefore have come from tank number 610 just as the chemical in that tank was beginning to react. It hypothesized that the reaction in tank number 610 had been noticed by employees earlier in the evening, and that they had discharged some of the chemical from the tank to the Sevin facility in a futile effort to reduce the amount of chemical or to remove the water in the tank. No witness or log entry confirmed this hypothesis, but Union Carbide's investigators attributed the absence of corroborating evidence to fear by the employees of criminal sanctions and a 'massive cover-up' in which 'log after log' had been altered in order to obscure the time of the leak.

Union Carbide's investigators did, however, later claim to have one witness – Sunder Rajan – who noticed, on the morning after the leak, that a pressure indicator on tank number 610 was missing and that no plug had been inserted in the opening, as should have been the case if the instrument had been removed for maintenance. This witness also claimed to have noticed a water hose lying nearby. While other witnesses contradicted both these statements, Union Carbide argued that the only possible explanation was sabotage. Their scenario is as follows. At 10:20 p.m. all was normal at the plant. At 10:45 the shifts changed, at which time the storage area would have been deserted. During the shift change, a disgruntled employee must have entered the storage area, removed the pressure indicator from the tank, attached a water hose, and turned on the water. The reaction began at 11:30 p.m. While the early leaks were noticed by some employees, they believed that the problem was a minor one and, after fixing a fire hose to spray in the direction of what they believed to be the source of the leak, they returned to their stations. Later, after midnight, the pressure in tank number 610 increased radically, and the employees returned to the storage tank. They saw the hose attached to the tank, disconnected it, and tried to transfer some of the chemical to the Sevin unit. When this effort failed, the employees agreed on a cover-up plan to avoid incurring personal responsibility, and the next day altered the logs to obscure their role in the disaster.

The Union Carbide investigators later claimed to have a 'likely candidate' for the role of saboteur – an employee who was bitter about his recent transfer from the MIC unit, which he took to be a demotion, and who also claimed that he had been 'tortured' by Union Carbide – though no confession was ever forthcoming. Company investigators hypothesized that he was simply trying to spoil a batch of the chemical, without realizing the consequences of his actions, and they pointed out that 'minor incidents of process sabotage by employees had occurred previously at the Bhopal plant.'[11]

There are gaps and anomalies in both versions of how the disaster happened. Neither is supported by direct evidence. While some of the logs may have been altered, it is difficult to imagine that an incident of sabotage could be as easily covered up as Union Carbide suggested. Nor, for many years, did Union Carbide ever release the name of the sabotage suspect; and, even when he was identified, he continued to live peacefully among his alleged victims in the town of Bhopal. Yet neither was direct evidence of the water-washing theory forthcoming from the government of India. Whichever of these scenarios is correct, one thing is certain: the facility at Bhopal was a disaster waiting to happen.

Union Carbide characterized the Bhopal incident as 'a unique combination of unusual events.'[12] But one of the purposes of this book is to suggest that it would be a mistake to treat the Bhopal disaster as an isolated 'accident.' Instead, I posit that the Bhopal scenario is not at all unusual, and that the combination of managerial, technological, and legal failures that prefigured the tragedy reveals a pattern that can usefully be used to analyse many industrial hazards and disasters more systematically. The introduction of water into tank number 610 – however it occurred – may have *triggered* the event, but it did not *cause* the disaster that ultimately took place in Bhopal. Instead, the disaster was the result of the failure of interdependent systems of information, technology, and law. The true causes of a disaster such as that which occurred in Bhopal can be understood, therefore, only by examining the structural dynamics of industrial production within a given social and regulatory regime. The Bhopal case, involving as it did a multinational corporation in a developing country, is particularly instructive because it reveals those dynamics in an especially clear light.

In Search of a Systematic Explanation: The Nature of Industrial Risks

'Risk' may be an inevitable part of modern life. However, some risks are neither justifiable nor tolerable. When we examine the conditions at the Bhopal plant and in the city on the day before the disaster occurred, we see that the Bhopal 'scenario' is a classic example of an operation that was allowed to deteriorate to the point of unacceptable risk.

All industrial facilities impose a degree of risk to human health and the environment. The level of this risk is a function of the severity of the potential consequences of an incident and the probability of one's occurring. No single analytical framework provides an easy method by which to assess and manage risks, but important variables can be identified and analysed to help us better understand why incidents like that in Bhopal happen. In the case of a hazardous-chemical facility, the severity of the consequences is a function of the following factors:

1) the toxicity of the substance
2) the effectiveness of warning systems
3) plant siting and population densities
4) emergency systems
5) medical knowledge and facilities.

Probability of an occurrence is difficult to quantify, but important factors include:[13]

1) the volume of the chemical present;
2) the conditions of its confinement and storage;
3) equipment- and system-engineering design criteria;
4) manufacturing processes;
5) routine safety precautions;
6) reliability of engineering principles and techniques in use at the location;
7) secondary containment;
8) maintenance practices and employee training; and
9) atmospheric conditions at the location.

When analysed in terms of these factors, the systematic neglect of health and safety at Bhopal provides a tragically perfect example of risk mismanagement. This theme is elaborated upon in more detail below.

Risk Assessment and Hazard Communication: Information and Planning Failures

The inexorable movement towards disaster can be traced to a time even before the Bhopal plant was constructed. Too little thought had gone into the economic and environmental implications of the decision to manufacture the particular pesticides in the first place. Estimates of the social benefits of the operation were wildly off the mark, and the technology chosen was inappropriate in relation to local needs and circumstances. With the benefit of hindsight, the decision to manufacture these pesticides at all can be seen to have been an error. Even during construction of the facility, the company began to have second thoughts about the wisdom of both the location and the plant, and the processes chosen. The plant never operated at full capacity, and better alternatives were available.

Perhaps more importantly, almost no attention was devoted to analysing the potential social costs of the operation. Little research had been done on the risks associated with methyl isocyanate or its properties and treatment. No one appears to have had adequate information about its characteristics, its effects on human health, or the proper form of medical treatment. No information was made available on the hazards associated with the operation, and there was insufficient attention to health and safety concerns. Too little effort was expended on anticipating the hazards of the Bhopal operation or on developing safety systems. Union Carbide's Indian headquarters had only one employee responsible for the coordination and supervision of safety at all its Indian operations. That employee's task was confined mainly to keeping safety manuals up to date rather than inspecting the Company's plants.[14]

CHOICE OF TECHNOLOGY

The Bhopal plant was owned and operated by Union Carbide of India Ltd. (UCIL) of which, in turn, 50.9 per cent was owned by the Union Carbide Corporation (UCC), a multinational company with headquarters in the United States. Indian government financial institutions also had a significant ownership share in the Indian company. UCIL had fourteen plants in India and had been operating in the country for fifty years. Its best-known product was the Eveready battery. The Bhopal facility, which was a more recent undertaking, had been formulating pesticides since 1969, but the MIC unit did not begin operations until 1980.

The UCIL plant manufactured Sevin and Temik, which are carbaryl-based pesticides. Carbaryl is produced from a mixture of alpha naphthol and methyl isocyanate (MIC). MIC, in turn, is produced from phosgene, which itself is a product of carbon monoxide and chlorine. UCIL had been *formulating* carbaryl-based pesticides since 1969 and did so by importing alpha naphthol and methyl isocyanate and mixing them at the Bhopal facility. In 1974 Union Carbide was granted a licence to *manufacture* pesticides, though not until 1979 did the Bhopal facility begin manufacturing MIC itself. This decision to 'backwards integrate' was made in an effort to reduce reliance on imports and to enhance economies of scale to meet increasing competition.[15]

The change in technology in 1979-80 was critical, giving rise to a host of risks that were not accounted for in planning the Union Carbide plant. The new technology required the storage of extremely large quantities of lethal MIC. Edward Munoz, a former Union Carbide employee who was initially in charge of the Indian project, has said that he warned Union Carbide officials of the danger of storing such large quantities of the chemical and that he recommended storage in smaller amounts. That recommendation, he said, was overriden by the parent corporation.[16] Ironically, notwithstanding aggressive lobbying by Union Carbide, the U.S. Environmental Protection Agency has now recommended banning or strictly regulating Temik, the other pesticide manufactured in Bhopal and the United States, on the basis that it presents an unreasonable risk to children. Residues in food products are estimated to affect up to 50,000 children a day, causing stomach cramps, nervous disorders, and headaches.[17] Local communities in the United States had been battling Union Carbide for years to have this product removed from the market on the basis that it was contaminating groundwater and drinking-water wells.[18]

More generally, the choice of technology was arguably inappropriate, given the technical, legal, and industrial environment in India. The plant itself may initially have been well designed, incorporating some 'state of the art' technology (though also containing less-sophisticated components). However, the local infrastructure in Bhopal was simply unsuitable for such a hazardous operation, and that fact should at least have alerted Union Carbide to the necessity of a much greater degree of ongoing supervision and improvement. Yet the skills level of employees and managers was poorly maintained, technological support was missing, and emergency measures were altogether inadequate. In India communications are unreliable, and governmental regulation of health and safety is almost non-existent. The decision to go ahead with the Bhopal project in such an environment either ignored or seriously underestimated the importance of these factors in the process of assessing risks and choosing technologies. Roger Aitla, a former Union Carbide engineer who was involved in the early planning, later said, 'There is no question that they [Union Carbide] knew what they were dealing with.'[19]

SITING

From the point of view of risk management, the UCIL plant could hardly have been located in a worse place. Built less than two kilometres from the centre of the old city, the plant was surrounded, except on its northern side, by densely populated hutments. The prevailing winds on the night of 2 December were from the north, and they blew the toxic gas immediately into the adjacent slums and, indeed, into the centre of the old town.

In 1977, at a conference on environmental law at the Indian Law Institute, H.C. Dhalakia, as if scripting the Bhopal scenario that was to occur seven years later, said, 'The location of industry has been selected on several considerations such as availability of power, water and other services, manpower, proximity of the residential areas and proximity of the market. This has resulted in the intermingling of industry and residential areas, leading to industrial emissions adversely affecting the residential areas.'[20]

The choice of Bhopal as the site of the plant was influenced by a variety of factors. The city is located in the geographical centre of India at an important rail junction of lines that extend to most other parts of the country. The plant was practically beside the station. The large 'Upper' lake provided a reliable source of water, and Bhopal offered sufficient electricity and labour to sustain a large scale industrial plant.

Densely populated slums had been allowed to grow in the vicinity of the plant, and there was no 'green belt' buffer between the plant and residential areas. When the plant's use was changed, and more dangerous production methods were instituted, little thought was given to its location. Bhopal had grown quickly as a result of the continuous migration of people from the countryside. The thousands of people who populated the slums worked as construction workers, sweepers, cleaners, and scavengers, and in the hundreds of cycle-repair and tea shops that line the roads in the city. With no public transport, and no alternative source of housing, these poor daily-wage labourers naturally occupied the nearest vacant land around the source of their livelihood.

The high density of the population around the factory, and the previous accidents, should have put both the company and the government on the alert. But, in 1975, when the state government prepared a master plan for the city of Bhopal, the plant was classified as 'general' rather than 'obnoxious' and was left in its original location notwithstanding the fact that sixteen other industrial facilities were relocated.[21] In that same year M.N. Buch, the municipal-planning administrator, issued a notice to Union Carbide to relocate the plant. Instead, Buch himself was relocated. In 1982, when the issue was again raised in the state assembly and it was suggested that the plant be moved, the labour minister replied, 'There has been an investment of rupees 25 crores [about $15.5 million (U.S.)]. It is not a small stone that can be removed just like that.'[22] Nor did the company or the government do anything to prevent the growth of slums around the plant or to remove them. In fact, just several months before the disaster, the state government had bestowed deeds upon the squatters in Jayaprakash Nagar, hoping perhaps to increase its political popularity in future elections.

COMMUNITY INFORMATION AND EMERGENCY PREPAREDNESS

The technological, social, and regulatory infrastructure in Bhopal was insufficiently adapted to accommodate a hazardous industry. There was an almost complete failure by the company to liaise with the community and to convey information about the plant. There was practically no knowledge in the community of the nature of the operation or of the materials that were stored on site. Had the local residents even known to place a wet towel over their faces, hundreds of lives might have been saved. Had they known where the gas was coming from, or that they should have run against the wind, many injuries might have been avoided. There was no warning system. Telephones in India are scarce and unreliable. Communications are poor. On the night of the accident there was simply no way to alert or inform the masses of people sleeping in the path of the gas. The plant's warning siren, which was muted during the explosion,[23] meant nothing to the residents of Bhopal in any event.

Neither industry nor government had prepared an evacuation plan, an emergency response system, or a medical plan. Panic reigned during the first twenty-four hours following the accident. There was little police, army, or government assistance or organization. The local hospital, with some 760 beds, was swamped with 20,000 patients within a few hours of the leak.[24] For the first several hours, doctors did not know that the chemical in the ruptured tank had been MIC. Initial requests to Union Carbide officials for information about the nature of the poison and the appropriate antidote were met with denial or ignorance. Company policy forbade employees to speak for the company without authorization, especially in emergency situations. Upon wiring both

UCC's U.S. headquarters and the Atlanta Centers for Disease Control, doctors were told that the gas was 'harmless' and later that there was 'no known antidote.'[25] They were able to provide treatment of symptoms only, washing the victims' eyes with cold water, administering steroids to manage inflammation, and giving oxygen to patients. As the Indian Supreme Court would later say, the horror of the injuries caused by the chemical was 'matched only by the lack of a prepackage of relief procedures ... based on adequate scientific knowledge as to the ameliorative medical procedures for immediate neutralization of its effects.'[26]

On 4 December, the national government sent a medical team to Bhopal. Medical personnel continued to be hampered by an almost total lack of knowledge about the nature of the injuries that the victims were suffering and the appropriate treatment for this type of chemical poisoning. Even when the authorities learned that the ruptured tank had contained MIC, they still did not know the precise chemical composition of the gas that had been released as a result of the chemical reaction. Indeed, there is still considerable controversy over the nature of the poison released. Autopsies revealed large amounts of cyanide in the blood and tissues of many victims, indicating that they had been exposed to thiocyanate or hydrogen cyanide. Sodium thiosulphate is an effective remedy for this poison, but business and government officials denied its effectiveness, fearing that such an admission would confirm the worst suspicions of the populace about the poisoning and cause further panic.[27] Several doctors did administer the drug to themselves and to a limited number of victims, with a good rate of success.[28] The sodium thiosulphate controversy in fact continued for two years after the disaster.[29]

How could such serious deficiencies in information generating, information sharing, and industrial planning come about? It seems that neither the company nor government officials were willing even to consider, much less plan for, such an 'unthinkable' catastrophe. In the resolution of the competing interests of the Government of India and UCC, safety and environmental factors were virtually ignored.[30] Industry and government failed to develop or share information, or to delineate responsibility for health, safety, and environment. They did no worst-case planning. In seeking to maximize their share of the gains from production, the parties failed to account properly for risks or to plan for negative contingencies. None of this is meant to deny that heroic efforts were made. But they were ineffective, owing to the almost complete lack of information and preparedness.

Technological Failures: Double Standards?

Union Carbide owned and operated a similar MIC facility in Institute, West Virginia. The company denied the existence of any double standard with respect to safety systems at the Bhopal plant and its home operation. The UCC claimed – inconsistently – first, that the accident could never have happened at the home plant and, second, that the safety and storage systems at both plants were identical. Both of these claims are dubious.

The first claim – that the accident could never happen in the United States – was intended to allay fears in the United States that Union Carbide's West Virginia operation imposed similar risks on U.S. citizens, and also to imply that the exclusive cause of the Bhopal disaster was slipshod management by Indian nationals. This claim was thoroughly rebutted by the fact that, even at its superior operation in Institute, there had been a series of gas leaks. Indeed, on 9 August 1985, a bare eight months after the Bhopal disaster, a leak at this plant injured more than 100 people. This accident occurred *after* the Institute plant had been thoroughly overhauled following the Bhopal disaster; yet it was remarkably similar to the Bhopal incident.[31] Steam entered a chemical storage tank, raising its temperature and pressure sufficiently to breach the tank's gaskets. A mixture of methylene chloride and aldicarb oxime floated into the atmosphere, and over the local community. The flare tower and water spray were insufficient to neutralize the gas, and community-warning systems failed; as a result, 135 people required hospitalization. Again, eight months later, in April 1986, Union Carbide was found by the Occupational Safety and Health Administration to be in violation of hundreds of U.S. safety standards and was fined $1.4 million.[32]

Union Carbide's second claim – that the Indian and U.S. plants were identical – was designed to deny that it applied a double standard to its Third World operations, and to minimize its responsibility for the disaster. This claim is rebutted by technical comparisons of the two plants. Union Carbide was thus wrong to claim either that the plants were the same or that such a disaster could never occur in the United States. Perhaps it would be more accurate to say that both plants were underdesigned for safety and, of the two, the Bhopal facility was by far the worse.

Investigators have compared the safety systems at the Bhopal plant with those of Union Carbide's plant in Institute, West Virginia.[33] While the latter plant had computerized warning and monitoring systems, the former relied on manual gauges and the human senses to detect gas leaks. The capacity of the storage tanks, gas scrubbers, and flare tower was greater at the Institute plant. Finally, emergency evacuation plans were in place in Institute, but nonexistent in Bhopal.

Nor was the Bhopal technology properly maintained. Specific problems at the Bhopal plant at the time of the leak (though in themselves probably not sufficient to cause or prevent the accident) included:[34]

TECHNOCAL FAILURES

a) the refrigeration unit designed to cool the MIC and inhibit chemical reactions had been shut off for three months;

b) there were no effective warning systems; the alarm on the storage tank failed to signal the increase in temperature on the night of the disaster;

c) the temperature and pressure gauges were so unreliable that they were routinely ignored (as they were on the night of the accident);

d) the gas scrubber, designed to neutralize toxic gases, had been shut off for maintenance;

e) the flare tower, designed to burn off escaping gases, was shut off;

f) water sprayers, designed to neutralize escaping gases, were insufficient to reach the flare tower;

g) MIC storage tank number 610 was filled beyond recommended capacity; and

h) a storage tank which was supposed to be held in reserve for excess MIC already contained the MIC.

While each of these technical failures is serious enough, what is perhaps of greater significance is that even had the safety systems been working perfectly on the night of the disaster, they would not have been sufficient to contain the reaction. The plant was simply not designed to meet a worst-case scenario.

Management and Operational Failures

Not only was there a failure during the early planning stages to investigate the risks associated with the operation, but a host of management and operating failures following the plant's start-up further compounded those risks. The local and foreign managers of the UCIL facility consistently failed to recognize and anticipate obvious and recurring dangers. When they did recognize these dangers they failed to investigate fully, and when they did investigate them they failed to implement their own recommendations. Safety information was not properly communicated from the head office, and what information was communicated was ignored.

Almost from the time of the original start-up of this 'high-tech' operation, the level of training, expertise, and morale among the Bhopal employees had steadily eroded, and safety standards were allowed to deteriorate. The plant was never an economically viable operation, and its management, like its profit slope, reveals a steady downhill slide towards disaster. Indeed, Warren Anderson, the president and chair of Union Carbide at that time, later admitted that the Bhopal facility operated at a level below standards that would have been acceptable in the United States.[35]

The plant's short history provided ample warning of the dangers. Three years earlier, on 26 December 1981, a leak of phosgene killed one worker at the plant, and seriously injured two others. On 9 February 1982, twenty-five workers were hospitalized, following another gas leak at the plant. After these mishaps an official inquiry was ordered,[36] which took two years to complete. In the meantime, on 5 October 1982, a further leak occurred, affecting nearby residents. The inquiry report, which had been released seven months prior to the final tragedy, had been effectively ignored by both government and Union Carbide officials.

Since 1982, local journalist Rajkumar Keswani had been writing articles in the local press, warning of the hazards associated with the plant.[37] The first article, which appeared in September 1982, was titled 'Please Save This City.' He later wrote 'Bhopal Sitting on Top of a Volcano' and 'If You Do Not Understand This You Will Be Wiped Out.' His final article, which appeared just five months before the disaster, was titled 'Bhopal on the Brink of a Disaster.' No one took any notice. Keswani himself was seriously injured by the gas, and since 1984 has been under constant medical treatment for breathlessness, fatigue, memory loss, and deteriorating vision.

In May 1982, a team of U.S. experts had been sent to Bhopal to inspect the UCIL plant. Their report concluded that there was a 'potential for release of toxic materials' as a result of 'equipment failure, operating problems, or maintenance problems.'[38] The report identified the following specific problems: 'Deficiencies in safety valve and instrument maintenance programs. Problems created by high personnel turnover at the plant, particularly in operations. Filter cleaning operations are performed without slipblinding process lines. Leaking valves could create serious exposure during this process.'[39] The inspection team also warned of slipshod operating procedures at the plant, but nevertheless concluded that 'no situations involving imminent danger or requiring immediate correction were noted during the inspection.' This report was forwarded to Jagannath Mukund, the works manager of UCIL, but little or nothing appears to have been done in response. Another report prepared in September 1984 canvassed safety concerns at the U.S. plant, and warned of the danger of a 'runaway reaction' of MIC resulting from contamination. This report was apparently not communicated to Bhopal management. There appear to have been serious communication problems and management gaps between Union Carbide and its Indian operation. This failure to communicate hazards was the result of UCC's hands-off approach to its overseas operation, and perhaps may also be traced to cross-cultural barriers. As one analyst of multinational business and environmental hazards suggests, disruptions and flaws appear in multinational operations because of 'the absence of common values, norms, and expectations among managers in different nations, from tendencies towards ethnocentric attitudes, from psychological impediments to cross-cultural understanding, and from obstructions and deficiencies in the flow of information within the transnational system attributable to distance and shared ownership.'[40] The fact that the operating manuals at Bhopal were printed only in English is an emblematic example of these problems.

There is another reason for the deterioration of operating standards at Bhopal. Many investigators have suggested that, in the plant's last few years of operation, its labour force had been progressively reduced and demoralized.[41] Well-trained staff had been leaving the plant in large numbers since 1981. The operating shifts were cut in 1983 from eleven to six, and the maintenance shift from four to two. On the night of the disaster there were no trained engineers on site. The company itself was aware of the dangers resulting from 'high personnel turnover' at the plant.[42]

The plant had been making little or no profit in its last years of operation and had never operated above 50 per cent of its original capacity. The unit's failing economic health can be traced to the collapse in the market for expensive pesticides and to the failure of another UCC project involving the manufacture of alpha naphthol (another pesticide).[43] When UCIL began formulating pesticides in India in 1969 the outlook for pesticide production over the next decade looked bright. Considered a corner-stone of the 'green revolution' and of India's policy of agricultural self-sufficiency, pesticide production and use increased dramatically during the late 1960s and early 1970s. During this period, pesticide consumption in the developing world more than doubled.[44] It was in response to this picture of the market that the decision was taken to expand the Bhopal facility.

However, the company's optimistic projections were well off-target. During this period agricultural production in India was actually declining, and the demand for pesticides grew at a far slower rate than projected.[45] In 1977 a severe drought had reduced the capacity of many farms and burdened their owners with a high debt load. By the time the Bhopal plant began manufacturing pesticides, cheaper products had entered the market, and demand had diminished. Early predictions of massive profits from pesticide production turned into gloomy projections of financial losses in the millions.[46] Ironically, immediately prior to the accident UCC had been considering ways in which it might divest itself of the Bhopal operation or dispose of the plant.

Regulatory Failures

Many industrial and environmental economists suggest that the essential obstacle to encouraging firms to invest in environmental and worker safety is the simple fact of business competition. While the harm caused by industrial accidents and environmental degradation is part of the full social cost of production, competitive pressures tend to encourage firms to ignore these costs in making investment and management decisions. In the absence of some reason to take account of these additional costs of production there is an inevitable tendency for producing firms to allow worker safety and environmental protection to assume a low priority. Social costs not taken into account by producing firms are known as 'negative externalities' and are one of the reasons why legal regulation is required. The absence of such regulation is an implicit subsidy to production that skews risk assessment and results in an underinvestment in safety.

However, even the best-intentioned regulation of risk will often reveal a gap between the promise and the reality of law. This may be particularly true in developing nations in which the bureaucratic and legal infrastructure is, by comparison, overburdened, undersupported, and torn between competing constituencies. As Charles Pearson of the World Resources Institute argues: 'It may be particularly difficult to exercise effective control of workplace hazards in developing countries. Responsibility for occupational health and safety usually falls to the country's Department of Labour or Public Health, which often has grossly inadequate resources for monitoring and enforcement. Lack of coordination and overlapping responsibilities are serious problems. Labour unions, a major source of pressure for protection legislation in industrial countries may be weak or absent.'[47]

Indian environmental and industrial safety laws are outdated and, more importantly, poorly implemented.[48] India, like many other developing countries, has a relatively recent colonial past, not emerging from colonial control until the middle of this century. The content of its law is historically derived from the resource-exploitive policies of the English colonial government. Those policies placed the highest priority upon the protection of private property and the preservation of law and order for the purpose of maximizing economic extraction. Little effort went into the creation of safe and sustainable long-term development. Mahatma Gandhi's cotton spinning and his trek to the sea to collect salt in violation of the British salt tax and monopoly were both symbolic protests against colonial policies that repressed the development of indigenous skills and resources.

It takes time to develop indigenous legislation, systems, and practices that suitably fit the unique social and economic environment of a particular country. And social pressures in India have traditionally militated against the rapid development of such laws and practices. Lacking any significant middle class from whom the pressure for environmental and industrial safety usually emanates, these issues have not figured prominently on the government's agenda. In an impoverished country that gives high priority to rapid industrialization as a means of alleviating widespread poverty, the goals of environmental protection and industrial safety are often subordinated to those of economic development. The government has tended to expend its energies on efforts to attract capital, build plants, and create jobs. The result of this regime is the inequitable distribution of risks and benefits of industrialization. As Bhopal illustrates, the failure to regulate health and safety enriches a small class while leaving the poor to shoulder the enormous human and environmental costs.

Economic power in India is concentrated in the hands of a very few individuals and organizations. Powerful business lobbies have the ear of government and constantly emphasize the cost and inconvenience of industrial regulation. At the time of the accident, the principal legislation concerning health and safety was contained in the Factories Act of 1948.[49] This legislation dealt primarily with mechanical problems and physical injuries as opposed to toxic substances and complex technology. Although there are approximately 5,000 chemical facilities in India, at the time of the disaster there was no mechanism in place for collecting information on the nature and quantities of stored substances, and almost no regulation of their storage and transportation. It was not until 1981 that India enacted the Air Pollution Act,[50] and not until 1986 that it enacted comprehensive environmental-protection legislation.[51]

Of more obvious consequence, the existing laws are underenforced. The city of Bhopal did have a development plan and zoning regulations. The former was outdated and the latter were not enforced. And the environmental and industrial regulatory agencies were poorly funded and understaffed. In 1983, for example, the entire budget for the Department of the Environment was $685,000 – this in a country with a population of 800 million people.[52] Inspection, the heart of public regulation, has simply not kept pace with the introduction of new substances and processes. Inspections are rare and superficial. At the time of the disaster, the state of Madhya Pradesh had only fifteen factory inspectors.[53] Compliance is low, owing primarily to sporadic enforcement practices and minimal fines.[54] Low rates of pay in the public service contribute to low morale and corruption and, as in other countries, regulatory agencies are not immune from political interference and 'capture' by the very industries they are intended to regulate.

Three years after Bhopal, experts at a conference on Indian environmental law continued to express considerable scepticism about the ability of formal legal mechanisms to reduce environmental risks. They concluded that, 'in the absence of effective political will to enforce them, the laws merely create illusions and mystifications. The laws create an image of social progress which is constantly belied by the everyday reality of non-enforcement.'[55]

The recent development of judicially sponsored public interest litigation in India has had some success in addressing specific problems of environmental and industrial degradation.[56] Article 51 (A) (g) of the constitution articulates the fundamental duty of all citizens to 'protect and improve the natural environment, including forests, lakes, rivers and wildlife.' Aided by such constitutional ideals the courts have sought to ensure the right to a safe workplace and a clean environment. In one case the court ordered the closure of a number of tanneries that were polluting the Ganges.[57] It ordered the public authorities to complete proposed work on sewage treatment in a timely fashion, to remove dairies from the side of the river, to provide facilities for waste removal, and to refuse new industrial licences in the absence of proof of waste-management facilities. It also ordered the local schools to teach environmental awareness for one hour per week and required the central government to have texts on the subject written and distributed free of cost. In another case the Supreme Court ordered the closure of a chemical plant that leaked oleum gas, allowing it to reopen only after it satisfied a stringent set of conditions.[58] But these developments have been primarily of symbolic value. They address specific rather than structural problems and there is no guarantee that the orders will be complied with. The difficulty of prosecuting complex litigation and the impossibility of supervising compliance mean that successes will be few and far between.

Nor is there any indication that the ordinary law of tort in India offered any incentive to invest in industrial safety. Even if we accept the theoretical argument that tort law forces industry to internalize the social costs of accidents, the basic point that legal theory and legal reality never coincide perfectly is ignored. One need not rely on ethnocentric observations to recognize that there is always a significant gap between the law in the books and the law in action. This gap is simply more obvious in a country like India where vast portions of the legal superstructure simply float about, entirely disconnected from the socioeconomic substructure. While the law in the books in India is roughly similar to that in England, Canada, and the United States, tort law has not played a large role in encouraging safety. Indeed, as one prominent student of Indian law has concluded, 'disasters large and small in India typically have no legal consequences.'[59]

Despite such gloomy assessments, many saw in Bhopal an opportunity to galvanize the Indian legal system and to provide some substance to the formal promises of law. Much of this book is devoted to analysing the process of the tort claims spawned by the Bhopal disaster. Yet, notwithstanding the incredible energies devoted to the case by judges, lawyers, and social activists, the final message of the litigation is that human life in India is cheap.

How Many Bhopals?

The Bhopal episode was unique in the magnitude of its consequences. But it would be a mistake to ignore the systemic problems of which it is but one ghastly illustration. In the years since the tragedy, dozens of other serious chemical leaks throughout India have occurred, resulting in hundreds of injuries. An International Labor Organization project undertaken in the wake of the Bhopal tragedy has identified 400 chemical facilities in India that constitute major industrial hazards.[60] 'Little Bhopals' occur nearly every day.

Nor should Bhopal be analysed exclusively as a 'Third World problem.' While India's level of development was certainly an important factor, hazardous incidents resulting from the leak or misuse of toxic chemicals occur on a frighteningly regular basis in all countries, regardless of their state of development. Just seven months after Bhopal, another Union Carbide plant in the United States experienced a similar though far less catastrophic incident, sending 135 people to hospital. In 1976 the Givaudan chemical plant (a Hoffman-Laroche subsidiary) in Seveso, Italy, underwent a similar exothermic reaction, releasing large amounts of dioxins into the locality.[61] The chemical cloud floated several kilometres over three local towns. It polluted the soil and water, killed more than 100,000 animals, and caused serious skin irritations in hundreds of people. As in Bhopal, there had been previous complaints in Seveso about safety equipment and operating procedures, there was inadequate knowledge about the hazards, and a failure by plant officials to sound a warning or inform local officials. On 20 November 1984, just two weeks before Bhopal, 300 people were killed in Mexico City when a liquified natural-gas storage facility exploded in a slum area in the suburb of Tlalnepantla. And just over one year after Bhopal, in April 1986, the explosion and fire at the nuclear reactor at Chernobyl spewed deadly radiation into the atmosphere over twenty-six countries. In November 1986, a fire at the Sandoz chemical warehouse in Basel, Switzerland, released hundreds of tons of insecticides, herbicides, and fungicides, and 1,000 kilograms of mercury into the Rhine, the surrounding soil, and the atmosphere, alerting the European Economic Community to the possibility of a 'European Bhopal.'[62] Similar events, though often on a lesser scale, have occurred in every country of the world. Dangerous leaks and spills of potentially deadly chemicals occur every day. Between 1980 and 1985, the U.S. Environmental Protection Agency (EPA) discovered and registered a total of 6,928 toxic incidents, resulting in an estimated 150 deaths and 1,500 injuries.[63]

The chemical industry is an enormous industrial sector in most developed countries, and in many developing countries.[64] The public record is good, but the risks are high. Canadian government regulations list some 2,400 dangerous products, 300 of which are considered to be potentially hazardous in the event of an escape or spill because of their toxicity, volatility, or the fact that they may easily mix with air or water and disperse rapidly and widely into the environment. Chemical risks arise out of everyday use of dangerous substances in production, faulty handling and storage, transportation incidents, and improper disposal.

The huge petrochemical industry, for example, is a source of Bhopal-type risks. At the refining stage, toxic leaks, fires, and the risk of explosion are major concerns. An explosion at a German chemical plant in 1921 killed more than 550 people, and another in Texas in 1947 had equally catastrophic consequences.[65] But perhaps the most significant risks from the public's point of view are those associated with transportation. A number of recent oil spills off the west coast of North America – including the *Exxon Valdez* disaster in Alaska, which may have caused in excess of $1 billion in damage – have given rise to complex legal proceedings to secure compensation and increased public demand for new transportation standards.

One spectacular example of the dangers arising out of the transportation of hazardous materials was the 1979 derailment of a freight train in Mississauga, Ontario.[66] At midnight, Saturday, 10 November 1979, a train carrying thirty-nine cars of chemicals derailed because of a burned-out axle. Initially, no one, including the railway company, knew that the train was carrying propane, butane, and chlorine. Two cars carrying propane exploded, creating a leak from a chlorine tank and producing a deadly cloud of chlorine gas. More than 200,000 people were evacuated from the area over the next twenty-four hours, though police and army efforts were hampered by the absence of an emergency plan and a total lack of coordination. By incredible good fortune, the derailment occurred in the industrial area of Mississauga, just outside the residential areas, and the winds did not blow large amounts of the gas towards those more heavily populated areas. By more incredible good fortune, the leaking chlorine tank, along with seventeen others containing the same chemical, did not explode. Amazingly, while some residents suffered from nausea and stinging eyes, no one was seriously injured, though it was estimated that the dislocation caused well in excess of $25 million in losses per day.

The Mississauga derailment uncannily paralleled the Bhopal disaster with one significant difference – spectacular good luck. While a few people had been warning of the danger of carrying hazardous chemicals through a residential area, the precautions were entirely inadequate. In the year before the Mississauga derailment there had been sixty-two railway accidents involving hazardous chemicals. Legislation concerning the transportation of dangerous substances had been drafted years earlier but was never passed, and the Canadian Transport Commission conceded that it did not have enough inspectors even to enforce existing regulations. At the time of the derailment no one knew what the train was carrying. Whereas the manifest showed the chlorine cars to be at the back of the train, several were, in fact, located at the front. It took five days for emergency workers to stop even the small chlorine leak. Local residents were unaware of the magnitude of the danger posed by the derailment and many refused to leave their homes. There was no community emergency plan, local residents were taken entirely by surprise, and the evacuation effort was delayed and disorganized. As the mayor said, 'It could have wiped out thousands of people. It's a miracle it happened where it did. Today we were lucky.'

Of equal concern are the dozens of less spectacular incidents that occur every day. The Canadian Environmental Protection Service has developed a database of spill statistics called the National Analysis of Trends in Emergency Systems (NATES), which, while far from exhaustive, has recorded more than 21,000 spills in a ten-year period.[67] Many of these events represented relatively minor incidents, yet they also reveal the incredible pervasiveness of chemicals in modern society and the everyday nature of potentially lethal incidents.

Risks are generated not only by producers and transport companies, but by industrial users and consumers as well. In Canada, pulp and paper production, for example, utilizes chlorine, hydrogen sulphide, and sulphur dioxide – all chemicals that could lead to a Bhopal-type incident. Workers at these plants are frequently taken ill from inhaling leaking vapours. On a day-to-day basis, air pollution from pulp and paper plants and their release of mercury, chromium, and titanium into the water are matters of significant public concern. Mercury discharge from the Chisso chemical plant into Japan's Minimata Bay during the 1950s killed an estimated 1,000 people and injured many thousands more. Today the victims of Minimata are still battling for compensation. Similar poisoning from industrial mercury has seriously affected aboriginal people in northern Ontario and Quebec.

Apart from these single-issue concerns, perhaps the greatest environmental problem today relates to the storage and disposal of hazardous wastes. Both industrial and household waste is building up at an alarming rate. The disposal of even 'ordinary' garbage is becoming increasingly problematic, to say nothing of industrial by-products, chemical wastes, PCBs, arsenic leavings from mining operations, and so on. The Love Canal is but one high-profile toxic dump site among thousands identified by the U.S. Environmental Protection Agency (EPA). In this case nearly 20,000 tonnes of toxic wastes, including dioxins, were discovered leaking into the local environment, requiring the removal of an entire community. Among its other responsibilities, the EPA has the responsibility to clean up toxic sites under the Comprehensive Environmental Response, Compensation and Liability Act. Its initial estimate of the number of such sites rose from 400 in 1980 to 2,000 by 1985, and estimates of the clean-up costs now exceed $100 billion.[68] At one site alone, in Oak Ridge, Tennessee $1.2 billion have been spent cleaning up radioactive materials and mercury dumped directly into water systems and unlined burial pits, and it is estimated that a residual 13.6 million kilograms of toxic substances remain in the soil.

It has been estimated that in 1980 alone, 57 million tonnes of hazardous wastes were generated in the United States, and the EPA has concluded that nearly 90 per cent of that waste was improperly disposed of, thus creating 'significant imminent hazards' to public health.[69] On 23 August 1988, a warehouse in St Basile Le Grand, Quebec, storing 117,000 litres of waste oil laced with polychlorinated biphenals (PCBs) caught fire. A cloud of toxic smoke passed northeast, causing thousands of people to flee from their homes. Chemical compounds with good insulating properties, PCBs had been widely used until 1977, when they were banned because of fears about their health hazards. Exposure can lead to respiratory illnesses, liver dysfunction, birth defects, and possible cancers. The burning chemical may also produce dioxins and furans, which pose an even more serious hazard to health and the environment. In 1968, 15,000 people in Japan had eaten rice contaminated with PCBs. Hundreds suffered from nausea, blindness, and nerve damage; some died.

Like Bhopal's, the St Basile operation appears to have been a disaster waiting to happen. As a condition of renewing his licence, the owner had been required to instal an alarm and sprinkler system; however, neither was in working order on the night of the fire. The warehouse was unfenced and openly accessible to anyone; it was in violation of its operating permit and was storing nearly 30,000 litres more than it was licensed to. While some local residents and government officials had been aware that the facility posed a hazard, they did not know the extent of the danger, and nothing had been done to bring the operation into compliance with the law.[70] Little is known about the long-term health or environmental effects of a PCB fire, or what will be the economic and physical repercussions of the incident. Following the St Basile Le Grand fire, several other PCB warehouses were discovered to be operating in violation of the law. Neither the provincial nor federal government had any plan for the disposal of these hazardous chemicals.

These and other examples illustrate how neither the information failures at Bhopal nor the legal failures it exposed are unique to situations involving Third World countries. While chemicals represent about 10 per cent of total world trade,[71] we know far too little about their risks to health and environment. For example, information on health hazards is available on only 10 per cent of all pesticides[72] – this notwithstanding that there may be as many as a million acute pesticide poisonings per year in the world, and many more minor cases.[73]

Nor is the failure of law unique to the Third World. Despite the almost bewildering array of environmental and industrial regulations in developed countries, the success of any legislative regime depends ultimately upon political will and fiscal backing. But regulatory resources are limited, and the bargaining power of industry is large. Environmental objectives, standards, and compliance timetables are the product of negotiation between government and industry. Government departments may be understaffed and underfunded. As the former chief of enforcement for Environment Canada stated, the main problem is 'lack of resources and experience.'[74] The impoverished resources of many government agencies, even in the industrialized world, create a relationship of dependency between the regulators and the industries they regulate. The latter have the best access to information on their products and processes and are in a strong bargaining relationship when it comes to negotiating standards.

Numerous studies have confirmed that governmental agencies rely heavily on industry for information and self-monitoring, that enforcement is sporadic, and that minimal fines for environmental offences are treated as a cost of doing business.[75] Despite the existence of legislation creating a multitude of criminal and regulatory offences, sanctions have not traditionally played an important role, the departments preferring to rely on persuasion.[76] In 1986, for example, Canada's minister of the environment acknowledged 'the country's appalling record of enforcement and compliance.'[77] It is true that some governments are adopting tougher policies with respect to environmental hazards. Environmental legislation in Canada and the United States has dramatically increased the penalties for offences, and in some jurisdictions more public resources have been channelled into the prosecution of offenders. The result may be a gradual enhancement of environmental and safety consciousness.[78] Similarly, new legislation imposing liability for clean-up costs may also provide significant deterrence. Yet the prosecution of corporate offenders is enormously complex and expensive. Judges still do not view corporate or 'white collar' crime as a serious offence and do not perceive the creation of systemic risks to health and environment as seriously as other forms of criminal behaviour. When sanctions are applied, they tend to concentrate on actual harm, rather than risk, and, even then, are often inadequate to achieve deterrence. For example, a recent study of waste management in British Columbia, found that 'a substantial number of firms habitually violate environmental and occupational health and safety regulations'[79] and that they are virtually immune from punishment. The minimal fines imposed for violations could easily be treated simply as a cost of doing business. Another recent review of workplace-safety regulation in the United States reached a similar conclusion. Individual workplace inspections take place only once every twenty years, the regulations and standards are not consistently or comprehensively enforced, and penalties are 'clearly too small to constitute a deterrent when compliance imposes any significant cost.'[80]

Environmental legislation in all countries is increasingly acknowledging the need for the development of information on toxic substances and hazardous processes for the purposes of risk assessment and standards setting.[81] Gradually, industries are being encouraged to engage in ongoing safety auditing and risk communication. Yet regulatory enforcement and industrial compliance are still viewed as expensive and bothersome. Bhopal serves as a reminder of the costs of not incurring these expenses. Municipalities have been slow off the mark in developing emergency response plans. Most local communities do not yet have a 'right to know' of the hazards in their immediate locales, or the ability to participate effectively in environmental decision making. Again, community input is often resisted by both government and industry on the basis that it is poorly informed and overly meddlesome. Bhopal may teach us that public education and participation may be a more positive response than secrecy.

2

The Political Economy of Industrial and Environmental Hazards

In order to take any lessons from what happened at Bhopal, it is necessary to recognize that the catastrophe was not an 'accident.' The event was neither unforeseen nor without identifiable cause. Nor was the risk only the result of callous indifference. It was the product of a systematic series of failures in planning, operating, and regulating the pesticide facility. These failures, which can occur in all countries, are vastly magnified in the Third World as a result of the way in which business is done there. The Bhopal 'syndrome' can and must therefore be understood in the broader context of the political economy of industrial development.

Planning a Disaster

The relationship between Union Carbide and the Government of India is a textbook-perfect illustration of the evolving nature of the relationship between multinational corporations (MNCs) and their host countries in the developing world.[1] The terms and conditions of this relationship are fundamentally determined by the interests and abilities of the parties, which include the relative poverty and developmental needs of the host state, balanced against the power and economic imperatives of multinational business organizations. In this dynamic, workers and communities are rarely considered to be parties.

Union Carbide began planning the Bhopal operation during the 1970s. Its investment and integration strategy at the time mirrored what other multinational companies were doing in response to the globalization of business. As international business scholar Robert Gilpin explains, the first stage of the 'product cycle' – the simple export of goods from industrialized countries to the Third World – was over. In their effort to industrialize, the countries of the Third World had implemented tariffs, import-substitution policies, and foreign-exchange controls in order to promote indigenous manufacturing. These barriers to entry, combined with increasing international competition, had created strong incentives for companies to shift production to locations that offered cheap pools of labour and large markets. Thus, during the early 1970s 'the United States had become more of a foreign investor than an exporter of domestically manufactured goods.'[2] Such direct investment enabled multinationals to avoid trade barriers, to 'thwart the emergence of foreign rivals,'[3] and to compete effectively against local firms by exploiting economies of scale, technological sophistication, and marketing experience.

The relationship between Union Carbide and the Government of India replicated this pattern. India had in place a regime of tough import controls and foreign-currency restrictions designed to promote its goal of industrialization. Additionally, pesticides were viewed as a vital part of India's 'green revolution' in agriculture and its attempt to achieve self-sufficiency in food production. The government's policy of industrialization, and its effort to minimize the country's dependence on imports, made the idea of a technology transfer attractive. The goal was to promote the development of an indigenous manufacturing facility, contribute to the industrial infrastructure, provide employment, and save foreign currency that would otherwise be spent on chemical imports. While the Bhopal facility had been producing pesticides for a decade, it had done so with imported methyl isocyanate (MIC). It did not begin to manufacture MIC itself until 1980.

In the aftermath of the Bhopal disaster, Union Carbide was to insist time and again that it had been 'forced' to produce MIC in India by the Indian government's foreign-investment policies. It claimed that, because of these policies, it had 'no option but to launch upon indigenous manufacturing of MIC-based pesticides and to set up a plant for that purpose.'[4] Certainly, it is true that India's policies were designed to encourage indigenous industries, but the company's claim that it was 'forced' to do anything is disingenuous. India was an extremely attractive place for Union Carbide to do business. It offered the company a skilled but inexpensive labour force and an enormous market for its products. During the planning period, India's population of 600 million people, its huge agricultural base of cultivated land (50 per cent of the country), and the widespread use of pesticides seemed to promise a market ideally suited to further investment in the chemical-pesticide sector. India also offered an industrial base, work skills, and a transportation system that were all relatively well developed by Third World standards.

In sum, the most important factors influencing the negotiations between India and Union Carbide were India's desire to develop a domestic pesticide industry, its policy of foreign-exchange conservation and import substitution, and its antagonism to multinational control of domestic industry. Union Carbide's primary aim was to exploit a new and large market, to maintain control over affiliates through majority ownership, and, of course, to maximize its share of the profits. Unfortunately, the different needs and interests of the two major parties to the negotiations were to create a dynamic within which considerations of health and safety were all but excluded.

Development and Environment

When India emerged from its colonial status in 1947 it was one of the most populous and poorest nations in the world. With an almost feudal agricultural system, the country, along with other post-colonial nations of the Third World, had been excluded from the first industrial revolution and was a late starter in the postwar economic explosion enjoyed by developed countries. Even today, with a population of more than 800 million people, India does not feed all its people, much less offer them the hope of the affluence enjoyed by many citizens in the industrialized world. Multitudes live in absolute poverty without adequate nutrition or shelter. Throughout the 1970s India experienced slow economic growth. Its annual per-capita income, about $75, was one of the lowest in the world.

As India's former prime minister Indira Gandhi frequently argued, the dominant environmental problem in the Third World is the 'pollution of poverty.'[5] Her father, Jawaharlal Nehru, was India's first prime minister. He had set India's course upon independence towards the goal of agricultural and industrial self-sufficiency as the only guarantee of the country's hard-won independence and as the only way of alleviating the misery of the 'millions who suffer.'[6] During the 1950s and 1960s India managed to enhance its industrial base and to encourage large-scale manufacture of consumer goods, machinery textiles, fertilizers, and transportation equipment. Accordingly, the country has moved some way towards creating indigenous industry and self-sufficiency and maintained an economic growth rate of about 3 per cent. However, this economic improvement has been practically neutralized by the failure of government efforts to redistribute the benefits of economic growth to the poorer members in society. Industrialization has concentrated enormous wealth in the hands of a very small élite without significantly improving the lot of the majority of citizens. As Atul Kohli argues, 'the perpetutation of poverty [in India] ... has resulted from an increasingly institutionalized pattern of domination involving an alliance between a loosely organized national elite and entrepreneurial classes.'[7] Sixty per cent of the population continues to scratch out a living in subsistence agriculture. And while industrial growth has encouraged massive urban migration, the standard of living in Indian cities has deteriorated alarmingly.

Perhaps the greatest developmental problem in India is posed by a population that is growing by an estimated 20 million people per year. The vicious cycle of poverty and population growth is a result of the fact that 'families poor in income, employment and social security need children first to work and later to sustain elderly parents.'[8] Nor has India become a major exporting country. Its exports account for less than 1 per cent of world international trade, and its foreign-exchange deficit is still perceived as a major problem. Scarce funds are used up in the effort to service foreign debts, and long-term planning too frequently gives way to short-term needs.

Moreover, what progress has been made has been achieved at a high cost to environmental quality and industrial safety. Rural areas have been permanently deforested, making them unfit for habitation. Enormous areas of land have been removed from agricultural production to make way for such mega-projects as hydroelectric dams. Lakes and rivers, including India's sacred Ganges, have been rendered unfit for human use by the unfettered discharge of household and industrial effluent. Massive increases in air pollution resulting from industrialization have rendered many urban environments almost uninhabitable. As the Brundtland Commission concluded, the 'pressures of poverty and rising populations make it enormously difficult for developing countries to pursue environmentally sound policies even in the best of circumstances.'[9] The concept of 'sustainable development,' new even in the developed world, is at best a future ideal in the developing world. At worst, the newfound concern for the environment of developing nations may be viewed as another strategy of oppression by developed nations. As the economist Robert Dorfman has suggested, the poorer countries of the world confront tragic choices. They cannot afford drinking water standards as high as those the industrial countries are accustomed to. They cannot afford to close their pristine areas to polluting industries that would introduce technical know how and productive capital and that would earn urgently needed foreign exchange. They cannot afford to bar mining companies from their unexploited regions. Nor can they afford to impose antipollution requirements on these companies that are as strict and as expensive as those in richer industrial countries. They should always realize that environmental protection measures are financed out of the stomachs of their own people; the multinationals cannot be made to pay for them.[10]

It is little wonder that many in the Third World (as, indeed, in the industrialized countries) share the perception that development and environment (including health and safety) compete; that there is an inevitable trade-off between the alleviation of poverty and the protection of workers, consumers, and the environment. While attitudes may be changing, there is a sense in which the environmental and safety ethic is seen to be an unaffordable luxury. In 1972, Prime Minister Gandhi said, 'The rich countries may look upon development as the cause of environmental destruction, but to us it is one of the primary means of improving the environment of living ... How can we speak to those who live in villages and in slums about keeping the oceans, rivers and air clean when their own lives are contaminated at the source.'[11]

These attitudes not only apply to issues concerning the quality of the physical environment, but also extend to working conditions and industrial safety. The reduction of pollution and the management of workplace risk are both costs, and not insignificant ones. One study has estimated that, between 1972 and 1981, $380 billion was spent on pollution abatement and control in the United States.[12] And according to a study prepared for the Brundtland Commission, had developing countries been required to meet the standards established in the United States, the cost for one year would have been between $5.5 billion and $14.2 billion.[13]

The massively unequal distribution of global wealth and resources therefore places even the most welfare-sensitive host states in an inherently contradictory position when they seek to regulate industrial safety and environmental quality.[14] Industry provides not only the materials of development but also a large portion of state finance. Domestically, the government is under pressure to create jobs and wealth, while at the same time protecting the environment and worker safety. Thus, the state seeks to regulate industry in a manner suited to the welfare of the citizen, without alienating the owners of capital. At the very least, these two functions create tensions in the formation of public policy. Perhaps more accurately, they place the state in a contradictory position. This is especially true in situations where, as in the Bhopal case, the state is a part owner of the very enterprise that is to be regulated.

As the previous chapter revealed, what formal legal efforts are made by developing countries to police industrial safety are bound to be limited. Decisions are made by government in consultation with business élites, with little input from labour groups or the public. The regulations that do exist are only sporadically enforced and are unable to keep up with the pace of technological change. Departments are understaffed, underfunded and ill equipped to regulate complex technological processes. Laws and policies that are intended to improve the welfare of impoverished people put a high premium on short-term economic gain and, as in the case of Bhopal, simply exacerbate their hardship.

As a result of the perceived trade-off between short-term development and long-term environmental protection, scarce development capital is used for the construction of industrial plants and little is invested in safety or environment. As one Indian environmental expert noted several years before the Bhopal disaster, 'in licensing a new industry, low priority in foreign exchange is given for selecting the control equipment. The procurement of control equipment is often delayed or even cancelled, thus resulting in new industry coming up without proper control or monitoring facilities.'[15] Environmental-impact and industrial-risk assessments are not done, and industries tend to be located in areas with an insufficiently developed infrastructure.

The development–environment trade-off must be carefully interrogated. Union Carbide's operation in India cannot, of course, be said to be an unqualified evil. Indeed, it created significant benefits in terms of employment and the provision of products that were at least thought to be needed. But the Bhopal disaster reveals the other side of the equation and provides a tragic illustration of the true social costs of importing hazardous technologies and products. Moreover, while there must be some trade-off between the costs and benefits of industrialization, too often the way in which those costs and benefits are distributed is ignored. Bhopal is merely one example of the way in which the economic benefits of a hazardous technology are reaped by a small élite, while the enormous costs to health and the environment are visited upon the disempowered poor.

There is a real paradox in policies that aim at improving the quality of life in a country by importing technologies that impose enormous risks on human health and the environment. Ironically, the Bhopal facility was part of India's 'green revolution.' Considered an essential factor in the effort to achieve self-sufficiency in agricultural production, pesticide production and use increased dramatically during the late 1960s and early 1970s. Investment in chemical-based agriculture was further encouraged by lending institutions hoping to see rapid returns on their investments.[16] The decision to manufacture the pesticides in India as opposed to relying on imports was based on India's goal of preserving foreign exchange and its policy of industrialization. But while the green revolution may have been a qualified success, its costs to current generations should not be underestimated. As the previous chapter explained, the Bhopal facility was misconceived from the outset, relying as it did on the large-volume production of an expensive chemical. More importantly, as Bhopal illustrates, industrial 'quick fixes' too often have unintended adverse impacts. To improve agricultural development, and thus the quality of life, by creating an ultra-hazardous industry is too much like squeezing putty. The problem simply reappears in a different shape. The Bhopal disaster is not the only incident to demonstrate the long-term repercussions of the massive use of pesticides in an effort to improve short-term agricultural production.[17] The World Health Organization estimates that there are 10,000 pesticide-related deaths yearly, and that annual cases of acute poisoning are as high as one million or more.[18] Most of this human carnage takes place in the developing world.

Multinational Capital and the Nation State

Even where there is a recognition by host countries of the need to regulate hazardous industries, their efforts are constrained by the realities of the global political and economic system. After the Second World War, many countries emerged from colonial control only to discover that direct political domination had been replaced by a new form of international power in the form of multinational corporations. At the time that Union Carbide was planning the Bhopal operation, an influential book, *Global Reach*, was published which argued that 'the survival of the poor nations of Asia, Africa and Latin America now depends upon how and on what terms they can relate to the world industrial system ... the three essential structures of power in underdeveloped societies are typically in the hands of global corporations: the control of technology, the control of finance capital, and the control of marketing and dissemination of ideas.'[19]

The future of the lesser-developed countries (LDCs) of the world is tied to their ability to attract technology and capital from the developed world. These resources are controlled by the industrialized countries and, in large part, by multinational corporations (MNCs). Many of these companies rival their host countries in economic power. For example, in 1974, one study of Union Carbide discovered that, of the 125 countries in which it marketed its products, 75 (60 per cent) had a gross domestic product smaller than the gross sales of the company.[20] And, in 1980, the governments and companies of the industrialized world owned 65 per cent of all patents, compared with the 6 per cent owned in the developing world.[21] In so far as economic growth requires large-scale capital investment and technology transfer from MNCs, LDCs must compete with each other to provide an attractive resting-spot for capital in search of a home. The development potential of the LDCs is therefore seen to be contingent upon the maintenance of a congenial relationship with international capitalism.

The control by MNCs of capital, technology and information therefore gives them enormous power in the developing world. In return for their participation they receive industrial concessions, cheap labour, raw materials, and access to enormous markets. They are allowed to maintain ownership of their information and intellectual property, and control over their technology and operations. When the state threatens to alter fundamentally the conditions of production, capital responds in a number of ways. There is evidence that multinationals will occasionally resort directly to bribery, blackmail, and violence in order to protect their interests in the communities in which they operate and to influence government policy.[22] Indeed, throughout the Bhopal litigation, the other major story dominating the pages of Indian newspapers was the 'Bofors Scandal' in which a European arms manufacturer was alleged to have bribed officials in Prime Minister Rajiv Gandhi's government in order to secure an arms-procurement contract. But of even greater significance is simply the economic power of large domestic and multinational corporations. Because they are essential to economic development, their negotiating positions are strong and, in the last instance, they are able to shut down factories and lay off employees. Capital may threaten to 'go on strike' or, indeed, migrate to more hospitable climates. In India, two familiar examples of this phenomenon are the departure of IBM and Coca-Cola Ltd from the country. The former chose to leave rather than to comply with India's requirement of majority Indian ownership. The latter left rather than disclose its secret formula to its Indian partner.[23] Union Carbide's continued majority ownership of Union Carbide of India Ltd (UCIL), as an exception to the Indian government's usual foreign-investment regula-tions, attests to the power of the company.

None of this is meant to suggest that MNCs are unqualifiedly bad for the developing world. Their participation is inevitable, and in many instances desirable. Indeed, prior to the accident, Union Carbide was considered by many in India to be a good corporate citizen. In its thirteen plants it employed about 10,000 Indian citizens, paying them decent wages. It did introduce into the country a desired (though ultimately deadly) technology. The point, however, is that the exercise of the enormous power of MNCs is guided by the profit motive, and ultimately multinationals will do business only on their own terms. Unfortunately, those terms fail to include a sufficient regard for the welfare of workers and local populations. As Union Carbide's critics have pointed out, the pattern of irresponsibility revealed in Bhopal was not the only example of the company's disregard of health hazards.[24] In its operations in other parts of the world, including the United States, it has frequently placed profits above safety. For example, when Temik (Union Carbide's other pesticide) began to show up in the drinking water of twenty-two U.S. states, and as residue on fruits and vegetables, the company denied that it posed a health hazard and lobbied to have standards lowered. The product was subsequently severely restricted. At its operations in West Virginia, Puerto Rico, and Indonesia, the company has also consistently denied the health hazards to workers and communities from pollution and exposure to chemical substances.

As long as state priorities require the reproduction of capital within a particular geographical unit, its economic and environmental policies are, in the last instance, constrained by the demands of capital. Countries compete to attract the capital, technology and skills MNCs have to offer. So long as there is a perception that MNCs are highly mobile, environmental and safety concerns will inevitably be balanced against the danger of capital flight. What limited power the state does have to respond to the demands of workers and social activists is just that – limited.[25]

Throughout the Bhopal case, social-activist groups have repeatedly called for the expropriation of Union Carbide's assets in India, for its expulsion from the country, and for a crack-down on other multinationals. It is significant that, while the government might have achieved short-term political benefits from taking some kind of action against the company, it chose not to do so. Officials recognized the country's dependence on foreign capital and the danger of limiting MNC operations in the country or appearing overly punitive. As one government official said, 'Why should we condemn all multinationals because of bad decisions taken by Union Carbide?'[26] Other officials in the Department of Chemicals confirmed that multinationals were monitoring the way in which the government treated Union Carbide and that the government felt it was necessary to maintain a favourable investment climate in the country.

The 'New Order': The Power of Host States and the Safety Gap

The preceding analysis is not intended to indict all multinational business corporations, or to imply that the behaviour of multinational business is necessarily worse than that of national industries in the Third World. MNCs have played an often valuable, and probably inevitable, role in the gradual development of Third World countries. Paradoxically, the prominent role played by multinationals in developing countries is, in part, the direct result of the successful trade policies of those countries. What the analysis does reveal, then, is the contradictory nature of the relationship between MNCs and their host countries, resulting in significant constraints on the promotion of values other than immediate economic returns.

Nor should it be concluded that the host countries of the developing world are entirely powerless in the face of multinational economic clout. Over the past twenty years, in their effort to enhance their control over economic development and to increase their share of the gains from production, host countries have exercised increasing bargaining power and sophistication and have managed to assert greater control over multinationals. In India, tough foreign-investment regulations limit foreign ownership of industry, and collaborations must be approved by the government. Increasingly, direct control of industry by MNCs through equity participation and operational management has given way to contractual relationships with domestic partners. These take the form of joint ventures, minority ownership, management agreements, licensing agreements, and simple sales of technology.[27] Through such devices the control exercised by foreign owners and management is thought to be reduced, and local control enhanced. The industry becomes increasingly indigenous, contributing more significantly to the development of the local infrastructure and becoming more susceptible to governmental influence.

Union Carbide's operation in India illustrates the evolving nature of the balance that is struck between multinationals and their host states. When the Indian company began more than fifty years ago, the operation was owned and operated entirely by Americans and relied on importing component parts and materials. But, over the years, Union Carbide had diluted its ownership share in the Indian company and had gradually turned over responsibility for local management to Indian nationals. Its backward integration into manufacturing its products entirely in India was also consistent with government policy. Union Carbide did not initiate its pesticide operation in Bhopal simply because India was a classic 'pollution haven'; it also received the encouragement of the Indian government. Its 'high-tech' Bhopal facility was located on government land leased to it for forty dollars per acre. And though Union Carbide retained majority ownership of the Bhopal operation, Indian public financial institutions were also major equity participants. While Union Carbide had exclusive control over the necessary technology, and was responsible for the transfer of technology and the initial design of the plant, the Union of India had sufficient bargaining clout to ensure that the construction of the plant and of much of the necessary equipment was undertaken in India by Indian firms. And while Union Carbide initially assumed responsibility for employee training and plant management, at the time of the accident the plant was operated and managed exclusively by Indian citizens.

To a certain extent, the increased control by host countries of MNC-sponsored industry gives the host greater control over environmental and workplace regulation. However, a number of facts militate against too optimistic a view of this 'new order.' In the first place, it is important not to exaggerate the control achieved by the host country over multinationals. Union Carbide remained the majority owner of the Indian operation, with full power to direct its policy and operation. Second, the development of indigenous industry does not eliminate the environment–development contradiction, but simply shifts the economic dependence of the state to local capital and local management. And, in many developing countries, including India, local capital has almost as much power as multinational companies. Wealth is concentrated in the hands of a very few actors, and only a small number of firms have the capacity to participate in large industrial projects. Government policy and investment itself may tend to encourage monopolization. As a result, two or three companies may wield great power and their quest for profit is unlikely to differ much from that of their foreign counterparts. As Charles Pearson of the World Resources Institute argues, 'One should not be too sanguine about the trend toward national control of natural resources, however. Responsibility for controlling abuse in resource exploitation is simply shifted to local state-owned or private enterprises. There is no evidence that they behave better than MNCs and indeed some evidence indicates that their record may be worse.'[28] Pearson suggests that, because of their size and sophistication, and because of the ability to transfer information and technology from their operations in developed countries, multinational corporations may, in fact, be better able to manage industrial risks.

Third, while contractual relationships may give the host country greater control over undertakings in which multinationals are involved, they may also create a danger that the MNC will abdicate its responsibility or that environmental and safety concerns will 'slip between the cracks in the newer forms of joint venture, subcontracting, and management-contract arrangements ... the increasing prevalence of joint ventures – often with state enterprise partners – and the use of subcontractors pose special difficulties. MNCs may be tempted to ignore environmental responsibilities if they hold a minority ownership and if the local partners are uninterested.'[29]

This is precisely what happened in Bhopal. Each of Union Carbide, the Indian company, and the Indian government exercised partial, and extremely imperfect, control over the facility. And each would later blame the other for the resulting disaster.

There is a further danger that, in the wake of Bhopal, the 'safety gap' may be widened. In their public pronouncements, multinationals and chemical companies assured the world that, after Bhopal, steps would be taken to improve safety standards and reduce risk. And some advances have been achieved. However, in their internal deliberations, these same companies are also concerned to reduce their own legal and financial exposure. Ironically, there may be a perception that the best way to achieve this is to further *reduce* their participation in operations and safety in the developing world. As the general counsel for a large multinational said in reference to the legal exposure of a parent company operating subsidiaries in other countries, 'Ironically the existence of pervasive and intrusive regulation by the foreign jurisdiction may have the effect of reinforcing a district court's willingness to dismiss a case brought by foreign plaintiffs. This type of regulation, while bothersome as a compliance matter, may have the unintended benefit of reinforcing the local interest in the controversy [and thus excusing the parent company for liability for the negligence of its subsidiary].'[30] This lawyer concluded that in order to reduce its legal exposure, the parent company should delineate more clearly the 'responsibility between headquarters management and subsidiary personnel, with delegation to subsidiary management of as much autonomy as possible concerning of *operating* matters and restriction of headquarters management to *strategy* and *policy* issues.'[31] Thus, control can be maintained while responsibility is avoided. Arguably, this was precisely the problem at Bhopal.

Global Problems, Global Solutions

The central tension in the relationship between multinationals and their host countries is over who is to control the enterprise and how to divide the gains from production.[32] There is no doubt that the transfer of technology from industrialized nations to industrializing nations is a practical necessity with real benefits. But it is not an unequivocal good. Along with the export of technology goes the export of danger. In the context of transnational transfers, technology may get out of control. The multinational may abandon responsibility, and the new host may be incapable of immediately filling the void. Transnational corporations are not regulated by the law of their home state, or by international law. And, as the later chapters make clear, they may even be beyond the reach of the law of the country in which they do business.

The Role of International Law

Given the problematic nature of host-country regulation, the question arises whether international law or the law of the MNC's home country might better respond to the problems created by the internationalization of hazardous industry. Developing countries need to attract new technology, yet are not always well situated to deal with the resulting hazards. The power of multinationals and the inadequacy of domestic laws reduce lesser-developed countries (or their citizens) to the status of mere passive importers of high-risk technologies, or even dumping-grounds for dangerous processes and substances that are no longer tolerated in the developed world.[33] This status quo can be altered only by international efforts that recognize the transborder nature of the problem. Given that there is a domestic 'accountability deficit' whereby corporate conduct is not sufficiently checked by government agencies, workers, or communities, perhaps that accountability could be enhanced on the international level.

Yet international law at present plays almost no role in a Bhopal scenario. Substantive international law remains weak in the area of pollution, industrial hazards, and multinational business regulation. This situation is not the result solely of a lack of goodwill (though indifference does, of course, play a part). International efforts are limited by the contradictory interests of developed and developing countries, by traditional notions of sovereignty, and, most of all, by the world's inability to redress the root problem – the vast disparities in wealth and power that characterize international relations.

Traditionally, international law is organized around agreements between sovereign nation-states and leaves the regulation of industry to the host state. The subjects of international law are nation-states, and its focus is upon their obligations. Indeed, multinational corporations and other non-governmental entities are assimilated to the status of 'private citizens.' They are not legal entities recognized by international law and are therefore not accountable to the international community. The interests of national governments tend to reinforce this situation. Comprehensive international regulation of multinational business might be insensitive to the needs of local economies, inconsistent with the policies of local governments, and, indeed, a violation of national sovereignty. For example, Principle 21 of the 1972 U.N. Declaration on the Human Environment provides that 'states have in accordance with the charter of the United Nations and the principles of international law, the sovereign right to exploit their own resources pursuant to their own environmental policies.'[34]

Thus, so long as there are no apparent transboundary effects, international law will not interfere with the domestic policy of the state (where there are transboundary effects, international law may be more potent as, for example, in the Canada–United States dispute regarding pollution from the Trail Smelter).[35] International law may, in fact, be hostile to the regulation of multinational business. The free-trade orientation of the General Agreement on Tariffs and Trade (GATT) might, for example, characterize the regulation of multinational business, or restrictions on the import or export of hazardous goods and technologies, as non-tariff barriers to trade.[36] Certainly the general orientation of modern international trade regimes has been to facilitate rather than to restrict the flow of products and technologies, however hazardous.

This is not to suggest that industrial safety and environmental concerns are entirely absent from the international agenda. International organizations have sought to come to terms with multinational hazardous industries and technology transfer, but their efforts, by and large, are limited to the production of voluntary codes of conduct and non-binding guidelines that are further limited by the reluctance of many countries to enforce them.[37]

The Organization for Economic Cooperation and Development (OECD) has twenty-four member countries, mostly from the industrialized world. In 1984 it revamped its Guidelines for Multinational Enterprises. Under these guidelines the member states agree to regulate their multinationals doing business abroad; to ensure, for example, that their operations 'are in harmony with national policies of the countries in which they operate.' However, as Robert Lutz points out, such efforts are in reality only limited measures and 'soft law.'[38] They are voluntary, apply only to several specific industries, and are framed in very general terms. Specific prohibitions are limited to non-controversial norms such as banning bribery and improper political interference. Similar voluntary codes and non-binding guidelines have been promulgated by the United Nations, the European Economic Community (EEC), and the International Labor Organization. The U.N. Conference on Trade and Development (UNCTAD) has been studying the regulation of transnational business and technology transfer for years with little result.[39]

The Chernobyl disaster demonstrates the practical non-existence of an international law of liability for industrial hazards. The nuclear meltdown that occurred in Chernobyl on 26 April 1986 caused extensive local and international damage. At least 34 people died immediately, and 40,000 people were evacuated. The radiation affected at least twenty-six other countries and it is estimated that thousands of people in those countries will die from cancer as a result of their exposure. Economic losses, resulting especially from agricultural damage, were suffered by both governments and individuals.[40] Production losses, clean-up costs, environmental monitoring, medical studies, and modest compensation from governments amounted to hundreds of millions of dollars.

Given the transnational consequences of the Chernobyl disaster, it is an even more obvious candidate for an international solution than is Bhopal's. Yet almost nothing happened. In the first place, it is unclear that any international law was violated. As Phillipe Sands, of the Centre for International Environmental Law, explains, there is neither a universally acknowledged principle of international law that requires states to prevent such a disaster, nor any clearly defined treaties or conventions regarding liability or compensation.[41] Even if there were such obligations, there is no agreement on the standard of care that a state must exercise in controlling its nuclear operations, or the level of harm that must be proven in order to trigger liability. The quantification of losses, especially those resulting simply from environmental degradation, would be enormously complex. Political considerations also militate against international responsibility. Most states are implicated in the creation of transboundary hazards, whether they result from their own nuclear installations or industrial facilities, or from the transportations of toxic wastes and hazardous materials.

A variety of international conventions regarding nuclear energy exist. Both the OECD Paris Convention on Third Party Liability in the Field of Nuclear Energy and the International Atomic Energy Commission Vienna Convention on Civil Liability for Nuclear Damage[42] require the member states to implement legislation controlling nuclear energy and to establish mechanisms for compensation for resulting damage. The difficulty with these conventions (to which the former USSR was not, in any event, a party) is that they place responsibility solely upon the 'operator' of the facility and set very low levels of compensation. As Phillipe Sands concludes, 'In terms of environmental protection the two conventions are arguably worse than nothing. They encourage negligence by telling operators that even if an accident occurs they will be held liable only for a minuscule fraction of its consequences, the remainder to be borne by the governments, citizens and future generations.'[43] It is perhaps not surprising that no claims were brought against the former USSR in respect of the Chernobyl disaster. Sands concludes that, 'after more than two centuries' development in international law, thirty years' experience with nuclear power, and two international conventions designed to deal with precisely the sort of issues raised by Chernobyl, not a single successful claim has been brought against the USSR, and this despite the USSR's implied acceptance of its own negligence in the incident. International law will have had absolutely no effect in preventing the next accident and protecting the environment from its transboundary consequences.'[44]

Exporting Danger: Home-State Law

Given the current inability of international organizations to deal with transnational hazards one might think that there is room for individual action by the more developed countries to ensure that their industrial citizens do not recklessly export danger to the Third World.[45] Those international initiatives in place rely, at any rate, on the good-faith participation of individual nations. But the commitment to date has been disappointing. The moment industry moves beyond the borders of its home state it ceases, for most purposes, to be subject to its laws. Home states are generally reluctant to give their domestic regulations extraterritorial effect, and importing states are reluctant to relax their sovereignty by importing foreign laws along with foreign technology. The result is that U.S., European, and Japanese corporations doing business in the Third World need not meet the standards of safety established for their domestic operations. So, for example, while the asbestos industry is now strictly regulated in the developed world, production has shifted to the developing countries, including India. In these countries, workers are exposed to uncontrolled hazards in deadly workplaces, often owned by or run with the collaboration of multinational companies.[46]

This situation is condemned by many because it licenses a double standard of safety for MNC operations in developed and developing countries. Yet it is defended by others who point out that the host state may regulate the industry if it wishes. Extraterritorial regulation by the home state would be difficult to enforce, and would reduce the benefits of comparative advantage often associated with transnational business. It would reduce the competitive edge of multinationals and could cause them to relocate in more congenial environments. Of equal importance is the fact that developing countries are themselves resistant to the idea that another country's regulations might apply to business operations within their own borders. Extraterritorial regulation of industry would be overly paternalistic, potentially overriding the balance struck by the host state between environment and development. Ultimately, it risks being a new form of legal colonialism.

Of course, the industrialized countries have made some efforts to regulate the transfer of hazardous products and technologies to the developing world.[47] Strategies include the requirement of 'informed consent' whereby an exporter is obliged to give the importer information on the dangers associated with a product or technology.[48] Some laws go even farther and either ban the export of certain products altogether or impose a condition that such products may not be exported unless they meet standards comparable to those set in the exporting country. Such initiatives were undertaken in response to the scandalous dumping of hazardous products (such as children's sleepwear coated with cancer-causing chemicals) on unsuspecting Third World consumers.[49] However, these ostensibly promising approaches are limited. First, they are neither comprehensive nor consistent; they apply mostly to *products* and do not reach technology transfers, industrial *processes*, or foreign *operations*. Second, they are neither guided by a coherent policy nor perfectly implemented. The moral interest of the exporting state not to inflict damage on other countries is continuously balanced against other economic interests and state imperatives, such as the encouragement of free trade and the growth of the exporting nation's own economy. Indeed, in 1982 the United States voted against a U.N. resolution expanding the informed-consent approach to hazardous exports; and, tellingly, during the same period that the Bhopal plant was coming on line, the Reagan administration in the United States, in line with its laissez-faire ideology, was rolling back existing export regulations.[50] The resulting situation is illustrated by the fact that almost 30 per cent of all chemical pesticides exported from the United States are either banned or severely restricted in their country of origin.[51]

Finally, while environmentally friendly, export regulation may also be characterized as 'environmental imperialism' by developing nations. Why, they ask, should they not be left entirely free to make their own import decisions, based upon their better appreciation of their needs and aspirations? The well-meaning paternalism of the industrially developed countries may simply echo or reproduce the relations of the previous colonial era.

One way in which multinationals might be made more accountable for their operations in developing countries is if, in the event of environmental damage or an industrial catastrophe, they might be liable for the consequences under the private law of their home country. This was, in fact, the main strategy adopted by the Indian government in the Bhopal case. As the remainder of this book makes clear, however, there are enormous obstacles in the way of such an approach. Unless the government takes over the litigation, the burden is upon the individual victims to prosecute the action. What hope have they against the massive financial and legal resources available to the multinational? Even where there are sufficient resources to prosecute the action, the courts of the home country may be reluctant to entertain litigation in respect of an accident that took place outside its boundaries. In most cases, including Bhopal's, the immediate damage will have been caused by a local operation that is a separate legal entity from its parent company. It will, therefore, deny responsibility on the basis of the theory of independent corporate personality. Finally, even if successful, such litigation may have unintended effects. Again, the threat of liability may lead to the flight of capital, or may encourage the company to assert greater control over the economy of its host country than that country desires. These difficulties, combined with a host of other procedural and substantive limitations on private law, make it unlikely that private litigation can contribute a great deal to the reduction of international hazardous risk.

A Smaller World

The many impediments to reform should not cause us to give up on the search for cooperative solutions. The international dimension of the Bhopal disaster affects us all. While Bhopal did not involve transborder physical harm, it did implicate a multinational corporation. It also involved and interrogated the laws and policies of another state, and captured the attention of the world community. Bhopal brought into question the individualistic assumption that moral and legal responsibility for such a disastrous legacy can be confined within national borders. The internationalization of business has more closely linked the economies and cultures of all the world. If nothing else, the Bhopal disaster was a foreign-relations setback for both the United States and multinational business.

This chapter has emphasized the ambiguous nature of the relationship between MNCs and the countries of the Third World. For the people of the developing world, multinational corporations and their home countries do not simply deliver economic development; they deliver death. The 'Killer Carbide' slogans on the wall of the Bhopal plant remind us that multinationals are hardly goodwill ambassadors from the developed world. The people of the Third World know that their countries are used as a dumping-ground for hazardous substances such as pesticides, medicines, and food products. They are aware of the pattern of development whereby affluent countries gradually shed their dangerous industries, moving them to regions where the cost of 'dirty business' is lower. They know that their lives are considered cheap. It is no wonder that, in the wake of Bhopal, the victims feel a 'desire for revenge.'

The global trade in toxic wastes reproduces this pattern of exploitation. The developed world produces an estimated 300 million tonnes of industrial waste per year. There are more than 12,000 transborder movements of such materials per year, many to developing countries who, desperate for foreign exchange, become cheap disposal sites. Each one of these sites is a disaster waiting to happen. Leaking drums of toxic or explosive chemicals are stacked in open yards, contaminating groundwater and food, and risking explosion. Recent efforts such as the United Nations (Basel) convention on toxic wastes go some way towards reducing these risks, but they also continue to be based upon the idea of *trade* in waste. There is no doubt that the developing countries are in need of foreign exchange, but the idea that they are able to achieve social advancement only by accepting the rest of the world's toxins is hardly likely to break the cycle of poverty and human and environmental degradation.

Citizens in the industrialized countries also feel the power of international business. Ships flying flags of convenience spill tonnes of oil onto the coastlines of Europe and North America. Their domestic industries also are controlled by companies that have grown to international proportions and are in a position to eliminate jobs, close plants, and remove their operations to less-expensive countries. The chemical industry, for example, is the fifth-largest industrial sector in Canada,[52] and is dominated by multinationals. In a brief presented to Canadian environ-mental authorities, the Canadian Chemical Producers' Association urged that environmental controls not be tightened, suggesting that 'it is a fact that if unnecessary or excessive costs, delays or uncertainty are introduced unilaterally by any country (or province), innovation and development will simply cease or be transferred to jurisdictions with a more favourable business climate. Should this happen in Canada, it could be very quickly reduced to a warehouse economy for chemicals.'[53]

The world community now firmly recognizes the global nature of many environmental and industrial hazards and has at least affirmed the need to develop cooperative regimes. Progress has been slow, and is obstructed by the competing interests of the main players. Bhopal reveals clearly the obstacles that must be confronted and the factors that must be taken into account. Any successful process must first of all interrogate, and at least rebalance, the development–environment trade-off. Official recognition of the norm of 'sustainable development' in the wake of the *Brundtland Report* is a welcome change, and must be translated into concrete action. Human safety and environmental quality must be given greater weight in government and corporate decision making. Second, any process will have to negotiate carefully the tension between international cooperation and national sovereignty. While national control of resources remains a reality, the internationalization of business and of industrial hazards has tilted the balance towards cooperative regimes, so long as those regimes are suitably tailored to local conditions. Finally, any solution will have to confront the vastly unequal distribution of wealth and power among different nations and their differential capacities to control risk, and to acknowledge the power of multinational business. At a minimum, the lessons of Bhopal require that we turn our attention to questions concerning the allocation of responsibilities among the various governmental and non-governmental actors in hazardous industrial sectors. Especially in the case of joint ventures, technology transfers, and multinational undertakings, responsibility can too easily fall through the links in complex chains of command. Similarly, we should re-examine the content and effectiveness of international codes of conduct and guarantees of financial and industrial responsibility by multinational actors. The world's commitment to free trade and national sovereignty should be continuously measured against the requirements of public safety and environmental quality. The informed-consent approach should be strengthened and broadened, risk assessment and emergency preparedness must become an integral part of any investment or development, and the regulatory infrastructure of host states must be strengthened.

While the immediate human consequences of the Bhopal disaster were confined to India, the problem is not simply a domestic one. The international economic system and government policies of both the developed and developing world are fully implicated, and Bhopal bespeaks the need to develop new models of multilateral cooperation, planning, and assistance if such catastrophes are to be avoided in the future. Later chapters return to these themes in more detail, and the final chapter elaborates on international processes. Chapter 3, however, returns to the Bhopal story and the more immediate question that it raised: how to respond to the plight of the victims of the world's worst industrial disaster.

3

Repairing a Disaster

Mass Disasters and the Law

Two thousand five hundred people died in Bhopal almost instantly. During the following years more than a thousand more of the worst-affected victims would also perish. Hundreds of children were orphaned, and surviving family members were left without means of subsistence. At least 20,000 people were seriously injured and left without the ability to work or care for themselves. Tens of thousands of others suffered from other physical injuries, economic losses, and social dislocation. All of these victims demanded and deserved relief and rehabilitation. They also demanded that the responsible parties be brought to justice and that the law be developed to ensure that such an incident never again happened.

Immediately following the Bhopal disaster, local, national, and international agencies began to respond to the plight of the people of Bhopal. The governments of India and the state of Madhya Pradesh promised to mount massive relief efforts. Individual doctors, the Red Cross, and other relief organizations entered the city to do what they could. Even Union Carbide, through its president and chair, Warren Anderson, accepted moral responsibility for the disaster and promised immediate assistance and compensation. Yet underlying (and undermining) all these promises and efforts was a single assumption: that any full and final resolution of the problem would have to be a *legal* one. The Indian and international press immediately began to speculate on what shape 'the world's biggest lawsuit' would take. While the Union Carbide Corporation had accepted moral responsibility, it had also stated that the 'legal details' would have to be sorted out later; and both the company and the Indian government began immediately to marshall their legal resources. U.S. lawyers moved rapidly to sign up Indian victims as clients, and social activists and victims' groups in Bhopal itself began to demand compensation, retribution, and 'justice.' With an inevitability reflecting the cultural dominance of law even in countries as different as India and the United States, the victims' expectations, and indeed the world's attention, gradually began to fix upon the promises of law; Bhopal was to become the severest test of those promises.

The Bhopal incident raised a multitude of questions about the role of law and the design of legal institutions. The first set of questions concerns the basic goals and objectives to be achieved, and how they are to be ranked. Is the goal to compensate the victims, to penalize wrongdoing, to reduce future risks, or to encourage industrial development? In so far as these goals are incompatible, how are they to be priorized, balanced, or compromised? To what extent does the desire to encourage industrial safety come into conflict with the other goals of state policy, such as economic growth? If one of the objectives is to assess responsibility, it must be determined which actors are involved and against what standard their actions are to be measured. How is the process to deal with the realities and complexities of modern business organization, which, as in the case of Bhopal, involve numerous governmental and non-governmental actors? What are the various responsibilities of multinationals, the local operators, and the Indian authorities?

The second set of questions has to do with the design of an appropriate process through which these questions are to be answered. Is the Bhopal dispute simply one between an injurer and the victims or are wider state interests implicated? Given the enormity of the tragedy, the large number of victims, and their overwhelming poverty, is it appropriate to treat the problem as involving a series of isolated and individualized contests between the victims and Union Carbide? The transnational nature of the tragedy raised equally difficult problems. The disaster crossed national borders and implicated Indian, U.S., and international law. Where was the dispute to be resolved, and according to whose rules and values?

In Search of Criteria for an Adequate Solution

In seeking answers to these questions, most lawyers and policy makers would probably agree on two *general* principles or goals: first, that the process should guarantee some form of remedial assistance to the innocent victims of industrial harms; and, second, that it should be designed so as to reduce the risk of such occurrences in the future. These two goals – compensation and deterrence – must themselves be sensitive to other considerations. They must take into account the realities, costs, and complications that inevitably accompany complex litigation. They must also be understood in terms of prevailing social values, including the desire to treat all of the parties fairly while, at the same time, designing efficient mechanisms whereby the solution to the problem does not itself create further damage or impose unnecessary social costs.

In the case of Bhopal, the goals of compensation and deterrence may be elaborated in the following manner. At bottom, the process should be designed to provide timely and adequate assistance to the victims. Of all the parties involved, it makes the least sense to leave the victims to bear the costs of the disaster. They are blameless. They cannot be said to have been direct beneficiaries of the operation and they were in no position to prevent the disaster.

The design of a compensation process must take into account the realities of the situation. The large number of victims and the complexity of the dispute mean that the final resolution of the question of legal responsibility would take time. Moreover, the victims in Bhopal were overwhelmingly poor and would be unable to pursue compensation on their own, or to provide for themselves in the meantime. These circumstances indicate that there would have to be provision for immediate emergency and interim aid to the victims while facts were investigated and individual needs determined. Equally importantly, the process would have to take into account the inability of the individual victims to pursue compensation without assistance. Given the massively uneven distribution of resources and the overwhelming poverty of the majority of victims, some means would have to be devised whereby the victims might be empowered rather than revictimized by the process.

The compensation must be adequate to repair the damage to the individual victims and to the community. Given the complexity of the factual and medical evidence, means would have to be devised to begin processing individual claims at an early date, before the facts became impossible to determine. Individual injuries would have to be assessed in a fair and accurate fashion, taking into account the likely future consequences of the disaster and the victims' ongoing medical needs. In the case of Bhopal, it must also be remembered that the disaster did not simply cause a number of discrete individual injuries, but virtually destroyed a community. The calculation of necessary compensation funds and the implementation of a relief plan would have to take into account the full social costs of the damage, and means would have to be found to provide the victims with not only a monetary substitute for what they had lost, but some way to care for their ongoing needs and, indeed, to sustain the effort to rebuild the community.

Especially problematic in the Bhopal case is the task of locating sufficient funds to compensate the victims, and determining the appropriate allocation of both legal and financial responsibility for the disaster. At least four major parties were involved in the creation of the hazard, including Union Carbide of India Ltd (UCIL), the Union Carbide Corporation (UCC), and the governments of India and Madhya Pradesh. While the first priority is simply to locate sufficient funds to achieve the goals of relief, rehabilitation, and compensation, most would also agree that the costs of a hazard should be placed upon the party who imposed those costs and benefited from them. This latter principle reflects the moral notion that the beneficiaries of a hazardous operation should also bear the costs. Theoretically, this principle also encourages safety and provides a better basis for social-cost accounting in so far as it forces economic actors to factor in the social costs of production in their economic decisions. By 'internalizing' the cost of industrial hazards, operators have an incentive to reduce (non–cost justified) risks, or, where the risks outweigh the benefits, to terminate production.

Finally, the process must strike an appropriate balance between the goals of fairness and efficiency. The structure for a solution should be cost-effective. It should maximize the value of the available compensation funds and minimize 'transaction costs' – in particular, the administrative and legal costs that are bound to be incurred in any attempt to resolve a dispute. Yet the desire to develop an efficient solution must also accommodate the demands of all the parties to fairness and due process.

When stated as the goals of a compensation system, these criteria would be widely affirmed. However, it must be admitted that, while these principles are easy to state, they are difficult to apply in practice, and may indeed conflict. In the case of Bhopal, no one denied that the victims deserved immediate and adequate compensation for their harm. But from whom would that compensation come – the Indian company, the government, or the multinational? While as a general principle it seems correct to specify that the beneficiaries of an industrial activity should bear the responsibility for the social harm it causes, it is not always easy to locate those beneficiaries. Clearly the owners of an industry are beneficiaries in so far as they reap economic rewards, but so, perhaps, are the employees of the company, local residents whose livelihood is dependent upon the industry, users of the product, and the government itself. While we may agree that compensation should be forthcoming immediately, the desire for timely action must be balanced against the practical necessity of determining who the legitimate claimants are and what the extent of their injuries is. The desire for a quick determination of responsibility must also be balanced against the demand of those potentially responsible for fair treatment and the notion that the burden of compensation should be commensurate with the degree of culpability. Thus, in Bhopal, the quest for a speedy and efficient resolution of the dispute would inevitably come into conflict with the value of due process and other traditional procedural safeguards.

Finally, the allocation of moral and financial responsibility for industrial and environmental hazards will have an impact not only on future levels of safety, but on investment, prices, and production as well. Should decisions about injury compensation take into account these wider questions of public policy? We live in a world in which risks are an inevitable part of everyday life. The decision to drive a car; to build a factory; to produce and distribute chemicals, medicines, and consumer products – all impose risks on workers, consumers, and others. As one author has suggested, we must make 'tragic choices' about which risks are tolerable.[1] But how are we to engage in this tragic calculus? Should considerations of human health and safety be traded off against other social goals and values? If so, what price do we place on human life, and how are the inevitable losses to be distributed? Do we leave these losses where they fall, requiring the victims to accept their fate as an inevitable incident of life in modern society, or somehow redistribute them across society more generally? Ultimately the answers to these questions can be found only in our convictions about the relative values of safety, industrial development, environmental quality, and the value of human life. These values, in turn, find their expression in law.

Mass Torts: The Legal Context

When the world awoke on the 3 December 1984 to the news of the

Bhopal disaster, what crossed most lawyers' minds was that it was one more example of what are becoming known as mass disasters or mass-exposure torts.[2] The U.S. lawyers who flooded India shortly after the disaster were, in particular, enthralled with the notion that the best remedy for the victims would be a giant lawsuit against the responsible parties. Such a lawsuit would not only secure compensation for the victims, but serve to punish Union Carbide and deter the undertaking of such hazardous activities in the future. These expectations were rapidly adopted by the victims, the press, and the general public.

While the magnitude of the Bhopal disaster was unparalleled, mass-disaster litigation has become increasingly common in the late twentieth century. Earlier cases, arising out of transportation disasters and fires, were certainly not unknown, one example being the 1944 circus fire in Hartford, Connecticut, that killed 169 people and injured hundreds of others.[3] However, in the past several decades, owing to the proliferation of chemicals and hazardous technologies, and new knowledge about their effects on health and the environment, such litigation has become far more common and has, indeed, spawned the emergence of new legal specialists and novel legal processes. Recent examples of such large-scale events include the nuclear incident at Three Mile Island, the *Amoco-Cadiz* and *Exxon Valdez* oil spills, and the PCB warehouse fire at St Basile Le Grand, Quebec. The litigation arising out of such events now also frequently displays a different character from that of the older 'single incident' disaster because the harm is often more creeping than immediate, more 'toxic' than traumatic. Thus, lawyers now frequently speak about mass-exposure problems and 'toxic torts.' Such events typically arise from contact with dangerous substances, either through product consumption or long-term exposure to hazardous substances in the ambient environment. Tragic examples of such incidents include the toxic poisoning of the Love Canal area and the injuries to consumers caused by products such as the Dalkon Shield,[4] and to the children of women who consumed thalidomide and DES during pregnancy.[5] Perhaps most tragically and dramatically in North America are the estimated quarter of a million people who have contracted cancer, asbestosis, or mesothelioma from long term exposure to asbestos, prompting hundreds of thousands of lawsuits against asbestos manufacturers such as Johns-Manville.[6] Similarly, thousands of Vietnam veterans brought actions against defence contractors such as Dow Chemical in an effort to obtain compensation for their exposure to the defoliant Agent Orange.[7] Whole communities in Canada and the United States have begun battling local industries over air pollution, heavy-metal contamination of soils, and pesticide-laced drinking water. Indeed, Union Carbide has itself been involved in such disputes in the United States as a result of contamination of groundwater (and food) by its pesticide Temik (after denying for years that there was any problem, the company was eventually forced to withdraw the product).[8]

Compared to other public schemes in the developed world, such as workers' compensation, universal health care, and income assistance, the private law of tort plays a relatively minor role in compensating victims of accidents and ensuring environmental and industrial safety. Nevertheless, to many in the legal profession it continues to represent the highest form of law, expressing the values of individual responsibility and corrective justice. The law of tort is said to reflect the moral principle that those who injure others are responsible for their actions and must provide adequate compensation to deserving victims. The law channels conflict, keeps the peace, and vindicates the rights of the ordinary citizen, even against large corporate bodies. The law of tort is thought to educate the public about their rights and responsibilities, and, as a part of the common law, it is flexible and responsive to new challenges. It is said to be 'efficient' in so far as it makes actors internalize the costs of their careless conduct, and thus deters careless and dangerous activities in the future. Therefore, to many in Bhopal, the law seemed to promise the possibility of relief to the victims and punishment of the wrongdoer.

The remainder of this chapter outlines the main contours of the law in relation to industrial and environmental hazards, and as it would likely apply to the Bhopal disaster. The discussion here is introductory, sketching the general legal background against which mass-tort actions such as Bhopal's are fought. Later chapters focus in more detail on the specific legal arguments made in the Bhopal case, and the unique features and peculiar circumstances that characterized the litigation.

Industrial and Environmental Hazards: The Common-Law Background

The law of tort, in India, Canada, the United States, and elsewhere, is part of the 'judge-made' common law. It derives originally from English law, supplemented and transformed since the colonial period by judicial decisions in the newly independent countries. The law of tort is not formally codified anywhere (though aspects have been altered by legislation), but rather has been developed on a case-by-case basis and is found in the reported judgments of the courts in civil litigation.

Article 372 of the Indian constitution provided, at independence, that English law would remain in force in the new country, subject to necessary adaptation. The law of tort in India is therefore based on the common law received from England during the colonial period, retained at independence, and developed since that time.[9] Because of the poverty of the population and the high cost of going to court, there has, in fact, been very little tort litigation in India. As a result, the law with respect to environmental and industrial hazards was, at the time of the Bhopal disaster, comparatively impoverished. Nevertheless, its formal structure and doctrine are similar to those of English law. Moreover, notwithstanding the (paucity) of tort litigation in India, Indian courts are, on occasion, remarkably flexible and creative compared with their Western counterparts. When ignited, Indian law can be the most dynamic in the common-law world, borrowing ideas from the legal systems of other countries and forging innovations uniquely suited to India.[10] In previous tort cases,[11] and especially in the case of Bhopal, they would inevitably consider developments in England, Canada, and the United States in relation to mass toxic injuries, and adapt them to meet the problems thrown up by the Bhopal case. This chapter thus develops a 'best-case scenario' by focusing on developments in England and North America, revealing at least the *doctrinal* possibilities in the Bhopal case. The next chapter develops a detailed critique of this best-case scenario, detailing how, even in the developed countries, the law of tort frequently falters in its goals of compensation and deterrence when confronted with the complex problems posed by modern forms of industrial and environmental harm. Later chapters then return more specifically to the Bhopal case and the unique problems that characterize the Indian legal system – problems that would compound and magnify the obstacles faced by the Bhopal survivors.

Negligence

Prior to the nineteenth century, the common law concerned itself primarily with intentional wrongs such as assault, battery, and trespass, rather than the more remote and factually complex forms of harm resulting from industrial hazards. However, with the advent of the industrial revolution, dangerous machinery, rapid transportation, and complex and impersonal patterns of production and distribution, the law came increasingly to be faced with a new paradigm of harm arising from proliferation of risks in a more complex industrial society. Even then, however, courts were slow to respond. Under the influence of a more strongly individualistic and laissez-faire temperament, the law took a narrow view of responsibility for industrial hazards. The law seems, during the industrial revolution and afterwards, to have been consciously moulded by judges to limit the liability of entrepreneurs and industrial actors in order to encourage risk taking and economic development.[12] It viewed with horror the notion that a manufacturer, for example, might be responsible for all the consequences of a minor (or even major) failure of attention or care. The high priority placed on industrial progress, and the values of individual responsibility and self-reliance, combined to produce a relatively narrow scope for recovery by individuals injured as a result of industrial activities. During the nineteenth century workers frequently went without compensation for their injuries on the basis that, by accepting employment, they had 'consented' to the risk of injury, or that their injury had been caused by a fellow employee rather than their employer. Consumers injured by defective products were unable to sue careless manufacturers on the basis that there was no 'privity of contract,' because the goods were not warranted to be free of defects or because the consumer might have protected himself from the injury (women frequently went without any recovery on the basis that, upon marriage, they lost their legal personality and property to their husbands).[13] Judges frequently referred to the 'absurd and outrageous consequences' of allowing actions for carelessness, fearing that 'if we go one step ... there is no reason why we should not go fifty.'[14] If liability became widespread, the floodgates of litigation would open to the detriment of industrial progress.

However, the law could not remain blind to the increasing incidence of injuries caused by remote actors and developing technologies, and the 'floodgates' did begin to open, if only a crack. Causes of action were developed to hold professionals responsible for carelessly executed undertakings, to deal with roadway accidents, and to allow recovery for injuries caused by 'inherently dangerous' articles. Finally, in 1932, in what may at first appear to be a trivial case, Anglo-Canadian common law recognised a more generalized theory of responsibility for personal injuries caused by carelessness (U.S. law had also been moving in that direction).[15] A Ms Donoghue, drinking a bottle of ginger beer purchased for her by a friend, claimed to have consumed a decomposed snail that had somehow got into the bottle.[16] She sued the manufacturer for her injuries. While prior to this time it was unlikely that she could have won compensation from a 'remote' manufacturer, the English House of Lords fashioned a new principle that was more responsive to the realities of modern industrial production and more consistent with the values of the emerging welfare state. Lord Atkin laid down the foundational principle of the law of negligence, based, he said, on a 'public sentiment of moral wrongdoing for which the offender must pay: The rule that you are to love your neighbour becomes in law, you must not injure your neighbour; and the lawyer's question, Who is my neighbour? receives a restricted reply. You must take reasonable care to avoid acts or omissions which you can reasonably foresee would be likely to injure your neighbour. Who, then, in law is my neighbour? The answer seems to be – persons who are so closely and directly affected by my act that I ought reasonably to have them in contemplation as being affected when I am directing my mind to the acts or omissions which are called in question.'[17]

This decision introduced a general regime of fault-based liability. However, under the law of negligence, a person will be responsible for harm to another only in certain circumstances. As Lord Atkin makes clear, negligence does not mean that actors will be liable for any and all injuries that they cause. In order to establish liability in negligence the victims of an injury must prove that the defendant owed them a *duty of care*. This duty is established when it can be demonstrated that the victims were a member of a class of persons who, had the defendant thought about it, might be foreseen as likely to suffer harm as a result of carelessness. Second, it must be shown that the defendant's behaviour was, in fact, careless, that it fell below the required *standard of care*. The law of negligence accepts some injuries as inevitable accidents and leaves the victim to bear the loss. For the actor to be liable, the accident must be caused by the actor's failure to take reasonable precautions judged by what a prudent person would have done, given the magnitude of the risk and the severity of the consequences. Third, the victims must establish *causation*: that their injuries were, in fact, caused by the actions or omissions of the responsible party. In other words, 'but for' the carelessness of the actor, the victim would not have suffered the injury. Finally, it must be demonstrated that the carelessness of the defendant was the *proximate cause* of the injury that was ultimately suffered (that the ultimate harm is not too remote or unforeseeable) and that the victims were not themselves guilty of contributory negligence.

The law of negligence has undergone enormous expansion in the latter half of the twentieth century. Its categories are not closed and almost any industrial or environmental hazard that causes actual injury might trigger negligence liability where the responsible party has failed to guard adequately against a foreseeable risk. The law of negligence now plays a major role in personal-injury cases whether such injury arises from road accidents, medical misadventure, defective products, toxic contamination of property, industrial hazards, or other activities creating risks to human health. Where an individual or firm creates a risk, or is responsible for overseeing safety at an operation, and fails to provide adequate precautions, that individual or firm will be held responsible for the resulting injury or illness to workers or communities.[18]

Negligence is part of Indian law, and in the case of Bhopal it might, at first, seem obvious that it would provide the victims with the remedy they desired. They would allege that the company had failed to research adequately the hazardous potential of the operation, that its safety equipment was underdesigned, that the decision to store such large quantities of the dangerous chemical disregarded reasonable safety standards, that maintenance procedures were inadequate, and that employee training had not been properly maintained. All of these failures have been held to constitute negligence.[19] But, as later chapters make clear, the task of the victims would not be so easy. While it may seem clear that, in the Bhopal disaster, *someone* was negligent, it would be difficult to demonstrate exactly who had a duty to prevent the disaster, what that duty was, and in what way it was breached. Union Carbide, presenting itself as a remote, overseas investor, would continue to claim to be only peripherally involved and not legally responsible for safety at the plant. The disaster would be portrayed as either an act of sabotage or an unavoidable accident. Designers would argue that the plant was well designed and blame the disaster on management. Management would claim that the plant was properly managed and in compliance with the customary and statutory standards of safety prevailing in India at the time.[20] The victims would be left with the task of proving *who* had a duty of care, *why* the accident happened, *how* it could have been prevented, and *what* injuries they suffered as a result.

Strict Liability

The most significant limitation upon negligence law is that an actor is not responsible for the harmful consequences of an act unless it can be demonstrated that those consequences could have been averted through the exercise of reasonable care. The law of negligence thus arguably favours industrial actors at the expense of victims. It essentially creates a presumption that the victims of injury must bear their own losses unless they are able to prove exactly how their injuries came about; that the defendant owed them a duty of care to prevent those injuries; that it breached that duty of care; and that, had it not been careless, the incident would not have occurred. The law of negligence, then, continues to be limited by its laissez-faire roots. The notion that there should be 'no liability without fault' may be an axiom of justice, but as John Fleming reminds us, this notion was also, 'best calculated to serve the interests of expanding industry and the entrepreneurial class, in relieving them from the hampering burden of strict liability and conducing to that freedom of individual will and enterprise which was at the forefront of contemporary aspirations.'[21]

In recognition of these difficulties, courts will sometimes dispense with the requirement of negligence and adopt, instead, a theory of 'strict' liability. In the old, but still important case of *Rylands v Fletcher*[22] the defendant, Rylands, operated a mill, and in the course of his business, excavated a reservoir. Unknown to Rylands, the reservoir was above an abandoned coal mine. The tunnels from this mine connected with another mine, operated by Fletcher. When the reservoir was filled, it flooded into the underground tunnels and, through them, into Fletcher's mine. While there was no finding that this accident was caused by his negligence, the court nevertheless held Rylands liable for the damage. Justice Blackburn said:

the person who for his own purposes brings on his land and collects and keeps there anything likely to do mischief if it escapes, must keep it in at his peril, and, if he does not do so, is *prima facie* answerable for all the damage which is the natural consequence of its escape ... The person whose grass or corn is eaten down by the escaping cattle of his neighbour, or whose mine is flooded by the water from his neighbour's reservoir, or whose cellar is invaded by the filth of his neighbour's privy, or whose habitation is made unhealthy by the fumes and noisome vapours of his neighbour's alkali works, is damnified without any fault of his own; and it seems but reasonable and just that the neighbour, who has brought something on his own property, but which he knows to be mischievous if it gets on his neighbour's should be obliged to make good the damage which ensues if he does not succeed in confining it to his own property.[23]

This judgment was upheld on appeal, though the principle was said to be triggered only by a 'non-natural' use of the defendant's property. This is the major issue in many strict-liability cases.

Strict liability would seem to fit many environmental risks arising out of industrial uses of land. As *Rylands* makes clear, it may apply to the collection of large amounts of water for industrial purposes, and has been invoked in cases where sewage or waste has escaped from tanks or drainpipes.[24] It has been applied in cases involving explosions caused by dangerous materials[25] and to smelter fumes.[26] Strict liability has been imposed in the case of herbicides and insecticides that blow onto neighbouring property, notwithstanding that their use was both legal and without negligence,[27] as well as in cases of noxious fumes from manufacturing operations.[28] In the United States, strict liability has been increasingly adopted to deal with the problem of consumer injuries resulting from defective products.[29] The doctrine has thus played an important role in prompting settlements in mass-tort cases involving asbestos, Agent Orange, chemical pollution, and nuclear radiation. For example, in 1982, 250 residents of Three Mile Island, whose lives had been disrupted and whose health had possibly been affected by a radioactive leak from a nuclear reactor, settled their case against the General Public Utilities Corporation for $25 million.[30] And, in 1984, about 1,200 people who lived in the vicinity of the Love Canal toxic dump site settled their lawsuit against the Hooker Chemical Company for $20 million.[31]

Strict liability is part of Indian law and would undoubtedly be invoked by the victims. The materials that were stored at the plant were extremely dangerous and the processes were obviously hazardous. In particular, the decision to store such large quantities of MIC proved to be fatal. As Stephenson LJ said in *Rylands*, it seems just that the operator and beneficiary should be liable for the consequences of an escape of these materials.

But even strict liability would not necessarily apply in the Bhopal case. In many countries, including England, Canada, and India,[32] strict liability has traditionally applied in a fragmented fashion only to particular forms of 'unnatural' or 'abnormal' activities. Indeed, there is some doubt (in England at least) that strict liability applies beyond property damage to include personal injury (creating the anomalous situations that the law provides more rigorous protection to property interests than to physical security).[33] Moreover, courts have offered a number of defences, all of which might apply in the case of Bhopal.

First, who is the 'owner' of the land upon which the hazardous materials were stored, and the 'operator' of the dangerous processes? UCIL? UCC? Or, indeed, the Government of India? Second, it would inevitably be argued by Union Carbide that the use of the land was neither 'non-natural' nor ultra-hazardous. Indeed, as the company would later stress, the plant was in place in accordance with Indian policy and operated under a valid licence. Finally, Union Carbide's sabotage theory was clearly devised to provide an important defence to strict liability – willful intervention by a third party.

Bhopal would test the limits of strict liability – whether it should be nourished and extended in order to provide compensation to the victims or constrained in order to protect industrial activity. Many judges and scholars have argued that the evolution of the concept of strict liability should be encouraged and that the principle should be applicable to all hazardous activities.[34] These arguments are based on principles of loss spreading and deterrence – the growing awareness that the fault-based negligence standard frequently fails either to compensate victims or to deter dangerous activities. The notion of strict liability expresses the increasing sentiment that, even where an industry has not been careless, it is nevertheless unfair to leave the victims of modern technology to bear their losses individually, and that it may be socially desirable and efficient to require industry to bear all the social costs of production.[35]

Strict liability is therefore part of the trend away from the focus on individual guilt and moral blame expressed by fault-based justice and towards a concern for distributive justice and the needs of the victims of social progress. In many countries, including India, in the context of injuries to workers, these concerns have prompted the enactment of workers' compensation legislation whereby the victims of industry are entitled to care and compensation, regardless of fault. Strict (or absolute) liability has been adopted by both North American courts and legislatures in environmental disputes. The U.S. Comprehensive Environmental Response, Compensation and Liability Act (CERCLA)[36] incorporates a strict-liability standard in respect of toxic dump sites, as do the provisions of the Ontario Environmental Protection Act.[37]

Nor has the common law remained static. Increasingly, judges and policy makers are beginning to accept the strict-liability argument in new contexts involving environmental and industrial hazards. While social and environmental damage may be an inevitable consequence of industrial progress, there is no reason why those costs should be borne by individual victims rather than by the industrial and consumer beneficiaries of the enterprise. By imposing liability on the industry, regardless of fault, those costs will be factored into decisions about production and risk management. The price of products, therefore, will reflect the full social costs of production.[38] There may, as a result, be a trend to ease the restrictions of the 'non-natural use' test, and to expand strict liability to any activity that is 'abnormally dangerous' or 'extra-hazardous.'[39] In Canada and the United States, the storage of hazardous materials and toxic-waste disposal have both been held to be abnormally dangerous and have both attracted strict liability.[40] In the U.S. case of *City of Bridgeton* v *B.P. Oil Inc.*,[41] strict liability was imposed upon the defendant for the improper storage of a hazardous chemical. The court held that 'this is the proper time to extend the concept of strict liability in this State to those who store ultra-hazardous or pollutant substances. This means that a defendant becomes liable for damages caused to a proper plaintiff. This rule is in reality neither new nor novel. For generations it has been the common law rule that an owner of realty is required to refrain from injury to the land of his neighbour.'[42]

Other legal principles that have been developed to deal with hazardous technologies and toxic substances would also come into play in Bhopal. These include the emerging 'duty to warn' of dangerous products, substances, or processes.[43] Where a manufacturer learns of a hazard, even *after* the product has been distributed, there may be an obligation to disclose the information.[44] It is possible that an intentional cover-up of such information might also amount to fraud. In a recent case against Monsanto in the United States, it was discovered that the company became aware of the presence of highly toxic dioxins in common household products, but knowingly hid the information so as not to lose sales. The jury awarded $16.25 million in punitive damages, and parallel litigation against Monsanto is under way in Canada.[45] Similarly, where a firm becomes aware of a health hazard at an operation, it must take steps to reduce the hazard or warn those who might be affected by it.[46]

The 'duty to warn,' and the even more general principle of the public's 'right to know,' are increasingly being incorporated into North American legislation. Many statutes governing the transportation of dangerous goods, environmental protection, and worker and consumer safety oblige those in control of dangerous substances to provide information on their toxicity, to report spills and releases, and to provide information regarding the health effects and appropriate medical treatment in the event of injury.[47]

Finally, the tort of nuisance – perhaps the predominant common-law remedy in environmental disputes – would also have some application in Bhopal.[48] Nuisance is an 'unreasonable interference with the use and enjoyment of another's property.' Nuisance, which requires courts to balance competing claims to scarce resources,[49] may be used to prevent a hazard from materializing (by injunction), or may be the basis of a damages claim following an environmental incident.

What is 'unreasonable' is a function of a variety of factors. Courts will look to the severity of the pollution, the character of the locale in which it takes place, the duration of the problem, its potential effect on health and comfort, and, more controversially, the social utility of the activity that gives rise to the annoyance. Where there is some physical damage to property the activity will likely be a nuisance. But less tangible interests are also protected. Almost any annoyance to a neighbour can amount to a nuisance. Noise, smell, fumes, vibration, and draining water have all been held to be nuisances, as have air, water, and soil pollution. Oil spills have been held to be nuisances,[50] as have the emission of gases and the escape of sewage. Similarly, nuisance law is playing a prominent role in the growing problem of groundwater contamination. In the case of *Ayers* v *Jackson Township*,[51] local residents received nearly $14 million compensation for diminished quality of life and medical surveillance when run-off from a toxic landfill site polluted their drinking water.

As with other bases of liability, the values of loss distribution and cost internalization are gradually influencing nuisance law. One example is the Canadian case of *Royal Anne Hotel Co* v *Ashcroft*[52] in which a municipal sewer backed up and damaged the plaintiff's property. The plaintiff sued the municipality for negligence and nuisance. The British Columbia Court of Appeal held that the blockage was a random accident and not the result of carelessness. However, the court did hold the defendant liable for nuisance. McIntyre J held that it was no excuse that the damage was not caused by carelessness, nor even that all possible skill had been employed to prevent the problem: 'The most carefully designed industrial plant operated with the greatest care may well be or cause a nuisance, if, for example, effluent, smoke, fumes or noise invade the right of enjoyment of neighbouring land owners to an unreasonable degree.'[53] To the defendant's argument that the sewer was for the benefit of the community, McIntyre J agreed that social utility must be taken into account. But, reflecting, perhaps, a new attitude to the question of social cost, he concluded that 'there is no reason why a disproportionate share of the cost of such beneficial service would be visited upon one member of the community by leaving him uncompensated for damage caused by the existence of that which benefits the community at large.'[54] Similar arguments would be urged in the case of Bhopal. Even in the absence of proof of negligence, there is no good reason why the damage caused by the plant, which was established for the benefit of its owners (and less directly for the community at large), should be left to be borne solely by the innocent victims.

These, then, are the legal doctrines and principles that would be brought to bear in Bhopal. This broad-brush account reveals a rather remarkable course of legal evolution in response to newly emerging hazards over the course of the last century. But legal doctrines and principles do not always provide clear and unequivocal answers to the hard questions raised by mass disasters such as Bhopal's. Indeed, because law is a relatively open and dynamic process, any description of the law 'as it is' should only be understood as a temporary compromise between competing visions of law 'as it ought to be.' Fixed legal principles would not, therefore, exclude the moral, political, and economic issues raised by the tragedy. Instead, these principles would provide only a framework within which a discourse about public values and policies would take place. In Bhopal, this discourse would rapidly focus in on the role of multinationals and hazardous technologies in a developing country. The courts would become not only a battleground for compensation, but also a forum in which the prevailing distribution of risks would be interrogated. The law of tort would be called upon to confront the issues of what are tolerable levels of risk in Indian society, and how the burden of those risks should be distributed.

Tort Law, Deterrence, and Tolerable Risk: The Economic Model

Tort law is a response to risk. The victims of Bhopal would argue that the 'prospect of exploitation of cheap labour and captive markets ... induces multinationals to enter into the developing countries,' and, once there, these companies exploit lax industrial regulations and ignore the health and safety of workers and communities. They would look to the law to alter this regime.

It has frequently been argued that tort law can play an effective deterrent role. By charging to industry the cost of unjustifiable harm to health and the environment, law can reduce risks to health and safety.

Yet there is no such thing as a risk-free world. The crucial issue of public choice, then, is to determine what are socially acceptable levels of risk. Such a determination involves the weighing of social values, and there is no single static model governing the law's approach to the question of 'tolerable risk.' However, it has recently been argued by many that the law reflects an economic logic; that the structure of its reasoning parallels the type of risk–benefit reasoning that goes into the formulation of public policy.

The school of 'economic analysis of law' suggests that legal decision making is guided by a quest for 'allocative efficiency' in the use of society's resources – by the desire to ensure that resources are put to their most highly valued uses in order that aggregate social welfare be maximized.[55] In the case of industrial hazards and other risky undertakings, this means that activities should be encouraged only when their benefits outweigh their costs. The law of torts, it is argued, achieves deterrence by charging to those who cause injury the cost of accidents. This, in turn, produces the 'optimal level' of safety by giving actors an incentive to take steps to reduce accidents, so long as the costs of safety are less than the costs of the accidents avoided. It is important to note that this recommendation entails a corollary: namely, that there is also an optimal level of danger. Society should tolerate risks and the inevitable harms that result when the cost of such harm is less than the cost of avoiding it.

There is some evidence that the law does in fact display an economic logic. In nuisance cases, for example, the concept of 'reasonable use' essentially requires the court to consider and weigh the social utility of a particular operation against the harm and annoyance that it causes, taking into account the costs of reducing that annoyance. An activity may be said to be a nuisance when the costs outweigh the benefits. This rationale has been expressly adopted in a number of cases, though the assessment of the full social costs of the activities is controversial.

This cost-benefit reasoning may be particularly apparent when it comes to fashioning remedies for nuisances where, in some cases, the courts may moderate the remedy against a polluting enterprise so as to preserve some of the social benefits of the operation. In the U.S. case of *Boomer* v *Atlantic Cement*,[56] the court granted damages instead of an injunction against a large cement plant that was polluting the locality. The court considered evidence that there was no technology available to reduce the pollution and that an injunction would in all probability shut down the plant, which employed 300 people and represented a capital investment of over $45 million. The majority in that case reasoned that the total damage to the plaintiffs was relatively small in comparison with the value of the operation and the social consequences of shutting the plant down.[57]

Perhaps not surprisingly, such explicit reasoning is controversial. To many, this cost–benefit reasoning seems to devalue human life. It makes health a commodity like any other and essentially allows the polluting enterprise to buy a licence to pollute. As the dissenting judge in *Boomer* said, the approach says to industry 'you may continue to do harm to your neighbours so long as you pay a fee for it.'[58] In a Canadian case dealing with industrial pollution of the Spanish River in Ontario, Chief Justice McRuer similarly rejected the economic argument, saying: 'Some evidence was given on behalf of the defendant to show the importance of its business in the community, and that it carried it on in a proper manner. Neither of these elements is to be taken into consideration in a case of this character, nor are the economic interests of the defendant relevant ... In my view, if I were to consider and give effect to an argument based on the defendant's economic position in the community, or its financial interests, I would in effect be giving to it a veritable power of expropriation of the common law rights of the riparian owners, without compensation.'[59] Significantly, in this case the Ontario legislature was more impressed with the company's economic argument and immediately passed a statute that dissolved the injunction granted by Justice McRuer.[60]

Courts take a similar approach when faced with the problem of what to do about an industrial risk *before* the hazard materializes or any damage is done. Where a court is asked for an injunction to prevent an environmental hazard from materializing, it also engages in a form of risk assessment informed by cost-benefit analysis. Injunctions will be granted where the risk is 'imminent,' balancing the 'magnitude of the evil against the chances of its occurrence.'[61] The more severe the potential consequences, the lesser the degree of probability that the court will require before granting the remedy.[62]

The law of negligence also reflects cost–benefit reasoning. In negligence law, individuals and firms are required only to take 'reasonable' care to avoid acts or omissions that may injure others. From the economic point of view the concept of reasonable care may be understood as a function of risk assessment and cost–benefit analysis. In setting the standard of care the courts must assess the *probability* that an accident will occur and the *magnitude* of the damage that would result from such an accident (together making up the total costs of accidents), and weigh these factors against the cost of taking precautions (accident-avoidance costs). The cost of precautions might include either the direct costs of investment in safety or the social benefits forgone from reducing or eliminating production. Thus the legal standard of 'optimal care' under this formula is the level at which the marginal cost of risk reduction equals the marginal reduction in social cost.

This method has been expressly adopted in some cases. In *United States* v *Carroll Towing Co.*, Judge Learned Hand explained how a company must take care if the expected benefits from reducing the danger outweigh the costs of the care: 'if the probability be called P; the injury L; and the burden B; liability depends upon whether B is less than L multiplied by P; i.e. whether B > PL.'[63]

Similarly, in product liability cases, many North American and European courts adopt a risk/utility test. Manufacturers must make design and warning decisions by determining whether the expected social benefits of a particular design or warning outweigh the social costs.[64] One case has expressed the test as follows: a product may be found defective in design 'if the plaintiff demonstrates that the product's design proximately caused his injury and the defendant fails to establish ... on balance, the benefits of the challenged design outweigh the risks of danger inherent in the design.' The relevant factors include 'the gravity of the danger posed by the challenged design, the likelihood that such danger would occur, the mechanical feasibility of a safer alternative design, the financial cost of an improved design, and the adverse consequences to the product and to the consumer that would result from an alternative design.'[65] This test has also been known as the 'excessive preventable danger' standard.

The economic model is an attractive one. It helps to explain the deterrence rationale of law and appears to offer an objective and scientific basis for making hard social choices about what constitutes acceptable levels of risk in society. It accepts that safety is a desirable goal, but also insists that risk-producing activities are necessary to maintain social welfare. It proposes a seemingly neutral formula by which the courts can balance these two goals. It promises to compensate the victims of antisocial accidents and to ensure levels of industrial production and safety that, in the long run, ensure aggregate social welfare.

Despite the attractions of the economic model, one should not conclude that it has been universally accepted. It is highly controversial and fraught with difficulty. While it does illustrate some of the choices that arise in tort litigation, economic analysis is only one form of discourse that may be brought to bear in the formulation of public policy. Even among those who accept that courts should balance the costs and benefits of industrial activities, there is little agreement about exactly how those costs and benefits should be measured and what legal rules best promote efficiency (for example, strict liability or negligence). In the next chapter some of the empirical and normative assumptions of the economic model are explored more specifically in the context of Bhopal. The analysis reveals that the economic model provides important insights into, but a radically flawed justification of, the actual operation of the tort system.

The Challenge and Promise of Law

At the end of this excursion into legal doctrine we are better able to summarize the challenge and promise of law. While law must be sufficiently certain to provide a degree of reliability, it must, at the same time, be flexible enough to respond to the needs of victims and to adapt to the new challenges posed by modern technologies and patterns of social interaction. In the case of Bhopal it would be variously expected to articulate required standards of safety and socially tolerable risk, to provide compensation, and to achieve deterrence. In making its 'tragic choices' the law would have to address the tension between safety and risk, environment and development, individual and collective responsibility, corrective and distributive justice. Through an adversarial contest, all the actors would demand the opportunity to participate in the ongoing articulation of these goals and values.

This is a tall order. When, in the next chapter, we turn to the concrete realities of the litigation process, especially in the context of mass disasters and toxic harms, we see that such cases are likely to strain traditional legal processes to their breaking-point. The phenomenon of toxic harm points to the need for a major reorientation in our thinking about law. What the analysis reveals is that while law promises to seek *shared* values, to treat all persons *equally*, and to achieve a *neutral* balance among conflicting goals and constituencies, the reality is that it systematically fails to keep these promises.

4

Mass Torts: From Rhetoric to Reality

The previous chapter outlined the general principles of tort law as it applies to environmental and industrial hazards such as the Bhopal disaster. The picture painted by this account is one of a dynamic body of law that is capable of engaging in a subtle social calculus designed to regulate unacceptable risks, to compensate the victims of wrongful injury, and to deter future hazards. Legal principles, first articulated in the eighteenth and nineteenth centuries, appear to have been adapted to meet the complex challenges of late-twentieth-century society, while at the same time affirming widely shared values of individual and social responsibility.

But this picture of law is drawn primarily from the law's self-description, relying upon relatively abstract statements of general principles, and upon the reported and partial accounts of the relatively few human tragedies that actually make their way into court in the first place, and then proceed to completion through the legal labyrinth. There is a world of difference between the law in the books and the law in action, and toxic incidents like that in Bhopal raise new issues that the law is ill equipped to solve. The previous chapter canvassed a few of the obstacles that the Bhopal victims would face, and this chapter turns to examine those obstacles in more detail. When we move from an abstract account of legal principle to a more concrete analysis of the realities of mass toxic litigation, we see even more clearly why the law's promise of compensation and deterrence in a case like Bhopal's would be so difficult to keep.

This chapter continues the analysis of mass torts like Bhopal under the 'best case' scenario. It demonstrates the tremendous difficulties that face the victims of toxic injuries in all common-law countries, even those with a well-functioning court system and dynamic body of tort law. It describes the difficulties encountered in previous instances of toxic litigation in North America, pointing to the specific problems and obstacles that would be faced by the Bhopal victims no matter where they launched a lawsuit. Later chapters introduce the further systemic difficulties that they would face in India.

Toxic Torts: A New Accident Paradigm?

While the law of tort has been substantially adapted to meet the conditions of life in the twentieth century, it remains fundamentally rooted in earlier social values and conceptions of human interaction. As many legal scholars have argued, the increasing prevalence of mass disasters, toxic injuries, and environmental damage not only throw up problems that the law is ill-suited to address, but, in fact, call into question the very presuppositions about social life upon which traditional tort law is built.[1]

Traditional tort law is *individualistic* and *mechanical*. It imagines a world that is populated by rational individuals pursuing their own self-interest. Occasionally such individuals may collide, in which case the task of law is to repair any damage done and to restore the boundaries between them by rearticulating the rights and duties that define their interactions. The paradigm of the traditional tort is a *traumatic* interaction between two *intentionalistic* agents. One person lights a fire that burns his neighbour's property; one person strikes another with her automobile. In such cases it is possible to say how the injury occurred and to assign liability for it upon the basis of individual responsibility. The dispute is bipolar and the goal is to achieve corrective justice between individuals rather than distributive justice between groups in society.[2] The wider community is not involved or implicated in the problem except to the extent that it supposedly provides the social norms that make up the concept of 'reasonable care.' Causation in such cases is specific and mechanical. It is easy to trace the victim's injury to the acts or omissions of the defendant and to exclude other possible causes. There is a clean line between 'inevitable' and 'avoidable' injuries; between the 'natural' misfortunes of life and those for which another person should be held accountable.

Legal scholars are beginning to explore how this picture of the way in which people are hurt, and the way society attributes responsibility for those hurts, is vastly inadequate to portray the reality of harm in modern society. They argue that the earlier model of accidents as traumatic collisions between individuals maintains its hold on the legal imagination and diverts attention from the far more serious problem of 'environmental' injury and illness. The trauma model accounts for only a very small fraction of human harm and ignores the 'social' or human-made source of most forms of disability.[3]

The modern epidemiological understanding of the concepts of 'risk' and 'harm' has exposed the inadequacy of an atomistic understanding of human interaction, an individualistic understanding of responsibility, a traumatic view of injury, and a mechanical view of causation. Social and technological complexity reveal the degree to which society is interdependent and how intricate systems are implicated in the production of accidents and sickness. The development of epidemiological and statistical knowledge about disease has undermined our ability to draw a bright line between 'natural' and 'unnatural' forms of disability. When dealing with toxic injuries, poisoning, cancer, and other forms of environmental and industrial harm, the paradigm of mechanical causation is replaced by a paradigm of 'statistical correlation,' and even the concept of injury gives way to one of 'risk.' The disparities in economic and social power between large corporate concerns and the victims of injury have exposed the inadequacy of the narrow model of corrective justice to address the more pervasive problem of distributive *in*justice.

The Compensation Promise

Identifying the Defendant: Proof of Causation and Fault

Many argue that the function of tort law is to provide 'corrective justice.' This means that the law seeks, as best it can, to 'right the balance' between a victim and the agent who caused the victim's injury. What it is important to note about the corrective-justice model is that the law intervenes only when there has been a 'wrong' done by one person to another. According to the traditional view, one person is not responsible for the welfare of another unless the victim, who has the onus of proof, can establish that the defendant had a duty of care, breached that duty of care, and thus caused the victim's injuries.

These legal requirements reflect the values of due process and individualism. A person is 'innocent until proven guilty' and does not have any general responsibility for the welfare of others. While these values are widely shared, they ultimately reflect a general presumption that individual victims must bear their own injuries *unless* they are able to overcome substantial evidentiary challenges and shift that loss to another party.

Mass-exposure problems are especially problematic in this regard. In the first place, they typically involve complex technology, dangerous processes, and toxic materials. The factual matrix is thus enormously complicated. Difficult scientific, technological, and medical questions may be involved. The collection of data and proof of technical and medical theories is time-consuming, controversial, and expensive.

In cases involving complex technology, such as Bhopal, even the apparently simple issues of mechanical causation and fault often prove to be enormously difficult. Ordinarily, a plaintiff must demonstrate that the incident was the result of carelessness; that, 'but for' the actions of the defendant, the accident would not have occurred. While little more than a straightforward factual investigation seems to be required, the matter is much more complicated. In the first place, as was the case in Bhopal, it may simply be unclear how the accident occurred at all. The 'facts' that must be investigated are all in the past. Indeed, they no longer exist. The incident must be reconstructed from physical evidence, much of which was destroyed or altered in the explosion; company records, which may be incomplete or misleading; expert testimony, which may be speculative or biased; and the recollection of witnesses, which is bound to be limited and contradictory, given the total chaos that reigned on the night of the disaster and the long period of time between it and a final trial. Given that the burden of proof is generally left to the plaintiff, who has little information about the hazardous substance, the nature of the technology, or the workings of the process, proof of mechanical causation is enormously difficult, if not impossible.

Even when it is clear how the accident occurred, the questions of fault and causation can never be straightforward, for the court must still make normative judgments and factual inferences. The normative judgment is whether the conduct of the defendant fell below a reasonable standard of care. The factual inference is whether, through the exercise of reasonable care, the accident could have been prevented. This latter question is essentially hypothetical, often requiring that the court make a guess at determining the unknowable.

In the case of Bhopal, there was not only very little physical evidence concerning the cause of the disaster, but almost none on how it might have been prevented. While both sides agreed that the explosion was caused by the introduction of water into the MIC tank, Indian authorities theorized that this was a result of employee carelessness or a design flaw, while UCC stood by its sabotage theory. The normative issue of whether Union Carbide had been negligent would raise intensely political issues. The victims would focus on the double standard of safety that emerged from a comparison of the company's operations in different parts of the world, while Union Carbide would emphasize that, by 'local standards' and regulations, it had taken all reasonable precautions. The tension between these positions is found frequently in toxic cases, especially those involving 'socially beneficial' activities. While courts may sometimes set the standard of care high in order to ensure safety and compensation, there is a competing concern to avoid unduly impeding the development of new technologies and products.[4] The victims may thus face the utilitarian sentiment that, in the name of 'social progress,' they must privately bear their injuries.

Even in situations where the defendant was clearly negligent, the victims must still demonstrate that the negligence was the effective cause of their injuries. The fact that they carry this burden of proof will often be fatal to their claim.[5] The victims of Bhopal would argue that the disaster could have been avoided or mitigated by the storage of smaller quantities of the chemical and by a better cooling system; Union Carbide would assert that such a view was entirely hypothetical and unproven. While it was clear that the existing safety precautions at the plant were inadequate to prevent the disaster, little evidence was available to indicate what further precautions would have insured prevention. And while none of the warning systems and emergency devices at the plant were capable of minimizing the damage, it was by no means clear what specific steps would have been required to eliminate the danger.

Courts are not entirely insensitive to the problems encountered in attempting to prove causation and fault and, in some circumstances, will make inferences in the plaintiff's favour. Where, for example, substandard precautions may have 'materially contributed' to the risk, the court may shift the onus of proof to the defendant.[6] Similarly, the principle of res ipsa loquitor (the thing speaks for itself) will sometimes be used to shift the burden of proof in situations where the plaintiff is unable to establish exactly how the accident occurred but is able to satisfy the court that the accident probably would not have happened but for the defendant's negligence.[7] In a technologically complex case like Bhopal's, where the disaster could have been caused by a number of factors, these principles are unlikely to prevail. The only meaningful way in which the burden of proof could be lowered is if the courts were willing to apply a standard of strict liability.

Multiple Defendants and Systems Accidents

The issue of factual causation in Bhopal and other mass-tort scenarios is further complicated by the large number of parties involved in complex industrial undertakings and the peculiar characteristics of toxic harms. Under the tort system, claimants must be able to trace their injuries back to the actions or omissions of a responsible party. But this individualistic orientation is ill-suited to disasters and toxic torts, which typically involve multiple actors interrelating through intricate chains of command and decision. It may simply be impossible to attribute responsibility to isolated individuals or firms. Thus, while the victims alleged that UCC was responsible for the disaster, the company in turn sought to remove itself from the sphere of responsibility, first by suggesting sabotage, second by distancing itself from the Indian operation, and third by reflecting blame back upon the government itself for failing to implement proper safety standards and for allowing a large population to settle so near to the plant. One of the parent company's most potent arguments would be that it was a virtual 'stranger' to the Indian operation; that it was merely a passive investor in the Indian-operated enterprise, having no control over its day-to-day operations and therefore no responsibility for its safety practices.

The problem of identifying a responsible party is a result of the structure of mass industrialization, the complex organization of modern business enterprises, and the peculiar characteristics of toxic harm. Numerous parties are involved in the design and operation of complicated technological processes that no one individual understands or controls. Intricate systems of production, control, and distribution make the lines of causation like the strands of a spider's web rather than the linear chain envisioned by tort law.

Several of these problems were confronted in the U.S. case of *Sindell* v *Abbott Laboratories*,[8] which involved the drug DES. This drug, which was taken by millions of pregnant women, was shown to have increased the risk of cancer in the children of the women who used it. Dozens of firms manufactured and marketed the product, and hundreds of young women are now suing for their resulting injuries. A major stumbling-block is the fact that the victims were often unable to say which brand of the drug their mothers used during pregnancy, and were therefore unable to trace liability to a particular manufacturer.

In the *Sindell* case the plaintiff established that she suffered from a malignant bladder tumour caused by DES, which her mother had taken during pregnancy. She could not, however, demonstrate which of a number of manufacturers of the drug was responsible for producing the drug that her mother actually took. She launched a class action on behalf of herself and other women in a similar position against five manufacturers. In its landmark decision, the California Supreme Court allowed the action against all of the manufacturers. The court reasoned that the law had to evolve to meet new technologies and new market conditions and that the defendants, as manufacturers of a dangerous product, were in a better position to discover and guard and warn against the hazards associated with their drug. In a case involving numerous producers and mass marketing, the traditional rule requiring the plaintiff to prove the identity of the particular manufacturer would effectively bar any recovery. Instead, the court held all of the manufacturers liable to the victims in proportion to their market share. The court held that the approach should be to 'measure the likelihood that any of the defendants supplied the product ... by the percentage which the DES sold by each of them bears to the entire production of the drug sold by all ... Each defendant would be liable for that share unless it could demonstrate that it did not make the product which caused the plaintiff's injuries.'[9]

This theory, which has come to be known as 'market share' liability, is one of a variety of principles that shift the onus of proof in cases of multiple wrongdoers (other theories include alternative liability, concerted action, and enterprise liability).[10] Yet the relaxation of causal requirements has by no means been unequivocally accepted by the courts. In a vigorous dissent in *Sindell*, Richardson J stated that the decision was offensive to the basic principles of tort law and involved a 'drastic expansion in liability' that would threaten basic medical research. He felt that the court had overreacted in order to achieve a 'socially satisfying result.'[11]

The decision certainly did go against traditional notions of individual responsibility. While it is likely that only one of the manufacturers made the drug that caused the plaintiff's injuries, all of the manufacturers were held responsible to her. From an individualistic perspective it may seem 'unfair' to hold a company responsible for injuries that it probably did not directly 'cause.' Nevertheless, the court's decision was probably made easier because it was a class action involving many of the women who had been injured by the drug. Thus, there was a good chance that all of the manufacturers had, in fact, 'caused' a portion of the total harm suffered by the class.

In the case of Bhopal, the problem is somewhat different. In *Sindell* the difficulty was to find the *one* actor responsible for the injury in a situation where *all* of the defendants were negligent. But, in Bhopal, there may simply be no single responsible actor, and all the parties involved would argue that they had not been (equally) negligent. Instead, a large number of actors – designers, workers, managers, and company and government officials – may each have contributed in some way to the disaster. Traditionally, the law attempts to allocate responsibility in such a case according to the notion of contributory negligence. Liability is traced to individual agents and assessed against each actor according to comparative fault. But, in the case of a major industrial disaster, this attempt to simplify reality may be futile. In the first place, in complex business organizations, which include numerous individuals, interlocking departments, and linked companies, it will be extremely difficult to attribute responsibility to particular individuals or units, or to assess their relative contribution to the harm. As one analyst of corporate responsibility points out, the irony is that, 'at the same time that these organizations serve to amplify human power, they also divide and diffuse the accountability of the humans who labor within them.'[12] Moreover, Bhopal is an example of what organizational analyst Charles Perrow, in his study of the Three Mile Island nuclear accident, calls a 'systems accident.'[13] Systems, he explains, are complex organizations of people and technology with special characteristics that make the assignment of 'blame' for an accident almost meaningless. Systems are characterized by their 'interactive complexity,' which makes the entire system incomprehensible to any one individual. Indeed, the increasing specialization and expertise prompted by the technical division of labour may make systems even more unstable by limiting the scope of each person's knowledge. Any one part of a system can fail in a trivial and unanticipated way and, in conjunction with other components of the system, such failure can lead to catastrophic results.

The narrow causal focus of both the government and Union Carbide – the former upon design defects and employee carelessness, the latter upon sabotage – were a natural, almost reflexive effort, to squeeze the facts of Bhopal into the traditional individualistic framework of tort responsibility. But individualistic conceptions of legal responsibility and causation do not fit well when the incident is the result of a complex combination of individual, corporate, and governmental decisions, actions, and omissions. It will often be impossible to isolate responsibility by focusing on the individual actions or omissions of only a few actors, and blame can easily be shifted from shoulder to shoulder *ad infinitum.*

Identifying the Victims: Medical Causation

The Bhopal victims would encounter other serious obstacles in their quest for compensation. Perhaps the most complex problem thrown up by environmental and toxic harms is the difficulty of establishing a link between particular toxic substances and specific harms, and tracing injuries to their source.[14] Under the tort system, claimants must demonstrate that their injuries were, in fact, caused by exposure to a particular substance or source of harm. But, in the case of diseases resulting from toxic substances, strict proof of causation may be impossible. There are two interrelated problems. The first is the immediate difficulty of identifying 'hazardous substances.' Science has by no means established with any certainty the various health hazards associated with the thousands of chemical products currently in the stream of commerce. Second, even where we know with certainty that a particular substance is hazardous, it is often impossible to determine that the injury or disease suffered by specific individuals is attributable to their exposure to the substance. Where a person contracts cancer, for example, it is often impossible to say with certainty that the condition was caused by exposure to a specific substance or source of pollution. Where a person uses or consumes a number of products, all of which turn out to have negative effects, it may be impossible to demonstrate which of those products caused the effects.

Both of these problems presented serious hurdles in Bhopal and, as a result, the estimates of the number of people dead and injured as a result of their exposure to MIC varied by tens of thousands. Little research had been done on the human consequences of exposure to MIC. Union Carbide put the victims to strict proof of their injury, maintaining that the lung was the only organ showing 'significant long-term damage from acute exposure to MIC.'[15] The company denied that exposure to MIC caused birth defects, cancer, or eye damage, or that it had any effect on human reproduction. Doctors and medical researchers in Bhopal confirmed that many of the symptoms from which the gas victims suffered, such as fatigue, breathlessness, gynaecological damage, and depression, were indistinguishable from the health problems that occur naturally in the city. For many of the victims, MIC poisoning left no obvious physical or physiological marks. Was the tuberculosis suffered by seven-year-old Pati Ram the result of inhaling MIC, or is he simply one more victim of a disease common in the slums of Bhopal? And while the rate of infertility among women increased, how could it be determined with certainty that a particular case was caused by the effects of the gas leak? The only way in which to establish causation with more certainty would be if there were comprehensive and accurate medical files on each of the victims *before* the disaster – an unlikely possibility for the majority of the poor victims – and if MIC exposure could be isolated as the sole cause of their affliction.

The long-term consequences of the Bhopal disaster are perhaps even more problematic. Cancer, for example, does not ordinarily appear for seven to twenty years after exposure to a carcinogenic substance. While exposure to MIC may thus create a risk of cancer, there is simply no way of knowing how many victims, if any, will be so affected. And given the long latency period for the disease, it would be nearly impossible even for victims who did incur cancer to isolate their exposure to MIC as the single cause of their disease.

Causal problems such as these reveal the inability of the present law of torts to deal with hazardous and toxic substances. As medico-legal expert Troyen Brennan suggests, common-law causation doctrine was developed under the Newtonian scientific paradigm that characterized causation in terms of 'mechanistic chains.'[16] Causal relations could be understood as collisions between discrete particulate objects, following scientific laws. This understanding of causation is congruent with the liberal-individualist moral premisses of tort law. Since it presupposes that harm may be conclusively traced to a discrete source, it coincides with the law's insistence on proof of a linear causal nexus between a substance and an injury, or between injurer and victim.

The problem, as Brennan explains, is that the scientific view of causation has changed, while the legal view has not. Especially when dealing with hazardous substances, scientific proof of causation now relies upon probabilistic rather than mechanical evidence. Medical hypotheses are based, not upon uncontroversial scientific laws, but upon experimental and statistical data. Our understanding of the relationship between human health, environmental factors, and toxic substances is based upon animal studies and epidemiological surveys.

These techniques reveal statistical *correlations*, which suggest *probable* causal relationships; but they do not produce concrete evidence of individual causation.

In cases involving chemicals, drugs, pollution, and other toxins, so long as the burden of proof of causation lies with the victim, the law will systematically underrate risks. Agricultural chemicals such as those involved in Bhopal provide a classic illustration of this problem. In Nova Scotia, an environmental group sought an injunction against the spraying of the herbicide 2,4,5-T. This product contains a dioxin described by the judge as 'one of the most toxic chemicals known to man.'[17] The data on the chemical, however, were derived from animal studies and cases involving massive exposure. Little information was available on its effects on human beings in low dosages. The judge, noting that the complete burden of proof rested upon the plaintiffs, refused to prohibit the spraying. A court of law, he said, 'is no forum for the determination of matters of science ... If science itself is not certain, a court cannot resolve the conflict and make the thing certain.'[18] As one commentator noted, scientific uncertainty in these cases 'results in the benefit of the doubt being given to the chemicals. In a court of law, chemicals are presumptively innocent.' This, in turn 'values the right to produce and use chemicals over possible adverse human health effects.'[19]

Even where it can be established that a particular chemical *is* clearly harmful to human health, causal problems do not go away. Particularly problematic is what Brennan calls the problem of 'individual attribution.'[20] Because epidemiological studies are based upon groups, it will often be impossible to reach definite conclusions about particular individuals. This is, in fact, the causal paradigm in toxic torts. In these cases the wrongdoer and the harmful substance may be clearly identified, but there will be only statistical and not individual evidence of the harm done; in other words, it is impossible to separate victims from non-victims. For example, leaking chemicals may have contaminated the water supply or leaking radiation may have contaminated the air. As a result, the incidence of diseases such as cancer in the community has increased by 20 per cent.[21] The problem, of course, is that it is impossible to isolate those individuals among the total population who have contracted their disease from the activities of the defendant.

How is the law to deal with such a scenario? Traditional views of causation give rise to a paradox: while we know that 20 per cent of the incidences of cancer in the population can be attributed to the defendant's negligence, in any individual case there is a less-than-even chance that the defendant is responsible. The traditional rule about causation forces us to the legal conclusion that the defendant did not cause any of the injuries.

These problems were acute in the case of Bhopal. Numerous epidemiological studies indicated that the mortality rate and the incidence of blindness, miscarriage, and respiratory illness increased dramatically following the disaster. A study by the Indian Council on Medical Research found, for example, that the mortality rate in the gas-affected areas of Bhopal was 12 in 1,000, compared with a city-wide average of 7 in 1,000, and that infant mortality in the city was 112 in 1,000, compared with a state-wide rate of 90 in 1,000.[22] Another study confirmed a dramatic increase in the number and severity of eye diseases in the community.[23] The damage to the victims' lungs resulted in increased respiratory afflictions such as emphysema, bronchitis, and infection. But even assuming that these studies do demonstrate conclusively that the gas incident was the cause of these startling increases, few of the individual victims were in any position to demonstrate that their afflictions were caused specifically by the gas and not by any of the other 'natural' sources of disease and illness in an Indian city.

If the courts insist on clinging to traditional notions of causation in toxic-tort cases, the compensation and deterrence justifications for the tort system simply cannot be maintained. For, where epidemiological or statistical evidence indicates that a toxic incident has increased the risk of disease by a percentage amount, the usual requirement of proof of causation in individual cases would nevertheless force the courts to deny compensation altogether, unless that amount is greater than 50 per cent. Thus, even in situations where there is virtual certainty that a toxic incident has caused widespread and serious injury, the victims go uncompensated and the defendant goes undeterred.

The Agent Orange litigation, described by Peter Schuck in his book *Agent Orange on Trial*,[24] provides an example of how the problems of factual and medical causation can combine to make recovery a near impossibility. This was an action brought by Vietnam war veterans against Dow Chemical and other companies who produced Agent Orange, a herbicide used during the war. The product, to which numerous U.S. troops in Vietnam had been exposed, contained dioxins, which may be carcinogenic or cause birth defects. According to basic tort theory, the claimants in such a case must first prove that they were exposed to Agent Orange; that the chemical actually caused their injuries; and that the batch they were exposed to was manufactured by the particular chemical company being sued. An additional problem in this case (as in that of Bhopal) was that, although the government was arguably negligent, it could not be sued. The military contractors also claimed that they could not be held liable because they had simply manufactured the product to government specifications and had no better knowledge about its health risks than did the government.

While many observers were convinced that Agent Orange was responsible for the injuries suffered by the veterans, it was unlikely that the victims would ever have been able to prove their cases. Animal studies indicating that dioxin is carcinogenic and teratogenic are not necessarily applicable to humans.[25] Many of the data on the health risks of the product demonstrated only a statistical correlation between exposure and sickness, and most of the veterans were unable to demonstrate that they had suffered or were likely to suffer damage to their health as a direct result of their exposure. Indeed, many would be unable to demonstrate that they had been exposed at all as they wandered through the jungles past the chemical residues. Even if they could prove exposure, they would have no way of demonstrating its frequency or severity. Equally problematic was the fact that Agent Orange was supplied by a number of defence contractors. How, then, would the victims demonstrate which defendant was to be held responsible for their injuries?

The case dragged on for more than five years and never reached trial. The lawyers on both sides had been multiplying and costs had been escalating obscenely. The delays were gradually exhausting the resources of the plaintiffs who had to finance not only their lawyers, but a host of expert witnesses in 'biochemistry, toxicology, epidemiology, internal medicine, statistics, oncology, occupational medicine, genetics, immunology, neurology and plant physiology.'[26] Given the enormity of the costs faced by the plaintiffs, and the near impossibility of establishing the requisite elements of their case, it is perhaps not surprising that an estimated 120,000 claims were settled before a trial in 1984 for a mere $180 million.[27] It has been estimated that this figure provided less than $6,000 for each person who had been permanently injured as a result of exposure and less than $2,000 in death benefits to the surviving family members of the veterans who had died.[28]

In the course of a hearing to determine whether the settlement was fair, Judge Weinstein canvassed each of the scientific and legal hurdles that the victims would have faced had the litigation continued. In addition to a detailed analysis of each of the causation problems, he noted that the victims would have been unlikely, at any rate, to be able financially to sustain the litigation. The settlement, he concluded, 'gives the class more than it would likely achieve by litigating to the death.'[29] As one commentator pointed out, given the near impossibility of proving the victims' case, one wonders why the companies bothered to settle at all. The answer, he suggests, lies with the defendant's legal costs – estimated at the time as $75 million and rising.[30] Several individual plaintiffs who had opted out of the class action fared even worse. In 1985 their actions were dismissed entirely on the basis that they had failed to prove causation.[31]

Courts in England and North America have slowly sought to grapple with the problems of medical causation and individual attribution. A variety of proposals and innovations have been mooted. The first possible solution is to relax the onus of proof faced by the victim. One example is the English case of *McGhee* v *National Coal Board*.[32] The plaintiff, who was employed to clean out brick kilns, developed dermatitis. The condition was likely caused by exposure to coal dust and aggravated by the fact that the employer did not provide washing facilities. At trial, the plaintiff's action was dismissed on the ground that he had not demonstrated that the provision of washing facilities would have prevented the condition. However, on appeal the House of Lords held that the absence of such facilities had materially increased the risk. Lord Reid said that a plaintiff will succeed 'if he can show that the defender caused or materially contributed to his injury. There may have been two separate causes but it is enough if one of the causes arose from the fault of the defender. The pursuer does not have to prove that this cause would of itself have been enough to cause him injury.'[33]

Essentially, in such circumstances, the court is asking whether the defendant negligently created an unreasonable risk of harm to the plaintiff. If so, then the court may be willing to infer that the risk was, in fact, the cause of the plaintiff's injuries (so long as those injuries come within the area of risk created). From a policy perspective, this makes good sense. Ordinarily the plaintiff will not be in a good position to demonstrate conclusively that his or her injuries were caused by a particular product or process. The defendant has better information about the technology and the risks, and is better situated to take precautions to prevent harm. By shifting the onus of proof to the defendant, the court ensures that the plaintiff receives the benefit of the doubt, and is not left helpless because of the inadequacy of medical and technical knowledge.[34]

A similar approach was adopted in the U.S. case of *Allen* v *U.S.* in which the plaintiffs sued for cancer allegedly caused by nuclear testing.[35] The court shifted the burden of proof on the basis that the negligence created a risk and the plaintiffs' injuries were consistent with that risk. The court stated: 'This shift in the burden of proof reflects a sound application of important legal policies to the practical problems of trying a lawsuit: where a strong factual connection exists between defendant's conduct and the plaintiff's injury, but selection of actual cause in fact from among several causes is problematical, those difficulties of proof are shifted to the tortfeasor, the wrongdoer, in order to do substantial justice between the parties.'[36]

These cases deviate significantly from the individualistic emphasis of the law on proof of fault and causation and, as such, are controversial. Indeed, *Allen* was overruled on appeal on the basis of sovereign immunity.[37] And, because individualistic assumptions about moral responsibility run deep in the law of torts, many courts are reluctant to relax the onus of proof against the defendant. Indeed, in 1988, the same court that decided *McGhee* arguably emasculated it in the medical-negligence case *Wilsher* v *Essex Area Health Authority*.[38] The plaintiff was unable to establish that his retinal condition was caused by the admittedly negligent treatment, and was not a preexisting condition. The House of Lords overruled the lower courts, which had relied on *McGhee* in favour of the plaintiff. Reasserting the traditional individualistic requirements of proof, Lord Bridge concluded: 'whether we like it or not, the law, which only Parliament can change, requires proof of fault causing damage as the basis of liability in tort. We should do society nothing but disservice if we made the forensic process still more unpredictable and hazardous by distorting the law to accommodate the exigencies of what may seem hard cases.'[39]

Other courts in Canada and the United States have shown a similar reluctance to relax too far the rules of causal proof.[40] Yet, while such rules protect defendants against unfounded lawsuits, they also serve to bar many deserving plaintiffs from compensation.

Unless the law can accommodate the new paradigm of causation, it will remain unable to deal with the problem of harm in an increasingly complex environment. Numerous other proposals have been offered. Some academic commentators have suggested that the concept of 'lost chances' might be utilized to solve the problem of statistical causation.[41]

On such a theory, the victims might be entitled to some discounted amount to compensate them for the chance that they would not have suffered their injury 'but for' the act of the defendant. This approach has been followed in some medical negligence cases where, for example, there is a 25 per cent chance that a course of treatment would have prevented the plaintiff's injury.[42] Not surprisingly, it has also been rejected by many courts because of fear of a 'flood of litigation.'[43]

Related to the 'lost chances' doctrine is the notion of 'statistical' or 'proportional' liability whereby the victims of a particular illness would receive compensation in proportion to the probability that their injury was, in fact, caused by the negligence of the defendant. So, for example, in a case where toxic contamination has increased the rate of a disease in a community by 20 per cent, every person who suffers from the disease would receive 20 per cent compensation from the defendant. One commentator has elaborated this theory of proportional liability whereby 'courts would impose liability and distribute compensation in proportion to the probability of causation assigned to the excess disease risk in the exposed population, regardless whether that probability fell above or below the fifty-percent threshold and despite the absence of individualized proof of the causal connection.'[44]

Still another way to deal with the problem of causation is to provide damages for 'enhanced risk.' This approach would apply in situations where a group has been exposed to a toxic substance, but the future effects remain uncertain. For example, in *Ayers* v *Jackson Township*, $13.5 million was awarded to a class of individuals whose drinking water had been contaminated by toxins leaching from a landfill site.[45] While the effects of the poisoning were still uncertain, the court accepted that there was a real risk of illness as a result of exposure, and the damages were intended to provide for diminished quality of life and the expense of future medical surveillance and testing.[46] In the face of causal uncertainty, medical-surveillance costs have also figured prominently in the settlement of other toxic incidents such as the Three Mile Island litigation and the Agent Orange tragedy.[47] Nevertheless, like other efforts to solve the causation problem, these approaches are far from settled, and are not without their critics. In *Anderson* v *W.R. Grace and Co.* (another water contamination case) the court rejected the argument, saying that there must be at least proof of a reasonable probability of harm.[48] The court expressed its concern that there would be a flood of speculative lawsuits, and that to 'award damages based on a mere mathematical probability would significantly undercompensate those who actually do develop cancer and would be a windfall to those who do not.'[49]

The Bhopal victims would inevitably confront all of these causal dilemmas, and would have to resort to innovative strategies in order to establish their injuries. But, as the foregoing account makes clear, even the most imaginative reforms in this area are controversial and imperfect. Even those judges who have promoted reform in this area recognize that the possibilities are limited. Many of these judges have called for removal of such cases from courts and the establishment of no-fault compensation schemes in their place. As one judge said, after finding that a plaintiff had failed to prove on the balance of probabilities that a child's devastating injuries had been caused by a vaccination, 'The slightest difference in the evidence,' or a new scientific advance on any one of several fronts, or even the different intellectual makeup of a different trial judge, might easily ensure a different result ... Surely it would be worthwhile for our society to agree to a certain adequate, though not lavish, standard of compensation upon proof of prior good health, the administration of vaccine and catastrophic damage within a limited period of time.'[50]

Not all judges are so sympathetic. Many remain wedded to fault-based ideas of individual responsibility and traditional notions of fairness. They point out that it is inappropriate to hold a defendant responsible for an injury in a case where there is only a (small) statistical probability that it caused (or will cause) the plaintiff's injuries. Indeed, some argue that statistical causation is also 'unfair' to plaintiffs in so far as it does not distinguish between 'natural' and negligently caused injuries. For example, if, following a radiation leak, the incidence of cancer in the community rises by 30 per cent, the approach theoretically requires that all cancer victims receive 30 per cent compensation. On the basis of the individualistic fault-based morality of the tort system, this result appears to 'undercompensate' that portion of the population whose cancer was the result of exposure to radiation and 'overcompensate' those whose cancer was caused by other means. But the only alternative that the law at present contemplates – and the one that is, by and large, embraced by most courts – is that *none of the victims* in such a case receives compensation. Is this fair? And from the point of view of deterrence, not to hold the defendant responsible for that portion of the cancers caused by the operation is simply to encourage, indeed subsidize, an unsafe industry. Tort law and civil litigation, as they stand at present, cannot resolve these dilemmas.

The Adversarial System

The doctrinal problems thrown up by traditional law are compounded by procedural barriers and the uneven capacities of the parties in the litigation process. The existing system of tort compensation presupposes an adversarial system of justice. This system is often defended as the best guarantee of truth. Through a vigorous contest between the interested parties and their advocates, before an impartial judge or jury, it is said that the facts will emerge, and justice will be done.

It does not take much analysis to show that, even in relatively simple cases, this model entirely ignores, or at least obscures, the material reality of social life. The resources of plaintiffs and defendants are never equal. Their access to legal services and information will diverge greatly, depending upon their expertise, and especially upon their wealth. From this point of view, the adversarial system is based more upon the model of the free market – the parties have access to the facts, and ultimately to justice, according to their ability to pay.

The large number of victims and potential victims means that the litigation will be difficult to organize and enormously expensive to sustain. In mass disasters the defendant can achieve economies of scale in the preparation of the lawsuit that are unavailable to individual claimants, thus tilting the tactical balance against them. Class actions, in which the claims of numerous victims are consolidated, provide a partial response to these difficulties. But these procedures are restrictive and often unavailable to plaintiffs because their claims or injuries differ too widely. In Canada and England the class action is virtually unknown. Proceeding from a highly individualistic perception of the lawsuit, courts are extremely reluctant to allow claims to be aggregated. The plaintiffs are required to have the 'same interest' in the litigation, and courts have essentially held that 'same' means 'identical.' Even in apparently simple cases, this requirement may bar a class action.[51] In cases involving personal injuries resulting from toxic exposure, the class action is especially problematic. No two individuals in Bhopal were exposed to exactly the same amount of the chemical, and no two suffered identical injuries. The losses incurred by the victims varied widely, as do their likely future conditions.

U.S. law concerning class actions is more liberal than Canadian law, yet the availability of the class action is still restricted by the requirement of 'commonality.' The U.S. Ninth Circuit Court of Appeals, for example, refused to allow a class action for Dalkon Shield victims on this basis, thus throwing the burden of the litigation back on the individual claimants.[52] Class actions stemming from the toxic contamination of the Love Canal area and the Three Mile Island nuclear disaster ran into similar difficulties.[53]

Thus, in the case of Bhopal, an insistence on individualized justice would likely bar a class action. Yet, if action was to be launched on a case-by-case basis, most victims would not even initiate litigation, and many of those who did would fall by the wayside. The process could last for years, involve a redundant and wasteful relitigation of similar issues, and generate legal fees into the hundreds of millions of dollars.

This is not meant to suggest that class actions are a panacea. Even where claims can be consolidated, enormous problems are encountered. Lawyers may spend more time jockeying for position to control the litigation than preparing cases. Organization of the class remains expensive. Members of the class lose control of their lawsuit and may feel that their individual interests are being overridden by the group. Class solidarity is difficult to maintain, and many members will choose to opt out. These were all acute problems in the Agent Orange litigation.[54]

The prospect for quick and adequate compensation is further reduced by the adversarial nature of litigation. The large potential damage award creates a strong incentive for the defendant to assume the most rigidly defensive posture in an effort to use all means to avoid, or at least postpone, a final finding of liability. Lengthy delays and enormous costs sap the power of the victims to pursue their legal remedies in the traditional fashion. For example, one of the first asbestos lawsuits brought against the Johns-Manville Corporation began in 1961 when Claude Tomplait, an asbestos worker, hired lawyer Ward Stephenson to secure compensation for pulmonary fibrosis caused by the inhalation of asbestos fibres.[55] Stephenson was unable to secure any compensation for his client until 1968, when the five defendants agreed to pay $15,000 each to settle his case. Tomplait was left, after the payment of legal fees, with a sum of $37,500. At the time of the settlement he could no longer work. He weighed just 100 pounds and could move around only by carrying a portable oxygen bottle. And it was not until three days after Stephenson's own death in 1973 that a court of appeal ruling finally paved the way for compensation for his other asbestos clients. Similarly, the Agent Orange litigation took nearly ten years to settle – a delay that served the purposes of the defence contractors to exhaust the ability of the victims to pursue their cases. Even in routine cases such as automobile accidents, the average period of time between injury and settlement is three years.[56] Even longer delays are typical in more serious cases, thus placing tremendous settlement pressure on those victims whose needs are greatest.

The potential liability of the defendant in a mass disaster is often enormous and well beyond its insurance coverage. An adverse judgment may affect the economic health of the defendant, and there may be insufficient funds to meet the claims of the victims. This is true even in the case of enormous companies such as Johns-Manville, which, in response to an estimated 50,000 claims by workers relating to asbestos related illnesses, successfully applied to be put into bankruptcy in 1982. As a condition of entering bankruptcy, Johns-Manville was required to create a trust fund out of which the victims would be compensated, but this fund has proved insufficient to meet these claims. Calculated on the basis of a modest $38,000 per victim, the fund underestimated the number of future victims of asbestos and is in serious jeopardy of becoming exhausted long before the 'asbestos problem' goes away.[57] With approximately 90,000 claims pending in 1990, payments from the fund were frozen to all claimants except those in the direst need.

Industry has other ways to minimize the impact and relevance of tort law. In the first place, companies are able to hire armies of lawyers to do battle on their behalf, and these lawyers are capable of sustaining – indeed, postponing – litigation almost indefinitely. On occasion, even plaintiffs' lawyers can be 'bought out' by corporate defendants in an effort to reduce their exposure in mass-disaster cases. Uncannily, an early example of such a strategy involved another mass industrial disaster in which Union Carbide was involved – a case that has been labelled 'America's worst industrial disaster.'[58] In the 1930s more than 700 workers (employed by a subcontractor) who had been building Union Carbide's Hawk's Nest Tunnel, in West Virginia, died from acute silicosis. The victims, who had been constructing a three-mile-long hydro-electric tunnel, were exposed, with practically no safety precautions, to silica dust from sandstone. A massive lawsuit claiming $4 million on behalf of 157 of the workers was settled for a mere $130,000, half of which went to their attorneys. It was later learned that 'the plaintiffs' lawyers had secretly signed a contract with E.J. Perkins [the tunnel contractors], providing for payment of another twenty thousand dollars to the lawyers in return for their agreeing not to engage in further legal action' and to turn over all their documentation to the defence.[59] A similar 'buy-out' and secrecy agreement was apparently reached by Johns-Manville with eleven of its workers in 1933, and the company was able to avoid any further litigation for three decades.[60] These types of arrangements serve to eliminate the continued involvement of the plaintiffs' attorneys in any further litigation and to bury the information obtained in the course of litigation. When future victims seek compensation for similar injuries, they, and their lawyers, must entirely reinvent the litigation. While considered unethical by many, such buy-out agreements continue to figure in mass-tort litigation.[61] In actions against A.H. Robbins Ltd, the maker of the Dalkon Shield contraceptive device (which caused serious, sometimes fatal, pelvic infections), such agreements were insisted upon by the company. In that case, Judge Miles Lord condemned the company for its 'delay and obfuscation.' The tactics, he said, were designed to deprive victims of the assistance of able and experienced lawyers and to 'put off payment for such a long period that the interest you earned in the interim covers the cost of these cases.'[62]

All of these problems would face the Bhopal victims. They were a heterogenous group who could not easily be organized. Individually, they had vastly insufficient means to sustain litigation against Union Carbide. Their demands could be put off indefinitely, or settled for very modest amounts. And even if they could sustain litigation, adequate funds would by no means be easy to locate. Though the company was an enormous multinational, its Indian operation had no insurance and total assets of only about $50 million.[63] The parent company would, throughout the litigation, present itself as a separate foreign company, with no responsibility for the disaster and over which the Indian legal system had no jurisdiction.

The Adequacy of Compensation

Even where the victim of an injury succeeds in proving causation and fault there is no guarantee that the damages recovered will be sufficient to 'compensate' for that person's injuries. In the first place, money can never adequately replace what has been lost as a result of a catastrophic incident. The most it can do is provide a fund to replace the victim's lost income and pay for medical care. But, in many cases, it cannot even do this. The tort system continues to rely upon once-and-for-all lump-sum awards. At the time of the trial, the victim must establish not only what has been lost already as a result of the injury, but what will be lost in the future. The court must estimate the severity of the plaintiff's injuries, his or her expected lifespan, future lost income, and future medical expenses. In other words, the court must look into a crystal ball to determine the life prospects of an accident victim for decades into the future. This task is clearly impossible and, as many judges have stated, is an irrational approach to the problem of caring for the victims of injury.[64] There is simply no way to say with certainty how long a person will live, how much that person might have earned had he or she not been injured, and whether his or her condition will improve or deteriorate. Lump-sum awards are therefore bound to be inaccurate. They are based on guesses about the lifetime effects of an injury on the victim and must take into account not only the chances that his or her condition will deteriorate further, but also guesses about the impact of interest rates and inflation upon the award.

These problems are particularly acute in cases like Bhopal where there is simply no accurate medical information on the long-term consequences of MIC poisoning. No one knows yet whether the chemical is carcinogenic. No one knows what its effects will be on the offspring of the women who inhaled the gas. As the head of the relief effort in Bhopal said, 'We really don't know what the future has in store for us.'[65]

The practice of awarding lump sums, combined with the inevitable delays that will accrue before the case is finally settled, adds to the victim's suffering. Many countries have no means whereby the victim of an accident can be cared for while litigation is under way. In Bhopal, the vast majority of the victims could never sustain themselves during that period. Indeed, the tort system, which is designed to repair the injury done to the victim, may, in fact, aggravate that injury. During the lengthy delay before trial, victims are encouraged to focus upon their loss rather than upon rehabilitation and to concentrate on 'legal' recovery rather than 'physical' recovery.[66] This phenomenon has become so common that it has been given a name – 'compensation neurosis.' As torts scholar Jeffrey O'Connell concludes, even the 'successful' claimant 'who makes it through the labyrinth of tort liability, with all its emotional and technical vicissitudes, often ends up defeated even when he wins. He wins the legal battle but loses the war he should have been fighting for maximum physical and psychological recovery.'[67]

A final point to notice about the present compensation system concerns its presuppositions about how law treats people fairly and equally. The task the courts set themselves is to estimate what the victim has lost. Doing so requires the court to determine what that person's life prospects would have been had the injury never occurred and then to make up the difference with a sum of money. So, for example, to determine lost earnings, the court looks to the victim's socio-economic status prior to the accident to make its best guess about what his or her future earnings would have been. It strikes no one as unfair or unequal that a person's life prospects are a function of such factors as sex, skin colour, familial socio-economic status, and so on. Traditional tort law thus ignores the problem of the maldistribution of wealth in society and the problem of social justice. It treats people 'fairly' when it replicates the result of a fundamentally unfair market. This difficulty is glaringly present in the Bhopal case where the majority of the victims were extremely poor daily-wage labourers.

The argument here is not that the tort system could or should be used as a means of directly redistributing wealth. But, by accepting the market as the measure of all things, law ignores productive and valuable human resources, discounts the damage awards charged to tortfeasors according to the economic status of the victim, and allocates compensation according to a scale of pre-existing social inequality. These problems are particularly obvious in the case of injured women.[68] Despite the fact that women in industrialized and less-developed nations work hard and productively, many are not wage earners and those who are earn far less than do men. Many work in the home, caring for their families and engaging in household work. They may work on the family farm or do hundreds of other tasks in the home or in the community for little or no money. Yet, because they do not earn a wage for much of this work, their economic losses have traditionally been ignored by the common law. Because law accepts money and the market as the measure of a person's loss, courts have often reasoned that women simply do not suffer significant economic losses when they are seriously injured.[69]

In the developed countries, under pressure from feminists and other progressive organizations, some courts have begun to recognize the value of non-market work. Yet no fundamental transformation is to be expected. Judicial attitudes and legal doctrines are firmly rooted in the notion that the market is the measure of all things, and we are unlikely to see non-market standards of equality and distributive justice take the place of market measures of value.

Finally, critics and defenders of the tort system alike frequently neglect to point out that even those 'lucky' ones who receive compensation must pay their lawyers, often as much as 33 per cent of the award. This fee, combined with defendant's legal expenses and the other social costs of maintaining the litigation system, leaves only a much-reduced portion of available compensation funds for the victim. According to one estimate, less than 40 per cent of the money spent by defendants in the U.S. asbestos litigation will go to the victims. A 1984 study found that claimants had so far received $236 million, while their lawyers had earned $164 million. Defence costs were estimated at $600 million.[70] Johns-Manville, the main defendant, successfully applied for bankruptcy, thereby placing a cap on its future liability. Even in the relatively straightforward area of automobile accidents, studies have estimated that, under the tort regime, only fifty cents of every compensation dollar ultimately goes to provide compensation.[71]

Controlling the 'Litigation Explosion': The Politics of Tort Law

Notwithstanding the many difficulties facing the victim of an injury, there is no doubt that the law regarding industrial and environmental hazards has been significantly 'liberalized' over the past several decades (especially in the United States). Courts have been somewhat more generous in allowing class actions in order to alleviate the burden on individual accident victims and to rebalance the scales of justice. The increasing availability of insurance has caused courts gradually to shift the emphasis in tort law from the fault of the defendant to compensation for the victim. This shift has been achieved in some cases by lowering the standard of proof of both negligence and causation and occasionally allowing stricter duties of care to displace the traditional standard of negligence. Some judges and lawyers have become more sympathetic to values of environmental cleanliness and industrial safety, and over time novel theories of liability that seek to promote those values have sprung up.

Yet it should not be forgotten that political and legal creativity is not monopolized by individuals and institutions acting on behalf of the victims of industrial risk and environmental degradation. Indeed, such efforts may be the exception rather than the rule. Judges, while often sympathetic to the plight of the victims they see before them, are drawn from the ranks of upper- and upper-middle class sectors of society and are schooled in the traditions of one of the most rigorously conservative professions in society.[72] And, for every lawyer who works on behalf of the poor, the environment, or the victims of industry, there is another, and usually better-paid lawyer working on behalf of industrial producers, insurance companies, and other corporate interests.

Powerful interests are also capable of effective political action through advertising campaigns and lobbying efforts. For example, over the past two decades, manufacturing groups and insurance companies in North America have responded with considerable success to the perceived litigation explosion. The increase in personal-injury litigation and an escalation in the level of damage awards have led to an 'insurance crisis' whereby coverage for certain activities has become prohibitively expensive or completely unavailable. This crisis has, in turn, led to a concerted campaign of 'tort reform' to restrict personal-injury law.[73] For example, in a full-page advertisement in the *Wall Street Journal*, insurance companies described products-liability law as an 'undisguised wolf who has entered corporate headquarters everywhere ... The American public seems intent on going to court. 'Sue the bastards' used to be a joke. Now it's a battle cry. With the help of eager attorneys, plaintiffs are not only quick to demand justice, but 'extra' justice, because their chances of success are great.'[74] The advertisement, which emphasized the 'frightening increase' and enormous cost of personal-injury claims, called for 'major changes in tort laws ... to correct a disastrous trend.'

The North American debate about whether there really is an 'insurance crisis' rages on.[75] It is true that both the frequency of tort claims and the quantum of awards have increased dramatically over the past decade (especially in the United States). It is also true that, in some sectors, insurance has become extremely expensive (for example, medical-malpractice insurance). Indeed, for a period, it became practically unavailable for certain forms of environmental harm. Some commentators have laid the blame for these developments solely upon the tort system, and have even gone so far as to argue that tort law has made the world a more dangerous place by impeding technological innovation in such fields as pharmaceutical development and toxic disposal.[76] They argue that tort law has gone too far and must return to more traditional standards of liability, even if that means leaving deserving victims with no compensation.

These concerns are, perhaps, somewhat removed from the Indian context. As later chapters reveal, Indian tort law has not been anywhere near as aggressive as its U.S. counterpart. Moreover, Indian legal culture may not be so accommodating of such laissez-faire arguments. The Indian judiciary is a heterogeneous group, committed to the social-welfare orientation of the constitution and including members who openly espouse socialist ideology.[77] Yet the same 'liability explosion' arguments would likely confront the Bhopal victims in a slightly different form. As chapter 2 indicated, Indian state policy does not unequivocally lean in the direction of environmental cleanliness and industrial safety. Competing goals of capital formation and economic development also weigh in the balance. Faced with the prospect of an expansive tort liability prompted by the Bhopal litigation, industrial interests would likely warn of the danger of capital flight and, at least in some government and judicial circles, those warnings would receive a sympathetic hearing. The North American debate on the liability explosion therefore deserves a brief examination.

Overall, while there are clearly problems in the way law deals with toxic injuries, the concerns of the North American critics are overstated and, more importantly, misdirected. Insurance and product prices have risen, but liability expenses do not represent a significant cost to business.[78] Moreover, those higher prices do not reflect new 'social costs.' Instead, they simply reflect the fact that already-existing costs (of injuries) are being transferred from victims back to producers and consumers more generally (though in an extremely inefficient fashion). Most important, to the extent that there is a problem, it is not attributable to the tort system's compensating *too many* people. Indeed, in most developed countries, the law of tort plays a relatively minor role in compensation. While some individuals do receive spectacular tort awards, most injury victims receive nothing at all. A study conducted in England, for example, found that nearly 90 per cent of all accident victims receive no compensation at all through the tort system; and if the definition of 'accident' were broadened to include the victims of non-traumatic (but socially caused) illness and injury, this figure would be much higher.[79]

The insurance problem may be more a result of the *uncertainty* created by exploding technology and an unpredictable legal system than of 'huge settlements.' Frightening discoveries about past and existing industrial practices, new scientific knowledge about the impact of substances on human health and the environment, and changing public values have exposed industry to new forms of potential liability. The judicial response to such a rapidly changing landscape *is* unpredictable and always after the fact, particularly when dealing with latent injuries and long-term hazards. When faced with the tragic consequences of 'social progress,' judges will, on occasion, promote doctrinal innovations to deal with new forms of injury; and, when faced with a system that relies so heavily on private insurance, they will look for a defendant with 'deep pockets.' The tort system *has* therefore made it difficult for insurers to predict risks in advance.[80] This uncertainty, and not simply 'overcompensation,' is what has driven up the price of insurance. As the president of the Canadian Institute of Actuaries has noted, insurers do not dislike liability; rather, they dislike uncertainty. Indeed, expanded liability rules create new markets for insurance, and as those rules become more certain (without necessarily becoming more restrictive) insurers will re-enter the market.[81]

Most of those who accept the seriousness of the insurance crisis do not conclude that the problem lies in an overly generous approach to compensation. Indeed, they also conclude that, as a system of compensation, 'the current tort system is, on most criteria, an abject failure.'[82] The system gets compensation to only a tiny portion of the injured population, and even then is thoroughly inefficient. Instead of 'blaming the victims,' these commentators have suggested that we re-examine our excessive reliance upon litigation and private insurance to care for the sick and injured. Everyone admits that litigation is an incredibly expensive way to provide compensation. And many have pointed out that private insurance suffers from contradictory goals. Its 'social' function may be loss spreading and compensation; however, its economic function is to make a profit. Its economic function thus tends to exclude it from those very sectors where it may be most needed.[83]

Nevertheless, there is also a narrower view that sees the solution simply in terms of retaining purely private mechanisms, while at the same time cutting back on compensation. Peter Huber, for example, calls for a return to a rigorous burden of proof of causation even while recognizing that the 'practical consequence would be to cut off virtually all environmental lawsuits,' and admitting that even under existing law, 'total environmental payments are lower than the total external environmental costs their activities generate.'[84] Such views have met with some success. A large number of U.S. states have passed or proposed laws that tighten limitation periods, legislate special defences for manufacturers, and limit damage awards. As Michael Trebilcock points out, tort liability has in the past been legislatively restricted, as in the case of workplace injuries. But these restrictions have been accepted only in exchange for alternative methods of caring for injured workers, such as workers' compensation regimes. But too many of the current proposals to curtail tort 'reflect no similar social contract.'[85]

Judges, too, have been influenced by the so-called crisis. For example, in 1978 the Canadian Supreme Court effectively legislated a $100,000 maximum ceiling for damages for pain and suffering for the victims of personal injury, no matter how severe their pain and how debilitating their injury.[86] The Court referred to the danger of 'extravagant claims' and the fact that such awards had 'soared to dramatically high levels' in the United States. It concluded that the 'social burden' of large damage awards should be guarded against by setting an upper limit. And the New Jersey Supreme Court recently rejected market-share liability in a vaccine case, in order to avoid a 'regressive effect' on the 'social policy of encouraging vaccine production and research.'[87] It is perhaps worth noting again that setting a limit on personal-injury damages does not in itself reduce 'social costs.' Rather, it simply leaves the victims to bear those costs themselves. The particularly candid remarks of an Australian judge, reacting to judicial efforts to reduce damage awards, are instructive on this point:

The judicial policy of depressing damage awards means that insurance premiums are kept within tolerable limits even with very high rates of death and injuries. It obscures the true social costs. The unintended result is a social acceptance of a high rate of road and industrial deaths and injuries, which would not be acceptable if the premiums reflected the implementation of full restitution. In practice therefore, this judicial policy has contributed to the high rate of deaths and injuries ... The sensible answer to this very serious social problem lies not in artificial transfer of social costs to the injured persons, but in reduction of the avoidable causes.[88]

The Deterrence Promise

Many commentators accept that if the only goal of tort law was to compensate the victims of injury, the current system could not be justified. It compensates only a few 'lucky' ones and even then is costly, inefficient, and unfair. However, defenders of the current system argue that tort law serves other goals better, particularly the goal of deterrence. This would certainly be one of the objectives of the victims of Bhopal, but the assertion that the law of tort provides effective deterrence, even in the developed countries, must be more closely inspected. The question is whether communities, workers, and activists should, in the wake of Bhopal, expend their limited energies and resources on the tort system or seek to devise alternative mechanisms to ensure safety.

One of the most important contributions to the theory of deterrence was Guido Calabresi's book *The Cost of Accidents*.[89] Calabresi argues that exposure to risk is an inevitable part of life in the modern world. All of our production and consumption, and nearly every activity in which we engage involve a trade-off between the benefits of engaging in the activity and the risk of the activity. Risks cannot be eliminated, but they can be controlled so that they are 'reasonable' or 'tolerable.' Calabresi says that, by imposing the costs of accidents on risky activities, the law will promote 'general' or 'market deterrence,' thus regulating risks at a socially acceptable level. So, for example, by requiring the drivers of automobiles to compensate persons who are injured, the law forces drivers to bear the full social costs of their activities. These costs will, in turn, be reflected in the 'price' of driving, which will reduce risks by giving drivers an incentive to substitute safer forms of transportation, to drive more slowly, or to invest in safer automobiles.

The economic theory of deterrence has gained widespread support as the rationale for tort law and as a potentially effective method of ensuring industrial safety and environmental cleanliness. The theory hypothesizes that firms underinvest in safety when they are able to avoid taking account of the full social cost of production in their decision making. These social costs include the damage to health and environment caused by industrial activity. The function of the law, therefore, is to force firms to 'internalize' those costs. By imposing the costs of pollution and accidents on firms, those costs are shifted from victims to the industry itself and become factored into prices. Thus, an implicit subsidy to hazardous activities is removed and an incentive to invest in greater safety is provided.[90] Industrial actors will make rational/optimal production, environmental, and safety decisions based upon an assessment of the total costs of production, including environmental and accident costs, compared to the benefits of the activity or the costs of reducing environmental and human damage.[91] Yet as good as this sounds in theory, there is little evidence that the goal of optimal safety can be achieved through the traditional processes of private tort law, especially in a case like Bhopal's.

Economic Assumptions

The economic theory of tort relies upon a number of spectacular assumptions and, more covertly, upon several highly controversial normative presuppositions. Perhaps the most problematic assumption is that the tort system is itself efficient.[92] Optimal deterrence can be achieved only if firms really are, in every instance, forced to pay *all* the costs of injury. From the preceding account, it is clear why this simply does not happen in practice. The tort system, in fact, ensures that the full costs of injury are not internalized by industry.

In the first place, most victims of accidents simply do not sue, or when they do, they do not prosecute their cases to a final judgment in court. Accident victims have neither the information nor the resources to sustain litigation and tend, instead, to settle their cases at a low figure, to rely upon public-welfare schemes, or simply to accept their injuries.[93] Second, as the discussion of statistical causation makes clear, we are now in a position confidently to say that the legal understanding of causation and injury vastly underestimates the quantum of illness and disease produced by industry. In a particular population group we may know from epidemiological studies that a certain percentage of illness and disease is attributable to toxic exposure, but because the victims cannot legally establish individual causation, none of the members of the group is in a position to recover damages. Third, even where victims do recover damages, there is no guarantee that those damages reflect the full cost of their injuries. The current lump-sum system of damage awards requires the courts to predict perfectly the long-term effects of the damage, including the victim's future injuries and needs.

The deterrence theory further assumes that firms will respond perfectly to the threat of a damage award. This also is unlikely. Even those costs that are imposed upon industry are usually absorbed by insurance. This fact alone would not undermine the deterrence rationale *if* insurers based their premiums upon a perfectly accurate form of experience rating whereby premiums were calculated on the basis of the insured's risk. This assumption also, however, is unrealistic. In the case of a corporate defendant (like UCC) other forms of 'insurance' include the legal notions of separate corporate personality and limited liability. Under these doctrines, individual owners and managers and parent companies are not responsible for the debts of companies under their control. The threat of a large damage award against an undercapitalized affiliate may be deprived of all deterrent effect if the human beings who control that undertaking are confident that they will not have to pay. Finally, deterrence theory assumes that firms will be able, in every instance, to factor the likelihood and size of future tort liability into their safety and production decisions. But this kind of risk analysis is neither accurate nor costless. Firms are not able to estimate perfectly the degree of risk associated with their operations, the likelihood and severity of future accidents, and the cost of those accidents, and even those imperfect equations are expensive to obtain. Indeed, it is for this reason that firms prefer to purchase insurance.

The final problematic assumption is that business managers are as 'rational' as the theory supposes; that they do, in fact, respond to the threat of a damages award and do carefully weigh the social costs of accidents in their decisions. This assumption is highly questionable in a case like Bhopal. Large business enterprises like Union Carbide are extremely complex organizations without a single 'directing mind.' They are managed by numerous decision makers, each with a degree of autonomy, and all operating from a variety of motivations, of which 'efficiency' is only one. There is evidence that managers of particular units, whose performance may be judged by short-term profit, may be tempted to take socially unjustifiable risks in order to improve their unit's performance (and thus their own position) within the enterprise.[94] This phenomenon seems clearly to have been an important factor at Bhopal where, in the face of a failing project, decisions were taken to make drastic cuts in operating and safety expenses in order to improve the profit picture.

The debate about the deterrence impact of tort law rages on. In some areas, such as medical malpractice, there is some evidence that tort law does play a modest deterrent role. In other areas, such as environmental risk, it plays almost no role at all. Thus, in a recent comprehensive survey of the North American evidence, D. Dewees and M. Trebilcock reach 'a relatively bleak judgment about the properties of the tort system as a deterrent mechanism and an even bleaker evaluation of the tort system as a compensatory mechanism.'[95]

Efficiency and Equity: Economic 'Rationality'

The final question is whether promoting the 'efficient' level of safety (and also of danger) is the desirable goal. There are two problems here. The first is the ethically questionable proposition that the aim of the law is not to reduce harm, but rather to make sure that it is efficient. The second problem is, even accepting that we do have to trade off risks and benefits, whether we should be satisfied that current estimates of risks and benefits provide a satisfactory and equitable means of social accounting. Have we properly answered the question, 'what is the value of safety, and ultimately of human life?'

The case against the Ford Motor Company provides a spectacular example of the public's dislike or misunderstanding of 'cold-blooded' cost–benefit analysis.[96] This case may also provide some insight into the type of corporate decision making that gives rise to unacceptable levels of risk, as in Bhopal, and to explain why traditional legal responses have often been defective.

In the early 1970s the U.S. government proposed standards for fuel tank leakage in automobile accidents. Ford determined that compliance with these standards would result in the prevention of 180 burn deaths per year and 180 serious burn injuries. It also estimated that the necessary design change would cost $11 per car. Using figures from the National Highway Traffic Safety Administration, Ford determined that the 'value' of the lives saved and injuries prevented would be $49.5 million per year (based on average per-accident costs of $200,000 for fatal injuries and $67,000 for injuries). The cost of complying with the standards was, however, $137 million. Ford argued that the standards were too high, and as a result they did not come into force until six years later.

The issues raised in this regulatory encounter came up again several years later in the context of litigation when a young man was seriously burned in an accident involving a Ford Pinto.[97] Evidence was introduced that, when designing the Ford Pinto, Ford learned that the placement of the gas tank behind the rear axle increased the risk of fire consequent upon a rear-end accident. The evidence indicated that the problem could have been remedied at a cost of about $4 to $8 per car. But Ford made the decision to defer the correction and instead simply to absorb the costs of the resulting injuries, reasoning that by paying damages it would realize a savings of $20.9 million. Upon hearing this evidence an outraged jury awarded $125 million in punitive damages. This sum was reduced to $3.5 million by the court. Ford sought to have the award further reduced on the basis that it had done nothing wrong or out of the ordinary in using cost–benefit methods to determine the acceptable level of risk. But the Court of Appeal upheld the award. It noted that punitive damages may be necessary in commercial torts because a 'manufacturer may find it more profitable to treat compensatory damages as part of the cost of doing business rather than to remedy the defect.' The court concluded: 'There was evidence that Ford could have corrected the hazardous design defects at minimal cost but decided to defer correction of the shortcomings by engaging in cost-benefit analysis balancing human lives and limbs against corporate profits. Ford's institutional mentality was shown to be one of callous indifference to public safety.'[98]

While, in this particular case, the award of punitive damages may have acted as a deterrent to such future indifference on the part of Ford, such awards are rare. Indeed, according to traditional notions of tort law, while Ford may have used the wrong figures in its calculations, or may have attempted to hide its findings from the public, its attempt to 'balance human lives and limbs against corporate profits' is precisely what economic analysis applauds and what deterrence theory assumes. Ford calculated the value of the expected benefits of a design change, weighed those against the costs of the change, and concluded that the change was not 'optimal.' The cost of producing more safety was greater than the cost of the expected accident, and it was therefore 'rational' to produce the car as it was.[99]

This concept of 'rationality' explains the logic at work in Bhopal and, more generally, serves to illustrate in formal and 'scientific' terms the reasons for the double standard of industrial safety in the Third World. Economic analysis measures human welfare in terms of current costs and market prices. As Richard Posner suggests, the 'value' of anything, including safety, is measured by what a person is willing to pay for that thing.[100] Private and social resources, then, are most 'efficiently' deployed when they are traded and allowed to gravitate into the hands of those who are willing to pay the most for them (i.e., those who 'value' them most highly). But willingness to pay is, of course, a function of *ability to pay* and, economists by and large accept the current distribution of wealth as a given. In specifying social policy and measuring efficiency, economics thus substitutes the notion of market value (measured by wealth) for the more problematic concept of human welfare. This substitution is attractive because wealth is easier to measure and compare than welfare. It is less attractive because it systematically confirms and reproduces the maldistribution of wealth in society. Posner offers the following example: 'Suppose that pituitary extract is in very scarce supply relative to the demand and is therefore very expensive. A poor family has a child who will be a dwarf if he does not get some of the extract, but the family cannot afford the price ... A rich family has a child who will grow to normal height, but the extract will add a few inches more, and his parents decide to buy it for him ... the pituitary extract is more valuable to the rich than to poor family, because value is measured by willingness to pay.'[101]

Posner admits that such examples demonstrate that efficiency 'has limitations as an ethical criterion' but goes on to argue that they are not serious and that the examples are rare. But an analysis of the economic logic of law demonstrates that they are both serious and common. The law of tort, like economics, measures most values in reference to market prices. So, as we have seen, the legal value placed on human life is, in part, based on the victim's preaccident income. What does this mean in terms of 'optimal deterrence'? The logic is brutally simple. The 'social cost' of injury or death is a function of income. The death of a poor person does not, therefore, diminish 'aggregate social wealth' to the same extent that the death of a rich person does. It is therefore rational to spend less on preventing accidents involving the poor than on those involving the rich. The 'efficient' level of safety is clearly inconsistent with the equitable distribution of care and concern for human life.

In North America, average annual income is about fifty times larger than average annual income in India. The cost of industrial accidents, measured by income loss, is therefore vastly less expensive in India. To the extent that the expected cost of accidents is a factor in the decision of where to locate a dangerous plant, and how much to spend on supervision, updating, and safety, the calculations will be very different in the two locations. In India, the maximum 'rational' outlay is fifty times less than in North America. Thus, by accepting the current distribution of income and wealth as the basis for determining social costs, law and economics both reproduce and aggravate the basic problem of distributive justice and the inequitable distribution of risks to human health and safety.

It is precisely this economic logic that so offended the victims in Bhopal. Speaking through their activist organizations they expressed their conviction that the Union Carbide disaster had occurred only because Third World life is cheap. For them, the looming legal battle was about equality, and the maldistribution of wealth and power between the developed and developing nations of the world. As one of the victims' groups stated, 'We are fighting for our right to be compensated by the multinational corporation for the damages caused by it. We are fighting to make the multinational realize that human life is not a thing to be dealt with so casually, negligently and cheaply. We are fighting to make them understand that life of an Indian is no less precious than that of an American.'[102] Yet, these groups placed their hopes in a system of law that not only is limited in its instrumental impact, but, in fact, presupposes and reproduces the very patterns of inequality under which they suffer. The following chapters, which relate in detail the story of the Bhopal litigation, illustrate why this is so.

5

Legalizing a Disaster

The sheer magnitude of the disaster at Bhopal invited all those affected by it – the government, the victims, the Indian company (UCIL) and its multinational parent (UCC) – to consider non-traditional approaches to its solution. The transnational nature of the dispute, its technical and legal complexity, the enormous number of victims, and the international public horror at what had happened might have prompted the main players to devise some quick and adequate response to the disaster. Most observers recognized that the pursuit of litigation would be slow and expensive, and that, at the end of the day, existing legal mechanisms could offer no guarantees to the victims. Many voiced the hope that a quick settlement could be achieved, with Union Carbide and the government sharing the costs of relief and rehabilitation. Others suggested the establishment of alternative dispute-resolution mechanisms. One commentator, for example, suggested a bilateral agreement between India and the United States to establish a claims tribunal funded by India, the United States, UCC, and UCIL.[1] Others suggested the creation of special courts with expedited procedures, or the establishment of arbitration facilities that might provide speedier and more cost-effective compensation to the victims. Few observers expected that a traditional legal response would prove adequate to meet the needs of the case.

However, so-called non-traditional solutions to the problem of personal-injury compensation – especially in mass-disaster cases – have been criticized in many quarters. An early settlement of the dispute, legally binding on the parties and excusing the UCC from any further liability, seemed clearly out of the question. Union Carbide initially estimated that full compensation would require less than $100 million, while citizens groups in Bhopal put the figure at well over $1 billion. The extent of the damage in Bhopal – the number of victims and the severity of their injuries – would not be known for years. Early predictions, based on scant scientific and medical evidence, vastly diverged and were hotly contested. It was not clear how many people had died; and the continuing toll on human health and the local environment would require intensive monitoring and scientific investigation. An early settlement would risk overlooking these contingencies. It would likely underestimate the full social costs incurred at Bhopal, undercompensate the victims, and sacrifice the goal of deterrence.

Other models of non-judicial compensation – such as publicly funded no-fault compensation and informal mechanisms of alternative dispute resolution – were publicly mooted, but found wanting. Such schemes had, for example, been attempted in the U.S. asbestos litigation, which was still ongoing at the time of the Bhopal disaster. In 1981, Senator Gary Hart had introduced a bill to provide 'no-fault' relief to the victims of asbestosis. This bill, modelled on the concept of workers' compensation schemes, would have eliminated the need (and right) of individuals to sue asbestos companies. But, in his book on the asbestos saga, Paul Brodeur describes how the bill came to be perceived as a cynical political bail-out for the companies.[2] Its meagre benefits, and the immunity it conferred upon the industry, amounted to little more than a pact between government and industry that 'institutionalized' cancer and licensed 'outrageous misconduct.'

During the asbestos litigation another compensation model had been tested – a voluntary claims resolution facility that would provide mediation and arbitration services for the rapid and inexpensive provision of compensation on a no-fault basis. This proposal had considerable support from people who doubted that the court system could handle the rising tide of claims, who were appalled by the astronomical legal costs, and who sympathized keenly with the needs of the victims and their families for more effective compensation. Yet the fact that the facility was sponsored by the asbestos industry and their insurers put the victims and their lawyers on early notice that the claims facility was more likely to evolve into an organization simply for the coordination of the defence effort of the asbestos industry.[3]

One of the problems in Bhopal, therefore, was that there were no ready, 'on the shelf' models available to be deployed and any effort to depart significantly from traditional litigation models would have met with resistance. Special tribunals may become overly bureaucratic, and expedited procedures may require a significant departures from traditional notions of due process. So long as there is the possibility of an appeal from the tribunal into the court system, the use of compensation tribunals may simply add one more level of proceedings to an already complicated judicial system. In the case of Bhopal, the opportunities for innovation may have been even more limited because of the transnational nature of the dispute. Because any judgment against Union Carbide would likely have to be enforced in the United States, efforts in India would have to take into account the insistence of U.S. courts on 'due process of law.'

Legalizing the Dispute

Whatever the merits of the alternatives, a traditional legal response was precisely what the victims got. It was assumed almost from the beginning that the solution to Bhopal would be a *legal* one, involving a mass claim by the victims against the Union Carbide Corporation. This assumption was the result of two main factors: the internal imperatives of the main parties to the dispute and the involvement of U.S. lawyers.

The rapid legalization of the Bhopal disaster forced the parties to assume an adversarial posture and quickly to entrench into positions designed foremost to protect their interests and only secondarily to respond to the plight of the victims. Both the Government of India and the UCC immediately adopted defensive strategies designed to control damage to their own position. Each sought to focus public attention away from its own potential responsibilities and to shift the locus of legal and moral blame to other parties. As a result, compensation to the victims remained a low priority.

Positioning

The morning after the disaster, Indian police arrested five management and supervisory personnel, including works manager Jaganath Mukund, charging them with causing death by negligence under the Criminal Code.[4] Warren Anderson, the president and chair of Union Carbide, later flew to India and was also summarily arrested, though he was released soon after and sent home. The Indian Central Bureau of Investigation (CBI) assumed responsibility for investigating the gas leak. It sealed off access to the factory and seized some 100,000 pages of UCIL documents. Union Carbide lawyers complained that the CBI was denying them access to records and witnesses that the company would need to mount an effective investigation and a legal defence. They would later to accuse the government of deliberately suppressing the facts and failing to disclose the medical information that it was acquiring.

The company, however, adopted a similar stance. Anticipating the forthcoming litigation, it became enormously cautious in its public statements, denying all allegations against it. While UCC expressed sympathy for the victims, its primary objective was 'damage control' – to deny any legal responsibility and to deflect attention away from its own involvement and on to other parties. Warren Anderson publicly stated that the company accepted 'moral' responsibility for the disaster, saying that legal responsibility could be sorted out later, but at the same time the company immediately hired public-relations consultants to manage the media and forbade its employees from speaking to the press. The company retained lawyers Bud Holman and William Krohley of the law firm of Kelley Drye and Warren to represent them. This firm was skilled at defending tort claims, and Holman's team included up to thirty lawyers. The company also retained Indian lawyers, including Fali Nariman and Nani A. Palkhivala, India's former ambassador to Washington. Union Carbide's position thus rapidly hardened into an effort to disassociate itself entirely from the Indian operation and to promote a version of the Bhopal disaster that would absolve it entirely of any responsibility.

What modest technical and financial assistance UCC did offer in the months immediately following the disaster was rejected by an adversarial Indian government on the basis that too many strings were attached and that the offers were simply public-relations gestures. The company's efforts to set up medical organizations in Bhopal were interpreted by the government as attempts to fabricate evidence that would support its case. There was some basis for this concern. One of the more prominent members of UCC's medical team was Dr Hans Weill, who had been a central researcher and witness for Johns-Manville in its attempt to deny the health effects of asbestos.[5] The company refused to acknowledge the dangers of MIC or to reveal any information about the disaster or the operation of the Bhopal plant. The government would later accuse the company of hiding documents that demonstrated its involvement in Bhopal and fabricating evidence about the disaster.

The state government of Madhya Pradesh did order a public enquiry into the disaster, setting up the Bhopal Poisonous Gas Leakage Enquiry.

But this commission's activities were marginalized by the greater efforts being devoted to the preparation of the case. Moreover, with the prospect of the lawsuit looming on the horizon, it was unrealistic to expect much cooperation or disclosure from the antagonistic parties. Instead, the enquiry served at most as a rehearsal stage for the litigation. On 9 March 1985, just one week before the deadline for the commission's report, UCIL presented its sabotage theory. The submissions from the state and central governments were not received until much later, after the commission's mandate had been extended. Finally, a year after the disaster, having made almost no progress, the commission was dissolved. Union Carbide was later to point to the commission's failure as evidence that the government had no interest in discovering the true causes of the gas leak. Perhaps more realistically, the commission's failure can be attributed to the fact that its access to facts was constrained, indeed undermined, by the antagonism and secrecy generated by the forthcoming litigation.

The legalization of the disaster did not, of course, entirely divert attention away from the needs of the victims, but it did redefine those needs and how they would be satisfied. The government did mount a massive relief effort, described in a later chapter. It established the Relief and Rehabilitation Department and made some early cash payments to the victims, though these were suspended within four days because of the impossibility of identifying bona fide claimants.[6] The government instituted a food-distribution program and began to provide medical facilities that would be needed for the long-term treatment of those who had been permanently injured by their exposure to the gas. Yet the long-term efforts of the department were made far more difficult because they were seen to be, at least partially, contingent upon the outcome of the litigation. Funding remained uncertain, and no mechanism was set in place until much later to undertake the laborious process of collecting information that would become pertinent to claims assessment. The government also feared that its own expenditures on Bhopal might be taken as an admission that it had some legal responsibility, or might reduce the ultimate liability of Union Carbide. Perhaps not surprisingly, the victims, who were forced to battle for every rupee of interim compensation, gradually began to perceive the government as an adversary. The longer-term relief effort is described in greater detail in subsequent chapters.

The prospect of adversarial proceedings, and the very structure of tort law, thus forced both the Government of India and the Union Carbide

Corporation to narrow their range of inquiry to the legal requirements for causation and fault, and to compete for public acceptance of their version of the 'truth' of what had happened in Bhopal and who was responsible. The prospect of litigation also resulted in an obsession with secrecy. Information that might leave prompted an earlier solution, assisted the medical effort, allayed the fears of the victims, or at least enhanced communication and understanding, was 'privatized' to satisfy the needs of litigators, rather than being used for the benefit of the victims.

Ambulance Chasing

The legalization of the Bhopal tragedy was most immediately accelerated by the entry of U.S. lawyers onto the scene. Directly following the disaster, personal-injury lawyers from the United States began to flood Bhopal, and within a few days hundreds of lawsuits had been filed in various courts in India and the United States. On 7 December, for example, the well-known U.S. attorney Melvin Belli had filed a $15-billion class action on behalf of several of the victims. Other lawyers were even faster off the mark and just as optimistic. These 'ambulance-chasing' legal entrepreneurs were roundly criticized in the U.S. and Indian press for their unseemly enthusiasm for profiting from a disaster caused by a multinational company. Belli, and others, responded that capitalist lawyers were 'needed in a capitalist society' and that 'I am a good capitalist.'[7] Controversial legal ethicist Monroe Freedman argued, 'What else but the profit motive could have brought to the doorsteps of the impoverished people of India some of the finest legal talent in America?'[8]

The presence of the U.S. lawyers in India confirmed the victims' view that the Bhopal disaster was an international incident and further focused their anger on the multinational corporation. It also gave rise to a lively debate in both India and the United States about the lawyers' role and ethics. It can plausibly be argued that the presence of the U.S. lawyers did galvanize both the victims and the government to speedier action. Their resources far exceeded anything possessed by Indian lawyers, and their experience with U.S. law and previous disaster litigation contributed to the way in which the dispute was framed and the legal process was initiated. As Marc Galanter, a specialist in Indian law, has argued, the U.S. legal profession 'includes specialists who pioneer new forms of accountability – entrepreneurs who, for economic gain or for ideological motives, bring marginal constituencies into the marketplace for remedies.'[9] They conveyed to the victims the promises of law – that they were entitled to compensation, that life in the Third World is not cheap, and that the multinational would be held account-able for the tragedy.

Nevertheless, as one U.S. judge said in later proceedings in the United States, 'those members of the American bar who travelled the 8,200 miles to Bhopal in those months did little to better the American image in the Third World – or anywhere else.'[10] The reports of their conduct while in India, measured against conventional professional or moral standards, left much to be desired. They placed advertisements in local newspapers and hired local agents to secure retainer agreements from large numbers of victims in record-breaking time. In many cases the victims were paid small sums of money to retain lawyers and were being signed on at a rate that suggests they were receiving no individ-ual advice, nor even being informed of the nature of their agreements.[11]

The story of John Coale, a Washington DC, lawyer, is notorious. His Bhopal odyssey is chronicled by John Jenkins in his book *The Litigators*.[12] Coale ran a flourishing assembly-line practice in Washington, DC, defending drunk drivers. For some time he had wanted to get into the 'mass-disaster business,' and the Bhopal tragedy seemed to offer the perfect opportunity. Within three days of the gas leak, he had hired C.S. Sastry, a Virginia tailor originally from Bangalore in India, and had arranged travel to India. He arrived in Bhopal on 9 December and found, to his delight, that he was the first U.S. lawyer on the scene. He and Sastry met with R.I. Bisarya, the mayor of Bhopal, and after some discussions Coale was hired as the city's lawyer. He then wasted no time in having a retainer agreement drawn up. He originally planned to charge the 'customary' 33.3 per cent contingency fee, but upon being informed that such agreements were illegal in India, settled for 'compensation in accordance with United States customs in personal injury cases.' He had thousands of copies of the agreements printed at a local shop and immediately set out, with the help of several local lawyers and students, to wander through the slums near the Union Carbide plant, signing up clients. Other lawyers, including Melvin Belli, Federico Sayre, and Jay Gould, now arrived on the scene. The competi-tion for clients soon manifested itself in slinging matches between the lawyers, each accusing the others of ambulance chasing and sharp practice. By this time Coale had attracted the interest of the police in his activities and, coming under increasing pressure from the local authorities, was forced to leave Bhopal quietly, but not before he had signed up 30,000 clients.

Within a month of the disaster, Coale claimed to have 60,000 clients. Other lawyers purported to have even more. In all, the various lawyers claimed to represent nearly 500,000 claimants. This number was no doubt vastly exaggerated since many of the victims, desperate for some kind of help, entirely confused by the antics of the lawyers, and hoping to improve their chances of recovery, signed retainers with every lawyer or tout who offered one. On their return to the United States, the U.S. lawyers promptly filed about 186,000 actions against UCC, claiming billions of dollars.

While the involvement of U.S. lawyers in the Bhopal case may have 'broken the pattern of legal resignation'[13] in India, it probably also reduced the prospect of a quick, non-traditional solution. Given the strategies adopted by the main players, it is questionable whether such a solution could have been devised, even in the absence of the U.S. lawyers. That it could not be devised in their presence is certain. The problems were individualized and legalized. The anger of the victims was exacerbated, and their expectations were raised impossibly high by reports that the lawyers had filed $50-billion lawsuits on their behalf. A hundred different lawyers presented themselves as authoritative spokespersons for the victims, and filed suits against UCIL, UCC, and the Government of India in every jurisdiction imaginable. Yet, with so many players, there was no unified or coherent strategy. More legal energy was spent on attempting to obtain control of the Bhopal cases than in pursuing them. Settlement negotiations were begun by one group and rejected by another. Confusion reigned.

Devising a Process for Mass Claims

For several months after the appearance of the U.S. lawyers it seemed as though a multitude of class and individual actions would be prosecuted by U.S. lawyers in the United States and Indian lawyers in India. The lightning speed with which U.S. lawyers had initiated the actions appeared to exclude any role for the Indian government and any alternative form of dispute resolution. But this strategy (or non-strategy) would be extremely hazardous.

The most obvious problem arose simply because of the sheer number of people affected. At least 3,500 people were killed in Bhopal and at least 40,000 others were seriously injured. Livestock was destroyed, and massive economic losses were suffered. In all, there were well over half a million claims. It seems obvious that, in an incident of such proportions, traditional individualistic legal processes make little sense. The poverty of the victims would exclude many from any formal legal redress whatsoever. With hundreds of lawyers, the litigation would be extremely difficult and expensive to organize and carry through against the legal artillery possessed by a multinational corporation. To litigate each case separately would be inefficient and so wasteful of public and private resources as to be absurd. The length of time it would take to achieve and enforce a final verdict would leave the victims suffering for years with no interim support. And lawyers' contingency fees of up to 33 per cent would further erode any compensation that would eventually be forthcoming. Yet this was precisely the course that the disaster seemed to be taking, until the Indian government was mobilized to action.

The Bhopal Act

In response to this gloomy prospect and to the demands of the victims and volunteer organizations for some kind of action, the government acted relatively quickly and effectively to reassert its interest in the litigation. In March 1985 it passed a presidential ordinance, and later a statute, giving itself authority to devise a scheme for the compensation of the victims.

The Bhopal Gas Leak Disaster Act[14] was designed to confer powers on the central government to ensure that claims arising out of the Bhopal disaster were dealt with 'speedily, effectively equitably and to the best advantage of the claimants.'[15] Perhaps most importantly, the statute made the Indian government the exclusive representative of the victims in legal proceedings for compensation *whether within or outside of India*. The act applied retroactively to actions already initiated by individual victims, although it preserved their right to retain counsel and required that the government 'have due regard to any matters which such persons may require to be urged with respect to his claim.' The act further authorized the establishment of a claims scheme as the primary mode of redress for the victims. It authorized the appointment of a claims commissioner whose function would be to administer the litigation process, registering, recording, and processing individual claims. Finally, the act declared that any amounts paid by the government to the victims would be without prejudice and would not be taken into account in determining the level of damages, but would be deducted from the amount disbursed to the victims under the scheme.

This statute thus gave the central government *parens patriae* control over the Bhopal case. It purported to all but eliminate the pursuit by individuals of claims and the involvement of U.S. lawyers. It proposed to substitute an administrative framework for the disbursement of any compensation monies. Of more immediate importance it allowed the Indian government to take over the litigation already commenced in the United States, to dictate litigation strategy, and to scuttle ongoing settlement negotiations. With the authority of this statute, the Government of India, on 8 April 1985, joined in the litigation already commenced in both the United States and in the Bhopal District Court.

The Bureaucratization of Justice

The Bhopal Act was an important, but limited measure. While it left open the establishment of a compensation commission, it by and large presupposed that the solution to the disaster would be achieved through the traditional litigation process. And although it contemplated that the commission would provide interim relief and assistance to the victims, any final compensation funds received from Union Carbide would go, first, to reimburse the government for its expenditures. The statute's primary importance, therefore, was to consolidate all of the Bhopal claims and to remove the burden of the litigation from the individual victims to the government. Even this limited innovation proved highly problematic.

In the first place, the very legality of the statute was a problem in both India and the United States. Union Carbide and the private lawyers for several of the Bhopal victims argued that the government had no authority to declare itself the exclusive representative of the victims, suggesting that doing so violated the individual's right to due process of law. The statute was, therefore, immediately challenged in both India and the United States. U.S. courts have held that the *parens patriae* power is appropriate only when the state's interest in the litigation is independent of the individual interests of the citizens, and that the procedure is not appropriately exercised simply to collect damages for a person who is legally entitled to an individual claim.[16] These same arguments were later to be raised in the Indian courts by victims and groups dissatisfied with the government's conduct of the litigation. They argued that the statute violated the victims' rights to equality before the law and access to justice in so far as it deprived them of the ability to pursue compensation through ordinary channels.

The hostility to the Bhopal Act was based upon the same individual-istic concerns that underlie the traditional distrust of class actions in mass-injury suits. Opponents argue that the class action 'bureaucratizes' justice by taking the conduct of the litigation out of the hands of the victim.[17] The class form cannot respond to the individual needs of the victims and cannot produce a remedy tailored to the individual. The aggregation and collectivization of claims 'achieves administrative goals of efficiency, consistency, and maximum substantive output by sub-ordinating the interests of individual victims (although not of defendant firms) to the interests of the class as a whole.'[18]

The use of *parens patriae* power is further questionable when we recognize that the Indian government was in a situation of considerable conflict of interest. It is arguable that various government bodies at both the national and the state level were legally implicated in the tragedy. The Government of India, itself an indirect shareholder in the Bhopal enterprise, and the state of Madhya Pradesh, were arguably lax in administering their own health and safety requirements, in allowing slums to grow in the vicinity of the plant, and in approving the dangerous technology. Even apart from the Indian government's potential legal liability in the case, the Bhopal disaster quickly was to become a major political liability for it. To what extent would the imperatives of political damage control come into conflict with the best interests of the victims?

Objections to the bureaucratization of justice become especially clear during settlement negotiations, when, inevitably, at least some members of the class will be dissatisfied with the proposals. The purpose of the class action is to empower individual victims who would not otherwise have access to justice by consolidating their claims. But the irony is that, as the process nears success, it comes under tremendous disaggregative pressures. Each time the government and Union Carbide were to come close to a settlement, the news would be met by massive protests, charges of incompetence and collusion, and occasional violence. With so many victims, and a large number of activist organizations claiming to speak for the victims, no common front is possible. Disempowered by the process, denied a voice, and suspicious of government motives, the victims will inevitably feel betrayed.

The Politicization of a Disaster and the Need for Public Responsibility

The response to the defects of the act was perhaps predictable. Modern India has developed an extremely vigorous tradition of social activism, which, in the case of Bhopal, manifested itself in the grass-roots organization of aid to the victims, the focusing of political pressure on government through media and organized protest, and the formation of medical and legal action groups to work on behalf of the victims. As the government took increasing control of the litigation, these social-action groups began to play an important role as watch-dogs and agitators on behalf of the victims. Groups such as the Bhopal Gas Peedit Mahila Udyog Sangathan, led by Abdul Jabbar Khan; the Zahreeli Gas Kand Sangharsh Morcha ('Poison Gas Disaster Struggle Front'); and the Jan Swasthya Kendra (the 'People's Health Clinic') were increasingly to become thorns in the side of the authorities. Outside of Bhopal, other groups included the Bhopal Group for Information and Action, the Society for Participatory Research in Asia, the Delhi Science Forum, and the Medico Friends Circle. Internationally, organizations, including the Bhopal Action Resource Centre, the International Coalition for Justice in Bhopal, and the Council on International and Public Affairs, became intensely involved in the Bhopal dispute.

These groups distrusted both the Indian government and Union Carbide, and were frustrated by the lack of support for the victims. They, more than anyone else, focused and articulated with extraordinary intensity the victims' hatred of the multinational 'Killer Carbide.' This approach increased pressure upon the government to take an extremely hard line. But the relationship between the victims' groups and the government was anything but amicable. Fully cognizant of the government's conflict of interest, and of the rampant corruption in the Indian bureaucracy, these organizations feared that the welfare of the victims would be subordinated to political imperatives and personal opportunism. Through their work with the victims and their vigorous advocacy, the voluntary organizations were able to use the media effectively and to mobilize widespread grass-roots support.

Jabbar Khan, in particular, held together a group of some 12,000 victims, mostly women who had suffered in the tragedy, through his charisma and energy on their behalf. On two hours' notice he could mobilize thousands of victims for a demonstration in the front of the Bhopal Gas Tragedy Relief Department's offices, the court house, or the chief minister's office. With the assistance of public-interest advocates, including Vibhuti Jha, Shanti Bushan, and Indira Jaising, the victims' groups also frequently petitioned the Indian courts to have their voices heard and to require the department to take a particular course of action.

Thus, while the problems were in one sense 'legalized,' they were also politicized. Although collective action was undoubtedly essential to safeguard the interests of the victims, it was also to complicate the process even more by further alienating the victims from the government and from one another. The government's sporadic crack-down on the victims' organizations, its closure of the People's Health Clinic, the arrest of 'agitators,' and police beatings of demonstrators exacerbated these problems and simply confirmed that it was not to be trusted.

The bureaucratization of claims, India's potential conflict of interest, and the disempowerment of the victims were major defects in the scheme framed by the government. But the failings of the Bhopal Act do not argue in favour of a return to individualized justice. Serious though the problems are, it is crucial to remember that the majority of victims were poor and had no other effective means of legal redress. The preference for individualized justice is based on the wholly untenable assumption that the victims could be empowered through more traditional channels. But the model could have been improved by a more thorough-going acceptance by the government of the concept of *public* responsibility, as opposed to the hybrid scheme of *private* litigation.

The defects of the act were the result of the fact that it was an attempt to graft a public model of administration onto a private model of litigation. The government, itself a potential litigant, simply substituted itself as the victims' lawyer, thereby assuming only partial responsibility for their welfare. By providing only limited and conditional interim relief, it left the victims as stakeholders in the litigation, at the same time denying them an effective say about their future. What this teaches is that, at a minimum, the agency responsible for the conduct of the litigation should have greater autonomy from government. It should also be structured in such a way as to allow more effective communication and participation by the victims. In the case of Bhopal, representatives of the victims' groups should have been made part of the process and given a voice in the litigation. Otherwise, their adversarial role becomes inevitable.

Even more ambitiously, the mechanism should have separated entirely the process of compensation from that of litigation. The government could assume greater legitimacy as *parens patriae* only by adopting more comprehensive responsibility for the victims' welfare. Doing so would require an approach whereby the victims are guaranteed at least a minimum of compensation out of public monies or a special fund, irrespective of the outcome of the litigation. Under such a model, the task of compensation and rehabilitation need not be subject to the delays of litigation. Any recovery simply goes to reimburse the fund out of which the victims were compensated. By accepting unequivocal responsibility for the victims' welfare, the government becomes the main stakeholder in the litigation and enhances its legitimacy as representative of the victims.

The Americanization of a Disaster

The most immediate result of the involvement of the U.S. lawyers in the Bhopal saga was that it focused attention almost exclusively upon the liability of the U.S. multinational and the promises of U.S. law. Upon their return to the United States, these lawyers began to file their suits. Within two months, individual claims totalling $250 billion had been filed in various state courts.[19] The U.S. lawyers denied that the Bhopal Act applied to their actions in the United States. However, most of them recognized that the case could not be prosecuted on a purely individualistic basis and they began to attempt to organize class and representative actions. The thousands of individual lawsuits that had been filed in different state courts would have to be consolidated under the U.S. rules for multidistrict litigation, and a team of lawyers would have to be appointed to steer the litigation. At this point the initial skirmishing moved to a new phase whereby the lawyers began jockeying for position to control what would undoubtedly be the world's biggest lawsuit ever.

There then developed a complex and fractious battle among the plaintiffs' lawyers to determine who would become members of the steering committee that not only would call all the shots, but would receive the greatest portion of the fees. More than 100 lawyers were now involved in the Bhopal cases, and during the two months following the disaster they held a series of meetings in Washington, New York, and New Orleans. Alliances were formed and broken; various factions strategized. Finally, at a meeting held on 9 February, a committee was formed that included one member of each of twenty-eight law firms involved in the cases. John Coale, who had returned from India to represent more than 60,000 clients, had not actually filed suit on any of his cases and was excluded entirely from the process. But Coale's involvement was not quite over.

In the meantime, Indian government lawyers, directed by the attorney general, K. Parasaran; the law secretary, B.S. Sekhom; and Shyamal Gosh of the Ministry of Chemicals had begun to develop India's litigation strategy. They retained Michael Ciresi, of the law firm of Robins, Kaplan, Miller and Ciresi, to represent India in the United States. The Judicial Panel on Multidistrict Litigation had previously (on 2 January 1985) ruled that the cases would be heard before Judge John F. Keenan of the Southern District Court of New York and on April 8 1985, India formally joined the U.S. litigation. Later that month, on April 25 1985, Judge Keenan appointed three lawyers to act as an executive for the steering committee for the purpose of the litigation. These three were F. Lee Bailey, Stanley Chesley, and Michael Ciresi. The first two of these men had a substantial number of Bhopal clients. Bailey, in particular, had a high and carefully cultivated media profile. Ciresi, as lawyer for India, was a natural choice since neither the litigation, nor an early settlement of the dispute, could be pursued without his participation. Each of these lawyers had been involved in previous mass-tort litigation, including the Dalkon Shield, Agent Orange, MGM Grand Hotel fire, and other high-profile tort cases.

The problems were by no means solved once the executive committee was struck because there was an impossible conflict of objectives and interests between Bailey and Chesley, on the one hand, and Ciresi on the other. Ciresi represented the Government of India which, under the provisions of the Bhopal Gas Leak Disaster Act, claimed the exclusive authority to represent the victims and to decide upon litigation strategy. This fact threatened to exclude the other lawyers from the litigation (and their fees) altogether. Nevertheless, the other U.S. lawyers reasoned that if they could keep the case in the United States, and achieve a quick settlement, the act might not be enforceable. Alternatively, they reasoned, Ciresi and the Indian government might be convinced to go along with their plan to settle the case.

In late July 1985, lawyers for Union Carbide moved for the U.S. court to dismiss the action on the grounds *forum non conveniens*. During the summer and fall of 1985 the parties entered into discovery proceedings to begin the long process of obtaining the evidence they would need for a trial. The lawyers for the plaintiffs were increasingly worried that they were losing control of the case and were confronted with the possibility that Judge Keenan might send it back to India, thereby excluding them altogether. Throughout the fall of 1985 and the first several months of 1986, the Indian government and Union Carbide had been conducting settlement negotiations, and by March 1986 the company had raised its settlement offer from $80 million to $350 million.[20] The private lawyers were in favour of accepting this offer, but it was unequivocally rejected by the Indian government.[21]

The wrangling among the plaintiffs' lawyers now assumed the proportions of a full-scale media battle in both the United States and India. In his book *The Litigators,* Jenkins describes how the other lawyers began to make desperate plans to sell the settlement to the people of Bhopal before it could be undermined by Ciresi on behalf of the Indian government. John Coale, who had been excluded entirely from the plaintiffs' steering committee, realizing that he had lost the main battle, had earlier turned over his cases to Chesley in exchange for reimbursement of his expenses and a right to 45 per cent of whatever fee those cases might finally generate. Now the prosettlement forces called upon him once again to go to Bhopal in order to convince the victims to accept the settlement. He and the government of India then engaged in a propaganda contest to capture local opinion. Coale circulated a leaflet entitled *Compensation Settlement for Gas Victims: Truth and Reality,* in which he advised the people of Bhopal that 'this settlement is the largest ever given in a personal injury case.' He did not mention how modest the offer was on an individual basis. The government responded with newspaper advertisements and a leaflet of its own, entitled *Gas Victims – Beware of the Temptations Offered by Suspect Middlemen.*[22] Coale in turn wrote a letter to the government, challenging them to guarantee compensation to the victims of at least $350 million if they were so confident that a better verdict could be achieved.[23]

Judge Keenan was outraged by the antics of the lawyers. He directed them to stop speaking to the press, and ordered Coale to return to the United States. The possibility of a settlement was now remote, and Judge Keenan began to write his judgment as to whether the case should be tried in the United States.

6

Finding a Forum: The U.S. Litigation

The Migration of a Disaster

The decision of the Government of India to seek compensation in the courts of the United States was greeted in India with reactions ranging from resignation to outrage. While to some the spectacle of the sovereign country of India seeking U.S. justice seemed to add insult to injury, to others it seemed the best strategy. In the first place, hundreds of individual lawsuits had already been commenced in the United States, and if the government was to implement the scheme under the Bhopal Act it had to find some way of taking over that litigation. Second, and equally important, the government's action was against the Union Carbide Corporation (UCC) and not simply against Union Carbide of India Ltd (UCIL). UCIL's assets in India (about $50 million) were far too meagre to satisfy the multibillion-dollar claim.[1] The UCC, with assets of $6.5 billion and insurance of $200 million, was headquartered in the United States. If India was to obtain jurisdiction over the U.S. company, and to enforce a final judgment against it, proceedings in the United States would be more direct, eliminating the complexities involved in enforcing an Indian judgment against the company later. A trial in the United States might have additional strategic advantages. U.S. tort law was perceived to be more 'liberal' than that of India. It offered the possibility of a jury trial and the prospect of more substantial damages, including punitive damages. Finally, many Indian lawyers entertained honest doubts that the overburdened Indian judicial system could provide timely and adequate relief for the victims. The Chief Justice of the Supreme Court of India said, 'It is my opinion that these cases must be pursued in the United States ... It is the only hope these unfortunate people have.'[2] At the same time, Union Carbide ridiculed India's attempt to have U.S. courts 'solve the world's problems.'[3]

India's decision to sue in the United States re-emphasized the transnational dimensions of the Bhopal tragedy. The internationalization of business has also internationalized potential harm to human health and the environment. The distribution of dangerous products and the diffusion of hazardous technologies know no boundaries. Despite the apparent novelty of India's strategy, such cases are not rare. One example is a case arising out of the crash of an Air India plane near Bombay in 1978.[4] The plane, a Boeing 747, crashed on New Year's Day, killing nearly all on board (almost all of them Indian citizens). Lawsuits were brought against both Air India and Boeing, the manufacturer of the plane, on the basis that the plane had malfunctioned. The case against Boeing was brought in the state of Washington, where the company was headquartered. The company argued that the case should be heard in India rather than the United States, pointing out that the accident had occurred in India, that the victims were Indian nationals, that the evidence was in India, and that Indian law would likely apply. Nevertheless, the Washington court allowed the case to proceed in the United States. In the case of Bhopal, Indian government lawyers reasoned that the same principle should apply, since the disaster had been 'manufactured' by the U.S. multinational.

Commencing the Action

The actions in the United States had been consolidated by the Judicial Panel on Multidistrict Litigation and were scheduled to be heard in the Southern District of New York in front of Judge John F. Keenan. The Union of India filed its initial complaint on 8 April 1985. Bringing the action on behalf of all the victims, it claimed an unspecified amount of damages to compensate individual victims and to reimburse the government for its relief expenditures, as well as punitive damages. It asserted that Union Carbide controlled the Indian operation 'from cradle to grave.' It alleged that UCC had knowledge of the dangerous properties of MIC; that it had responsibility for the faulty design and supervision of the plant in Bhopal; and that, as a multinational, it must in any event assume responsibility for the damages caused by one of its corporate arms. The claim relied upon absolute liability, strict liability, negligence, breach of warranty, and misrepresentation.[5]

On 29 July 1985, Union Carbide entered a preliminary motion to dismiss the actions on the grounds that the U.S. courts were the improper forum for the actions, and on 31 July filed a long memorandum of law in which it both denied any connection with the disaster and expanded on its argument that the case should be sent back to India for trial. Thus, before the litigation could even begin to address the substantive issues at stake in the case, the preliminary question of where the trial should take place would have to be decided. Throughout the rest of the summer and fall the parties began to collect evidence and prepare the affidavits required for arguing the forum issue.

The main strategy adopted by lawyers for the Government of India was to emphasize the 'U.S. connection' by demonstrating the degree of control exercised by Union Carbide over its Indian subsidiary; to explain the difficulty that would be faced by the plaintiffs if the case was to be tried in India; and to convince Judge Keenan that the disaster should be of great public concern to the citizens and courts of the United States. Chesley and Bailey, acting for the individual plaintiffs, filed documents in support of India's claim, and they were joined by a coalition of U.S. church groups, and environmental and other public-interest organizations who submitted an *amicus curiae* brief urging Judge Keenan to retain the case in his court on the basis that the United States had a strong interest in the particular case, and in ensuring the good behaviour of its corporations abroad.

All of the submissions for the plaintiffs sought especially to demonstrate that the end of justice to the victims could not be served by forcing the case back to India because the Indian legal system was simply not capable of dealing with a disaster on the scale of Bhopal's. Supported by an affidavit from Professor Marc Galanter, the foremost U.S. authority on Indian law, the plaintiffs' lawyers argued that Indian law on mass torts was undeveloped; that the system was overburdened to the point of breaking down; that the legal profession was not organized to pursue such a massive claim; and that its civil procedure was incapable of accommodating and expediting such complex proceedings.

Lawyers for Union Carbide responded in kind. They sought to minimize the connection between UCC and the Indian operation and to demonstrate the inconvenience that they would suffer if the action was to be tried in the United States. They emphasized the fact that the Bhopal plant was an Indian operation, that the victims were all Indian citizens, and that the relevant witnesses and evidence were located in

India. Nor did they accept the plaintiffs' contention that the Indian legal system could not effectively deal with mass litigation. Supported by affidavits from two eminent Indian lawyers, N.A. Palkhivala and J.B. Dadachanji, they sought to minimize the limitations of the Indian legal system and to emphasize its virtues. Palkhivala, the former Indian ambassador to Washington, prefaced his evidence by saying, 'I am constrained to say that it is gratuitous denigration to call the Indian legal system deficient or inadequate.'[6] He proceeded to defend the Indian legal profession and judiciary from the 'slanderous' charges made by the plaintiffs, arguing that the Indian legal system was capable of dealing with complex technology and that if 'the Bhopal litigation represents an opportunity for the further development of tort law in India, that chance should not be denied to India merely because some might say that the American legal system is ahead in development.'[7]

Inconvenient Forum

Judge Keenan, recognizing the enormous complexity of the litigation regardless of whether it took place in the United States or in India, and genuinely desiring that compensation be made quickly, strongly pressed the parties to achieve a settlement. Earlier in 1985 he had urged Union Carbide to contribute $5 million to the Red Cross for the purpose of providing interim relief, but the parties, were unable to agree on how the money should be disbursed. Throughout 1985 he viewed with growing concern the mounting antagonism of the parties, the manoeuvring of the lawyers, and the increasing complexity of the case. He knew that the litigation would likely drag on for years and was of the opinion that a settlement was probably the best option. He delayed entering his judgment while the parties sought to negotiate a settlement. These negotiations took place throughout the fall of 1985 and the spring of 1986, but to no avail.

On 12 May 1986, when it became apparent that all efforts at achieving a settlement had fallen through, Judge Keenan announced his decision. He dismissed the action from his court on the ground of *forum non conveniens* and decided that the case should be heard in India. He felt that the Indian legal system provided an adequate alternative to the U.S. courts and, weighing all the factors together, he concluded that India would be a more convenient location for the trial. He did, however, make this order subject to three conditions:

1. Union Carbide shall consent to submit to the jurisdiction of the courts of India and shall continue to waive defences based upon the statute of limitations;

2. Union Carbide shall agree to satisfy any judgment rendered by an Indian court, and if applicable, upheld by an appellate court in that country, where such judgment and affirmance comport with minimal requirements of due process;

3. Union Carbide shall be subject to discovery under the model of the United States Federal Rules of Civil Procedure after appropriate demand by the plaintiffs.[8]

How and why did Judge Keenan reach this conclusion? The determination of the proper forum for a case is a two-step process. The court must first ask whether there exists another adequate forum. If the answer is no, then the case must be tried where brought. If the answer is yes, the court must then go on to determine whether, in its discretion, the private and public interests at stake favour the alternative forum.

The Adequacy of Indian Law

India had argued that the U.S. courts should give a preference to their choice of forum. In the earlier case of *Koster* v *Lumbermens Mutual Casualty Co.*[9] the U.S. Supreme Court had held that U.S. courts should pay great deference to a plaintiff's choice of forum. And in *Gulf Oil* v *Gilbert*, the Court had said that 'the plaintiff's choice of forum should rarely be disturbed.'[10] However, the case law had been changing since those cases and was not unequivocally on their side.

Judge Keenan held that the later case of *Piper Aircraft Co.* v *Reyno*,[11] involving the crash of an airplane in Scotland, made it clear that the normal deference to the plaintiff's choice of forum did not apply when the plaintiff was a foreign resident and simply seeking to have the trial conducted according to more 'liberal' U.S. laws. He stressed that the fact that U.S. law might be more favourable to India's case was not something that should be taken into account. To give weight to this factor, he reasoned, would involve the court in the extremely complex exercise of comparing the laws of the two jurisdictions. Moreover, he feared that if substantive advantages to the plaintiff were taken into account, they would almost always favour the U.S. forum with its more generous approach to personal-injury victims. Quoting from the *Piper* case, Keenan concluded that, because of the renowned liberality of U.S. remedies, 'the American courts, which are already extremely attractive to foreign plaintiffs, would become even more attractive. The flow of litigation into the United States would increase and further congest already crowded courts.'[12]

Having dispensed with India's contention that its choice of forum should be deferred to, Judge Keenan then turned to examine the plaintiffs' arguments about the substantive inadequacies of the Indian legal system and the contention that justice could be done only in the United States.

The plaintiffs had argued that the Indian legal system continued to be fettered by its colonial past, was slow to innovate, and would have difficulty putting in place mechanisms to expedite such massive litigation. But Judge Keenan preferred the defendant's evidence. He referred to the active enforcement by the Indian Supreme Court of citizens' fundamental rights under the constitution and accepted that the 'examples cited by the defendant's experts suggest a developed and independent judiciary.' Thus, he concluded there was no evidence that 'the Indian legal system has not sufficiently emerged from its colonial heritage to display the innovativeness which the Bhopal litigation would demand.'[13]

The plaintiffs had further argued that the Indian legal system is vastly overburdened, that backlogs and delays of Bleak House proportions were commonplace, and that the victims could not therefore expect timely compensation. They relied on the Bombay Air Crash case to support their position that this justified the retention of the case in the United States. However, Judge Keenan noted that delays were a problem in U.S. courts as well, and that there was every possibility that the Bhopal litigation might be expedited in India. He pointed to the Bhopal Act itself as evidence that the litigation could be dealt with effectively, and referred to a recent case in which the Supreme Court of India had dealt swiftly with another gas-leak incident.[14] These developments satisfied him that 'the most significant, urgent and extensive litigation ever to arise from a single event could be handled through special judicial accommodation in India, if required.'[15]

To the plaintiffs' argument that India lacked a specialist bar with sophisticated fact-finding and research competence, Judge Keenan noted that the Indian Central Bureau of Investigation would be doing much of the investigation and that the government as nominal plaintiff would be able to marshall the legal resources that would be necessary to prosecute the case. And in response to the plaintiffs' argument that the law of tort in India was underdeveloped and ill equipped to deal with complex issues of technology and causation, he responded: 'With the groundwork of tort doctrine adopted from the common law and the precedential weight accorded to British cases, as well as Indian ones, it is obvious that a well-developed base of tort doctrine exists to provide a guide to Indian courts presiding over the Bhopal litigation.'[16] He accepted the defendant's argument that 'the complexity of the technology cannot be equated with the complexity of the legal issues ... Well settled law is to be applied to an unusual issue.'[17]

Judge Keenan was not entirely unsympathetic to the difficulties that the plaintiffs would face in India. He recognized that the primary difficulty with the Indian forum was that it might have no jurisdiction over Union Carbide as a U.S. corporation. However, he concluded that this difficulty was overcome by the defendant's acknowledgement of such jurisdiction and he included their submission to Indian jurisdiction as a condition of the dismissal of the case. He also accepted the argument that Indian civil procedure, especially with respect to pretrial discovery, was very limited and that the plaintiffs would have difficulty obtaining evidence from Union Carbide. To overcome this problem he suggested that it should be a condition of dismissal that the UCC agree to abide by U.S. discovery rules. He added, in a footnote, that it would only be fair if Union Carbide was given the same rights of discovery, but concluded that it was beyond his jurisdiction to make such an order. With these conditions in place, Judge Keenan concluded that "the courts of India appear to be well up to the task of handling this case ... Differences between the two legal systems, even if they inure to the plaintiff's detriment, do not suggest that India is not an adequate alternate forum.'[18]

The Public and Private Interests

The decision that India did offer an adequate alternative forum did not end the matter. It remained necessary for Union Carbide to demonstrate also that the Indian forum was *preferable* to that of the United States; that is, that the private interests of the litigants and the *public* interests of the different countries favoured India as the location for the trial. Once again, the company's arguments prevailed.

In addressing the question of the 'private interests' of the parties, Union Carbide argued that virtually all the relevant witnesses, records, and evidence were in India. They suggested that the plant was managed and operated by Indian personnel and that the operating records were located there. They admitted a U.S. connection in so far as there had been three safety inspections of the plant by U.S. personnel, occurring in 1979, 1980, and May 1982. But Judge Keenan accepted that these were only a 'very small fraction of the thousands of safety audits' conducted at the plant, and were well in the past.[19] Thus, he concluded that victims, witnesses, and documentary evidence were located almost exclusively in India and could be more conveniently examined there.

Turning to the 'public interest,' Judge Keenan also concluded that the relevant considerations favoured India as the forum for the trial. He noted the tremendous burden on his own court, which was already a 'congested centre' of litigation, and pointed to the comparative administrative convenience of holding the trial in India. Quoting from another recent case in which the republic of Iran sought to sue the Shah and his wife in New York, he agreed that 'the taxpayers of this State should not be compelled to assume the heavy financial burden attributable to the cost of administering the litigation contemplated when their interest in the suit and the connection of its subject matter ... is so ephemeral.'[20]

The plaintiffs had sought to argue that, despite the administrative inconveniences to the U.S. courts, U.S. citizens had a compelling interest in the conduct of large corporations operating outside of the United States, and that Union Carbide should be compelled to accept responsibility by U.S. law. They suggested that the Bhopal case offered an opportunity for the U.S. courts to set a precedent whereby multinationals might be controlled and future accidents deterred, and that a refusal to make it accountable in this way would have the effect of reinforcing a double standard of corporate responsibility in the developed and the developing world.

Keenan was not, however, persuaded that there was a strong U.S. interest in the case. He referred to Union Carbide's evidence of India's control over the Bhopal operation; to the fact that it was licensed and regulated by Indian law, subject to Indian environmental and safety laws and monitored by Indian agencies. He concluded that 'the recital above demonstrates the immense interest of various Indian governmental agencies in the creation, operation, licensing and regulation, and investigation of the plant. Thus, regardless of the extent of Union Carbide's own involvement in the UCIL plant in Bhopal, or even of its asserted "control" over the plant, the facility was within the sphere of regulation of Indian laws and agencies, at all levels.'[21]

Given the degree of Indian control over the Bhopal operation, there were, in Judge Keenan's view, no compelling reasons why the U.S. judiciary should impose itself into the dispute. He accepted the reasoning of an earlier case in which an action had been brought against Richardson Merrell, the U.S. parent of a UK drug company for injuries to UK citizens. The court in this case had dismissed the action from the United States on the grounds that 'this action involves the safety of drugs manufactured in the United Kingdom and sold to its citizens pursuant to licences granted by that government. The interest of the United Kingdom is overwhelmingly apparent ... [the U.S. forums in which the actions are brought] for that matter, have a minimal interest in the safety of products which are manufactured, regulated and sold abroad by foreign entities, even though development or testing occurred in this country.'[22] Judge Keenan concluded his judgment by emphasizing once again the overwhelming Indian connection with the Bhopal case and the strong public interest that the Indian government had in controlling its own industrial and environmental standards. It would, he said, 'be sadly paternalistic, if not misguided, for this court to attempt to evaluate the regulation and standards imposed by a foreign country.'[23] And while agreeing that double standards of industrial safety are not to be encouraged, Judge Keenan also noted that, 'when an industry is as regulated as the chemical industry is in India, the failure to acknowledge inherent differences in the aims and concerns of India, as compared to American citizens would be naive, and unfair to the defendant.'[24] He concluded his judgment by saying that, 'to retain the litigation in this forum ... would be yet another example of imperialism, another situation in which an established sovereign inflicted its rules, its standards and values on a developing nation. This Court declines to play such a role ... To deprive the Indian judiciary this opportunity to stand tall before the world and to pass judgment on behalf of its own people would be to revive a history of subservience and subjugation from which India has emerged.'[25]

Inconvenient for Whom?

The U.S. chapter of the Bhopal story is rife with ironies and contradictions. The sovereign state of India, proud of its hard won independence from colonial rule, resorts to the courts of a foreign nation to obtain justice for its citizens, arguing that its own legal system cannot meet the task. A major multinational corporation, whose objectives are to be 'realized through management of a mix, or portfolio of businesses in selected areas throughout the world,' with a management 'designed to provide centralized integrated corporate strategic planning, direction and control,' argues that it had little or no control over its subsidiary, and that foreign firms and authorities had ultimate responsibility for the construction, operation, and regulation of its enterprise. And, as one Indian commentator noted at the time, it is ironic that the courts of a country that is 'among the foremost exporters of effective liberal legal ideologies for the ex-colonial nations of the Third World'[26] concludes that the U.S. legal system is incapable even of assuming jurisdiction over a U.S.–based corporation, much less providing a remedy to the victims of the disaster.

While Judge Keenan's judgment sounds eminently reasonable, it contains a number of anomalies that require explanation. First, given his reluctance to export U.S. law and his finding that India was an adequate alternative forum, why did Judge Keenan feel it was necessary to include the three Union Carbide undertakings as preconditions to dismissing the case? Is the Indian legal system adequate or is it inadequate? Similarly, Keenan J pointed to the Bhopal Act as an example of the way in which the Indian legal system is capable of innovation and how the case might be expedited, but he did not mention that the act was, even at the time, being challenged as unconstitutional in the Indian Supreme Court[27] (and would, in all probability be considered unconstitutional under U.S. law).[28] If the Bhopal Act was unenforceable, then the vast majority of the victims would, as a practical matter, have no remedy at all in India. And it is at least ironic that the act, which was passed to *facilitate the prosecution of the claims in the United States*, is itself used as the *primary reason for refusing to hear the case there*. Finally, while Judge Keenan framed his decision in terms of a respect for Indian sovereignty, his judgment, not surprisingly, reflected a strong North American perspective. His denial that there was a U.S. interest in the case seems blind to the power that U.S. companies exercise in the developing world; and his reluctance to hear the case in the United States, because that would be a form of 'imperialism,' ignores the fact that it was the Government of India itself urging him to accept jurisdiction.

In a strongly worded critique of the judgment, Upendra Baxi, one of India's most eminent legal scholars, suggests that Judge Keenan had prejudged the case and was ultimately of the opinion that the UCC should not be held responsible for the disaster.[29] But, argues Baxi, given the world-wide focus of attention on Bhopal, it would have been impolitic for a U.S. court to make such a finding. The dismissal of the case on the grounds of *forum non conveniens* thus offered the ideal way out of this dilemma.

Baxi makes a number of points to support this thesis. First of all, Judge Keenan relied on the *Piper* case to support his conclusion, contrary to earlier principle, that the court need not pay great deference to the plaintiff's choice of forum when the plaintiff is a foreign national. But *Piper* does not unequivocally stand for this proposition. The court in that case was equally divided on this point. Apart from this technical point, even if *Piper* can be interpreted in this way, argues Baxi, *less* deference does not mean *no* deference.

Perhaps more importantly, the issue in *Piper* was whether or not the fact that the law in the alternative forum was less favourable to the plaintiff should be a relevant consideration in such a case. The court held, for good reasons, that an 'unfavourable change in law' should not be a relevant consideration as it would involve the court in a hopelessly complex comparison of the substantive law of different countries. But India's argument was not that Indian *law* was less favourable, but that the Indian legal system lacked the *institutional capacity* to deal with the litigation. Judge Keenan ignored this distinction. He accepted the defendant's argument that Indian tort law, based as it is on English law, was sufficient to deal even with mass litigation involving complex technology; that 'the complexity of the technology cannot be equated with the complexity of the legal issues ... Well settled law is to be applied to an unusual occurrence.'[30] This, suggests Baxi, belies either a hopelessly naïve, or downright distorted understanding of the relationship between law and technology.

Nor is the way in which Judge Keenan dealt with the adequacy of the Indian legal system entirely satisfactory. For example, in response to India's concern about delay, he responded that delay is a problem in U.S. courts as well. But, as Baxi points out, Keenan J ignored entirely the 1982 Bombay airline disaster case in which the endemic delays of the Indian legal system were taken to be a sufficient ground for allowing litigation to proceed in the United States.[31] And for Keenan to equate U.S. delays with the endemic backlog of the Indian legal system demonstrates an almost complete failure to take the government's evidence seriously. Many Indian legal commentators, including the former chief justice of the Supreme Court, have stated on numerous occasions that the inefficiency, delay, and overwhelming demands on the courts of India threaten the imminent collapse of the system. In 1985 there were 40,000 civil cases pending in the Indian Supreme Court alone.[32] Even ordinary tort cases frequently take well over a decade to come to a conclusion. Judge Keenan's concern for the welfare of the U.S. taxpayer and the congestion of U.S. courts seems a little crass in the face of the magnitude of human suffering in Bhopal. As another judge suggested in a later forum case, it is 'the height of deception to suggest that docket backlogs ... are caused by so called "foreign litigation."'[33]

Baxi is equally critical of the way in which Judge Keenan analyzes the 'private interest' factors. Keenan accepted that virtually all of the witnesses and evidence were in India and that, therefore, a trial there would be most convenient for the parties. Baxi argues that this conclusion ignores India's evidence of Union Carbide's participation in the design of the plant and its continued control over the operation. If the legal question in the case concerned the liability of the local owners and operators of the Bhopal plant, Keenan would be on solid ground here. But, as Baxi points out, the action brought by India was against UCC, not UCIL. The question that India had framed concerned the responsibility of a U.S. company for the design and control of a subsidiary; and the answer to this question does not so unequivocally lie outside the United States. Keenan J significantly obscures the fact that the defendant was Union Carbide and focuses almost exclusively on the potential liability of UCIL. This effectively localizes the issue, de-emphasizes the possibility of UCC responsibility, and severs the U.S. connection. The conclusion, which refuses in any way to acknowledge the U.S. connection, is softened by the rhetoric of Indian independence, sovereignty, and national pride.

Baxi reserves his most potent criticism for the way in which Judge Keenan dealt with the 'public interest' factors. Keenan had emphasized the Indian connection with the Bhopal operation and minimized U.S. involvement. He portrayed the disaster as a matter of local concern and expressed a reluctance 'to impose American standards and values on a developing nation.' What this obscures is that the plaintiff was not urging the U.S. courts to regulate Indian industries or to change Indian law, but to set standards for U.S.-based multinationals operating abroad – standards that could not effectively be policed by other than the multinational's home jurisdiction. While the spectre of the Indian government seeking U.S. justice might present a difficult domestic situation in India, of what concern is that to the U.S. courts? It is not unusual for foreign governments to resort to the legal processes of another country when necessary. There is, indeed, something paradoxical in suggesting to a foreign sovereign that to acquiesce in its policy decisions regarding litigation strategy would violate its national interests and further perpetuate a bygone colonialism. Moreover, from the perspective of many in the developing world, the primary means by which industrial colonialism continues to be perpetuated is through the consistent refusal of the countries of the developed world and the international community to control the behaviour of their nationals abroad.

Judge Keenan refused to acknowledge or interrogate the power of multinationals, or to recognize that the developed countries might legitimately play some role in ensuring safety in developing countries. From his perspective the U.S. connection with Bhopal was slender, 'ephemeral,' and therefore insufficient to justify the 'heavy financial burden' of the litigation to the U.S. taxpayer. Baxi suggests that this is 'Dow-Jones jurisprudence': 'As long as no harm occurs to Americans, the American legislators remaining vigilant to ensure that their regulatory effort at home is not contaminated by lower standards abroad, how can the public interest of the United States be ever adversely affected? Indeed it is best served by dumping dangerous technology on poor countries ... A more rigorously conservative view of the public interest concerns of the United States, and a more joyous surrender of power and discretion to do justice than Justice Keenan's would be difficult to locate in the recent annals of American jurisprudence.'[34]

The Politics of Choice of Forum

Baxi's potent criticism does not lead to the conclusion that Judge Keenan was *legally* wrong in the way he exercised his discretion. Indeed, it is the nature of judicial discretion that the guiding legal principles are vague and open to considerable interpretation and manipulation. What the criticism reveals is that the way in which discretion is exercised is largely a product of one's *perspective*. This perspective is, in turn, a function of the way in which the facts are filtered and constructed, and is based upon an understanding of the purposes and values underlying legal principles. Facts and laws are not pregiven. They must be interpreted; and the process of interpretation incorporates a host of personal, political, moral, and economic commitments.

Judge Keenan's decision was clearly informed by his particular experience and perspective. He had been strongly urging the parties to settle the litigation prior to announcing his decision. Their refusal to do so, combined with the antics of the lawyers on all sides and their tendency to fight their battles in the press, perhaps invited the response of 'a plague on both your houses.' Perhaps also of significance was the fact that, at the time, the corporate health of the UCC was on the line, and a damage award approaching the level demanded by India might bankrupt the company.[35]

More fundamentally, however, Judge Keenan's decision reflects widespread assumptions about how the international economy does and should work. His understanding of the facts was informed by the empirical assumption that businesses are autonomous, and the normative assumption that developed countries are not implicated in the problem of health and safety in the developing world. While declining to make any finding with respect to liability, Judge Keenan seems to have based his view of the case upon an unstated assumption that UCC should not be held responsible for the disaster. He accepted most of UCC's evidence regarding its lack of participation in the Bhopal operation. He seems also to have accepted that the relationship between the U.S. and Indian companies was at arm's length, that UCIL was primarily responsible for the construction and operation of the plant, that UCC had but a limited role and no continuing responsibility for health and safety. He appears to have accepted the defendant's evidence that the designs provided by Union Carbide were 'nothing more than summary design starting points.'[36] Judge Keenan's scepticism about the degree of UCC involvement in Bhopal is not simply a finding of fact (indeed, later chapters elaborate upon the extensive control exercised by UCC over its Indian subsidiary). It is, instead, a reflection of a *normative* position that the company *should not* be held responsible. While Keenan denies that he is making his decision upon the merits of the case, his factual assumptions clearly indicate that he did not think the parent company should be liable. His emphasis of the degree of Indian control over the operation reflects and reinforces a presumption of multinational non-responsibility. As he said, 'India no doubt valued its need for a pesticide plant against the risks inherent in such development.'[37] This may be true, but the exclusive focus on Indian sovereignty tends to reinforce the notion that developed countries have no responsibility in the developing world.

Judge Keenan simply did not want to create a precedent whereby

U.S.–based multinationals might be held responsible in the United States for damage that they cause abroad. Intervening religious and public-interest organizations had urged him to set a precedent whereby all U.S. multinationals would be bound by uniform obligations in respect to their offshore operations. 'Declining to undertake this challenge,' they argued, 'would allow a double standard to govern American corporations.'[38] While Judge Keenan decried the possibility of double standards of safety at home and abroad, double standards are precisely one of the attractions offered multinationals by the countries of the developing world. To set a precedent whereby a U.S.–based multinational is liable in the United States, according to the principles of U.S. law, for its activities abroad would significantly deprive those enterprises of major international competitive advantages. Significantly, only two years before Bhopal, business interests had successfully convinced the U.S. administration to relax its controls on exports of hazardous substances, on the basis that the controls were too 'burdensome.'[39] Is it any wonder that Keenan J suggested that 'the purported public interest of seizing this chance to create new law is no real interest at all. This Court would exceed its authority were it to rule otherwise when restraint was in order.'[40] Restraint, indeed, was in order. U.S. business breathed a sigh of relief, having been saved from the 'billion-dollar lottery' of lawsuits that would have resulted had Judge Keenan decided otherwise.[41]

None of this is meant to suggest that the Government of India was the helpless victim of the politics of the situation. It, too, was faced with domestic and international pressures, which may have had as much to do with its litigation strategy as any genuine concern for the victims of the disaster. At home, the government faced tremendous pressures to act swiftly and effectively against the UCC. It also faced mounting suspicion that the ineffectiveness of its own regulatory and monitoring agencies may have been contributing factors to the disaster. The action in the United States might have served to deflect some of this criticism by focusing attention on the international dimension of the problem rather than on any domestic failings. Perhaps more importantly, India faced precisely the converse economic pressures as those faced in the United States. Just as a finding of liability in the United States might have had a damaging effect on the international competitiveness of U.S. industry, so too a finding of liability in India might have a damaging effect on India's ability to attract foreign capital and industrial participation. India's foreign-trade laws and import-substitution policies aim at rapid industrialization through technology transfers requiring foreign collaboration. The development of a hospitable environment and liberalization of foreign-investment regulations are seen as corner-stones in this effort. An adverse finding of liability by an Indian court against a foreign-based multinational could be seen as inconsistent with this agenda. Thus, while India was forced to sue in the United States in order to pre-empt the litigation, this tactic also fit the political imperative of responding to the demands of the victims, while avoiding the assertion of contradictory industrial policies at home.

The Final Washing of Hands

Following Judge Keenan's decision, the U.S. lawyers for the private plaintiffs took a last gamble. Seeing the case, and their fees, slipping rapidly out of their hands, they sought to revive a U.S.–made settlement of $350 million. In an informal hearing on 20 May, Mr Ciresi for the Government of India stated that 'the case has run its course here'[42] and that India would probably not appeal the decision. F. Lee Bailey responded with anger: 'We learned two moments ago that the government of India obviously will abandon any appeal. We seriously question whether or not the entire effort [sic] because we were led to believe that they expected to win the [forum non conveniens case], they were very solid that they would win it – we now think maybe it was a maneuver to get Union Carbide by these maneuvers into India for trial.' Bailey and Chesley then went on to suggest to Judge Keenan that Union Carbide and many of the victims might still be willing to settle the case. 'A couple of pretty experienced lawyers have laboured long and hard to try and find a fair settlement,' said Bailey. 'I personally have a fair conscience about the amount I voted to accept on behalf of the clients.' He went on to argue that the victims should be given information about what the government was turning down on their behalf and that Judge Keenan should 'suspend' his decision long enough to finalize a binding settlement in the United States.[43] Once Keenan's order was final, and the case sent back to India, Bailey and Chesley's involvement would be over. Ciresi responded by saying that the government of India would move to have all the cases dismissed from the United States on the basis that 'Mr Chesley and Mr Bailey and the other attorneys don't represent anyone.'[44]

The following day, Bailey and Chesley submitted a motion for a fairness hearing on their proposed settlement. They asserted that a settlement had been reached; that it was beyond what the courts of India ordinarily awarded; and that, with the exception of those representing the Union of India, most of the lawyers involved agreed that it was fair and adequate. They claimed that the Government of India was merely posturing, claiming by virtue of the Bhopal Act 'the right to practise law' in the United States and that the court should not recognize the government's claim to represent all the victims. They argued that the Union of India had not offered 'a scintilla of evidence to show that the victims have been informed as to what they would receive if they elected to settle now, what problems they may face in litigation in India if remedies are pursued there, and when payment may be expected in view of India's historical difficulties in getting cases to trial within less than ten years.'[45] They asked the court to hold a further hearing to determine whether or not the settlement was fair.

At a subsequent hearing, the Government of India reiterated its new position – that it would not accept the proposed settlement, that it would accept Judge Keenan's ruling, and that it intended to return the case to India for trial. On 28 May Judge Keenan rejected Bailey's request for a fairness hearing on the basis that 'a settlement of this case is not practicable absent the agreement of the Union of India to accept and abide by the terms of a settlement.'[46]

In their final move, the private plaintiffs filed an appeal against Keenan J's judgment, opposing the dismissal of the U.S. actions. Both UCC and the Union of India filed cross appeals. In an interesting reversal of position, UCC argued that Indian courts do not observe the due-process standards that would be expected in the United States and that the condition requiring them to satisfy any Indian judgment was therefore unfair. The Union of India sought to have Judge Keenan's order affirmed in its entirety.

The appeal was argued on 24 November 1986, and on 14 January 1987 the Court of Appeal upheld the dismissal of the action from the U.S. forum. It was, if anything, even more dubious than Judge Keenan about the plaintiffs' theory of liability, stating that 'the plaintiffs seek to prove that the accident was caused by negligence on the part of UCC in originally contributing to the design of the plant and its provision for storage of excessive amounts of gas at the plant'; however, 'UCC's participation was limited and its involvement in plant operations terminated long before the accident.'[47] The Court of Appeal accepted entirely the defendant's argument that the Indian government controlled the terms of the agreements and precluded UCC from exercising any authority to 'detail design, erect and commission the plant.'[48] Indeed, the court concluded that 'it might reasonably be concluded that it would have been an abuse of discretion to deny a *forum non conveniens* dismissal.'[49]

The Court of Appeal went even farther in acceding to Union Carbide's arguments. Judge Keenan had imposed upon Union Carbide a condition that it would agree to satisfy an Indian judgment. The appeals court struck down this requirement. It noted that, under New York law, foreign judgments are regularly enforced as conclusive between the parties, subject only to the domestic court's power to review the judgment for a violation of due process or where the foreign court did not have jurisdiction over the defendant. The court thought that there was a danger that the wording of Judge Keenan's condition, that UCC satisfy any judgment so long as it conforms to the 'minimal requirements of due process,' might suggest a lower standard than would otherwise be required. It therefore deleted the condition, thereby remitting the plaintiffs to enforcement of any order by way of the usual U.S. procedures, warning India that 'any denial by the Indian courts of due process can be raised by UCC as a defence to the plaintiff's later attempt to enforce a resulting judgment against UCC in this country.'[50]

The Court of Appeal also deleted the third condition, requiring Union Carbide to abide by the broader U.S. discovery rules, on the ground this condition was not reciprocally imposed on the plaintiff and defendant. Union Carbide's victory was complete.

Conclusion

The refusal of the U.S. courts to hear the Bhopal litigation is entirely reasonable from one perspective. The immediate location of the accident was in India, the victims were Indian, and the U.S. connection with its Indian affiliate did not appear to give it an unusual degree of control. To say that the courts of India are inadequate to the task of settling the dispute would be insulting. To sit in judgment on Indian environmental and safety standards would be paternalistic or even imperialistic, and might threaten to interfere with India's policy priorities. To accept jurisdiction over the case would be to encourage forum shopping and increase the burden on U.S. courts.

Nevertheless, when measured against the criteria suggested in chapter 3, the U.S. chapter of the litigation can only be labelled a failure. It not only prolonged the litigation, but also resulted in a substantive principle denying that home states have *any* interest in the activities of their corporations abroad, or even to ensure that those corporations submit to the foreign jurisdiction and honour judgments given. This result may, indeed, encourage corporate irresponsibility. Judge Keenan was right to point out that the blanket imposition of U.S. standards on a multinational's overseas operation might be insensitive to the needs and policies of the host country. Indeed, this is one of the most problematic features of the ongoing attempts to formulate international codes of conduct for transnational business.[51] But the refusal to play any supervisory role simply entrenches the double standard of safety and confirms to the people of the Third World that their lives are considered cheap.

The *forum non conveniens* doctrine shields multinationals from liability for injuries abroad. Interestingly, the doctrine emerged with full vigour only after the Second World War, coinciding with the rise of multinational business. Originally, its scope was quite narrow, aimed only at preventing serious injustice or oppression to U.S. defendants, but since that time the doctrine has expanded in scope and changed in rationale. Now it seems designed simply to prevent 'inconvenience' to U.S. defendants and courts, reflecting the attitude that 'injuries done by American business to foreign nationals abroad are not America's problem.'[52] What little empirical evidence exists indicates that a finding of *forum non conveniens* is usually determinative of the outcome of the dispute. The vast majority of cases dismissed under the doctrine are either abandoned or settled for a small fraction of the claim.[53]

The refusal by U.S. courts and regulators to assert some interest in the activities of their corporations abroad, on the basis of a respect for sovereignty, is somewhat disingenuous. Extraterritorial regulation of foreign affiliates is an established instrument of U.S. domestic and foreign policy when it is deemed suitable, for example, enforcing antitrust policy or trading bans on 'hostile' countries. To treat health and safety matters as the purely 'local' concerns of the corporation and its host country ignores the fact that the most significant arena in which modern-day imperialism is played out is the international economy. The decision not to regulate multinational corporations does not avoid, but rather licenses this form of domination and confirms the non-accountability of international business. Indeed, in so far as the decision was based on an avowed deference to Indian law and the apparent autonomy of Union Carbide's Indian operation, it may in fact have the effect of encouraging the parent corporation to reduce even farther its involvement in supervising the safety of its operations in Third World countries. There is already evidence that Judge Keenan's message has not fallen on deaf ears. After considering the Bhopal decisions, the general counsel for a major multinational said, 'Ironically the existence of pervasive and intrusive regulation by the foreign jurisdiction may have the effect of reinforcing a district court's willingness to dismiss a case brought by foreign plaintiffs. This type of regulation, while bothersome as a compliance matter, may have the unintended benefit of reinforcing the local interest in the controversy.'[54] The conclusion drawn by this lawyer is that legal responsibility can be avoided by emphasizing local government regulation and delegating to the subsidiary 'as much autonomy as possible concerning operating matters.'[55] The advice to multinationals, then, is to maintain strategic control from afar, but to leave operations in the hands of local managers and safety in the hands of the host government. Control can thus be maintained, and responsibility avoided. Arguably, this is precisely what happened in Bhopal. As suggested in chapter 2, the partial assertion of regulatory authority of the host state may have the unintended effect of widening the safety gap. It is one of the further ironies of the Bhopal case that India has sufficiently emerged from its Third World status that it has a degree of bargaining clout when negotiating with and regulating multinational corporations. The degree of autonomous control that it was able to achieve over the UCIL operation is also the degree to which the rest of the world may refuse to acknowledge any share of responsibility for the tragedy.

Finally, while a 'hands-off' approach may be justified on the basis of a respect for Indian sovereignty and its legal process, U.S. law was to remain a brooding presence in the background and a significant limitation on the Indian legal process. Any judgment of an Indian court would have to be enforced in the United States; and, as the Court of Appeal had warned, any violation by the Indian courts of Union Carbide's due-process rights could be used as a defence by the company in enforcement proceedings. While the 'innovativeness' of the Indian courts was one of the reasons for returning the case to India, that same innovativeness was later to be characterized by Union Carbide as a failure of due process and a sufficient reason not to undertake to submit to Indian jurisdiction.

These considerations indicate that the courts of the industrialized world should reconsider the issue *forum non conveniens*. The Bhopal case was brought against the U.S. multinational, and it was neither oppressive nor unjust to bring the case on the company's own home ground. India wanted to demonstrate that the corporate conduct of Union Carbide, originating in the United States, imposed unreasonable risks on foreign citizens. India was not asking that the entire regulatory or tort apparatus of the United States be exported to India, but rather that the U.S. courts affirm that the parent company must, in its dealings abroad, maintain responsibility for its subsidiaries and live up to a humane standard of care. It would not be impossible for the courts to develop such a principle in a way that did not interfere with the sovereignty of the host country and that also made allowances for differences in local conditions and priorities. This principle could take the shape of a rebuttable presumption that the parent corporation will apply similar or equivalent safety standards in all its operations. Indeed, Union Carbide had maintained that this was its policy in any event. If the company sells defective technology, abandons its safety-monitoring obligations, or fails to provide safety information and warnings, it should be liable *anywhere* for the consequences. Differences in operational standards or levels of safety in the host country may be justified by local circumstances and requirements, and the presumption of responsibility may be rebutted where the parent can show that its method of operation was, in fact, required by the host state. Certainly the precise shape of this principle would be controversial, but the issues at stake are not fundamentally different from those that arise in tort litigation in any context. They are issues that should be resolved by substantive law and policy, not simply evaded through the application of the doctrine of *forum non conveniens*. India wanted the opportunity to demonstrate that UCC applied unjustifiable double standards to its Bhopal operation. It may be that U.S. policy is such that the U.S. courts would decide that U.S.–based multinationals are justified in adopting much-relaxed standards of safety in their foreign operations. But this is an issue that must be addressed rather than avoided. In the Bhopal case, U.S. law registered only an abstention, leaving the problem firmly in place.

Having successfully returned the case to India, Union Carbide reversed its position. Indeed, even before leaving the U.S. courts, it sought to revoke its consent to abide by Indian jurisdiction on the basis that 'Indian courts, while providing an adequate forum, do not observe due process standards that would be required as a matter of course in this country.'[56] Having expressed compassion for the victims, Union Carbide then refused to abide by orders to pay interim compensation.

Having glorified the sophistication and flexibility of the Indian legal system, Union Carbide was later to characterize the system as primitive, political, and bereft of minimal notions of justice. Having convinced U.S. courts not to export U.S. justice to India, Union Carbide then sought to export U.S. legalist notions of due process to stifle all attempts to do justice for the victims.

7

The Litigation in India

Problems and Possibilities

Judge Keenan had returned the case to India on the basis that the law of tort was similar in structure to that of the United States, confidently expressing his faith that the country's legal system was 'well up to the task at hand' and capable of dealing effectively with 'the most significant, urgent and extensive litigation ever to arise from a single event.'[1] The Indian legal system, he said, was capable of forging the type of innovations that would be required to deal with the Bhopal disaster, and indeed the case presented the Indian courts with an opportunity to 'stand tall before the world.' In many ways, Judge Keenan was right. A North American or Commonwealth lawyer would have little difficulty in understanding the *formal* structure and content of Indian law. Its doctrine derives from the English common law, its judges are widely respected, and its law makes similar promises to the victims of hazardous industries. But in many other, and more important, ways, Judge Keenan was tragically wrong – wrong in his optimistic faith in both tort law, generally, and the capacities of the Indian legal system, in particular.

The Indian Legal System

On its surface, India's political and legal system is not unlike that of Canada or the United States.[2] India is a federal republic with a bicameral parliamentary system of government and a strong central administration. Its court system is a three-level hierarchy, with state district courts at the bottom and a national supreme court at the apex as a final court of appeal. Lawyers are educated in university law schools, and judges, by and large, are selected from the élite of the profession. The working language of the law is English, and the categories of public and private law, including property and tort law, resemble Western models. An Anglo-Indian common law has been developed according to the principles of 'justice, equity and good conscience,' and modern legislation and codes regulate a broad spectrum of social arrangements.

As in Canada and the United States, a written constitution establishes the institutions of state, defines the division of powers among various levels of government, and contains a bill of rights. The preamble to the Indian constitution expresses a commitment to secure to all citizens of India 'justice, social, economic and political; liberty of thought, expression, belief, faith and worship; equality of status and opportunity; and to promote among them fraternity assuring the dignity of the individual and the unity and integrity of the nation.' The constitution also guarantees fundamental human rights, including freedom of the press, equality before the law, and the right to life. Unlike many Western constitutions, India's also contains non-enforceable 'directive principles' of state policy. These principles reflect a positive commitment to human-welfare measures. Article 38, for example, requires the state to 'promote the welfare of the people by securing and protecting as effectively as it may a social order in which justice, social, economic and political shall inform all institutions of national life.' Another article requires the state to direct its policy towards securing 'the right to an adequate means of livelihood ... that the ownership and control of the material resources of the community are so distributed as best to subserve the common good.'

In spite of these ringing promises, the very *similarities* of the Indian and U.S. legal systems noted by Judge Keenan were to ensure that the Bhopal litigation would still be enormously difficult. As demonstrated in chapter 4, there is a large gap between the promises and realities of law. At every stage the law places the burden upon the victims. They must demonstrate how the accident happened and that their injuries were caused by it. They must establish the defendant's legal liability, prove their damages, and, where successful, pursue the defendant again to collect any judgment. Long delays and enormous expenses sap the power of the victims to pursue recovery. Each of these obstacles would confront the victims of the Bhopal disaster in their quest for justice.

The doctrinal and procedural impediments that are part of all common-law tort systems are enormously magnified in India, where the gap between the formal structure of law and the substantive promise of justice is even more clearly revealed. As one Indian judge said of the law, only a few years before Bhopal: 'It is a finished product of great beauty, but entails an immense sacrifice of time, money and talent. This "beautiful" system is frequently a luxury; it tends to give a high quality of justice only when, for one reason or another, parties can surmount the substantial barriers which it erects to most people and to many types of claims.'[3]

India's 'modern' legal system operates in a country that could hardly be more different from North America. When India achieved independence, it was one of the most populous, and poorest, countries of the world. It had missed the first industrial revolution. The majority of the population eke out a subsistence-level existence in the countryside, quite untouched by modern institutions. Indeed, law in India is even expressed in a language that is inaccessible to a majority of the people. A large portion of India's incredibly diverse population has little contact with the modern legal system, and continues to be organized along age-old customary and caste-based patterns that are far more important in daily life than the national legal system.

India's own description and critique of its legal system in the New York courts did not inspire hope. In the first place, while this newly independent country has been enormously successful in establishing the largest democratic political system in the world, its legal system remains burdened with the legacy from its colonial past. As Marc Galanter testified in the Bhopal case,

India's common law system was imposed on it in the eighteenth century by British colonial rulers who were eager to have a legal system that would maintain law and order and secure property rights. It was designed to effectuate the interests of the colonial overlords rather than to be responsive to the emergent needs of the Indian people. Legislation was enacted by the Parliament in London or by the Governor General in Council. The highest court of appeal was the Judicial Committee of the Privy Council. Courts were relatively few in number; their use for civil cases was discouraged by steep *ad valorem* court fees ... It was – and to some extent remains – a version of the common law shaped by the imperatives of colonial rule.[4]

There are only 10.5 judges per million population in India, as compared with 107 per million in the United States and 75 per million in Canada. These judges are forced to work with impoverished physical and support facilities.[5] Delay and backlog are simply a fact of legal life in India. For example, in 1985, there were some 40,000 cases pending in the Indian Supreme Court alone, and an estimated backlog in the other courts of one million cases.[6] Complex rules of civil procedure provide for numerous interim and interlocutory motions in which the litigation can easily become bogged down. As one scholar of Indian law argued, these extensive appeal procedures were designed to ensure control by the higher (British) courts over the lower courts and were premised on the assumption 'that the lower courts are incompetent to do anything more than prepare a record of the evidence and that the real contest is in the first court of appeal.'[7] As a result of these judicial structures the trial process may be diverted through a maze of intricate proceedings, further exacerbating the problems of judicial backlog and delay. In a survey of Indian law conducted in 1971, ten tort cases were reviewed. Their duration ranged from six to eighteen years.[8] In his own survey of the *All India Law Reporter*, Marc Galanter found that the average time for a motor-vehicle accident case was over eight years and that other tort cases took over thirteen years.[9] Highly restrictive pretrial discovery rules make the collection of evidence extremely difficult.[10]

The substantive law is also problematic. While its formal doctrine, derived from English common law, is similar to that in the rest of the common-law world, it plays almost no role in accident compensation. Because it is almost never resorted to by the populace, its place in the legal system is peripheral at best. Unlike many other areas of law, it remains uncodified and is neglected in many works on Indian law. As a result, neither has the judiciary accumulated significant experience in developing procedures and doctrines for dealing with large or complicated cases, especially those involving complex technologies.[11] Various factors explain the very peripheral status of the law of tort in India. There are no contingency fees, and heavy *ad valorem* court charges that must be paid merely to initiate litigation (up to 5 per cent of the total damages claimed) serve as a serious disincentive to bring an action. This makes it virtually impossible for the ordinary Indian citizen to seek legal redress. Contrasted with the higher stakes involved in the many land disputes that clog Indian courts, damage awards in tort have traditionally been very low. There are no civil juries, and government has sovereign immunity.[12] The victims of injury typically settle their cases for a small ex-gratia payment. Most cases involving negligence therefore never find their way to court, or else are diverted into the criminal system. Galanter suggests that the impoverished state of the law of tort is in part the result of the desire by colonial rulers to discourage litigation and suppress accountability: 'As India acquired modern industrial technology and its products, with their injury-producing potential, the development of accountability through tort law was deliberately inhibited by its colonial rulers.'[13] As Supreme Court justice K.N. Singh was later to explain in one of the many Bhopal hearings, India has relied for its development since the Second World War on the development of science, technology, industry, and agriculture, yet its legal system has not kept pace, remaining 'bound by the shackles of conservative principles' laid down by English courts in the nineteenth century.[14]

The evidence presented by India in the U.S. litigation included a fifty-year survey (from 1914 to 1965) of the *All India Law Reports*, which discovered a total of only 613 tort cases. Of these, only 132 were negligence actions; indeed, cases of malicious prosecution outnumbered those for negligence.[15] And in his own ten-year survey, Galanter found only 56 reported cases, other than motor-vehicle accidents. Of these, only 22 were concerned with negligence, and none of those involved products liability or industrial or chemical mishaps. The duration of cases was on average twelve years and nine months. Average recovery of successful plaintiffs was 15,159 rupees ($1,263 U.S.).[16]

Galanter was equally sceptical of the ability of the legal profession to deal with Bhopal. There is very little specialization in the profession, and most lawyers are sole practitioners with almost no institutionalized fact-finding capacity. The prevailing model of legal practice is atomistic; lawyers provide reactive advocacy to deal with discrete problems and isolated interests, rather than providing programmatic planning for classes of interests and needs.[17] High court costs and the threat of cost awards further discourage innovative litigation. Some scholars have suggested that the virtual non-existence of legal redress for personal injuries is an aspect of the fatalistic approach to life that reflects the Dharmic vision of life in India. As one Indian scholar wrote, the law of tort has been influenced by the spiritual culture of India: '"Dharma" has for its objective the attainment of temporal welfare through spiritual well-being. In India, high regard is paid to "duty" which puts the concept of "rights" in the shade ... Negligence which is the typical modern tort was not recognized by the *Dharmasastras*.'[18] The author concludes that, while penal sanctions for the violation of duty are consonant with these notions, the vigorous assertion of rights to compensation are not. Whatever the case, it is fair to conclude with Galanter that 'disasters large and small in India typically have no legal consequences.'[19] At least until now, the law of tort in India is little more than a myth about how people would be cared for in a better world.

Notwithstanding this gloomy scenario, the systemic deficits strategically recounted by India in the U.S. litigation would not necessarily doom the victims. Indian tort doctrine, while underutilized, would be available to them. To the extent that Indian accident law had been inhibited by the country's colonial pro-industry heritage, Bhopal provided an opportunity to inject the law with a new vitality. Principles developed in other countries could be imported by way of analogy, or even adopted outright. Indian culture is noted for its genius for absorbtion, adaptation, and synthesis, and Indian law is no exception. In other areas of Indian law, judges have proved themselves adept at borrowing, synthesizing, and adapting new elements.[20] The sheer enormity of the tragedy would likely galvanize both the government and the judiciary to search for new means to alleviate the suffering of the victims. The government had, of course, already passed the Bhopal Act and thrown the weight of its resources behind the victims' cause. Its agencies and the judiciary would be further prodded by the victims' groups and public-interest lawyers already involved in the case. Their involvement is evidence that, in an industrial age, any residual patterns of Dharmic resignation are giving way to a more vigorous assertion of human rights to a clean and safe environment.

Indian law presents a paradox. While, on the one hand, it may be characterized by inertia, on the other it reveals tremendous innovation and activity. Indeed, when fully galvanized, the Indian legal system is one of the most dynamic in the common-law world. Over the past several decades, judges, lawyers, and social activists in India have demonstrated a remarkable degree of social and legal creativity and have expended enormous energy in an attempt to make law work for the poor. Especially under the banner of public interest litigation, courts have sought to enhance access to justice, expedite legal processes, and breathe some substantive life into the formal promises of law.[21]

The legal-aid and public-interest movements have been initiated and led by a small group of progressive Indian judges, lawyers, activists, and politicians who believe that, in a country like India, there is room, and the need, for forms of judicial innovation that go far beyond that typically practised in the developed world. Faced with the daily reality of the judicial process in India, these judges recognize the enormous gap between the formal promises of law and the reality of the lives of ordinary Indian citizens. As a result, they have, through a variety of strategies, sought to enhance the ability of the poor to use the courts. Through the use of law 'camps,' *nyaya panchayats* (village tribunals), and *lok adalats* (people's courts), India has experimented with legal-aid programs and systems of informal justice.[22]

In the case of public-interest litigation on behalf of poor and exploited groups, the courts have dramatically liberalized the rules of standing to allow third parties to bring actions on behalf of other groups. As former Supreme Court justice Krishna Iyer explained, the traditional requirement that individuals seek justice on their own behalf effectively bars the poor from the courts. The socio-economic circumstances of India, he concluded, require that individualized justice be rejected in favour of 'broadened forms of legal proceedings that are in keeping with the current accent on justice to the common man.'[23] Thus public-interest litigation has been initiated and pursued by social-action groups, academics, journalists, and public-interest lawyers on behalf of slum dwellers, labourers, untouchables, and other disadvantaged groups. The courts have allowed actions to be commenced through informal means, such as a simple letter or petition to a judge. Indeed, there are reports of judges who, upon receiving a postcard or seeing a letter to the editor in a newspaper about a group of bonded labourers, have ordered that the matter be converted into a legal petition.[24] Judges have provided funding for public-interest advocates, and have appointed commissions of inquiry or socio-legal committees to investigate the facts of particular cases in order to relieve individuals of the burden of proof.

Just as they have sought to enhance access for the poor, they have tried to increase their impact on the structural conditions that give rise to poverty. They will frequently treat individual cases as class or representative actions. In one case involving widespread pollution of the sacred Ganges, the court ordered that notices be published in the newspaper, informing all the local industries of the pending litigation and, in the end, ordered that dozens of offending firms be closed down.[25] In another case, brought on behalf of prisoners awaiting trial, the court ordered that legal aid be provided by the state, that prisoners be educated about their rights, and that a local judge monitor prison conditions by making surprise visits to the jail.[26] And in a case dealing with the horrors of bonded labour, the court instructed local officials to identify oppressed workers, have them released, and work towards their economic and social rehabilitation. It licensed local social-action groups to carry out surprise checks at quarries to inspect working conditions and to set up labour-education camps to instruct workers about their legal rights.[27]

As the former Chief Justice of India, P.N. Bhagwati, explained, judges must recognize that, given the socio-economic reality of Indian life, formal legal guarantees mean almost nothing to the masses of people. Without significant innovation, the promises of law are but a 'teasing illusion' for most people. 'We have therefore, to abandon the laissez faire approach in the judicial process ... and forge new tools, devise new methods and adopt new strategies for the purpose of making fundamental rights meaningful for the large masses of people.'[28] What the Indian legal system presents, then, is a series of startling contrasts between resignation and initiative, inertia and innovation. It is, therefore, no surprise, that, during the course of the Bhopal litigation, a number of innovations were attempted.

Commencing the Action

Preparing the Claims

The government had first to deal with the simple fact of the staggering number of victims at Bhopal. Officials in the Ministry of Chemicals and the attorney general's office had realized very early that, given the large number of victims and their overwhelming poverty, it would have been entirely unreasonable to expect the victims to pursue their claims on their own once the case was returned to India. The passage of the Bhopal Act was the first of a series of attempts to change the law to accommodate the challenges presented by the Bhopal litigation. However, as pointed out in chapter 5, this statute was a limited measure. It did not radically alter the compensation regime, but simply substituted the attorney general of India as the lawyer for all the claimants. It thus presupposed the necessity of proceeding through the traditional stages of litigation. Having made this choice, the next task facing the government was to find some way of identifying the victims, determining the nature of their injuries, and collecting the evidence that would be needed for what was bound to be a drawn-out and contentious court battle.

Under the authority of the Bhopal Act the central and state governments moved to establish the Bhopal Gas Tragedy Relief and Rehabilitation Department. This agency was headed by a principal secretary and relief commissioner, and included a directorate of claims, a directorate of health, and a relief and rehabilitation 'collectorate.' The department was to be generally responsible for the welfare of the victims, and was charged with the task of framing a scheme for the registration, documentation, and processing of the half-million claims that the government expected. Under the relief agency's plan, which was prepared during the summer of 1985, the claims would be registered, documented, and categorized according to the nature and severity of the victim's loss. The various categories (drawn from workers' compensation statutes) were (a) death; (b) total disablement resulting in permanent disability to earn a livelihood; (c) permanent partial disablement resulting in diminished earning capacity; and (d) temporary partial disablement resulting in diminished earning capacity. Additional categories included claims for dislocation, property loss, income loss to farmers, other economic losses, and government expenses.

Under the plan, deputy commissioners would be responsible for the task of registering claims and preparing the medical documentation that would ultimately be required for the litigation. Victims or surviving family members were to provide death certificates, medical documentation, and any other evidence of their condition in the aftermath of the disaster. Evidence would also have to be collected on their employment history, past income, and any expenditures incurred as a result of their injuries. The victims would then be put through a series of medical tests to determine the severity of their injuries and future prognosis. Finally, the files would have to be evaluated and placed into the appropriate categories, subject to the right of a victim to appeal that decision to the commissioner of claims.

The documentation process began in earnest in the summer of 1985. The enormity of the task facing the claims directorate can be gleaned even from a vastly simplified account of the process as it unfolded. The first stage, *registration*, required simply that the victims be notified and that their files be opened. Dozens of registration camps were set up, and notice went out to the victims by way of newspaper, radio, and television advertising. The realities of life in the slums of Bhopal – poor communications, poverty, and illiteracy – also obliged the department to rely on posters, mobile loudspeakers, and ultimately, word of mouth. By the end of the registration process, over a year later, more than half a million files had been opened in the directorate's offices. But this was just the beginning.

Once the files had been opened, the process of *documentation* of each claim commenced. The relief department established eighteen documentation centres, staffed and equipped for medical examination. One hundred and forty full-time process servers were employed to contact the claimants to return for examination. Each centre was staffed by medical and claims personnel who recorded reported symptoms and prepared an initial summary of their findings. At the peak of their operations, the claims centres were processing about 2,800 people per day.

At stage three of the process, *evaluation and categorization*, the files were returned to claims officers who, with the assistance of two hundred doctors, set about to evaluate the information collected in the files and then to fit the claims into the categories set up under the scheme. Staff were drawn from around the country, and each officer was expected to process ten to twelve files per day. Random checks were introduced to ensure consistency and to guard against corruption.

At the height of the documentation process the relief department employed more than four hundred doctors and one thousand support staff. In all, the documentation scheme required forty different steps, and each file contained an average of forty pages of documentation. The department's task was time-consuming, expensive, and unwieldy. With no model to work from the department was required to invent the process as it went along. Medical guidelines and documentation were not even prepared until 1987, and the process of evaluation would take more than five years to complete.

Relations between the victims' organizations and the relief department, already under strain because of the government's perceived mishandling of the case, were made worse by the long delay. Insufficient resources – the lack of trained staff, medical expertise, testing equipment, and medical facilities – further slowed the documentation process. For example, one of the major effects of MIC is pulmonary and respiratory damage, and the health branch was criticized for doing incomplete examinations. Full pulmonary-respiratory testing, however, takes approximately five hours and is very costly. Further criticism was aimed at the failure to examine the victims for the psychiatric consequences of the disaster – consequences that would later become widespread. Early studies had warned of this problem, but in response to the principal secretary's request for thirty psychiatrists, only one was made available.

The department's task was made more difficult by reason of duplicate and exaggerated claims, bureaucratic inertia, and the simple fact that it was unable to contact many of the victims. Additional problems were bound to surface. At each stage of the complex process, officials, including claims commissioners, medical personnel, and relief officers, were required to make judgment calls, allowing a wide exercise of discretion. In addition, many of the victims were uneducated and illiterate, requiring the assistance of officials to frame their claims and fill out the necessary forms. The power of the officials and the dependency of the victims thus raised the additional problem of corruption. Underpaid government officials in India work in a culture in which *baksheesh* (a tip or a bribe) is a widespread method of supplementing an otherwise inadequate salary. Government officials and medical personnel were frequently charged with corruption, demanding payments from deserving victims before processing them and accepting bribes from others to falsify documents. The principal secretary, S. Sathyam, realistically maintained an overriding concern to minimize the problem of corruption: 'We cannot take the goodness of humanity for granted. People tend to exploit disaster situations. We must assume the worst in order to protect the genuine victims.'[29] A system of cross- and random checking, and categorization appeals had to be implemented, thus adding an additional level of bureaucracy to the process, resulting in further delay and expense. The perception that they were being exploited by dishonest government workers added further fuel to the victims' criticisms of the department's efforts.

The long delay in documentation had several serious consequences. As intimated already, it inevitably strained relations between the victims and the government. It also made an early settlement of the matter, or expedited litigation, nearly impossible. With no information on the quantity or severity of the claims, the parties could not realistically hope to fix on a figure that might be used as a basis for negotiations. Lawyers for the social-action groups continually charged that official incompetence in completing claim forms, medical documentation, and loss estimates was stalling the progress of the litigation. The delays also played into Union Carbide's hands. Under the provisions of India's Fatal Accidents Act of 1855, the claimant must give full particulars of the nature and quantum of the victim's injuries. As Union Carbide was to argue throughout the litigation, the government had not yet complied with this requirement. The company took the position that a trial could not even begin until the extent of the injuries was disclosed in detail. Yet, in light of the magnitude of the disaster and the unknown medical consequences of MIC poisoning, the requirement of full particulars was entirely unrealistic. Supposedly 'fair' procedures, designed to ensure due process, thus clearly militated against the prospect of early relief for the victims.

Another consequence of the delay was that it compounded the already near-impossible task of establishing medical causation. As each day passed, the quality of the information obtained by the claims and health directorates deteriorated. As discussed in a previous chapter, the Bhopal disaster illustrates the difficulties inherent in establishing who are the 'real' victims of a toxic incident, and proving that their injuries were, in fact, specifically caused by their exposure to a particular substance. Exposure to MIC did not typically leave any obvious long-lasting physical or physiological symptoms that could easily be distinguished from other diseases common in the slums of Bhopal. The masses of poor victims had no medical documentation on the state of their health prior to the disaster, and little written evidence of medical treatment in the days immediately following. There was simply no way for most of them to prove that they were, in fact, victims.

Despite the valiant efforts of a few individuals, the documentation process did not fully get under way until 1987, and a meaningful examination of most of the 6 million claimants did not begin until 1988, more than three years after the disaster occurred. By this time, individual records had been lost or destroyed, and easily identifiable chemical residues were no longer detectable in blood and urine samples. As a result, the government was simply unable accurately to identify and classify the victims. As S. Sathyam confirmed, 'Today, yes, it is very difficult to say that this is a gas victim, this is not.'[30] The claims directorate sought to mitigate these problems by being flexible about the documentation that it required from a victim. Certificates of treatment, prescription forms, and other documents were accepted as proxies for proof of exposure. Still, many of the victims could produce none of these. Even those that might have once had a prescription form were unlikely to still have it four years later. And given that the entire process was driven ultimately by litigation, the problem could not, in any event, be solved by relaxing the standards of proof required of the victims; evidence of their injuries would inevitably be rechallenged by Union Carbide when the case eventually came to trial. As one official in the claims directorate explained, the government 'had to preserve the scientific character and ensure the credibility of the exercise of the evaluation ... to adhere to certain quality standards so that the exercise could stand up to scrutiny in any Court of law or in any scientific forum.'[31]

Paradoxically, greater speed in the documentation process would not itself entirely solve the problem of medical causation. Because the long-term effects of MIC exposure remain unknown, what evaluations were done in the early stages of the process would have to be continually reassessed. During the eight-year documentation process, many of the 100,000 people who had previously been classified as only mildly injured began to show symptoms of worsening condition. These included tuberculosis and other respiratory complications, premature cataracts and degenerating eye diseases, and gastro-intestinal problems.[32] Medical and social activists pointed out that almost no attention was paid to the increasing evidence of chromosome damage or immune-deficiency and mental-health problems in the gas-affected areas. As Principal Secretary S. Sathyam admitted, 'We really don't know what the future has in store for us.'[33]

At the beginning of 1990, approximately 350,000 of the 600,000 claimants had responded to notices for interim medical assessment and categorization of claims. Despite three rounds of notices, newspaper advertisements, drumming in the wards, radio and television announcements, and loudspeaker broadcasts, 250,000 claimants had not yet responded. Some of the lost claims were clearly fraudulent. Others were probably duplicates, a fact that can be explained simply by reason of the victims' attendance for multiple treatments and their completion of the documentation twice over. But many of the lost claimants were real. A survey prepared by the Medico Friends Circle provided evidence that many deserving victims were falling through the gaps of the complex system. In one sample, as many as 53 per cent of the families surveyed had not received any of the three notices. Another 18 per cent said that, while they had received notice, they were too ill to go to the medical centre for evaluation. Other claimants were peripatetic workers who had moved away and would never return to the city. Still others had died, or simply given up hope in the process.

The Initial Skirmishing

As the documentation moved slowly ahead, the litigation in India began in earnest, in a climate of distrust and antagonism. In September 1986, the Union of India formally revived its suit against UCC in the District Court of Bhopal.[34] The litigation would be coordinated by the joint secretary of the Department of Chemicals and Petrochemicals and undertaken by the attorney general. The statement of claim, filed on 5

September, was the first of what would become a torrential flow of documents that would last for two years.

During October 1986, even before the final appeal in the U.S. litigation, both the Union of India and Union Carbide brought a series of interlocutory applications to prevent each other from interfering with evidence or destroying documents. In addition, Union Carbide pressed the Bhopal District Court to require India unequivocally to elect Bhopal as the proper forum for the case in order to forestall appeal proceedings in the United States. And on 17 November 1986, even before the final decision in the U.S. litigation, India successfully requested Judge Patel of the Bhopal District Court to issue an injunction freezing Union Carbide's world-wide assets in order to preserve them in the event of a damages award.[35] Judge Patel took this step in response to India's concerns that Union Carbide was liquidating its assets. In December 1985, the company had become the target of a hostile takeover bid by the GAF Corporation. In order to fight off the bid, Union Carbide had liquidated or mortgaged a significant number of its assets, using the funds to buy back its shares from stockholders. Throughout 1986 it had continued selling off major properties as part of its restructuring, raising fears in India that it was seeking to avoid financial responsibility for the Bhopal tragedy.

Union Carbide officials protested that Judge Patel's order was unfair, and had even used it as evidence for its argument before the U.S. Court of Appeals that the Indian legal system did not have a sufficient guarantee of due process to justify its automatic submission to an Indian judgment. This characterization of Judge Patel's order was somewhat disingenuous since such injunctions are established remedies in the common-law world.[36] Nevertheless, the breadth of the order and its extra-territorial application were breathtaking, and threatened to interfere significantly with Union Carbide's ordinary business operations. On 30 November 1986, Judge Patel agreed to dissolve the injunction on condition of Union Carbide's undertaking to preserve at least $3 billion in assets to satisfy a potential judgment.[37] This enabled Union Carbide to carry on with its restructuring.

With the litigation returned to India, the voluntary social-action groups also saw an opportunity for increased involvement in the litigation. On 27 November 1986, both the Zahreeli Gas Kand Sangharsh Morcha and the Jana Swasthya Kendra applied in the Bhopal District Court for intervenor status in the case.[38] Foreshadowing later battles that would take place between themselves and the Indian government, these organizations expressed their fear that the interests of the gas victims were not being sufficiently protected and that their participation would be required as watch-dog organizations to 'thwart any attempt by the parties to come to a settlement unjust to the victims or to hide the culpability of the defendant or to suppress the actual magnitude and gravity of the episode.'[39]

Both the Indian government and Union Carbide were hostile to any public-interest intervention and opposed the application. This action confirmed to many that the litigation would ultimately become a three-way contest, or that the victims, as relatively helpless bystanders, would simply remain caught in the middle of the crossfire between the multinational and the Indian state.

8

Finding Fault: The Question of Liability

While in the city of Bhopal attention was riveted on the documentation process, hundreds of kilometres away, in New Delhi, lawyers and high-ranking government officials turned their attention to the requirements of proving their case. The issues that would have to be addressed in the Bhopal District Court were enormously complex. Exactly how was the leak caused? Was it the result of sabotage, as UCC claimed, or was it the result of equipment failure or employee negligence? To what extent did the faulty design of the plant contribute to the risk, and which of the two companies (UCIL or its multinational parent, UCC) had a duty to prevent the harm? Were Indian government agencies also implicated in the disaster? Should the risks have been discovered earlier, and what steps could have been taken to eliminate them? How many people in the city had been exposed to the gas and what would be the long-term consequences of that exposure? These issues were not only about facts, but also about law, and ultimately about values. The question of who is ultimately responsible for what happened in Bhopal, what steps they should have taken, and how the losses should be distributed could not be answered solely by scientists or technical investigators.

Framing the Issues

During the seventeen months from September 1986 until early 1988 the parties sought to address these questions, gradually burying each other and the court in a flurry of documents and interim applications. India's claim, now set at $3.3 billion, relied upon the general law of tort. It asserted that the Union Carbide Corporation not only was the majority owner of the Bhopal facility, but was in control of the Bhopal operation 'from cradle to grave.' In the first place it asserted that Union Carbide was liable for *breach of warranty* in so far as the design, construction, and operation of the plant were not maintained according to the best information and technology available. Similarly, India argued that Union Carbide was responsible for *misrepresenting* that the plant was designed and operated according to state-of-the-art specifications. The other counts in the complaint included *negligence, strict liability*, and *absolute liability*. India alleged that Union Carbide designed, constructed, owned, and operated the Bhopal plant; that it had provided a faulty design; that it was aware of the dangerous nature of the materials present; that it knew the plant was operated at a substandard level of safety; and that, none the less, it took no steps to manage or reduce the hazards.

Union Carbide entered its statement of defence on 10 December 1986.[1] Although the company did not accept any of India's allegations, it did not initially take any great pains to disprove them. Instead, it took the position that India's allegations were so vague and general that they were insufficiently detailed to respond to and did not disclose a basis of liability. In addition, because the documentation process was nowhere near complete, UCC argued that the suit was premature and that the litigation should not proceed until all of the injuries, and amounts claimed, were itemized with more precision. Company lawyers asserted that the government had massively overestimated the number and severity of injuries and, in a fit of lawyerly overkill, also challenged the government's authority to sue on the victims' behalf. Having previously used the Bhopal Act as an example of why the case should be tried in India, company lawyers now challenged the legality of the act and denied that the victims were 'physically, financially or otherwise incapable of individually litigating their claims' as alleged.[2]

The company then directed its energies to distancing itself from the Bhopal operation. Union Carbide conceded its majority ownership of Union Carbide of India, but pointed out that the plant had been constructed by Indian firms and that, at the time of the accident, it was managed, operated, and maintained entirely by Indians, in India. The 'Indianization' of the plant, it insisted, was in fact required by government policies intended to reduce reliance on imports, enhance indigenous manufacture, and increase employment opportunities. Union Carbide stressed the Indian government had approved all of the plans, that it was aware of the dangerous nature of the chemicals on site, and that the government had assumed responsibility for licensing and regulating the operation. The role of UCC, argued the company's lawyers, was merely as a 'contractual' provider of technology and knowl-edge. The process design that it provided was simply a 'starting-point' for the project, which was really carried out by the Indian company and other local firms.

Lawyers for Union Carbide argued that there was not a 'shred of evidence' that the disaster was caused by a defect in Union Carbide's design, which, they said, met or exceeded industry standards at the time. They again attacked the government's water-washing theory and reiterated the charge of sabotage.[3] The company claimed again to have solid evidence that employee misconduct was the cause of the disaster and that the other employees had engaged in a massive cover-up. The company was still not in a position to disclose the names of its witnesses or of the alleged saboteur, but it blamed its difficulties on an official conspiracy. Indian government scientific advisers and the Central Bureau of Investigation, the company said, 'desired not to reach a conclusion that the event was caused by a deliberate act,'[4] thus making it easier for the employees to maintain their deception and more diffi-cult for the company to obtain the evidence it needed for its defence.

In addition to its statement of defence, Union Carbide also counter-claimed against both the Union of India and the state of Madhya Pra-desh. The company alleged that both governments had knowledge of the toxic properties of MIC but failed to take adequate precautions. They argued that, notwithstanding its knowledge of the risks, the state gov-ernment had allowed the growth of slum areas in close proximity to the plant and that it was the responsibility of the government to design adequate warning systems, evacuation procedures, and other emergency and medical facilities in case of an accident.

While UCC continually maintained that it had almost no involvement in the construction and operation of the Bhopal plant, the history of the company's operation in India tells a different story, and helps to sort out the allegations and counter-allegations. At the time of the disaster, Union Carbide – through its subsidiary UCIL – had been operating in India for fifty years. In 1966, Edward Munoz, a technical representative of UCC, was sent to India to determine the feasibility of constructing a pesticide plant. He returned to the United States with a favourable report and was sent back to India as a general manager of UCIL, with responsibility for developing the project. In 1966, UCC applied for a permit to manufacture pesticides using MIC, and the Indian government issued a letter of intent to issue the licence. A trial project was begun in 1968, but the letter of intent lapsed in 1970, at which time Munoz reapplied in order to revive the project. For several years thereafter, Union Carbide formulated pesticides with imported MIC and then, in 1973, took the next step of entering into an arrangement to manufacture the MIC itself at the Bhopal facility.

Planning for the project was formally initiated in 1973 according to terms contained in a series of technology transfer agreements between UCC and its subsidiary UCIL. The 1973 agreements, which were signed on 13 November, included a 'design transfer agreement' and a 'technical service agreement.' They provided that UCC was to make available technology and supplies in return for a payment of $20 million. The technical service agreement provided that Union Carbide would make available services and information

generally connected with or specifically pertaining to the production and use of the Products which may reasonably be required by UCIL for the most efficient use of the production techniques that Union Carbide has developed or may develop in the future in Union Carbide's laboratories, plants and factories for the production and use of the Products as pesticides ... Union Carbide shall for this purpose, regularly make available to UCIL, from time to time, such technical data and findings of Union Carbide's laboratories which are actually adopted by Union Carbide in the commercial production and use of the Products as pesticides.[5]

The information was to include operating data and instructions, information concerning raw materials, production processes, and other such technical data 'as Union Carbide's present and future experience may indicate as being necessary or useful for the production and use of products as pesticides in India.'

Under the terms of the design transfer agreement, Union Carbide had agreed to provide process flow diagrams; instrument diagrams; performance and materials specifications for plant construction, equipment, and control systems; and equipment arrangements and descriptions of analytical instrumentation and laboratory quality-control equipment. These design packages, which were prepared by a team of seven UCC engineers in the United States, contained design reports for the safety systems, including the gas scrubber, flare tower, cooling system, and storage tanks.[6] India alleged that these systems had all proved to be inadequate and that it was at this stage that U.S. personnel made the fatal decision to store the MIC 'in large quantities at Bhopal despite the existence of alternative, safer methods of production and despite the position of UCIL, represented by Mr. Munoz, that MIC should be stored in only small amounts because of safety considerations.'[7]

The technology transfer agreements were signed by UCC and UCIL and approved by the Indian government; in 1975, permission was granted to carry on business.[8] Indian law, driven by a policy of foreign-exchange conservation and import substitution, required that, wherever possible, construction of the plant be undertaken by Indian firms. On the basis of specifications provided by UCC, the detailing and construction of the plant was undertaken by Indian firms, though reviewed by UCC personnel. Employees in the United States provided twenty-nine design reports, and John Couvaras, a UCC engineer, was assigned to UCIL as the Bhopal construction manager.[9] The plant was completed and operational by 1980, at a cost of $23 million. A team of eight UCC technicians, led by Warren Woomer, travelled to Bhopal several times in 1979 to conduct an extensive start-up review.

Initially the plant was run by U.S. personnel, and Indian managers and operators who had been trained in the United States. Following his start-up audit, Warren Woomer stayed on in Bhopal as works manager for a period of two years. During this time there were two serious incidents in which toxic gases were released at the plant. On 26 December 1981, a leak of phosgene killed one worker and seriously injured two others, and on 5 October 1982, another leak affected a number of residents in the nearby slums. Woomer left shortly after these accidents and was replaced by Jaganath Mukund who had previously been stationed at the Institute, West Virginia, facility. Union Carbide alleged that it requested the continued presence of UCC personnel at the Bhopal plant, but that the Indian government insisted that the management and work force be made up entirely of Indian nationals. At the time of the accident, there were no personnel in the direct employ of UCC at the plant.

This history, contrary to UCC's version, demonstrates the very close involvement of the company in the development and operation of the Bhopal facility. But, if India was to establish negligence, it would have to specify more precisely what went wrong at the plant. This was, of course, a difficult task, given that no one knew precisely how the water had entered into storage tank number 610. India's technical and legal team therefore focused on the more systemic problems at the facility, arguing that however the water had entered the tank, the disaster was ultimately the result of negligent design and operation. Over the course of three years they made the following more specific factual and legal allegations:[10]

a) Contrary to the advice of its own experts, and unlike the practices at other plants, Union Carbide recommended, encouraged, and permitted the storage of dangerously large quantities of methyl isocyanate. Had the chemical been stored in smaller batches, the disaster would never have occurred.

b) The design of the plant did not include an intermediate storage tank to prevent the possibility of contamination of the primary tank.

c) The storage tanks were not insulated and the cooling system was defective and improperly maintained. There was no back-up cooling system which might have maintained the stability of the stored chemical when the main system was out of operation.

d) The tanks were not equipped with dual temperature indicators to sound alarms or trigger warning lights in the event of a pressure rise.

e) The emergency relief system, including the vent-gas scrubber, was grossly underdesigned. Its capacity to neutralize gas was nowhere near sufficient to deal with the large quantities of MIC being stored, and the system was defective and improperly maintained. Either the system should have been capable of dealing with a runaway reaction in the huge tanks, or the chemical should have been stored in smaller quantities. The vent-gas scrubber was additionally defective in that it allowed the back-flow of caustic soda into the storage tanks.

f) The company failed to provide information on the nature of the materials at the plant, and on proper medical treatment in the event of an accident.

g) A 1984 safety report on the Institute plant warned of the danger of a 'runaway reaction' due to contamination of MIC, but this report was not disclosed to Bhopal management and was not acted upon.

Based on these allegations, Indian lawyers hoped to establish that Union Carbide's conduct in relation to the Bhopal facility fell below the legally required standard of care in negligence. The toxicity of the chemical and its catastrophic potential was, or should have been, known. Previous incidents at the plant demonstrated that the risks were foreseeable. Given the obvious risks, argued government lawyers, the company had an obligation to ensure safety, but failed adequately to do so. The lawyers argued that the design of the plant, especially of the emergency equipment and systems, was substandard and defective since it was so obviously incapable of dealing with a worst-case scenario. They further alleged that Union Carbide had the legal obligation, but failed to conduct sufficiently frequent and thorough safety audits, to respond to obvious dangers or to warn of the hazards associated with the operation. Government lawyers would argue that the company failed to ensure adequate training and supervision of plant personnel, and that it had failed to maintain sufficient staffing levels. Finally, the shoddy state of much of the equipment indicated that the company had failed to keep up a regular inspection and maintenance program.

Union Carbide, in turn, denied that the design was substandard or that any of the defects alleged by India were the effective cause of the disaster. The partial burial of the tanks was, they said, sufficient insulation. The vent-gas scrubber, they argued, was 'capable of handling all reasonably foreseeable conditions.' The company also rejected India's contention that it had mandated storage of such large quantities of MIC on the site, and it claimed that Edward Munoz, India's prime witness on this point, was simply an embittered ex-employee, now in the pay of the Indian government. Lawyers for the company argued that the storage of large quantities had been part of the original plans, which were approved by the government, and, by local standards, was not negligent – that storage in bulk was standard practice in the chemical industry and was common at many facilities in India. In their statement of defence, they detailed dozens of locations in just two states in which 'potentially toxic' materials were stored in similarly large quantities.

The company also pointed out that the agreement between itself and UCIL, and approved by the Indian government, contained a waiver-of-responsibility clause that provided that UCC would not be 'liable for any loss, damage, personal injury or death resulting from or arising out of the use by UCIL of the Design packages.' As India pointed out, this 'self-serving contract with a subsidiary' could hardly be binding on the victims of the disaster.[11] It was signed by UCIL on the instructions of the controlling parent. It was merely one more example of the efforts of the powerful multinational to avoid its responsibilities and to indemnify itself against its own negligence. Even if binding between the two corporate entities, the waiver could hardly affect the rights of the victims who were never parties to the agreement. Nevertheless, Union Carbide would continue to rely on this agreement as part of its more general position that, by virtue of Indian policy, its 'hands-off' approach to the operation was not unreasonable.

Union Carbide's simple denial of all of India's allegations demonstrates the way in which the burden of proof in tort law works against accident victims. In order to succeed in establishing negligence, India would have to prove not only that the catastrophe caused all of the victims' injuries but that the U.S. corporate entity Union Carbide had a duty to ensure the safety at the Indian plant, that the design it provided and steps that it took were in fact substandard or defective, and that those defects were the effective cause of the leak and its results. Doing so would require India to establish how the gas leak occurred and to demonstrate that it would have been prevented by the exercise of reasonable care by Union Carbide. Given that the parties did not know even the mechanics of the accident, they were hardly in a position to show how it could have been prevented. And, given that Union Carbide denied that it had *any* duty to oversee the Bhopal operation, tracing the catastrophe to a specific act of corporate negligence would be extremely difficult.

Given the complexities of the case, India sought to escape the heavy burden of proving negligence by relying on the theory of strict liability developed in *Rylands* v *Fletcher*.[12] According to this principle, an occupier of land is responsible for harms caused by the escape of a dangerous thing when the property is being used in a 'non-natural' manner. This liability exists even without fault.

At first sight, the *Rylands* v *Fletcher* principle would seem to apply. The chemical stored at the site was certainly dangerous, and its escape had caused massive harm. However, on closer inspection, the case is problematic.[13] Given that the plant was constructed with the permission and encouragement of the Indian government, UCC would argue a defence of statutory authority. As it stated in its defence, 'The Union of India, in deciding upon a deliberate policy of import substitution for carbaryl and other MIC-based products, themselves took the view that the manufacture and storage of MIC indigenously in the country would not by itself pose a clear and potential danger.'[14] The plant was located upon land set aside for the purpose and was extensively (though inadequately) regulated by Indian law. The company denied that MIC was 'ultra-hazardous' or that its storage for the purpose of pesticide production was a 'non-natural' use of land. Finally, UCC's steadfast insistence on the sabotage theory was also intended to provide a defence to strict liability based on the notion that the damage was caused by the 'willful intervention of a stranger' and was therefore not the act of Union Carbide.

Because of the restricted scope of the principle of strict liability in *Rylands*, India sought to establish an even more generalized theory of strict or even *absolute* liability. Because of the difficulties of proving the particulars of negligence in the circumstances or bringing the case within the technical requirements of *Rylands*, India argued that Union Carbide should be responsible even in the absence of proof of negligence. In its pleadings it explained this theory as follows:

The defendant, a multinational corporation operating the said plant at Bhopal had at all material times, an absolute and non-delegable duty to ensure that the said hazardous plant did not cause any danger or damage to the people and the State by the operation of the ultrahazardous and dangerous activity at the said plant. This included a duty to provide that all ultrahazardous or inherently dangerous activities be conducted with the required standards of safety and to provide all necessary safeguards, information and warnings concerning the activity involved ...

In manufacturing, processing, handling and storing MIC at its plant in Bhopal and in designing and putting the plant into operation, the defendant Union Carbide engaged in an ultrahazardous and inherently dangerous activity. This activity created the clear and potential danger of death, serious injury and damage to property in the event of the escape of lethal gas from MIC storage tank into the atmosphere.[15]

This 'heretical' theory had first been articulated in 1944 in a California products-liability case, *Escola* v *Coca-Cola*.[16] The majority in that case had allowed the plaintiff to recover in negligence for injuries resulting from an exploding bottle. Justice Traynor went farther, suggesting that negligence should no longer be considered an essential element of the plaintiff's claim. Instead, a manufacturer should be absolutely liable:

public policy demands that responsibility be fixed wherever it will most effectively reduce the hazards to life and health inherent in defective products that reach the market. It is evident that the manufacturer can anticipate some hazards and guard against the recurrence of others, as the public cannot. Those who suffer injury from defective products are unprepared to meet its consequences. The cost of an injury and the loss of time or health may be an overwhelming misfortune to the person injured, and a needless one, for the risk of injury can be insured by the manufacturer and distributed among the public as a cost of doing business.[17]

Government lawyers reasoned that the same considerations applied in the Bhopal case. The operation involved an extremely hazardous material over which the victims had no control. Nor were the victims in a position to establish exactly what had gone wrong. Union Carbide, however, was in the best position to control the risk, to mitigate the potential harm, and to absorb the loss as a cost of doing business. The principle of absolute liability was not clearly part of Indian law, but government lawyers hoped that the Bhopal case would provide the occasion for the same type of judicial law reform that had previously occurred in other path-breaking cases such as *Donoghue* v *Stevenson*, *Rylands* v *Fletcher*, and *Escola*. But they still faced two serious obstacles. The first of these was Union Carbide's sabotage theory, and the second was the company's corporate veil. If the disaster was caused by the intentional act of an employee, could it be said that the company was responsible for the event? And even if the Indian company could be held liable, could responsibility be traced even farther up the corporate hierarchy, to the parent company?

Vicarious Liability and the Sabotage Theory

India sought to meet Union Carbide's sabotage defence in a variety of ways. In the first place, government lawyers simply attacked the sabotage theory and put Union Carbide to strict proof. They claimed that the theory had been manufactured by the company, and denied that there was any physical evidence to support it (such as the allegedly missing pressure indicator). In their pleadings, government lawyers developed the sabotage scenario in such a way as to show how unlikely it was that a saboteur could have completed the operation without being observed. They challenged Union Carbide to disclose the name of the saboteur, but the company refused, stating that his identity must be guarded and that their witness on this point feared retaliation and harassment. Government officials pointed out that it was more likely that an appropriate candidate had still not been found. Finally, the government took the position that, even if the event had been caused by a saboteur, UCC was nevertheless liable, both vicariously and directly.

The question of when an employer is liable for the wrongful, or even criminal act of its employees is difficult and controversial, and is usually said to turn on the vague test of whether the employees are acting 'within the scope of their employment.'[18] As in other areas of tort law, considerations of public policy and morality provide no clear answers to hard questions such as that raised by Union Carbide's sabotage theory. While, on the one hand, it may seem unfair to hold one person responsible for the wrongful act of another, other considerations point in favour of an almost absolute vicarious responsibility. Where an innocent person suffers a loss because of the wrongful act of another's employee, as between the innocent victim and the employer, it seems fair that the victim should not be left to bear his or her own loss. The employer takes the benefit of its employees' actions and therefore should also be responsible for any resulting damage. The employer is in the best position to select, train, and supervise its employees, and must be held accountable for their wrongdoing.

As in other areas of tort law, the principle of vicarious responsibility has evolved over the years. In the nineteenth century, an employer's responsibility was frequently narrowed by the requirement that the employee's act be 'authorized' before attracting vicarious responsibility. However, consistent with the expansion of tort liability since that time, the principle of vicarious liability has also broadened to include unauthorized conduct. The principle is, however, still limited by individualistic notions of fault. Where the employee's wrong is entirely unauthorized and outside the scope of his or her employment, the conduct may be considered an 'independent act,' for which the employer should not be held responsible. As torts scholar John Fleming explains, this formulation represents a 'compromise between two conflicting policies: on the one hand, the social interest in furnishing an innocent tort victim with recourse against a financially responsible defendant and, on the other, a hesitation to foist any undue burden on business enterprise.'[19]

Union Carbide's sabotage theory was designed to take the case outside of the principle of vicarious liability. It argued that sabotage is an intentional wrong, unauthorized by the employer and independent of the employee's job. Here the company felt it was on strong ground. There are numerous cases in which employers have been excused from liability when the employee committed an intentional tort or a crime not obviously related to his or her work responsibilities. But the mere fact that the employee's wrongful act was intentional does not mean that the employer is not, in the end, responsible. Employers have, for example, been held responsible for acts of fraud and assault committed by their employees.[20] Some courts have indicated a willingness to go even farther. In the English case of *Photo Production Ltd* v *Securicor Transport Ltd*,[21] a night watchman, employed by the defendant, intentionally lit a fire that destroyed the very building he was hired to guard. In the Court of Appeal, Lord Denning held the employer liable to the owner of the building:

> It seems to me that Securicor [the employer] should not be able to avoid their liability simply because Musgrove [the employee] did a deliberate act ... Securicor were under a duty to give a careful and trustworthy service of night patrol. This was a duty owed to all the neighbourhood who were in sufficient proximity to the factory. Securicor are liable for the wrongful act of their service in the course of it ...
>
> By the same token, it is clear that any person who was injured or damaged by the fire would have a cause of action in tort against Securicor for the wrongful act of their servant. If a passer-by was burnt and injured in the fire, he would be able to sue them.[22]

The issue of vicarious liability would be a difficult one in the Bhopal case. Notwithstanding the *Photo Production* case, traditional legal principles probably favoured the company. From Union Carbide's point of view, an act of sabotage was certainly not within the scope of their employees' duties, and it would be 'unfair' to hold them responsible for the independent acts of a 'criminal.' However, the company would also have to prove that the sabotage did, in fact, occur. Moreover, if Indian lawyers were successful in persuading a court to accept an 'absolute and non-delegable' duty of care in respect of hazardous substances, they would be on stronger ground. Their arguments about loss distribution and deterrence also weighed in favour of placing liability on the company, which is in the best position to control the risk, even of sabotage, and to mitigate the harmful effects of an incident, however caused.[23]

Finally, Indian lawyers argued that, even if the company was not vicariously responsible for an employee's crime, it might nevertheless be directly liable for failing to take sufficient care to prevent the disaster or to design systems that would minimize its effects. Here they were on stronger ground. Where a person is in control of a hazardous facility, there is a duty, independent of vicarious liability, to establish precautions to avoid all foreseeable risks, including tampering and sabotage.[24] Where foreseeable, the misconduct of another person 'whether innocent, negligent, intentionally tortious, or criminal does not prevent the actor from being liable for harm caused thereby.'[25] Under Canadian environmental law, for example, vandalism is no defence where the company has failed to take adequate precautions to prevent access to a hazardous substance.[26] In the case of Bhopal, the employee had access to the premises only by virtue of his employment. According to Union Carbide's own theory, he was unaware of the consequences of his act because of inadequate training and knowledge about MIC. Further, it would be argued for the victims that Union Carbide itself had acknowledged that 'minor incidents of process sabotage by employees had occurred previously at the Bhopal plant.'[27] Why had steps not been taken to enhance security in light of these incidents? Why was it so easy for a person to gain access and introduce water into tank number 610? Why was the problem not noticed earlier and dealt with more effectively; and why were back-up warning and safety systems inadequate to deal with the gas discharge?

The Corporate Veil

Even if all of the Indian government's arguments on strict and vicarious liability were accepted, it still faced one major remaining hurdle. For as Union Carbide officials had been arguing throughout the litigation, while the *Indian* company (UCIL) might be held vicariously liable for the acts of its employees, and though the *Indian* company might be held to a standard of strict liability, the U.S. company (UCC) was a separate legal entity that was 'unconnected' to the disaster. In other words, they argued, India had named the wrong defendant.

India had strategic and political reasons for implicating Union Carbide in the disaster. Most importantly, UCIL's Indian assets (of about $50 million) were nowhere near sufficient to provide compensation for the victims.[28] In addition, especially from the point of view of many of the victims and social activists, Bhopal was simply a catastrophic illustration of the usual pattern of multinational exploitation of the Third World, and the only adequate legal response would be one that held the parent company to account. The government had lost its bid to achieve this objective in the U.S. litigation, but now sought to renew its efforts to establish a principle of multinational responsibility. It argued that, as a matter of fact, UCC owned, controlled, and managed the Bhopal operation and, as a matter of principle, parent companies must be held responsible for their foreign operations in order to provide adequate compensation to the victims and to deter the type of neglect that led to the tragedy.

Given the power of multinationals, and the degree of control that they enjoy over their operations in the developing world, it might be thought too obvious for argument that UCC, the parent corporation, should be held responsible for the damage caused by its Indian operation. Ironically, however, it is a testament to India's political and economic progress that UCC was not unequivocally in control of the Bhopal operation. India has been a leader in the Third World's drive towards industrial self-sufficiency. It has sought to reduce its reliance on imports and foreign-controlled business, and especially to encourage the development of indigenous technology and skills. Its policy of foreign-exchange conservation required that most industries be constructed by Indian firms, using Indian materials. Foreign-investment regulations required that companies be owned and managed by Indian citizens. While not entirely successful in implementing these policies, India has achieved a significant measure of local control, even over those industrial ventures sponsored by multinational companies.

Union Carbide sought to turn India's limited success in achieving economic control against the government's claim that the company should be held responsible for the Bhopal disaster. It argued that it was India's own industrial and investment policies that 'created a situation whereby UCIL had no option but to launch upon indigenous manufacturing of MIC-based pesticides and to set up a plant for that purpose.'[29] It further asserted that India's own policies strictly limited the role that the parent company could play in India and the control it could exercise over the Bhopal facility. The two companies were formally separate entities, and while UCC owned the majority of UCIL shares, the Indian company had its own management, which controlled the company's day-to-day activities. Thus, UCC maintained throughout that its relationship with UCIL was at arm's length. It presented itself as a passive investor in the Indian operation, exercising no control or authority over its day-to-day operations. UCC insisted that the relationship between itself and UCIL was so remote that it would be both unjust and illegal to hold it responsible for damage caused by faulty operation of the Bhopal plant.

The legal issues here are deceptively simple. First, does a parent corporation have a direct duty to manage its subsidiaries in a competent fashion? Does it owe a duty of care to the community arising out of its activities there? Second, apart from its direct duties to the community, is the parent company liable for the acts of its subsidiaries? Should the courts adhere to the traditional approach to separate corporate personality, or recognize the realities of multinational business organization and treat the two enterprises as part of a single monolithic concern?

Capital and the Law

According to conventional company law, an investor/owner of a limited-liability company is not liable for the acts or debts of the corporation, except in specified circumstances. This principle flows from the idea established in the case of *Saloman* v *Saloman*[30] that a corporation has a separate legal identity distinct from its shareholders and owners. This shield from legal liability applies also to related companies. They are said to have separate legal personalities, even where one owns the other and they are part of a larger group of companies.[31] In the case of a multinational enterprise, the theory of separate corporate personality creates the fiction that each of the interlocking companies is an independent entity within the country of its incorporation. This is the principle upon which Union Carbide relied.

One of the most notorious illustrations of the principle of separate corporate personality involved a New York taxi operator who ran a fleet of taxi cabs.[32] The owner had incorporated ten separate companies, each of which owned just two taxis. The plaintiff was severely injured by one of the cabs and sought to recover damages by suing the company that owned the cab. However, the plaintiff soon discovered that each cab carried only the minimum insurance required by law ($10,000) and that the company had no other assets. The plaintiff then brought an action for the remainder of the damages against the owner of all the companies on the basis that the entire business was, in fact, a single enterprise, and that the use of a series of separate companies was nothing more than an attempt to defraud members of the general public who might be injured by one of the cabs. The New York Court of Appeals refused to accept this invitation to 'pierce the corporate veil.' Judge Feld said that 'the corporate form may not be disregarded merely because the assets of the corporation, together with the mandatory insurance coverage of the vehicle which struck the plaintiff, are insufficient to assure him the recovery sought.'[33] The court felt that to pierce the corporate veil in order to obtain compensation for the victim of an accident would have a negative impact on business planning and investment.

One judge, Keeting J, dissented in this case. He felt that it was clearly unfair to deprive the plaintiff of compensation and that the corporate form was, in this instance, being used in an unjust fashion. He explained that 'the issue presented by this action is whether the policy of this State, which affords those desiring to engage in a business enterprise the privilege of limited liability through the use of the corporate device, is so strong that it will permit that privilege to continue no matter how much it is abused, no matter how irresponsibly the corporation is operated, no matter what the cost to the public.'[34] Judge Keeting held that the way in which the business was organized in this case revealed that the owner's sole purpose was to avoid financial responsibility for damages claims and that it would be against public policy to allow the corporate form to be used in this fashion.

This case reveals the basic conflict that arose in the Bhopal case.[35] On the one hand, separate corporate personality and limited liability are widely used instruments of state economic policy that encourage capital accumulation and investment in economic development. By limiting the potential liability of investors, the law provides an incentive for investment and avoids unfairly surprising remote owners with undue managerial responsibility or financial risk. On the other hand, the corporate form can too easily be used to avoid taking financial responsibility for risks not consented to. Indeed, in industries involving hazardous processes and materials, there is strong evidence that operations have been fragmented and segregated into smaller, thinly capitalized corporations in an effort to avoid liability.[36] Unlike commercial creditors, victims of corporate torts have no way of knowing in advance of the risk of dealing with a limited-liability corporation, or of protecting themselves against that risk.[37]

The problem is acute in the case of multinational organizations. By pursuing their global purposes through networks of legally independent subsidiaries, multinational companies can widely disperse their assets, placing them beyond the reach of the law. Through transfer pricing techniques, high-risk subsidiaries can be maintained on the borderline of solvency.[38] When a disaster does occur, the assets and insurance of the local company are insufficient to compensate the victims, while the assets of the parent are shielded from any claim. To hold the parent liable is often the only way in which to ensure full compensation for these victims and to encourage the parent companies to exercise greater responsibility in controlling their foreign operations.

Piercing the Corporate Veil

The principles of separate corporate personality and limited liability are not absolute. They are legal instruments created by the state and bestowed upon entrepreneurs and investors to achieve greater economic welfare. The favourable treatment of investor/owners is justified only because it is grounded in a calculus of the public good. There are times when this same calculus will compel a departure from limited liability, and in a long list of cases, the corporate veil has been lifted in order to do justice.

In the first place, Indian government lawyers reasoned that UCC could be *directly* liable for breach of a duty it owed to the victims itself. Such a duty would not depend upon vicarious liability or 'piercing the corporate veil,' but would be based on the concept that UCC committed a wrong, independent of any carelessness or tort committed by UCIL or its employees. This liability might be founded upon Union Carbide's initial provision of a defective design, its failure to monitor and supervise the operations of the Bhopal plant, its failure to upgrade safety systems, and its failure to insist on the implementation of safety recommendations or to warn of the risks of a 'runaway reaction.' This duty might be similar to a manufacturer's duty to warn of dangers of a product when a defect is discovered. The transfer of technology to a developing nation is not a simple sale of goods. Given the less-developed infrastructure of the host country, and the continued control and direction of the affiliate by the multinational, there is an ongoing relationship that gives rise to legal responsibilities greater than those assumed in a simple commercial exchange.

In addition to its direct liability, India argued that UCC should, as a matter of principle, be held vicariously responsible for the acts of its subsidiary, or that the two companies were so closely related that the corporate veil should be pierced. But these notions are traditionally limited to use in situations where the parent exercises almost complete control over the subsidiary or in order to prevent fraud or wrongful conduct. So, for example, where separate corporate personality is being used solely for the purpose of evading taxes or avoiding statutory obligations, the courts will frequently look behind the corporate form and fix liability upon the owner. Similarly, where one company is simply the agent or 'alter ego' of an individual owner or another corporation, the courts may infer an agency relationship and ignore their separate personalities. Ordinarily, agency is inferred not only from the fact of ownership, but from the extent of authority exercised over it by the owner, measured by the degree of day-to-day control and direction. The courts frequently state that they will disregard the corporate form only when the corporation is the 'creature' or the 'puppet' of its owner.[39]

Thus, the extent to which the courts will disregard the corporate form remains one of the most controversial questions in this area of the law. U.S. and European courts may go somewhat farther than their English and Canadian counterparts. Where, for example, the corporate tort-feasor is seriously undercapitalized or underinsured, and is simply being used as a mechanism to avoid responsibility for debts, the owner may be personally liable. Generally, however, the veil survives intact to protect owners, investors, and associated companies from liability for corporate torts.

India's Theory of Enterprise Liability

Because of the limitations of the traditional law, India invoked a more radical theory of 'multinational enterprise liability.' This argument is based upon the proposition that the web of companies under the financial control of the multinational are part of a single economic group with common objectives. Just as the parent corporation maintains control over the group, so must it maintain financial responsibility for its various endeavours.[40] The notion of group-enterprise liability has been substantially adopted in Germany,[41] and has found some favour in the common-law world in cases dealing with the tax liability of corporate groups and antitrust conspiracy issues. Indeed, Union Carbide itself has on occasion suffered from such an approach. In *Continental Ore Co.* v *Union Carbide & Carbon Corp.*,[42] the U.S. Supreme Court applied antitrust provisions in respect of a vanadium monopoly obtained by Union Carbide's Canadian affiliate.

India's principal contention was that, by virtue of the parent company's global structure, it had effective control over its foreign subsidiaries, and the acts and omissions of the parent company were ultimately the source of danger. It argued that, in the case of a complex and intricately organized international business, it is impossible to pinpoint responsibility to a discrete unit or individual within the enterprise, that the multinational alone has the power to prevent a disaster, and that it must therefore be held accountable for damage done at one of its subsidiaries. The argument is worth quoting at some length.

18. Multinational corporations by virtue of their global purpose, structure, organization, technology, finances and resources have it within their power to make decisions and take actions that can result in industrial disasters of catastrophic proportion and magnitude. This is particularly true with respect to

those activities of the multinationals which are ultra-hazardous or inherently dangerous.

19. Key management personnel of multinationals exercise a closely-held power which is neither restricted by national boundaries nor effectively controlled by international law. The complex corporate structure of the multinational, with networks of subsidiaries and divisions, makes it exceedingly difficult or even impossible to pinpoint responsibility for the damage caused by the enterprise to discrete corporate units or individuals. In reality, there is but one entity, the monolithic multinational, which is responsible for the design, development and dissemination of information and technology worldwide, acting through a forged network of interlocking directors, common operating systems, global distribution and marketing systems, financial and other controls. In this manner, the multinational carries on its global purpose through thousands of daily actions, by a multitude of employees and agents. Persons harmed by the acts of a multinational corporation are not in a position to isolate which unit of the enterprise caused the harm, yet it is evident that the multinational enterprise that caused the harm is liable for such harm. The multinational must necessarily assume this responsibility, for it alone has the resources to discover and guard against hazards and to provide warnings of potential hazards. This inherent duty of the multinational is the only effective way to promote safety and assure that information is shared with all sectors of its organization and with the nations within which it operates.[43]

Union Carbide hotly contested this theory of multinational-enterprise liability. Indeed, it went so far as to argue that 'there is no concept known to law as a "multinational corporation"' and it even denied that the U.S. company had any operations in India 'or elsewhere outside the United States of America as alleged.'[44] These were rather startling assertions, based more on legal fiction than business reality.

The UCC Connection

Union Carbide of India Ltd (UCIL) was 50.9 per cent owned by the U.S. Union Carbide Corporation (UCC). Of the remaining equity, Indian public financial institutions owned 22 per cent and the balance was traded on the Calcutta Stock Exchange. The two companies were separately incorporated – the former in India and the latter in the United States. The Indian company reported to the parent through Union

Carbide Eastern (UCE), which had its head office in Hong Kong, but was a wholly owned subsidiary of UCC and incorporated in Delaware.

As previously explained, the Bhopal facility was not a simple sale of technology from one company to another. While the relationship between UCC and UCIL was defined in 'contracts' between the two companies, these agreements were hardly the result of arm's-length bargaining between two independent entities. They were drafted by UCC, and UCIL management were instructed to approve them. Indeed, work on the design of the plant had commenced in the United States a year prior to these agreements. While the detailing and construction of the plant was done by other firms, it was subject to UCC supervision and approval.

The plant was originally managed and run by UCC personnel, though at the time of the disaster there were no personnel from the U.S. parent directly involved in the management of the plant. UCC did not, of course, oversee or manage the day-to-day operations of the Bhopal plant. In any large enterprise with numerous units, immediate operational control is delegated to a relatively autonomous local management. But this does not mean that UCC did not continue to exercise significant authority over the operation. While UCC had diluted its ownership share of the Indian operation, it was still in full control of the company. Indeed, the parent corporation had been granted an exemption from the usual foreign-investment requirements of India in so far as it was allowed to maintain majority ownership of UCIL. Control was further achieved through the promulgation of corporate guidelines and policy manuals, an overlapping board of directors, and a hierarchical system of reporting and responsibility. UCC's corporate charter stated that 'the UCC management system will be designed to provide centralized, integrated, corporate strategic planning, direction and control; and decentralized business strategic planning and operating implementation.'[45] Its corporate policy manual (section 1.5.4) provided that, 'except for certain special situations, it is the general policy of the Corporation to secure and maintain effective control of an Affiliate. Normally this is accomplished through ownership of 100% of the Affiliate equity where this is consistent with the laws, policies, and customs of the host countries.'[46]

UCC's policy manual also stipulated that the corporation had the duty and authority to issue technical policies, procedures, and objectives. It also placed responsibility on the U.S. divisions of the company to make periodic audits regarding health, safety, and environment, and to issue policies and procedures for legal services regarding laws and regulations pertaining to health, safety, and environment. It stated that the company would take positive steps to ensure superior standards of safe design and practices.[47] At least formally, headquarters in Danbury had responsibility for the development and communication of all safety and maintenance guidelines. India also claimed that UCIL did not have authority to spend more than $10,000 without clearance from the parent corporation.[48]

Union Carbide stressed that, at the time of the accident, none of its directors was on the board of UCIL. But this was somewhat disingenuous. Four of the directors of UCIL (including the chair) were officers of Union Carbide Eastern, which was, in turn, wholly owned by UCC. A fifth director was a vice-president of UCC.[49] While UCC sought to emphasize that UCIL was a 'free standing' and separate legal entity, its majority ownership and control of the board thus gave it full authority over the direction and management of the Indian company. The testimony of James Rehfield, a Union Carbide vice-president, offered in the U.S. litigation is instructive:

Q: In order to secure effective management control of an affiliate, Union Carbide need not have 100 per cent say on the board of directors, correct?
A: Union Carbide does not control its affiliate companies, period.
Q: Sir, who controls an affiliate company?
A: The board of that company.
Q: Who is the board elected by?
A: The Equity participants.
Q: And who's the major equity participant in UCIL?
A: Carbide's 50.9.[50]

Rehfield himself provides a good example of the way in which multinationals maintain effective control over their 'independent' affiliates. He was an executive vice-president of UCC, based in Danbury, Connecticut, with management responsibility for the division including UCE and UCIL. He was also on the board of directors of UCIL, as were four other former UCC directors.

Some indication of the degree of formal authority which UCC exercised over UCIL can be inferred from events that took place just shortly before the disaster. The UCIL plant had not been a successful operation financially. A series of policy suggestions and meetings resulted in a number of proposals respecting its future. One early proposal was that UCIL should start exporting its products in order to utilize its excess capacity. While this might have been in the interest of the Indian company, the idea was rejected by UCC headquarters on the basis that these exports would compete with other Union Carbide operations. Another proposal suggested converting part of the plant for other purposes. When this project fell through, there was a suggestion that the plant be sold outright. These plans, which received serious consideration from UCC officials, were apparently conceived with little or no input from Bhopal. They were abandoned when no buyers could be found. The final proposal, when no buyer could be found, was to dismantle the plant and sell it to Indonesia or Brazil. The first time the management of UCIL seems to have been consulted on this matter was when they were ordered to prepare a feasibility study in 1984. This study was completed on 29 November 1984 – three days before the tragedy.[51]

An Early Victory?

India's case was obviously a difficult one to make. Negligence would be difficult to prove, and even then, some way would have to be found to pierce Union Carbide's corporate veil. India's argument about enterprise and absolute liability, while not entirely novel, was based on slim precedential support, and would meet with considerable resistance. The principle of strict liability has, in some areas, seen considerable growth, particularly in the United States in cases regarding products liability. Yet, *Rylands* v *Fletcher* has not yet evolved into a generalized principle of responsibility for hazardous activities. Instead, it has been hedged about with various restrictions, exceptions, and qualifications.[52] Some legal scholars have suggested that the judicial reluctance to extend *Rylands* may be explained by the increased prominence of social-insurance schemes as mechanisms of loss spreading, and the lesser need for judicial invention.[53] If so, then it is arguable as a matter of social policy that, given the absence of such mechanisms in India, the Indian courts would be justified in adopting a more activist stance. And this is precisely what they have done.

Exactly one year after the Bhopal disaster, a leak of toxic oleum gas from the Shriram fertilizer factory in north Delhi killed one victim and injured hundreds of others. The Delhi administration immediately closed down the plant, and a public-interest application was brought to the Supreme Court. During the course of the litigation, the Court appointed four committees to investigate the accident and to make recommendations on necessary improvements before the plant could be reopened. In a hearing just over two months after the leak, the Court allowed the plant to reopen, subject to a number of strict safety conditions.[54] One of these conditions, signalling the Court's willingness to pierce the corporate veil, was that the managers would agree to be personally responsible for potential damages in the future and that they would deposit 1.5 million rupees as security. The Court also required the company to deposit security of 2 million rupees to satisfy compensation claims arising from the leak. The victims then brought a further petition to the Supreme Court to clarify the law regarding Shriram's liability to pay compensation.

In December of 1986, Chief Justice P.N. Bhagwati (now retired) gave the Court's ruling on the issue of liability.[55] While accepting that the chemical industry was necessary to the economy of India, he reasoned that the social costs of industrial development should not be borne by individual workers and citizens, and he concluded that injuries caused by hazardous industries violated the constitutional guarantee of the right to life. Obviously aware that he was extending the law as traditionally understood in the Anglo-Indian tradition, the Chief Justice said, 'We cannot allow our judicial thinking to be constricted by reference to the law as it prevails in England or for that matter of that in any other foreign country. We no longer need the crutches of a foreign legal order ... We in India cannot hold our hands back and I venture to evolve a new principle of liability which English Courts have not done.'[56] Justice Bhagwati held that an enterprise engaged in hazardous or inherently dangerous activities owes an 'absolute and non-delegable duty to the community' to ensure that no harm is done:

... if any harm results on account of such activity, the enterprise must be absolutely liable to compensate for such harm and it should be no answer for the enterprise to say that it had taken all reasonable care and that the harm occurred without negligence on its part. Since the persons harmed on account of the hazardous or inherently dangerous activity carried on by the enterprise would not be in a position to isolate the process of operation from the hazardous preparation of substance or any other element that caused the harm the enterprise must be held strictly liable for causing such harm as part of the social cost of carrying on the ... activity.[57]

The Court declared that this principle was not subject to the many exceptions that qualify the rule of strict liability in *Rylands* v *Fletcher*. It reasoned that, where a dangerous activity is permitted to be carried on for profit, the law should presume that it is allowed to operate only subject to the condition that the enterprise will absorb the social costs of any resulting accidents. It reasoned that the victims were in no position to prove negligence and that 'the enterprise alone has the resources to discover and guard against hazards or dangers and to provide warnings.'[58]

Finally, the Supreme Court observed that if the principle was to serve the goal not only of compensation but also of deterrence, the measure of damages should be such that it could not be treated by the defendant merely as a cost of doing business. 'The measure of compensation in such cases must be correlated to the magnitude of capacity of the enterprise because such compensation must have a deterrent effect. The larger and more prosperous the enterprise, the greater must be the amount of compensation payable by it for the harm caused on account of any accident.'[59]

The *Shriram* judgment was clearly written with Bhopal in mind. This was Chief Justice Bhagwati's last case, and he had been one of the most outspoken judges on behalf of the victims. The language of the decision was, in fact, taken in part from India's complaint in the Bhopal case, and he clearly wished to leave the victims with increased legal leverage in their battle against Union Carbide. As he wrote in the course of the judgment, this new principle is particularly appropriate when a large number of persons are affected or where, because of their poverty or socially disadvantaged position, it would be unrealistic and unfair to require the victims to pursue their remedies through normal channels.

One potential limitation of the *Shriram* case is that it is based upon rights enshrined in the constitution. According to the traditional understanding, such constitutional rights essentially govern the relationship between the citizen and the state, and not that between private citizens. The principle might, therefore, be limited to actions against the government, or at least against facilities that are under the control of the government. Nevertheless, the *Shriram* judgment was hailed as an important victory by all concerned. In the context of environmental and industrial hazards, a principle of absolute liability is consistent with the notion that the polluter should pay for any damage, and thereby ensures that the full social costs of production are taken into account in making risk-management decisions. From one point of view it may seem unfair to 'punish' a person or firm for an accident that was not their 'fault.' But, if we are to take safety seriously, it is necessary to move beyond the individualistic fault-based morality of traditional tort law. A principle of absolute liability places responsibility on the party best able to control risks, and ensures that that party will take steps to eliminate or mitigate the hazards. Their responsibility to do this derives from their authority and capacity to prevent disasters rather than from any 'fault' or wrongful intent. If we want to prevent future Bhopals, it is necessary to move beyond punishment and concentrate on prevention.

A principle of absolute liability affirms the primacy of compensation for innocent victims, relieving them of the near-impossible tasks of proving factual causation and negligence. Internationally, the *Shriram* judgment was acclaimed as an important contribution to the common law, and locally it was seen to have bestowed a significant bargaining endowment on the victims' side of the litigation. It was greeted with enthusiasm by many activist groups as providing a precedent that might hasten a speedy and more generous settlement of the case.

Shriram may have significantly boosted the morale, but it was far from being conclusive of the case against Union Carbide. In the first place, it was challenged by Union Carbide spokespersons on the basis that it was politically motivated and that it amounted to legislative reform, outside the scope of the Court's power. They argued that the decision went too far beyond the ordinary law of tort established by Indian courts, and that to apply the principle in the Bhopal case would be retroactive. Essentially what Union Carbide sought to do was to minimize the importance of the decision and also to preserve the option of refusing to honour any future judgment against them on the basis that it violated their rights of due process. In so far as any final judgment would have to be enforced in the United States, this was a potentially effective strategy.

The *Shriram* judgment closed out the second year of the Bhopal litigation. Throughout the following year the parties continued their efforts in the District Court of Bhopal to frame the case and to move ever so slowly towards a trial. But then, in February 1987, District Court judge G.S. Patel was removed from the case when it was discovered that he had filed a claim in the proceedings on his own behalf.[60] This embarrassing revelation was, at the least, a public-relations setback for India and its judiciary, adding fuel to Union Carbide's campaign to discredit the Indian legal system. 'The fix was on,' said one lawyer; 'it was like a kangaroo court over there.'[61] The new judge appointed, Mahadeo Wamanrao Deo, was the fourth to sit on the case.

On 3 July 1987, UCC again claimed to have solid proof of its sabotage theory, and a spokesperson for the company said, 'We will disclose his name at the appropriate time before the court.'[62] At the same time, the police and the Central Bureau of Investigation continued their criminal investigation, laying charges against Warren Anderson and a number of UCIL management personnel. As part of this investigation, they conducted a series of interviews with Sunder Rajan, the senior instrumentation engineer at the Bhopal plant, who was also Union Carbide's primary witness in support of their sabotage theory. Union Carbide took the view that this interrogation was intended to intimidate their witness and sought an injunction to prevent the police from further questioning Sunder Rajan, and especially from requiring him to submit to a lie-detector test.[63] Judge Deo rejected their argument that the witness was being harassed or intimidated and refused the injunction.

In mid November 1987, rumours of a settlement at between $500 million and $650 million were reported between UCC and the government. This report was followed by protests in front of the court-house and also by a group of eminent persons, led by the former chief justice of India, P.N. Bhagwati, demanding that the settlement include an admission of liability by Union Carbide to serve as a precedent for the future. The settlement fell through.

9

And, in the Meantime,
What of the Victims?

While the government and Union Carbide were fighting, the people in Bhopal were dying. The case had been in the U.S. courts for two years without result. Litigation had been initiated in India in September 1986, but for the next fifteen months was consumed by a series of interlocutory applications by both parties. Three years after the disaster, the trial remained bogged down in preliminary matters, and discovery proceedings had not even commenced. The injury documentation and assessment process was only just under way; and throughout 1987 Union Carbide continued to demand that India provide full details of the victims' injuries and refused to proceed further until the information was forthcoming. The company argued that it was in no position to defend itself against the claim until it was aware of the number of victims and the extent of their injuries. It would require information on the status of each victim, the medical treatment received to date, and the likely future injury and income loss. Yet, in light of the magnitude of the disaster and the unknown medical consequences of MIC poisoning, the requirement of full particulars was entirely unrealistic. By the end of 1987 neither Union Carbide nor the Government of India had even completed filing its pleadings.

In the meantime, the plight of the victims worsened.[1] Sajida's husband had been an operator at the Union Carbide plant and was killed in the 1981 phosgene leak. On the night of the disaster, her five-year-old son, Arshad, had been killed. Her other son, Shouyer, survived, but required frequent hospitalization, since the MIC had burned the linings of his lungs and stomach. Sajida herself was incapable of working since the gas leak because of respiratory problems. Another victim, Ali Bange, had been a trade-unionist working with rickshaw pullers and porters.

Before the accident, he earned about 300 rupees per month (about $22), out of which he supported his wife and three children. After the disaster, he was completely unable to work. 'I cannot carry a tiffin carrier more than ten yards. All my kids have been badly affected. My daughter cannot hold a glass of water.'[2]

Relief and Rehabilitation

For three years following the catastrophe, the government struggled to devise some way of caring for the victims until final compensation was obtained. The urgency of this effort was particularly acute because the majority of Bhopal victims were overwhelmingly poor, and existing social-welfare systems were incapable of providing even the basic food and medical care they required.

In the days and weeks immediately following the disaster, the relief effort was chaotic. Limited medical facilities were overwhelmed by the enormity of the problem and practically neutralized because of the lack of knowledge about how to treat the MIC-affected population. Doctors' efforts were confined primarily to treatment of symptoms. Relief agencies were similarly overwhelmed. Their resources were vastly inadequate to deal with the problems faced by the people in Bhopal, and, with almost no communication and coordination, their efforts were confined to the provision of ad hoc emergency assistance. Life in the city had come to a complete standstill. The victims, most of whom were subsistence labourers, lost all means of supporting themselves and their families. Many began to starve to death. The initial response was disorganized and a recipe for chaos and corruption. Indeed, for some time, relief officers simply walked through the community with briefcases stuffed with cash, making on-the-spot payments to persons in immediate and severe physical distress.

With the realization that a more comprehensive and organized relief plan would have to be devised, interim measures were put in place to ensure, at least, that the people who lived in the thirty-six most seriously affected wards had enough food to meet their daily consumption requirements. The government's first step was to set up a system of relief camps, responsible for ensuring at least the physical survival of the community. For five months, milk was distributed throughout the city, especially to young children. For thirteen months, sugar, rice, and other food grains were provided.

As the immensity of the tragedy at Bhopal dawned on the people of

India, the authorities sought to put in place a better-organized plan for relief, and ultimately a more systematic blueprint for the rehabilitation of the city. In addition to its efforts to document the claims in preparation of the litigation, the Bhopal Gas Tragedy Relief and Rehabilitation Department was given the responsibility to develop and coordinate a relief plan. The Indian Council of Medical Research (ICMR) was assigned the task of coordinating long-term medical research and treatment.

As the victims were processed through the documentation centres, small amounts of cash were made available to help them survive. In the most seriously affected wards, 78,000 families were provided with 500 rupees ($35) to help them to meet their daily consumption requirements; 762 widows received 200 rupees ($15) per month to alleviate the hardship resulting from the loss of a family income earner; and 5,600 destitute individuals received 60 rupees ($5) per month to help them survive.

The children of Bhopal were among the worst affected. Many were injured, and far more were left orphaned or were at least deprived of adult support as their parents and relations languished without work. In cooperation with the state Child Development Service, the relief department instituted five projects to provide care for the city's children. It set up hundreds of small child-welfare centres charged with responsibility for meeting the health and nutritional requirements of 73,000 children under the age of six. It arranged the adoption of orphans by family members. Dozens of children were made wards of the state in cases where there were no close relatives willing to adopt, or where officials were concerned that the adoption was being sought for opportunistic reasons. The family-relief centres also sought to minimize the impact of the disaster upon the 17,000 pregnant women and nursing mothers whose children had already begun to succumb to the effects of the gas and, then, starvation. These centres sought to provide a nutritional supplement of 500 calories per day for the children and 1,000 calories per day for the mothers.

Throughout 1986 and 1987, the relief department sought to transform its ad hoc approach to relief into a more organized 'relief action plan.' By now it was clear that the disaster had not simply caused a large number of individual injuries but had virtually destroyed the social infrastructure of the entire community. All economic and social systems had collapsed. The task was not simply to care for the injured people, but to attempt to reconstruct a community.

Under the proposed seven-year, 371 crore (3,710 million rupees; $250 million U.S.) action plan, the thirty-six most seriously affected wards would be turned into a new medical district to provide more accessible facilities to local residents. Because so many of the victims were daily-wage labourers with no means of transport, they were unable to make a trip to the hospital without losing a day's pay, or worse, being blacklisted from future work. Six new hospitals were to be constructed, with a total capacity of 1,000 new beds. In addition, the plan called for the construction of six local dispensaries, two diagnostic centres, and ten mobile hospitals.

It had also become apparent that the economy of the old city had been massively damaged by the disaster. Hundreds of small businesses were destroyed, and thousands of working people had been displaced. The action plan thus called for widespread economic rehabilitation. The department proposed to build forty 'work sheds' in which 7,000 youths would be trained in rudimentary trade skills, including plumbing, welding, carpentry, typing, and painting. Three thousand women were employed for 350 rupees per month to stitch school uniforms. In cooperation with the government's Special Training and Employment Program for Urban Poor (STEPUP), bank loans would be arranged to help small businesses re-establish themselves. The plan also called for the development of a special industrial area in which 120 small facilities would be installed to provide work for up to 10,000 persons. Businesses would be encouraged to locate here if they were 'labour intensive' and 'environmentally benign.' Since so many of the victims had become incapable of heavy labour, these businesses would also have to require only light work.

The department next proposed to undertake much-needed improvements to the local environment and infrastructure. Until now, many of the gas-affected areas had been unregulated slums. Following the disaster, these areas had deteriorated even further, becoming breeding-grounds for disease and infection to which the gas-affected population was now even more susceptible. Dividing these areas into eighty localities, the department built thirty-six public latrines and began to construct modest housing for the victims. Work was done to cover over the open sewers, collect garbage, provide fresh water, and pave the roads.

In spite of these ambitious and imaginative plans, the relief effort was plagued with problems, and the action plan became a political football. Contradictory statements by the government of its funding intent made it impossible for the department to fully commit itself to the plan. By late 1989, for example, only three of the medical facilities had been completed, adding only 165 of the proposed 1,000 beds. The government continually expressed its reluctance to provide full funding since it felt that this would be like giving an interest-free loan to Union Carbide. Indeed, funding was not finalized until the summer of 1991, and then was less than half what the department had anticipated. Realistically, it must be recognized that Bhopal was not the only disaster in India that public authorities had to cope with during the late 1980s. The turmoil in the Punjab continued unabated during these years, claiming thousands of lives and diverting the main focus of government attention to questions of law and order. The worst drought in decades had jeopardized the lives of thousands in central India, while communal violence in the north, a drawn out 'war' with Pakistan, and a 'police action' in Sri Lanka placed a heavy burden on extremely limited public resources. And, while the people of Bhopal were living on the wrong side of the edge of absolute poverty, this is a condition which thousands of other people in India are forced to endure.

Nor was the promised assistance from Union Carbide forthcoming. On the basis of the company's expressed desire to contribute to the relief effort, Judge Keenan had 'ordered' it to pay $5 million through the Red Cross. But the company and the government were unable to agree on how the funds should be administered. The government objected to the reporting requirements, which, it feared, were designed to obtain information that could be used against the victims in the litigation. This money simply sat in the Red Cross account for years.[3]

What limited relief funding did make its way into Bhopal was further dissipated through corruption and inefficiency. Local residents complained frequently that promised foodstuffs were diverted to the black market, and that they saw little of the hard currency that the government claimed had been given to them. Thieves, con artists, and middlemen appeared in the city to seek their fortune in the wake of the disaster. Official corruption was also a problem. Much though it is abhorred by all the people of India, the practice of *baksheesh* (bribery) is an inevitable consequence of the power that underpaid government officials wield over those who are dependent upon them. The experience of Basanti Bai is probably not untypical. Too weak to work, she had been in pain since breathing the gas. Two years after the leak, she learned that she was entitled to an interim relief payment from the government of 1,500 rupees (about $110). 'To get this money I had to spend nearly the same amount going from place to place.'

By late 1989, the department estimated that it had spent 115 crore rupees ($95 million U.S.) on relief and rehabilitation (25 crore from the state and 90 crore from the central government). However, much of this money was spent on administration and half-completed civic-beautification projects. In a series of interviews at the end of 1989, local residents in the gas-affected wards expressed their dissatisfaction with the relief effort. Half-finished buildings stood empty. The pits dug for work sheds had become cesspools and breeding-grounds for mosquitoes. Newly constructed sewage lines were not cleaned and were once again backing up and becoming sources of disease.

The relief department had become entrapped between politics on the national and state levels, on the one hand, and the demands of the victims, on the other. Much of the resentment that the victims felt against the government's conduct of the litigation was channelled into anger about the rehabilitation effort. Rumours of enormous settlements raised the victims' expectations and prompted their ire when they reflected upon the meagre assistance they felt they had so far received. 'There are no limits to the demands,' complained the principal secretary; 'whatever we do, it's never enough.'[4]

Relations between government authorities and victims' groups had been tightly strained from the very beginning. In particular, the 'sodium thiosulphate controversy' had created considerable distrust of the government. This drug, a partial antidote to cyanide poisoning, had been denied to the victims because the government refused to accept its efficacy. Social activists believed that the government's position amounted to a coverup, designed to obscure the extent of the harm suffered by the victims, and the controversy raged for two years. A study by the Indian Council of Medical Research did confirm that there were increased levels of thiocyanide in the urine of the victims, and they recommended the massive use of thiosulphate. Other authorities, especially Dr N.P. Mishra, head of medicine at Gandhi Medical College and a consultant to Union Carbide, attacked the scientific veracity of this study, and the Madhya Pradesh government not only refused to implement the ICMR recommendations, but shut down the only clinic administering the drug. On a petition from the victims and Dr Nisith Vohra, the Supreme Court ordered that the clinic be reopened and that an expert committee be formed to monitor the medical relief effort.[5] When the government finally changed its policy on the drug in 1988, it was too late for the drug to be effective, and many of the victims blamed both Union Carbide and the government for prolonging their suffering.

Notwithstanding these problems, the department claimed that at least its basic medical efforts were successful. Several new medical facilities had been built, and officials asserted that there was no longer a shortage of medicine. Special ophthalmic examinations and free eyeglasses were distributed to the victims. Dozens of medical and scientific teams conducted research in Bhopal on the human and environmental consequences of the disaster. These included the Indian Council of Medical Research, The Indian Council of Agricultural Research, and the National Institute of Toxicological Research. Yet activists and victims' groups claimed that these measures were never sufficient. The medical studies failed to produce concrete results that could be put to use for long-term treatment, and many of the promised medical facilities were never built.

The relief workers recognized that the issues in Bhopal had been politicized and sought to provide formal and informal channels whereby the victims could express their concerns and participate in the rehabilitation process. But these processes seemed simply to add to the bewildering array of bureaucratic structures already in place, and the victims remained distrustful. Social-action groups, such as the Zahrili Gas Kand Sangharsh Morcha and the Bhopal Gas Peedit Mahila Udyog Sangathan, took up the victims' cause. These groups presented themselves to the victims as watch-dogs. The more sincere and capable of them, through their energetic advocacy on behalf of the victims, were able to mobilize a great deal of public support. The victims, distrustful of government motives and disempowered by the bureaucratic structures they were required to deal with, readily adopted more direct tactics, including demonstrations, prayer meetings, and writ petitions to the Supreme Court. The reaction of government officials to the participation of the activist groups ranged from a grudging respect to downright hostility, though they were able to develop an uneasy working relationship.

The relief effort in Bhopal was a remarkable experiment, though defective in many ways. The delays and deficiencies were largely attributable to the simple fact that there are no standard models for this kind of social reconstruction. The system put in place was devised from the ground up by a few compassionate and creative individuals, trying to respond to the unpredictable consequences of a disaster that essentially destroyed the basic social systems in place in the city. As one of the department's commissioners said, 'Notwithstanding the fact that immediately after the disaster all systems collapsed and life was almost totally paralyzed in Bhopal, the Government provided prompt and comprehensive relief measures. Recovery from any disaster is always a slow process. Such was the severity of this disaster that the limp back towards normalcy could have been even slower and more harrowing ... If the Bhopal scene of disaster was not engulfed by a sense of fatalism, it was due in no small measure to the all round sympathy, support and particularly the assistance extended by government.'[6]

The failings of the rehabilitation effort were the further result of the program's partial nature and its linkage with the litigation. The government refused to separate the issue of rehabilitation from that of litigation. It continually reiterated that its hands were tied because to provide more full compensation to the victims 'would amount to giving Union Carbide an interest-free loan.' By failing to build its efforts upon a broader concept of public responsibility, the government could not earn the victims' trust. As one Indian editorialist argued, relieving the suffering of the victims should have been the prime consideration of the government, but, instead, the victims became invisible as government and legal élites 'rushed to pillory the American multinational who, they said, was playing cheap with Indian lives.' He concluded that assistance to the victims had 'taken a back seat to jingoistic America-bashing, anti-transnational sloganeering, and manipulation of the legal process that makes a laughing stock of Indian justice and undermines our economic development.'[7]

Antagonism towards the work of the department became especially virulent each time the case came close to settlement. Victims feared, with some justification, that in its effort to defend an inadequate settlement the government would seek to minimize the damage at Bhopal and would begin to deny just claims. As the department's principal secretary, S. Sathyam, confirmed, 'Because of the litigation, the course we have taken has always been molded around the requirements of the case. This may not always have been in the best interests of the victims or their rehabilitation.'[8] The litigation interfered with accurate documentation and rehabilitation in several ways. While a large number of medical organizations were involved in medical assessment, the requirement of secrecy meant that they were unable to publish their findings or effectively communicate with one another. Many private doctors were therefore unable to obtain the information that they needed to diagnose and treat their patients. Given the inevitably limited nature of the government's relief effort, it is perhaps not surprising that the victims' expectations focused increasingly on the courts as a means of obtaining interim relief.

Interim Compensation

For two years the victims had been watching the glacial progress of the lawsuit, first in the United States and, later, in the Bhopal District Court.

At the end of 1986, two of the social-action groups applied to the Bhopal District Court to order UCC to pay interim compensation to provide for at least the minimum survival needs of the victims.[9] The company responded by denying that it had any legal or moral responsibility for the victims' welfare, that it had already offered $5 million in aid which had been refused by the Indian government, and that, in the absence of a finding of liability, it could not be made to pay interim compensation. The application proceeded no farther, but it did prompt the District Court judge to begin thinking about some way of providing for the victims.

Throughout 1987, Judge Mahadeo Wamanrao Deo, the fourth judge to sit on the case in Bhopal, had become increasingly frustrated with the course of the litigation and had been pressing the parties to reach an out-of-court settlement. As he said, the 'victims of the ghastly tragedy have so far been left to look with somewhat justified dismay at the procedural proceedings in the court' and without any relief so far, 'the poor gas victims may find it difficult to hold heart to wade through the jungle of laws and legal battles.'[10] In April 1987 he urged the parties to work out some form of interim relief and presented them with a formal written proposal. Yet, it was not until four months later that Union Carbide responded.[11] The company reiterated its position that it had no liability and that the court had no authority to order interim compensation. It asserted that the victims' claims were grossly exaggerated and that their needs were, in any event, being met by government authorities. To show its good faith, however, it offered a sum of $4.6 million. This offer was rejected as insulting by India's attorney general.

Once again Judge Deo expressed his frustration with the parties and urged them to reconsider the possibility of a final out-of-court settlement. At the request of the parties, he again adjourned the case for several weeks in October in order that they might resume negotiations. In November 1987, it was rumoured that a figure of between $500 million and $650 million had been agreed to. The parties were scheduled to appear before Judge Deo on 18 November 1987 to report on the settlement, but before that time victims' groups, supported by social activists and retired Supreme Court justice Krishna Iyer, staged vigorous protests against the settlement, insisting that it was inadequate and must include an admission of liability. A group of eight hundred women victims from Bhopal travelled to New Delhi to demonstrate against the settlement. On the day the parties were to appear before Judge Deo to report on the result of their negotiations, the court gates had to be locked against a large group staging a *dharna* (sitting and fasting) outside. The International Coalition for Justice in Bhopal argued that 'the question of accountability of those responsible for the disaster is very important. Accountability must be established as a first step if further disasters are to be prevented.'[12]

The victims were not, of course, unanimous in their condemnation of the proposed settlement. Most were poor and in dire need of assistance. Having lost the family bread-winner, or having themselves become unable to work, they felt they had already waited too long for financial help. Judge Deo now accepted a new petition from the victims' groups, this time for interim compensation. The application was brought by Vibhuti Jha, the lawyer for two of the social-activist groups working with the victims – the Zahreeli Gas Kand Sangharsh Morcha ('Poisonous Gas Disaster Struggle Front') and the Jan Swasthya Kendra ('People's Health Clinic'). These groups chastized both the company and the government for their disregard of the welfare of the victims, claiming that 'whatever may be the inflated claims of the government both Central and State, in their publicity stunt, the fact is that the relief measures undertaken by them are almost zero.'[13] On 27 November 1987, Judge Deo told the lawyers for both sides: 'I have really been moved by the fact that the third anniversary of the disaster is drawing close,' and ordered them to prepare and submit arguments on the question of interim compensation.[14]

At the same time, another judge, B.M. Lal, hearing one of the numerous interim applications in the case, accused Union Carbide of delaying the proceedings and ordered the parties to show cause why the case should not be immediately transferred to the High Court for an expedited hearing.[15] Both Union Carbide and the government then presented arguments in the High Court as to why this should not be done. F.S. Nariman, the chief lawyer for Union Carbide, argued that Union Carbide's interim applications were legitimate requests for information so that it might mount its defence. The Court agreed and, on 3 December 1987, the third anniversary of the Bhopal tragedy, it refused to grant the transfer petition.[16] It accepted that, in such complex litigation, lengthy pretrial proceedings were inevitable as the parties sought to frame the issues for trial. The Court denied that UCC or the Government of India were unreasonably delaying and also noted the increased complexity that would result if the case was transferred to the High Court in Jabalpur, hundreds of kilometres from Bhopal. It concluded that the 'learned single Judge was swayed by the sufferings of the victims of the tragedy at Bhopal and the fact that the claim cases have not yet been set for trial, although three years have passed.'[17] The Court did, however, also say, 'Before parting, we must direct the parties to fully cooperate in the early disposal of the claim cases in order that the victims of the tragedy get justice without further delay. We also direct the District Judge to examine what interim relief can be granted to ameliorate the conditions of the victims and to minimize the human sufferings, especially of the legal heirs of 2500 or so persons who died in the tragedy and those who have been permanently disabled and are not in a position to earn their livelihood and having nothing to fall back upon.'[18]

Judge Deo of the District Court took this direction as his cue and, on 17 December 1987, the case took its most dramatic turn. Frustrated that the most recent negotiations had 'bogged down in the din of diverse voices' and after hearing the parties' arguments, Judge Deo ordered Union Carbide to pay 3.5 billion rupees ($270 million U.S.) in interim compensation to the Bhopal victims.'[19] He found his authority to make this order in the 'inherent jurisdiction of the court.' He acknowledged the novelty of the step he had taken, but noted that courts do frequently play an active role in preserving the rights of the parties during the course of the litigation by granting interim orders, interlocutory injunctions, and other pretrial directives. While interim compensation had not been granted before, he asserted that the law 'must also grow to meet the problems raised by such changes ... including the hazards of industrialization.'[20] He concluded that 'it cannot be denied that an unprecedented tragedy took place on account of a deadly leak ... Can the gas victims survive till the time all the tangible data with meticulous exactitude is collected and adjusted in fine forensic style for working out the final amount of compensation with precision ...?'[21] Quoting a famous English judge, he remarked that, 'if we never do anything which has not been done before, we shall not get anywhere.'

Judge Deo also suggested that the Supreme Court of India had opened up the possibility of interim compensation in the *Shriram* case and wryly noted that this case had been relied upon by Union Carbide's lawyers in their argument that the Indian legal system was sufficiently innovative that the case should be tried there. 'UCC relied upon this source of law in obtaining judgment on forum-non-conveniens and is, therefore, bound by it.'[22] The order required Union Carbide to pay the sum into court within two months and that it would be administered by the claims commissioner, Justice P.D. Muley of the Madhya Pradesh High Court. The order provided payments of 200,000 rupees ($15,385 U.S.) to the next of kin of each victim, 100,000 rupees ($7,690) to the permanently disabled, and smaller amounts to those with less severe injuries.

Judge Deo's order was met with joy by the victims. Crowds outside the court-room cheered when they heard the news and encircled Mr Jha, the victims' lawyer, anointing him with *tilak* (crimson powder, usually used to mark the forehead). Some sources suggested that the unprecedented decision was aimed at hastening a negotiated settlement. Whatever the intent, it was perceived to have bestowed an important bargaining endowment upon the victims who might otherwise have been forced to accept an inadequate settlement. The International Coalition for Justice in Bhopal commented that Deo's decision should be a model for world-wide reform. It was vital, they argued, 'that the provision of interim relief to victims of industrial disasters be delinked from the process of establishing legal liability. Unless this is done, victims will be forced not only to compromise their claims by entering into inadequate settlements but will also be forced to let the harmdoer escape unscathed and free to victimize others.'[23]

Union Carbide spokespersons responded with anger, issuing a statement that the 'court order amounts to awarding damages without a trial, which runs counter to legal principles in India and other countries.'[24] The order was immediately appealed to the Madhya Pradesh High Court where Union Carbide characterized Judge Deo's decision as 'arbitrary, harsh and burdensome,' 'wholly perverse,' and displaying 'a complete pre-judgment.'[25] Lawyers for UCC argued that the order had no basis in law, that it was punitive in nature, and that the judge had been coerced into making the order by public pressure.

The Revenge of the Colonies

The appeal of Judge Deo's order reached the Madhya Pradesh High Court within four months. UCC strenuously put forward two main arguments. First, it stated, the claim was misconceived and premature, violating the Fatal Accidents Act[26] and the rules of civil procedure that require a claim to be supported by particulars of the injuries suffered by the victims and the exact damages claimed. Second, the company argued, Judge Deo's order was judicial legislation. There was no provision under the Indian Code of Civil Procedure for the award of interim relief, and that the court had exceeded its inherent jurisdiction in making an order that affected the substantive rights of the parties before trial.

On 4 April, after two postponements, Justice S.K. Seth gave his judgment.[27] He upheld the decision of the lower court, but on different grounds, and awarded a reduced sum of rupees 250 crores ($170 million U.S.). In his decision, he responded to Union Carbide's arguments point by point.

Procedure

In an adversarial system of justice, it is important that the defendant have full information about the nature of the claim that it must meet. This requirement is enshrined in legislation providing that the plaintiff must disclose particulars of the nature of the claim and the individual for whose benefit the action is brought. This is something that had not so far been done in this case and, Union Carbide argued, it would therefore be unfair to make any compensation order until the company had an opportunity to challenge the government's evidence about the number of victims and the nature of their injuries.

However, as Justice Seth recognized, the individualization of the proceedings in the Bhopal litigation, according to the traditional rules of civil procedure, would hardly promote justice for the victims who were poor, disorganized, and unlikely to obtain adequate legal advice. If 'left to themselves the majority of the countless victims of the disaster would have hardly been in a position to secure justice.'[28] It was to overcome this problem that the Bhopal Act was passed. This statute, noted Judge Seth, contemplates new forms of procedure to deal with this unprecedented claim. Its creation of a claims directorate to collect and quantify the claims of the victims was an appropriate alternative to the usual form of civil procedure. Thus, in place of an adversarial determination of the facts regarding the number of victims and the extent of their injuries, Judge Seth felt that it would be appropriate to substitute the mechanism set up by the act and to rely on the evidence gathered by the claims directorate. While this deviates significantly from an ordinary understanding of due process, it is appropriate in such an extraordinary case.

Inherent Jurisdiction

Justice Seth did, however, accept UCC's second and more important argument – that Judge Deo had stepped beyond his jurisdiction in making the order that he did. A judge does have jurisdiction to control the *procedure* of a trial, but Justice Seth agreed with Union Carbide that Judge Deo's order was not simply procedural, but in fact affected the *substantive rights* of the parties and could not, therefore, be upheld on the basis of his procedural authority.

Judge Deo's order had been made pursuant to sections 94 and 151 of the Indian Code of Civil Procedure. The former section expressly authorizes the court to make interim orders in certain situations, and the latter provides: 'Nothing in this Code shall be deemed to limit or otherwise affect the inherent power of the Court to make such orders as may be necessary for the ends of justice, or to prevent abuses of the processes of the Court.' Section 94 specifically itemizes those circumstances in which the courts may make interim orders and it does not include a provision for interim compensation. Section 151, which reiterates the inherent jurisdiction of the court, is a broad and supplementary section, but Judge Seth accepted Union Carbide's argument that this inherent power must be exercised in a way that is consistent with principle and precedent. Following the reasoning in several earlier Supreme Court decisions,[29] Justice Seth held that section 151 was not intended to increase the court's jurisdiction over the parties' substantive rights, but rather to enable it to control its own procedures. He concluded that section 151 related to procedure only, and not to substantive rights, and that Judge Deo was therefore mistaken in finding in that provision authority to make an order affecting the private rights of the parties.[30]

At this point, Union Carbide must have been breathing a sigh of relief. For what Judge Seth was saying seemed to go entirely in their favour. But their relief was to be short-lived; what he had to say next was to take the case against Union Carbide even farther than Judge Deo had. Judge Seth had signalled to the parties that he intended to explore other avenues to resolve the case when, five days into oral argument, he had asked them to prepare arguments addressing the question of whether interim compensation could be ordered not as a matter of *procedure*, but as a matter of *substantive law*.

Substantive Relief

Having decided that the District Court had not had authority under the Code of Civil Procedure to order compensation, Judge Seth's judgment took a remarkable turn. Instead of striking down the order, he held that, as a matter of the substantive law of torts in India, the victims were entitled to immediate compensation. He reached this conclusion by holding that, in the circumstances of the case, it was appropriate to import into Indian common law a provision of English law that permits a court, in a situation where one party will eventually be held responsible to pay damages, to award interim compensation. Essentially, Justice Seth was telling Union Carbide that, as a matter of substantive law, it would eventually be liable for the Bhopal disaster.

The provision that Justice Seth was determined to make part of Indian common law is based on section 21 of the English Administration of Justice Act and the Supreme Court rules, which empower the Court to award interim compensation in certain circumstances. India has no such statute, but, argued Seth, it was appropriate in the Bhopal case to accept the principle as part of the Indian common law. But how can English law be imported in this fashion?

Seth began by discussing at some length the development of tort doctrine in British India. He first pointed out that there were never two separate systems of law and equity. Instead, the courts' general jurisdiction to try civil matters was found in section 9 of the Code of Civil Procedure (1908), and in the general principle that the law should be developed according to 'justice, equity and good conscience.' This principle, familiar to many ex-colonial nations, is generally understood to mean the rules of English law, if found applicable to Indian society and circumstances.

Justice Seth then noted the very interesting interpretation placed on this principle in the case of *Vidya Devi* v *M.P.S.R.T. Corp.*[31] The issue in that case was whether the court should apply the traditional common-law doctrine of contributory negligence, which barred plaintiffs from receiving damages if they had contributed to their own injury. This doctrine had been altered by the English Contributory Negligence Act of 1945, though there was no equivalent legislation in India. Nevertheless, in the *Vidya Devi* case, the court held that it was not strictly bound by the rules of common law, but was instead obliged to follow the general principle of justice, equity, and good conscience. This, in turn, meant that it should alter its common law to conform to the better principle contained in the English reform. The court explained: 'There is no doubt a presumption that a rule of common law is in consonance with justice, equity and good conscience. But how can that presumption continue if the country of its origin has itself rejected the rule and has made new rules in its place? If the new rules of English law replacing or modifying the common law are more in consonance with justice, equity and good conscience it would be open to us to reject the out-moded rules of common law and apply the new rules.'[32] The court departed from the common-law rule and apportioned damages. Other Indian cases have taken a similar approach, adopting as part of the common law statutory reforms forged in England.[33]

Taking this approach as his springboard, Justice Seth then referred to and adopted the rules enacted under the English Administration of Justice Act as providing common-law authority for the award of interim relief. He explained: 'It does not require much of an argument to accept that the intervening period between commencement of an action and its ultimate trial in a suit for damages especially when based on a tort caused a greater hardship in a developing country like India than in a developed country like England. As such, there existed no valid ground why the abovesaid set of statutory rules ... could not be adapted with suitable modifications as a part of Indian common law and applied to the Bhopal suit.'[34]

According to the English rules, interim compensation may be appropriate where: (a) the defendant has admitted liability; or (b) the plaintiff has obtained judgment against the defendant; or (c) if the action proceeded to trial, the plaintiff would obtain judgment for substantial damages against the defendant. The defendant must be: (a) a person who is insured in respect of the plaintiff's claim; (b) a public authority; or (c) a person whose means and resources are such as to enable him or her to make interim payments.

Justice Seth had no doubt that the Bhopal case satisfied the second set of requirements. It was on record that UCC was insured to the extent of rupees 262 crores ($200 million U.S.) and had substantial resources ($6.5 billion) to meet the claim. The more difficult question was whether the case satisfied the first set of requirements. Union Carbide had certainly not admitted liability, nor was there any outstanding judgment against it. Thus, interim compensation would only be granted against it if it could be demonstrated that, if the case proceeded to trial, the victims would obtain judgment against UCC. Justice Seth suggested that this requirement could be satisfied if it could be shown, first, that the victims had a *prima facie* case, and, second, that UCC could be held responsible for the damage caused by its subsidiary UCIL; that is, that it was legally appropriate in this case to 'lift the corporate veil' between the two companies.

Justice Seth was satisfied that the victims did have a *prima facie* case against one of the two companies. The *Shriram* case, he said, made it clear that, in India, the victims of hazardous industries have an absolute right to compensation. 'It is thus unquestionable in the Bhopal suit that whichever was the enterprise [the UCC or UCIL] engaged in the hazardous or inherently dangerous activity at the plant ... is liable to pay damages/compensation to the gas victims in accordance with the rule of absolute liability without exceptions as mentioned above.'[35] But, which of the two companies would be held liable under the *Shriram* principle? Union Carbide had been insisting throughout the litigation that its relationship with UCIL was at arm's length, that they were separate legal entities, and that it should not be held responsible for the defaults of the Indian company.

The Corporate Veil: Water Down the Ganges

In the United States, Judge Keenan had not been impressed by India's argument that the parent company should be responsible for the operations of its affiliate. During the course of his judgment, he had accepted Union Carbide's argument that it was not intimately involved in the Indian operation. He had emphasized that UCIL had been built primarily by Indian firms and that, at the time of the disaster, it was operated and managed by Indian citizens. The plant was, he said, extensively controlled and regulated by Indian law and, he implied, quite autonomous from its U.S. parent. Keenan's judgment was, on this score, hostile to India's theory of multinational liability and a real victory for Union Carbide.

Armed with Judge Keenan's findings, Union Carbide had unswervingly maintained the position that the principle of separate corporate personality, first articulated in the English case of *Saloman* v *Saloman*, would protect it from liability for the disaster caused by its 'independent' affiliate. But, perhaps not surprisingly, Judges Deo and Seth let Union Carbide know that Indian judges do not entirely agree with the U.S. perception of the realities of multinational business operations in the Third World. As Seth J suggested, 'much water has flown down the Ganges since it was first held in *Saloman* v *Saloman and Co.* as an absolute principle that a corporation or company has a legal and separate entity of its own.'[36] In the course of five pages of his judgment, he dramatically swept away the company's single most important defence.

Justice Seth began his analysis by noting that the principle of separate corporate personality was subject to a growing number of exceptions. He referred to *Tata Engineering and Locomotive Co. Ltd* v *State of Bihar*,[37] which recognized these exceptions, and suggested that such developments revealed a changing attitude in the law. 'It may be that in course of time these exceptions may grow in number and to meet the requirements of different economic problems, the theory about the personality of the corporation may be confined more and more.'[38] As Chinnappa Reddy explained in the case of *Life Insurance Corp. of India* v *Escorts Ltd*,

Generally and broadly speaking, we may say that the corporate veil may be lifted where a statute itself contemplates lifting the veil, or fraud or improper conduct is intended to be prevented or a taxing statute or a benevolent statute is sought to be evaded or *where associated companies are inextricably connected as to be in reality part of one concern. It is neither necessary nor desirable to enumerate the class of cases where lifting the veil is permissible, since that must necessarily depend on the relevant statutory or other provisions, the objects sought to be achieved, the impugned conduct, the involvement of the element of public interests, the effect on parties who may be affected*, etc. (emphasis of Seth J).[39]

Justice Seth referred also to developments in other countries that reflect a growing willingness by the courts to pierce the corporate veil, even in situations not involving fraud or improper conduct. In particular, he suggested that where the businesses are, in fact, tightly interconnected, they may be treated as a single enterprise.[40] Seth J concluded that, if the corporate veil can be lifted in these circumstances, and to enforce welfare measures relating to workers,[41] there is no reason why it should not be lifted 'in a case of tort which has resulted in a mass disaster and in which on the face of it the assets of the alleged subsidiary company are utterly insufficient to meet the just claims of a multitude of disaster victims.'[42]

Justice Seth expressed his confidence, on the basis of the evidence adduced so far, that UCC had real control over the Bhopal plant. The parent company was the majority shareholder, and it controlled the composition of the board of directors and the management of the Indian company. UCC's corporate policy revealed that it was a multinational concern with the purpose of managing and running industries throughout the world. It exercised full and effective control over its subsidiaries, and had full authority to act for the Indian company. It had control over technology and information, and the Indian company was entirely dependent in this respect on UCC. Even after the promulgation of the Foreign Exchange Act,[43] the UCC had managed to maintain control over the Indian company, and at any rate, the purpose of this act was to regulate, and not prohibit, business in India by foreign concerns. Most importantly, Judge Seth took a very different view than had Judge Keenan of the company's evidence that it took a 'hands-off' approach to the Indian operation. 'If, as alleged by the defendant, UCC, it chose to follow the policy of keeping itself at arms length from the Indian company in certain respects, it was entirely its choice and such policy could not absolve it from its liability.'[44]

Administration of the Fund

The final problem facing Justice Seth was to determine the amounts of compensation and to devise some mechanism for its distribution. He was of the opinion that the trial judge had been wrong to leave to the commissioner the task of determining the amount payable to the victims. Displaying some frustration with the government's procedures, he noted that the payments made so far had been only a 'pittance' and that any further delay 'would have grave and tragic consequences.'[45] Instead, he held that compensation amounts could be worked out by the court itself, based on the figures so far collected by the Gas Disaster Relief and Rehabilitation Department.

By this time, the department's figures indicated that 2,500 people had died and that 30,000 had been seriously injured. Judge Seth noted that the *Shriram* case required that the amount of compensation be reasonable, but also related to the wealth of the defendant in order to have a deterrent effect. He suggested that, if the case came to trial, the damages would likely be: (a) death, 200,000 rupees ($12,500 U.S.); (b) total permanent disability, 200,000 rupees ($12,500); (c) permanent partial disability, 100,000 rupees ($6,250); and (d) temporary partial disability, 50,000 rupees ($3,125). He then suggested that half of these amounts would be reasonable as interim compensation and ordered Union Carbide to pay a total sum of rupees 250 crore ($157 million). He ordered the Government of India to execute his order as though it were a 'decree passed in its favour' and emphasized once again that 'the payment is not for interim relief, but as damages under the substantive law of torts on the basis of more than a prima facie case having been made out.'[46]

Seth J recognized that the proper registration of all the claims would take some time and granted UCC two months to deposit the funds in the trial court. He then ordered the commissioner of claims to have the registration work completed within four months from the date of the deposit. Finally, he ordered the trial court to proceed with the trial 'with advertance to the findings on the relevant questions of law given by this court.'[47]

Consequences and Controversies

Essentially, Judge Seth had gone even farther than had Judge Deo. While he reduced the amount of the interim award, he had made significant findings of fact and law against Union Carbide. As he said, his order was not simply for interim relief without reference to the merits of the case, but was, in fact, a finding that there was a *prima facie* case against the company. He had essentially concluded that the *Shriram* case applied and that Union Carbide would be held to a standard of absolute liability. He had held that Union Carbide exercised sufficient control over its Indian subsidiary that it could not hide behind its corporate veil. In the eyes of many, he had vindicated the Indian judicial system. Indeed, he himself had remarked that 'this Court cannot restrain itself from expressing its shock over the manner in which with the sole object of getting over what appeared to be an incontrovertible plea of "forum non conveniens" ... the plaintiff – Union of India under-rated its own judiciary and made it a subject matter of ridicule so publicly before a foreign Court.'[48]

Union Carbide spokespersons, however, responded to Judge Seth's ruling with hostility. They argued that he had effectively decided the issue of liability before a trial. Doing so, they alleged, violated the company's right to due process under both Indian and U.S. law. Moreover, they suggested, Seth J's order was based upon a retroactive application of the *Shriram* decision, unfairly subjecting them to liability on the basis of a principle that did not exist at the time of the accident. Essentially, they argued, the decision amounted to a form of judicial legislation that violated the principle that judges should declare what the law is rather than make the law. These reactions clearly indicated Union Carbide's intent to take a further appeal to the Indian Supreme Court and, if unsuccessful there, to resist enforcement of the judgment in U.S. courts on the basis that it failed to conform to the requirements of due process.

The order granted by Judge Seth was, perhaps, defective in that, while it was interlocutory in nature, it envisaged no mechanism whereby Union Carbide could claim reimbursement in the event that it should win at trial. In seeking a basis for ordering interim compensation,

Justice Seth felt obliged to rule decisively on the merits of the case before hearing all of the evidence and arguments, thus leaving his decision open to the charge that he had prejudged the case and thus deprived Union Carbide of its rights of due process in the adversarial system. The simple expedient of requiring an undertaking from the Union of India, guaranteeing repayment of the award to the company in the event that it later prevailed at trial, would have made the interim order far more palatable. Such an approach would affirm the concept of *public* responsibility, whereby the government assumes not only the right to represent the victims, but the responsibility to ensure their compensation, regardless of the outcome of the litigation. However, this was not the model that the government had built the Bhopal Act and its compensation strategy upon. Because the application had been brought by an intervenor and not the government, and because of the government's unwillingness to assume ultimate responsibility for the large sum at stake, the requirement of a guarantee was not feasible.

Thus, the solution fashioned by Judge Seth was imperfect, and its imperfections were the inevitable result of the fact that the case continued to presuppose a model of adversarial justice and tort liability instead of a model of public responsibility. Even in India, the decision was not greeted with universal acclaim. Some commentators agreed that he had stretched both the law and the facts too far. Some felt that Union Carbide might have legitimate defences and that it deserved its day in court. Others, while unsympathetic to Carbide, recognized the reality of the situation. The decree would likely be appealed again, adding further to the delay; even if upheld by the Supreme Court, the order might not be enforceable against the company in the United States. They feared that 'Conservative American judges who have in mind American industrial interests' would likely dismiss the decree as a denial of due process.

Tearing the Corporate Veil

Perhaps the most striking aspect of Judge Seth's decision was the way in which he determined not only that interim compensation must be paid, but that the responsibility for payment lay unequivocally with Union Carbide. His ruling marked a dramatic departure from the traditional respect that courts show to the principle of separate corporate personality. And while his decision to pierce the corporate veil was an unequivocal victory for the claimants, its long-term implications are more problematic. Multinational corporations play a pivotal role in much Third World development. The open question is whether an outright abolition of the notions of corporate personality and limited liability might have serious adverse consequences for a developing nation's ability to attract international investment. Multinationals will cry foul and will threaten capital flight. They will argue that enterprise liability would penalize off-shore investors and make it impossible to evaluate the level of financial risk on any investment or project. The enterprise-liability approach threatens to rewrite the responsibilities undertaken by the parties, for example, by turning a simple technology transfer into a joint venture or partnership. It fails to recognize that affiliates and subsidiaries sometimes *do* operate in an autonomous fashion and threatens to force multinationals to take a role in domestic management beyond what it, or even the host state, desires.

But both the benefits of limited liability and the objections to enterprise liability are overstated. Indeed, some commentators have argued that limited liability could be entirely abolished without serious adverse consequences.[49] The principle of limited liability is an instrument of public policy and is ultimately justifiable only when grounded in the public good. It should therefore be ignored 'when it is used to defeat an overriding public policy.'[50] In the case of Bhopal, the calculus of public benefit points towards a finding of liability. Union Carbide was the primary economic beneficiary of the hazardous activity, and the victims were blameless. The parent company's control of technology, finances, the board of directors, and company management gave it complete control over the direction and operation of its subsidiary. As Judge Seth reasoned, if the parent chooses to abdicate this power, that is as much a reason for imposing liability as denying it.

Especially in the case of hazardous industries and complex multinational business organizations, limited liability and the corporate veil can too easily be used to avoid taking responsibility for risk. By organizing its operations through a network of formally independent subsidiaries, a multinational can widely disperse its assets and place them beyond the reach of the law. Through minimum capitalization, inadequate insurance coverage, and transfer pricing techniques, high-risk subsidiaries can be maintained without assuming financial responsibility. The immunity from liability offered by the corporate veil means that too little is spent on safety precautions and insurance.[51] There is, in fact, evidence that larger corporations have been segregating their more hazardous activities into smaller, financially unaccountable companies in order to shield their assets from damage claims.[52] A doctrine of enterprise liability would, therefore, go some way towards reducing the double standard of industrial safety in the developing world.

From a more individualistic point of view, it may seem 'unfair' to hold one person or firm responsible for the acts of another. But, if we are to take safety seriously, it is necessary to move beyond the narrow notion of individual responsibility embraced by traditional tort and company law. Vicarious or enterprise liability places responsibility upon the party best situated to control risks, and most able to remove or reduce hazards. If the goal is to prevent future Bhopals, it is necessary to broaden our concept of responsibility. The point is not so much to focus upon and 'punish' a single responsible actor, but to develop a principle that will encourage responsible risk management and reduction. On this view, the responsibility of the parent company derives not from fault or wrongful intent, but from its authority, control, and capacity to prevent harm.

The principle of enterprise liability is equally justified from the point of view of compensation. As between the parent company and the subsidiary, it is often impossible to pinpoint responsibility for particular risks. Victims are not in a position to isolate which part of the monolithic concern caused the harm or should have prevented it. To hold the parent liable is often the only way in which to ensure full compensation for these victims and to encourage the parent companies to exercise greater responsibility in controlling its foreign operations.

The concept of multinational enterprise liability is one whose time has come. As J.L. Westbrook argues, it is not an idea that 'the developed world can dismiss as another Third World brainstorm.'[53] It has been affirmed by the U.S. Supreme Court as a legitimate device in a number of taxation cases.[54] However, most advocates of this notion recognize that the principle should not be absolute. For some purposes, the foreign affiliate *will* be an independent company, and to ignore its autonomy in some spheres of operation would be inappropriate and lead to a flight of capital, or at least a slowdown in the rate of new investment. However, in other spheres, especially those concerning workplace safety, hazard communication, and risk management, there should be minimum standards of parent-company responsibility. Thus, for example, David Aronofsky has proposed that there should be a presumption that multinational companies are liable for the activities of their subsidiaries and that this presumption can be rebutted only where the parent corporation can show that 'its conduct and economic status within an enterprise are completely unrelated to the dispute before the court.'[55]

Westbrook similarly acknowledges that the unequivocal adoption of a theory of enterprise liability would probably promote the flight of capital from India, or at least slow the rate of new investment.[56] Instead, he suggests a more modest theory of 'multinational management responsibility' whereby the parent company would be legally responsible only if it failed to live up to certain standards of responsible investment, management, training, and supervision. The source of these duties might be found in the contracts entered into between the parent company and its subsidiary and the host country, or in the emerging international codes of conduct for multinational enterprises.

A suitably defined theory of enterprise liability would not significantly increase investor risk. Indeed, some commentators have argued that the currently chaotic nature of the law on limited liability poses greater potential harm than the 'chilling of investor activity through increased risk of shareholder liability.'[57] A carefully crafted doctrine of multinational liability would put the parties on notice as to what their obligations were and would remove the incentive to allow an orphan operation to run on while imposing unacceptable hazards. The theory might allow, and indeed encourage, the parties to spell out more carefully in the initial agreements what their respective obligations were.

It is too early to say what will be the effect of absolute and enterprise liability decisions on the investment climate in India. In recent negotiations with the Union of India, potential investors have raised the Bhopal judgments as a concern.[58] It has been reported that one company has postponed its investment decision partly out of its concern on these grounds, and the government has been urged to relax the law. While changing the law is not politically feasible at this time, officials have noticed a slowdown in the rate of growth of U.S. investment in India (though not necessarily related to the Bhopal litigation) and acknowledge the possible costs of the Bhopal judgments. However, it should also be realized that these 'radical' reforms have not yet translated into any cost for industry, and as one director of a large multinational said, 'I doubt whether any chemical company in the world defers an investment in India on this ground. Investments are more of an economic question.'[59]

Playing by the Rules: Indian Activism and U.S. Legalism

Another set of criticisms, more ideological and political in nature, were levelled at Justice Seth's decision. These criticisms echoed what Union Carbide had been saying about the Indian legal system throughout the litigation. Relying upon the notion of the 'rule of law,' they suggested that the Indian courts were going beyond 'the law as it is' and basing their pronouncements upon their perception of 'the law as it ought to be.' This approach, argued Union Carbide, demonstrated the arbitrariness and, indeed, 'lawlessness' of the Indian legal system. The principle of absolute liability announced in *Shriram*, the courts' willingness to pierce the corporate veil, and the provision of interim compensation went beyond what Indian courts had done before. From Union Carbide's point of view, these decisions were arbitrary and amounted to judicial legislation. The courts' critics claimed that the judges had gone beyond their traditional function, which is to *apply* rather than *make* the law. UCC lawyers complained that 'you can't go into a country and have them totally change the law in order to convict a specific company. We have a right to full due process.'[60] They argued that the interim compensation decisions showed that the Indian judges were not impartial, but had, in fact, 'descended into the dust of the conflict.' So, following the decision of the High Court, Fali Nariman, Union Carbide's principal Indian lawyer, asked Judge Deo to remove himself from the case because of the bias he had shown in making the original order. Deo's decision, argued Nariman, 'was not only without jurisdiction but wholly arbitrary, perverse and displays a complete prejudgment.'[61]

Much of this rhetoric was strategic positioning by UCC, designed to enhance its bargaining power against the government by implying that any final judgment would be unenforceable against it in the United States. By emphasizing the lack of 'due process,' lawyers for Union Carbide were building an argument against later enforcement of an Indian judgment against Union Carbide in the United States. As Bud Holman, UCC's lead counsel in the litigation, had said earlier, 'In the long run we're going to be better off because if these things they're doing succeed, they'll get a judgment that is unenforceable worldwide and worthless.'[62]

It is true that, during the course of the Bhopal litigation, the Indian judiciary extended the frontiers of Indian law. Yet, while it is technically correct to say that the Indian courts sought to change both the procedural and the substantive law during the Bhopal litigation, such innovations were arguably no more novel than the reforms fashioned by courts in other countries to do justice in particular cases. Judicial innovation is certainly not unusual. It is, in fact, often celebrated by lawyers as proof of the continued viability and responsiveness of the common law to new social problems and changing social values.

The development of a generalized remedy for negligently caused personal injuries was itself an obvious and much-loved judicial innovation, overruling a number of clear past precedents. This change, and others in the law of tort, do apply retroactively, without undermining the legitimacy of the judiciary.[63] Nor did the Indian courts pull out of thin air the notions of absolute liability and enterprise responsibility. These concepts have a respectable toehold in North American common law and legislation. The development of more stringent remedies for injuries that are caused by hazardous activities, and the expansion of responsibility to a larger number of parties and firms are both well within the realm of the 'judicially possible.' To criticize the Indian courts for seizing the opportunity to accelerate the evolution of law in these areas is simply to assert that Indian law should remain static; that it is somehow 'naturally' at its proper point of development.

Similarly, the decisions by Judges Deo and Seth to award interim compensation may have been novel, but they were no more novel than many of the other pretrial remedies that English, U.S., and Canadian courts have invented to protect the rights of individuals facing the prospect of a long and drawn-out trial. For example, in 1975, without precedent and without any legislative basis, English and Canadian courts developed the *Mareva* injunction[64] which essentially allows the court to freeze a defendant's assets in order to preserve them to satisfy any judgment that the plaintiff might obtain. In that same year these courts also developed the *Anton Piller* order[65] which allows a plaintiff to search the defendant's premises for evidence that may be important in upcoming litigation. Again, these orders were essentially forged by judicial legislation, without precedent and without any statutory basis.

Thus, while there is no doubt that the Indian courts did display considerable activism during the course of the Bhopal litigation, they did not so radically depart from the judicial role as Union Carbide suggested. One might also be excused for thinking that it ill-behooved Union Carbide to object to India's judicial creativity when it formed a major part of their argument for having the case dismissed from the United States that the Indian legal system was capable of substantial innovation and that it could effectively deal with a disaster of such large-scale proportions. As Vibhuti Jha, a lawyer for one of the victims' groups, asked, 'If they do not trust the Indian courts, why did they insist the case be tried in India?'[66]

Notwithstanding this defence of the Indian courts, many Western-trained lawyers would still agree with Union Carbide's less-than-flattering description of Indian courts. Indian judges *are* more openly activist than their North American and English counterparts and they *did* seek more energetically to respond to the plight of the victims by pushing the law to its limits. To understand why these efforts might be called 'wrong' it is necessary to understand something about the dominant premisses of North American legal culture.

The political and legal culture of Western countries cherishes the notion of the rule of law and the idea of the separation of legislative and judicial power. Because we value individual freedom, we tend to distrust the authority of the state and require that it be exercised only in accordance with the 'rule of law.' What this means is that our legal rights can be affected only by properly enacted legislation, and that state power, including the power of the courts, can be exercised only in accordance with previously announced rules. The basic idea is that judges, who are unelected and unaccountable, must be content to *apply*, but never *make* the law. They are required to be unbiased and impartial, and ideally their decisions must conform to the rules as they are written in legislation or found in previous judicial precedents. While sometimes the law will appear to be unjust, it is thought to be better in the long run to leave legal reform to elected legislatures. The expression 'hard cases make bad law' ultimately means that if judges were licensed to base their decisions simply upon their personal views of the justice of a case, the 'law' will simply wither away and be replaced by the arbitrary rule of personal authority.

This is an appealing model of justice. Who, after all, disagrees with the notions of individual liberty and equality before the law? Who, after all, would be content to leave the formulation of law entirely to a small number of unelected judges? But the model is overstated and, perhaps more importantly, there is a real ethnocentricity in imposing the North American legalistic understanding of the judicial function upon Indian courts. The wholesale application of the ideology of legalism to the Indian legal system betrays a failure to appreciate the workings of that system and ultimately amounts to a form of cultural imperialism.

In the first place, the rule of law ideal tends to overstate the ability of pre-existing 'legal rules' to determine concrete results. It tends to imply that courts never 'make' law, but only apply it. Nothing could be farther from the truth. Most of our basic legal concepts were fashioned, in the first place, by the judiciary, and over time have been modified by the judiciary. Certainly in the context of the Bhopal case, the crucial questions concerning the standard of care, the scope of the corporate veil, and the ultimate allocation of legal responsibility rely on concepts that find their origin in the common law. Even where there appear to be well-developed legal rules, these rules are stated in general terms. The 'open-textured' and ambiguous nature of legal language leaves enormous room for human choice.[67] Indeed, many critics of North American law insist that such choices lie at the heart of the legal system and that ideas about precedent, *stare decisis*, and the rule of law are little more than ideological artefacts designed to obscure the fact that judges wield enormous personal power. These critics argue that 'legalism' in fact delivers the opposite of what it promises. By portraying judicial decisions as the result only of legal 'logic,' legalism tends to obscure the *politics* of law, and thus privileges judges and the legal system from criticism. Legalism remains blind to the fact that law is not about logic, but is about the struggle between interests, and it closes its eyes to the fact that that struggle is carried out on an unequal footing. Instead of improving the welfare of the disadvantaged, the purely formal notion of equality embraced by legalism simply entrenches the existing maldistribution of wealth and power in society. By characterizing justice simply as a process of 'playing by the rules,' legalism simply excludes from legal comprehension those very aspects of social life that ensure injustice.

More importantly, the simple application of Western legal ideology to judge the Indian system is ethnocentric. While formally built on the basis of imported English law, the Indian legal system also retained the more flexible and accommodating characteristics of traditional Indian law and society. As the foremost U.S. authority on Indian law has explained, the country's modern legal system is in fact an 'indigenous synthesis' of foreign and local elements, modern and traditional features.[68] Indian judges do not adhere so closely to precedent as do their English or even U.S. counterparts. The system has retained considerable flexibility and diversity when compared to Western models, remaining open to fresh ideas, adopting and absorbing new elements as needed. Indeed, Indian courts are among the most 'activist' in the world, without sacrificing credibility or legitimacy.

While many judges in India are trained in the methods and values of English and U.S. law, and thus share a commitment to the notion of the rule of law, they have also been unwilling to close their eyes to the suffering of Indian people, or to ignore the failure of law to reduce that suffering. In their effort to make law work for the poor, Indian judges have therefore departed considerably from the traditional positivist or legalistic understanding of law, rejecting the 'bureaucratic tradition' of rule-bound adjudication. As former chief justice P.N. Bhagwati said, legalism is a myth designed to insulate judges from popular scrutiny.'[69] Instead, many Indian judges perceive their task to be that of alleviating human suffering and achieving social justice. As he said, 'The judges in India have asked themselves the question: can judges really escape addressing themselves to substantial questions of social justice? Can they ... simply follow the legal text when they are aware that their actions will perpetuate inequality and injustice? Can they restrict their inquiry into law and life within the narrow confines of a narrowly defined rule of law?'[70]

Thus, in seeking to give some substance to the promises of law, Indian judges may frequently go beyond the judicial role as it is understood in England and North America, openly pursuing social justice. To characterize this activity as 'lawless' or even 'illegitimate' is to misunderstand the role of the courts in Indian society and to impose a narrow, culturally specific, and potentially misleading definition of 'law' upon the institutions of another country. Indeed, it is through their judicial activism that Indian courts, and especially the Supreme Court, have been able to maintain their tremendous popular and political legitimacy.[71] Perhaps only lawyers could suppose that by trying to enhance the welfare of the poor the courts are behaving 'illegitimately.'

Finally, the circumstances of the Bhopal victims were such that the courts were required to be more 'activist.' They were caught between two monolithic litigants and had themselves almost no say in their fate. There is no room in these circumstances for the assumption that the courts merely need to mediate an adversarial dispute between formally equal parties. Instead, as is often the case in India, the courts were called upon to acknowledge the powerlessness of the victims and to act on their behalf. As lawyer Vibhuti Jha said on behalf of the Zahreeli Gas Kand Sangharsh Morcha: 'The victims have absolutely no say in the legal battle. In a case of such a magnitude, if the plaintiff Union of India falters or indulges in certain acts of omission or comission ... it becomes a bounden duty of the court trying the case to safeguard the interests of the victims. In such a case the court cannot be expected to be a silent spectator or simply an umpire, but has to undertake judicial activism in order to do justice to the hapless victims.'[72]

Perhaps not surprisingly, Judge Deo refused Union Carbide's request that he remove himself from the case, denying that his actions were biased. As he explained, his interim order was made in response to a suggestion from the High Court and was not an arbitrary or injudicious exercise of power. He also thanked UCC for providing him with 'an opportunity for introspection ... 'which we Indians have ingrained in us by philosophical and cultural heritage according to which prudence dictates to be equanimous in examining even our own life dispassionately from position of a trayastha i.e. as a third person.'[73]

10

Settling a Dispute

Following Judge Seth's dramatic decision in April 1988, Union Carbide repeated its now familiar line that the order was 'bound to lead to further litigation.' The company appealed the order to the Supreme Court and also carried on with its application to remove Judge Deo from the case.

Notwithstanding the fact that the High Court had upheld the result of Judge Deo's previous decision on interim relief, it also acceded to UCC's petition, and on 13 October 1988 it ordered that the case be transferred to Judge N.K. Jain, now the fifth District Court judge to preside over the Bhopal litigation.[1] In ordering the transfer the High Court did not expressly accept UCC's charge of bias, but it did agree that Judge Deo's conduct of the litigation could at least raise an apprehension that he had prejudged the case and that his 'intense empathic response' had overpowered his judicial reasoning. The High Court's concern, of course, was that the charge of bias would be used by Union Carbide against any later attempt by India to enforce a judgment in the United States. Oddly, the High Court felt that the gravest defect in Judge Deo's decision was that he had not gone far enough. Instead of recording a clear finding of liability against Union Carbide, said the appellate court, Deo had resorted to 'meaningless rhetoric' in searching for a basis for his order of interim compensation. Lawyers for Union Carbide were further emboldened by Judge Deo's dismissal, publicly declaring that even the Indian courts now admitted that the proceedings were without due process.

In addition to these tactics, Union Carbide continued to explore the possibility of circumventing the Indian courts by once again reopening the question of a final settlement. They reasoned that the necessity of paying interim compensation could thus be avoided and the damage figures apparently relied upon by Judges Deo and Seth might thus be reduced. Through their Indian lawyer, Fali Nariman, Union Carbide stressed that the Indian government had 'demonstrated repeatedly that it has no interest in resolving [the victims'] claims by settlement.'[2] Government officials responded that UCC was simply trying to subvert the process that had been established by the Bhopal Act and sought an injunction restraining individual settlement negotiations. On 29 June, before he was removed from the case, Judge Deo had ordered Union Carbide to refrain from seeking settlements without the consent of the Indian government.

Neither judge's order, however, put an end to the settlement strategy. In July 1988, a Connecticut court ruled that Union Carbide could settle cases in the United States and denied that U.S. courts were required to recognize the Bhopal Act or Judge Deo's injunction against individual settlements. Throughout September 1988, U.S. attorneys armed with the Connecticut decision purported to be settling their clients' cases with Union Carbide in the United States. They began to send large numbers of letters to the victims in Bhopal, reminding them that 'your legal representative (head of your family) engaged me under written retainer' to represent them in the litigation. The letter then explained how the case had been dismissed from the United States but went on to explain that the U.S. lawyers were still involved:

I was then invited by the lawyers for the government of India to join your claim in their lawsuit [in India]. I declined on the grounds that too many claims were involved (some 500,000). I reasoned that your claim would be lost amongst such a large number of claims and that you would never hear of it again. Additionally, I felt that even if a sum were awarded or a settlement made, the court would order the money divided among the 500,000 and your share, if you ever got it, would be so small it would be of no financial help to your family at all!

Instead I filed in the Court of the District Judge in Bhopal, on behalf of your family, a separate lawsuit, which lawsuit was independent of the litigation filed by the GOI. This way the damages awarded or the settlement made would have to be paid directly to you and not paid to the GOI to divide as it saw fit. Very clearly, this move insures that immediately awards are made or settlements concluded you will quickly, and directly be paid your lump sum compensation money.

On the 21st of September, 1988 in New York City, I conferred with the attorneys representing the defendant, Union Carbide Corporation. Mr. Bud Holman, Chief Attorney on the case went over your claim with me and he found no difficulty with its validity. The claim is recognized and Union Carbide is willing to pay it as quickly as possible![3]

This letter concluded by explaining that the family would need to forward documentary proof of their claim, which would be presented to Union Carbide, which would then make a settlement offer as quickly as possible. Government lawyers were infuriated by this intermeddling, fearing that it would undermine their position on appeal and interfere with their own ongoing settlement negotiations with Union Carbide. They sought further injunctions ordering the company to put an end to independent settlements.

The Settlement

Meanwhile, the appeal of Judge Seth's decision proceeded to the Indian Supreme Court. This was the first time this court obtained jurisdiction in the Bhopal case and, once again, the litigation was to take a remarkable turn.

In the Supreme Court the procedural and substantive issues merged. Government lawyers apparently decided that the only way to support Judge Seth's interlocutory judgment was to demonstrate that any final decision would clearly place liability upon UCC. They thus asked the Court to consider, 'as a pure question of law the liability of the UCC for damages for the gas leak disaster at Bhopal.'[4] The appeal thus assumed the proportions of a full-blown trial on the merits. All the parties were clearly unhappy with this development. The factual basis for the arguments was insufficiently developed to enable the Government of India to present its arguments, to allow UCC to respond, or to allow the Court to decide. The government was forced into a position of making a legal argument that, regardless of how the accident happened, and based solely on UCC's ownership of its subsidiary, the company was legally responsible for the accident.

Attorney General Parasaran began his arguments with the strong assertion that, on the basis of the evidence adduced so far, Union Carbide was liable under the rule in *Rylands* v *Fletcher*, especially as expanded in the *Shriram* decision. Even if the company's sabotage theory was correct, he argued, an employer is nevertheless responsible for the acts of its employees, especially where the risks are so obvious and the likely consequences so serious. He referred to the expansion of legal liability for personal injuries in England and the United States where, 'reflecting the moral, social and ethical values of the shift of their legal systems from protection of private property to protection of communities,' these countries had gradually been moving towards a general rule of strict liability for hazardous industries. He challenged the Supreme

Court to 'choose between judicial valour and judicial timidity.'[5]

For its part, Union Carbide objected to every point of India's legal argument, continuing to refuse even to agree to abide by any Supreme Court judgment.[6] It argued that the interim order was premature, pointing out that the case had not yet even reached discovery. It disputed the authority of the Indian courts to import English rules regarding interim compensation. It objected to the factual theory presupposed by Parasaran's argument, to the introduction of evidence in appellate proceedings, and to the legal theory presented by the government. Union Carbide's Indian attorney, Fali Nariman, argued that the Central Bureau of Investigation (CBI) had prevented Union Carbide from interviewing employees and collecting other evidence for its defence. In response to the government's reliance on *Rylands*, he repeated UCC's allegation that the disaster was a deliberate act of a third party, that the Bhopal facility was a 'natural use' of the land, and that it was properly licensed and in compliance with all relevant government regulations. He urged that there was simply no evidence that Union Carbide could have done more to prevent the disaster. During the course of Parasaran's argument, Justice Venkataramia reminded him of the *Shriram* case, suggesting that 'the only solution is that if you can't control the devil, don't manufacture the devil.'[7] Nariman in turn attacked the *Shriram* judgment as politically motivated judicial legislation that was out of line with Indian law. 'Even assuming the law of torts could grow,' he argued, 'it had to grow from precedent, and not from quantum leaps which are tantamount to judicial legislation.'[8] Nariman continued to insist that UCC had no control or authority over UCIL and that it was impermissible in the case to lift the corporate veil. He repeated the company's objection to Judge Deo's order on the basis that he had no authority to require interim compensation and that he had 'descended into the arena' and become 'touched by the dust of conflict.'[9] He insisted that Union Carbide could not be required to pay compensation without allowing its lawyers the opportunity to challenge the reliability of the evidence, the number of victims, and the severity of their injuries. Innumerable claims, he argued, were 'bogus.'

Then the case took its most dramatic turn so far. On 14 February 1989, after four months of written and oral argument, and without warning, Chief Justice Rajinder S. Pathak interrupted the proceedings and ordered Union Carbide to pay $470 million in damages.[10] He said that, in light of 'the enormity of the human suffering occasioned by the Bhopal gas disaster and the pressing urgency to provide immediate and substantial relief to victims of the disaster,' the case was 'pre-eminently fit for an overall settlement.'[11] Justice Pathak's order was in final settlement of all claims and would discharge Union Carbide from all future civil or criminal liability. Both sides greeted the ruling with enthusiasm. The victims, observers, and the general public were astounded.

That the final judgment was truly 'imposed' by the court is unlikely. While Indian courts do involve themselves more intimately in the litigation process than do their U.S. or Canadian counterparts, they do not impose settlements on the parties. Instead, the 'judgment' was, in fact, a deal that had already been worked out by the lawyers (in later years, even the Supreme Court would refer to its judgment as a 'court-assisted settlement').[12] The government and Union Carbide had been engaged in a series of secret talks for several weeks. Both accepted the court ruling immediately, without consulting their clients, showing that an agreement had already been struck behind closed doors. Indeed, one month earlier, Rajkumar Keswani, the journalist who had warned of the disaster before it occurred, had written an article in *Newstime*, predicting the exact terms of the settlement. Keswani had speculated that Union Carbide had the upper hand in the negotiations because the litigation had been going in its favour. The U.S. Court of Appeals had rescinded the requirement that Union Carbide submit to an Indian judgment, thus dampening the prospect of easy enforcement of a large final judgment. The Madhya Pradesh High Court had reduced the amount of interim compensation and had transferred Judge Deo from the case, allowing Union Carbide to create 'a favourable atmosphere for itself by publicizing that even the Indian courts feel that the Bhopal judge was biased in granting the relief against the multinational.'[13] Keswani noted that the only sticking-point was that Union Carbide was demanding dismissal of the criminal charges against it, and the amount offered would fall short of the high expectations of the victims, further revealing the incompetence of the government, which was facing national elections.

Thus, the interposition of the Supreme Court into the settlement negotiations was a formal move designed to enhance the credibility of the settlement and to protect the parties – especially the government – from criticism. A national election was approaching in India and, as one government official said about the settlement, 'We feel that once the Supreme Court says it's fair, the government will be on a strong wicket.'[14]

The settlement seemed clearly to be a victory for Union Carbide. On the day it was announced, the price of its shares on the New York stock market rose by $2. The amount of the award was paltry in comparison to the government's claim for $3.3 billion, and Union Carbide's share was, in the end, no more than the current value of the $350 million for which it had offered to settle the suit in 1986. It was less than the $500 million to $650 million lump sum that Union Carbide was rumoured to have offered in November 1987. These negotiations had collapsed in the face of protests organized by victims' groups and other social activists.

The Politics of a Settlement

Why settle? With elections approaching, the litigation was clearly a political liability for the Indian government. The case had still not come to trial in the District Court, and the litigation promised to drag on indefinitely. Even if it had won on the issue of liability, it is not clear what amount of damages the government would recover, or whether it would be able to enforce a final judgment in the U.S. courts. UCC had refused to undertake to submit to the jurisdiction of the Indian Supreme Court and had intimated that it would resist enforcement of any judgment in the United States, assuming (with some justification) that there was a good chance that U.S. courts would view such an order with suspicion and as failing to comply with the 'due process' requirement.

Opposition politicians, victims' groups, and social activists immediately condemned the settlement as woefully inadequate and simply confirming the fact that Third World life is cheap. The settlement provoked mass protests by victims' groups and prompted the opposition parties to walk out of Parliament. Twenty-five hundred survivors, mostly women, made the journey by train from Bhopal to Delhi, marching under the banner of the Gas Peedit Mahila Udyog Sangathan and staging a *dharna* at the Supreme Court. The Indian paper *The Patriot* described how many of these victims then marched upon Union Carbide's Delhi office, ransacking it within ten minutes. When they were confronted by the police, 'one of the women snatched a sten gun from an armed guard, then threw it back at him. Another chased a policeman until he jumped into a passing bus for safety.'[15] Several months later, at a similar demonstration in Bhopal, the police struck back, injuring three hundred people in a *lathi* (bamboo cane) charge.

Two prominent former Supreme Court judges joined in the condemnation of the settlement. 'The multinational has won and the people of India have lost,' stated former chief justice P.N. Bhagwati. 'UCC has got away cheaply at the victims' cost. The Supreme Court has lost the opportunity of advancing human rights jurisprudence from the Third World viewpoint and failed to meet the expectations of the people of India.'[16] And, in his usual inimitable style, former Supreme Court justice Krishna

Iyer said: 'Obviously the judges shared the concern for the victims and were worried by the tantalizing length of a looming, looney litigation with a foreign jurisdiction and keenan [Judge Keenan] jurisprudence to upset Bharat [Indian] justice. Probably, Carbide blackmail, in the context of UCI assets being but a poor sum, that battles would be waged in the U.S. to delay and defeat the Delhi decree oppressed the naive psyche of the brethren into greeting any settlement as a fair adjustment.'[17]

The critics of the settlement were, in turn, chastised for having unrealistically built up the hopes of the victims, being insensitive to their immediate needs, and placing the desire for a novel legal precedent above the necessity of alleviating suffering. Legal commentator Devendra Nath Dwivedi lamented that one of the unfortunate by-products of Indian judicial activism has been the growth of 'legal populism' and the rise of a caste of legal politicians who judge the court in non-legal terms. These sociolegal activists, he argued, have their priorities wrong. 'For the activists the important things are not the victims but their cause; not human suffering but the struggle to alleviate it. For them the rights of the human beings and human rights jurisprudence are more important than the human beings themselves.'[18] The Supreme Court, he argued, could have taken a legalistic or humane approach to the suffering it saw in Bhopal. To do both would have been impossible, and by opting for immediate compensation the Court made the right choice.

Nor were the victims unanimous in their condemnation of the settlement. The social-action groups divided over the issue, the Zahreeli Gas Kand Sangharsh Morcha reasoning that the certainty of some compensation now offered a more attractive prospect than the uncertainty of continued and drawn-out litigation. Many of the victims, like Kailash Pawar, had been sick and unemployed since the disaster. Pawar, twenty-seven, was so heavily hit by the gas that he had been taken for dead and placed in a truck full of corpses. Frequent trips to the hospital and expensive drugs had driven him and his family, and many like them, to the edge of starvation. Furious with both UCC and the government, and dissatisfied with the amount of the settlement, he nevertheless felt that 'at least there is some hope we will get the money.'[19]

The basis upon which the settlement was calculated was not known for some time. Its adequacy was attacked by comparing it to the Johns-Manville asbestos settlement of $2.5 billion (to 60,000 victims), and the A.H. Robbins (Dalkon Shield) settlement of $2.9 billion (to 195,000 victims). Critics alleged that the documentation of injuries was not complete and that the figures used radically underestimated the number of victims and the amount that would be needed to care for them. At the time of the settlement, fewer than 30,000 of the victims had been medically examined. Little was known about the long-term effects of the poison gas, how many more would die, and what new injuries would surface over time.

Many observers felt that the settlement simply confirmed the power of multinationals. The head of India's Consumer Guidance Society and a long-time advocate for consumer rights in India, saw the settlement as merely one more manifestation of the power of the multinational business lobby.[20] With no strong middle class, environmental and consumer issues simply do not figure prominently in the government's calculations, and India remains a dumping-ground for hazardous substances such as chemicals and drugs. Officials in the Department of Industry confirmed that multinationals had been responding negatively to the legal developments surrounding the Bhopal case, perhaps postponing investment decisions on this ground. Indeed, business lobbies had been urging the government to disavow its position on strict liability and multinational responsibility. And while this was not politically realistic at the time, officials confirmed that the government might 'reassess its position' on these matters in the future.[21] The settlement was thus condemned as a sell-out by both the government and the Court and as confirming the 'political economy of technological feudalism.'[22] As one commentator concluded, 'There seems to be no other explanation except that it [the government] desperately wants to propitiate foreign multinationals on which it has started relying more and more as the potent instruments for the fulfillment of its social, economic and political objectives ... The settlement sends out a clear message: multinationals can operate freely in the Indian market.'[23] Indeed, while relations between the Government of India and Union Carbide had been adversarial and antagonistic, following the settlement relations became amicable. UCC was given permission to liquidate its assets in Bombay.

Indian citizens were not the only people unhappy with the settlement. So were the U.S. attorneys who had watched the course of the litigation since it had been sent back to India. When word of the settlement hit the U.S. press, they were once again galvanized into action. On 15 February, the day after the settlement, Chesley and Bailey filed a new application with Judge Keenan. They suggested that he still retained jurisdiction over the case and, since the funds for the award were to come from the United States, he could properly scrutinize the settlement to ensure its propriety and the manner of its distribution. In particular, they suggested that he should pay them their fees out of the amount. They argued that they had rendered considerable services to the victims and to the Government of India during the course of the litigation and that, if they were not compensated for that effort, the Government of India would be unjustly enriched: 'if the Court does not grant the plaintiff's attorneys application for fees,' they argued, 'the practice of utilizing the services of American attorneys without any expectation of compensating them would be condoned and encouraged.'[24] Judge Keenan, who had never been particularly impressed with the conduct of these lawyers, refused to grant their application.

In light of the public furore over the settlement, the government felt compelled to issue a statement to the press, justifying its decision.[25] It claimed that the settlement was based on an accurate estimate of both the number of victims and the amounts necessary to provide for their injuries. It asserted that it had accepted the settlement figure because it was adjudged to be fair by the Supreme Court, and asked, 'Where else could the government go for a larger sum? Nowhere in India, of course. And to try to return to the courts in the U.S.A. would have been akin to a vote of no confidence in our own judicial system.' The government explained that Union Carbide had been intransigent and claimed that 'it was the government's assumption of "parens patriae" of the Bhopal victims and its tough stand which obliged UCC to raise its figure.' It pointed out that the case had not even reached discovery, and that to pursue the litigation would 'in the most optimistic circumstances need anywhere from 15 to 25 more years.' And, 'as for the government paying out the money first and claiming it from Union Carbide Corporation later, this would amount to giving UCC an interest-free loan for meeting its liability for the duration of the trial.' It claimed that the victims had been heard through various petitions to the court and concluded that 'if dealing with public interest litigations is the hallmark of judicial activism, the Supreme Court's Bhopal decision is a step forward in innovative judicial activism for which the court deserves to be praised. It is a matter of pride that where foreign courts refused to take a stand, our Supreme Court dealt with a difficult matter effectively and courageously.'

Vociferous public criticism was also levelled at the Supreme Court, causing one Supreme Court justice, E.S. Venkataramiah, to threaten to resign. 'Every day you open the newspaper and you find article after article; photograph after photograph against the court.'[26] Such criticism, he said, was 'worse than impeachment.' The Court also felt compelled to justify its decision and, on 4 May 1989, it issued a 'judgment' explaining the settlement.[27] The Court explained that its primary consideration had been the necessity of immediate relief for the victims. While the

Court acknowledged that important legal principles were at stake, it could not justify the length of the litigation. The 'niceties of legal principles were greatly overshadowed by the pressing problems of very survival for a large number of victims.'[28] And, in a stinging criticism of its detractors and the social activists in Bhopal, the Court said: 'It is indeed a matter for national introspection that public response to this great tragedy which affected a large number of poor and helpless persons limited itself to the expression of understandable anger against the industrial enterprise but did not channel itself in any effort to put together a public supported relief fund so the victims were not left in distress.'[29] The court also remarked that it would not be influenced by 'agitational measures.' 'Here, many persons and social action groups claim to speak for the victims, quite a few in different voices. The factual allegations on which they rest their approach are conflicting in some areas and it becomes difficult to distinguish truth from falsehood and half truth, and to distinguish as to who speaks for whom.'[30]

The Court explained that it had based its compensation calculations upon figures submitted to it by the parties, derived from previous settlement negotiations. It had apparently accepted Union Carbide's position that it would not pay more than the $350 million that it had offered two years previously (plus interest). The Court felt that this figure would provide reasonable compensation based on the estimated number of deaths (2,660) and injuries (30,000–40,000) accepted in the High Court. The Court felt that it was reasonable to discount the total number of claims because 'doubts that a sizeable number of them are either without any just basis or were otherwise exaggerated could not be ruled out.'[31] It pointed out that the total figure would provide compensation to the victims on a higher scale than the sums conventionally awarded in India in personal-injury and fatal-accident cases. Finally, the Court recognized that the opportunity to address important social, technological, and legal issues had been lost. But, it concluded, 'in the present case, the compulsions of the need for immediate relief to tens of thousands of suffering victims could not, in our opinion, wait till these questions, vital though they be, are resolved ... The tremendous suffering of thousands of persons compelled us to move into the direction of immediate relief which, we thought, should not be subordinated to the uncertain promises of law.'[32]

The Adequacy of the Settlement

The total amount of the settlement was 7,500 million rupees, which was the equivalent of $470 million (U.S.) at the exchange rate in 1989. This sum was intended to provide compensation for all of the victims in the different categories specified under the Bhopal Act, including the families of those who had died and the victims who had suffered permanent disability, temporary disability, and other forms of damage.

The Supreme Court based its settlement calculations upon the injury figures used by Justice Seth in the Madhya Pradesh High Court. These figures were, in turn, taken from a 1987 study done by the Indian Council for Medical Research. Of the total amount of the settlement, the Court concluded that the compensation required for an estimated 55,000 individuals who had been killed or injured in the disaster would be 5,000 million rupees. Of this amount, the Court first allotted 700 million rupees to compensate the families of 3,000 victims who the Court accepted had died in the gas leak. On average, each of these families would receive just over 233,000 rupees ($14,500). In the second category were 30,000 individuals who had suffered permanent disability as a result of their exposure to the gas. To this category the Court allocated 2,500 million rupees. While the severity of the injuries suffered by the victims in this category varied from minor to complete disability, the average award would be about 83,000 rupees, or $5,200. Third, the Court estimated that 1,000 million rupees would be required to compensate 20,000 victims who had suffered injuries resulting in temporary disabilities, providing an average payment of 50,000 rupees, or $3,125, each. To these figures the Court added on a sum of 800 million rupees to provide for an estimated 2,000 individuals who had suffered injuries of 'utmost severity.' Victims in this category would receive compensation of up to 400,000 rupees, or $25,000.

In addition to the figures for individual personal injuries, the Court specified that 250 million rupees ($15.6 million) would be used for the creation of facilities to provide specialized medical treatment and rehabilitation. Finally, a sum of 2,250 million rupees ($140.6 million) was to be set aside for another 150,000 claims, including less serious physical injuries, losses of livestock and other property damage, business losses, temporary dislocations, and other future injuries.

In assessing the adequacy of the settlement, two basic questions are immediately apparent. First, did the Court have the numbers of claims and victims right; and, second, if the numbers are right, are the amounts adequate to provide for the care and rehabilitation of the victims? Given the paucity of information on the number of victims and the severity of their injuries, neither of these questions is easy to answer, but several points deserve to be highlighted.

In the first place, while the Court had argued that the amounts were generous by Indian standards, it was those standards themselves that the victims had hoped to challenge. Those who had viewed the Bhopal litigation as an opportunity to alter the devaluation of human life in India were thus enormously disappointed. The individual amounts are minuscule in comparison with amounts awarded for similar injuries to persons in Western countries. And, even by Indian standards, there was no guarantee that the amounts would be adequate. Awards to the families of deceased victims might produce, after inflation, annual amounts of about $900 for twenty years, with nothing left at the end of that period. Awards to those who were permanently disabled might generate about $350 per year. These amounts can hardly be called 'generous.' While the lump sums are more than the ranges specified in Indian workers' compensation legislation, they would produce far less than the annual wage of an average Indian factory worker. Indeed, the income from the awards to individuals would likely fall short of total average per-capita income in India, and scarcely exceeds nationwide individual consumption.[33] Thus, while the awards might replace some income loss, they would certainly not guarantee the future cost of subsistence and medical care. Nor did they include any amount for pain and suffering, a usual head of damages at common law. Finally, the award included no sums to restore the community infrastructure, to provide for housing or job creation, or to reimburse the government for its own losses, or expenditures on the relief effort, which, even before the provision of monetary compensation to the victims, was estimated at about $90 to $100 million.[34] The final figure, then, could hardly be said to reflect the full social cost of the disaster at Bhopal.

Second, even these modest figures assumed that there would be no new claims or injuries. In its settlement calculations the Court had been forced to extrapolate from extremely tentative data, for the medical assessments of the victims had barely begun. Of the 600,000 claims that had been initiated, only 350,000 had so far been documented, and fewer than 30,000 of those had been medically evaluated. On the basis of this very limited information the Court estimated that only 3,000 of the claims would be for fatal injuries and just over 50,000 for serious injuries resulting in temporary or permanent disability. When these figures are combined with the Court's estimate of 150,000 minor injuries, we see that it had apparently discounted entirely approximately 400,000 claims. Nor did the award include any amount to hedge against the possibility of future contingencies such as the possibility that MIC exposure might have undetected long-term effects on human health or the environment.

What of the 400,000 claims that had been entirely ignored? Many of these were no doubt redundant, fraudulent, or at least unsubstantiated.

Social and medical activists asserted, however, that in the wake of the settlement the government had moved from exaggeration to minimization of the effects of the disaster – tailoring the size of the disaster to the amount of the settlement. They remained convinced that the government figures radically underestimated the extent of the suffering by minimizing the number of victims and the seriousness of the injuries. Even those assessments that had been done, charged the critics, were based on faulty and inadequate procedures. Doctors were processing 20–25 patients per day, only taking x-rays and doing urinalysis, rather than giving proper pulmonary- and respiratory-function tests, biopsies, and immune-system diagnoses. The critics argued that many of the victims who had been classified as only mildly injured were already beginning to show signs of worsening condition. These included tuberculosis and other respiratory complications, premature cataracts and degenerative eye diseases, and gastro-intestinal problems.[35] They also objected to the fact that government had closed down all but two of the medical facilities, thus making treatment and proof of injuries more difficult for the victims.

The figures employed by the Court should be contrasted with the estimates provided by some of the activist groups. Some agencies have placed the death toll at 20,000 persons, conceding that it is nearly impossible to link death definitively to MIC exposure, but pointing to epidemiological studies that indicate a vastly increased mortality rate in Bhopal.[36] An ICMR study conducted in 1988 found that the mortality rate in the gas-exposed areas in Bhopal was 12 in 1,000, as compared to an average in the city of 7 in 1,000. Infant mortality in Bhopal was 112 in 1,000, compared to 90 in 1,000 throughout the state of Madhya Pradesh generally. In late 1989, 43 volunteer doctors studied a sample of 400 Bhopal residents and discovered evidence of respiratory, gastro-intestinal, neuro-muscular, neuro-skeletal, gynaecological, and psychological injury far in excess of that officially estimated. Their report concluded that the government had 'grossly underestimated' the nature and extent of the injuries suffered by the gas-affected population.[37]

On the basis of these non-governmental studies, both the Bhopal Group for Information and Action and the International Coalition for Justice in Bhopal estimated that there were approximately 200,000 injured victims in Bhopal and that the cost of medical care alone would be 18 billion rupees ($1.125 billion). This sum would provide 250 rupees per month ($16) to provide medical treatment to the victims for a period of 30 years. The Zahreeli Gas Kand Morcha's estimate, based upon a study done by the Council on International and Public Affairs, was in excess of 50 billion rupees (the $3 billion originally claimed in the action).[38]

Nor could the victims rely on the continued assistance of government should the settlement prove to be seriously inadequate. While the Supreme Court had denied government the right to reimburse its own expenses from the compensation fund, in the wake of the settlement the government slashed its estimated expenditure on the relief plan from 3.7 billion to 1.6 billion rupees.

After the Settlement

Union Carbide complied with the Supreme Court's order in March 1989, producing bank certificates to prove payment. However, in the meantime, victims' organizations kept up the pressure against the settlement and began to file petitions to overturn the order. Following the settlement, Abdul Jabbar Khan, the organizer of the Bhopal Gas Peedit Mahila Udyog Sangathan, had threatened, 'We'll file 10,000 individual applications before the Supreme Court seeking a review of the decision.'[39] Activists began to pursue other tactics as well. Several shareholders sought (unsuccessfully) at Union Carbide's annual general meeting in the United States to have the corporation increase the amount of compensation. Activist groups in India and the United States, including the Bhopal Action Resource Center, organized a twenty-seven-day tour of the United States by three Bhopal victims. On 27 April, these victims tried to enter the Hyatt Regency hotel in Houston, Texas, where Union Carbide's meeting was being held, but were arrested for trespass.[40] While Union Carbide expressed its regret about these incidents, it was also outraged at the tactics adopted by the activist groups. Earl Slack, Union Carbide's assistant director of corporate communications, said it was 'far-out speculation' to think that the settlement would be nullified. 'We think that by using the victims for political ends, the activists are making them victims for the second time.'[41]

The Renewed Fight for Interim Compensation

Other victims' groups, exhausted by the litigation, accepted the settlement and devoted their attention to the immediate disbursement of interim compensation to the victims pending finalization of the settlement. People were still dying in Bhopal. Four days after the settlement, MIC claimed the life of Ashiq Ali; he died in the Hamidia hospital of multiple organ damage, liver enlargement and pulmonary oedema.[42] His condition had been steadily deteriorating since the accident. Ultimately he had been forced to quit his job. His family had spent their meagre earnings on medicines that seemed to have no effect. Thousands of other families were in similarly desperate situations. In addition, there were approximately 200 orphaned children in different institutions in Bhopal who lost all their relatives in the disaster, and the three major hospitals in the city were continuing to treat about 1,000 MIC patients a day.[43]

Yet, even interim relief was still not to be forthcoming. There were two reasons for this. First, the anti-settlement forces had not exhausted all their appeals and the government was wary of distributing funds that it might later be ordered to return to Union Carbide. Second, the necessary infrastructure was simply not in place. Hampered by a lack of funds, and virtually suspended pending the outcome of the challenges to the settlement, the development of claims-adjudication facilities and processes practically came to a halt. As P.D. Muley, the chief claims commissioner, lamented, 'We have no infrastructure to start our work.'[44] While the commission had been promised 5 million rupees, it had received only 1 million. 'Barring my appointment and the setting up of a nucleus office, not much progress has been made. And all this while, people who need help fast have been suffering,' Muley said.

The slow progress of the relief effort was not solely the result of bureaucratic inertia or a lack of will. The difficulties must also be traced to the structural features of the system created by the commission. Under the scheme, the disbursement of compensation would be accomplished in two stages. The commission would first have to complete the documentation, evaluation, and categorization of claims. Going strictly by the formal procedures established by the commission, each claim would have to go through forty stages, involving clerks, medical evaluators, and adjudicators. The commission had to develop a special code of procedure for the adjudication of claims that balanced efficiency and fairness. Doing so was especially problematic. To utilize a formal adversarial model would simply replicate the problems of the tort system. The commissioner estimated that the use of a formal model would take twenty-five years to process all the claims. Even assuming that the more than 500,000 claims could be adjudicated as quickly as one per hour, it would take over 200 work years to complete the task. The expense to the individual claimants would exclude all but the richest from the process. The delay would mean that compensation amounts would not go to relieving the misery of the victims, but merely to enriching their descendants. On the other hand, a failure to insist on proof would be equally impossible. Some of the claims were fraudulent or exaggerated. As the principal secretary of the relief department said, 'We cannot take the goodness of humanity for granted. People tend to exploit disaster situations. We must assume the worst in order to protect the genuine victims.'[45]

At the same time that it ordered the settlement, the Supreme Court sought also to hasten the compensation process. It ordered the government to come up with a scheme for both interim and final compensation of the Bhopal victims. But progress was slow. Final compensation was still years away, and practically no interim payments had been made. With more than half a million claimants to evaluate and too few medical resources to complete the task, the compensation process became bogged down.

In response to this delay, the victims brought a further set of petitions to the Supreme Court to obtain relief. The petitioners included Bharatiya Nav Chetna Manch, the Bhopal Gas Peedit Mahila Udyog Sangathan, and the Zahreeli Gas Kand Morcha. On 12 April 1989, Shanti Bushan, for the victims, suggested that every family should receive 1,000 rupees per month. The attorney general replied that the Government of India was not responsible for the disaster and had no legal liability to pay compensation on its own. He conceded that, as head of a welfare state, the government would provide some assistance, but that this obligation was not enforceable in the courts.

The Court, which had already put its popular authority on the line in assisting the government to settle the case, was less than satisfied with this response. Justice Venkatachaliah pointed out to the attorney general that the government had taken away the victims' cause of action and now proposed to further delay their compensation. The 'legal questions will take a long time to decide ... As a welfare state the government has to compensate the victims.' The suffering that had been caused by the relentless pursuit of economic gain was matched only by the 'government's ignorance of the means to relieve the hurt.'[46] The Court indicated that it wanted to explore the possibility of a national fund to care for the victims while the challenges to the settlement were pending and ordered the government to return in one week's time with information on the number of victims, the extent of their injuries, and a proposal on interim relief.

On 21 April the Supreme Court reconvened to hear from government lawyer Gopal Subramanian.[47] He informed the Court that the government had still not come up with a scheme for monthly assistance, pending the finalization of the litigation, but, apologizing for the delay, he suggested payment of 300 rupees per month to every victim. This amount was rejected as inadequate by lawyers for the victims. The Supreme Court agreed and ordered the state of Madhya Pradesh to pay 750 rupees ($45) per month to the families of the deceased. This order would apply to the survivors of 2,000 deceased adults. The Court also required Subramanian to report back to it at the end of the week with information on the 60,000 victims who had so far been medically examined and to prepare a proposal for their compensation.

On 28 April Subramanian revealed that, of the 326,000 victims who had so far responded to the government's call for medical evaluation, 83,625 had been evaluated but only 48,058 categorized. Of these, 15,222 were said to have no injury. Still dissatisfied with the results and requiring more information, Justice Venkatachallia told Subramanian, 'We do not want to dispute the results ... but what has been presented today is only a partial picture and not a representative projection of the nature and extent of injuries suffered by the victims.'[48] The Court again ordered the government to provide further information. It took the additional step of ordering further relief for an additional 773 gas victims[49] and ordering the authorities to speed up the process by increasing the number of medical-documentation centres from 18 to 100.

On 25 August 1989, the Supreme Court made further compensation orders and also required the central government to appoint fifty-six deputy commissioners to begin the compensation process. The Court rejected the government's argument that the process could not be started until the Court had ruled finally on the validity of the Bhopal Act.[50] The victims were pleased but cautious in response to these developments. They were right to be cautious. It would take the government another year to develop a more comprehensive package of interim relief, and another three years to begin the process of final compensation.

As of late 1989, government doctors pronounced 51,000 claimants as uninjured and another 64,664 as having only slight injuries. Only thirteen individuals so far had been classified as permanently and seriously injured and were awarded 500 rupees ($30) per month.[51] The government had earlier agreed to make a lump-sum ex-gratia payment of 10,000 rupees to the families of people who had died in the disaster. These payments were to be administered by a committee of three MLAs and one MP. As of late 1989, 3,650 payments had been made; 2,800 applications had been denied and 2,000 were still pending.[52] Many former Union Carbide employees had been re-employed by the government, but other victims, especially the slum dwellers and daily-wage labourers, remained without work. As a result of the Court's April orders, several thousand victims would now receive modest monthly payments. The relief department was employing about 2,000 women stitching clothes for 340 rupees ($20) a month, and claimed also to be rehabilitating about 10,000 workers by providing skills training and employment in work sheds. Apart from these efforts, tens of thousands of other victims had received very little or nothing.

The Zahreeli Gas Kand Sangharsh Morcha continued to insist that government figures radically underestimated the number of deaths and injuries. Victims lamented the delay and wondered why the government, even after five years, had been unable to categorize the victims' injuries. They were also sceptical about whether, and how much of the interim compensation they would ultimately receive. 'We know what happened when Rs 10,000 for dead and Rs 1,500 for those affected were distributed. We had to part with most of it to get the remainder,' said a woman, whose husband and son had died in the disaster.[53]

Unsettling

The long delays in distributing compensation and the government's consistently conservative categorization figures convinced many of the victims' groups that they were right in their view that their fight was now as much with the government as with Union Carbide. In their view, the government was seeking to minimize the harm done in Bhopal in order to justify an inadequate settlement.

In ordering the settlement the Supreme Court had left open the possibility of review, remarking that 'like all other human institutions, this Court is human and fallible ... the case equally concerns the credibility of, and the public confidence in, the judicial process. If, owing to the pre-settlement procedures being limited to the main contestants in the appeal, the benefit of some contrary or supplemental information or material, having a crucial bearing on the fundamental assumptions basic to the settlement, have been denied to the court and that, as a result, serious miscarriage of justice, violating the constitutional and legal rights of the persons affected, has been occasioned, it will be the endeavour of this court to undo any such injustice.'[54]

Responding to these remarks, several of the victims' groups kept up their campaign to have the settlement reopened in court. The challenges to the settlement fell into two categories. The first attacked the constitutional validity of the Bhopal Act itself, and the government's authority to approve a settlement without consulting the victims. The first of these petitions had been brought as early as 1986 by Shri Rakesh Shrouti, a Bhopal lawyer who had himself been injured in the gas leak. Shrouti had challenged the right of the government to exercise *parens patriae* power for the victims. Other petitions in this group were brought by the journalist Rajkumar Keswani and Charanlal Sahu, another Bhopal lawyer. These petitions asserted that the Bhopal Act deprived the victims of their constitutional right to equality and access to justice. They challenged the government's use of the *parens patriae* power on the basis that this power may be used only when the state is suing to enforce the rights of the state as opposed to those of individuals. They bolstered this argument by suggesting that the government's conflict of interest rendered it incapable of fairly representing the victims. The victims pointed out that Indian public financial institutions owned a substantial share of UCIL, and that a number of actions were still pending in the courts in which the victims were suing the government. The victims argued that the settlement was an attempt by the government to cover up its own negligence and to protect itself from liability.

The second set of petitions did not attack the Bhopal Act, but instead sought to have the settlement reopened and reviewed. These claims asserted that the victims had a right to examine the settlement and to show the nature and extent of their injuries in order to demonstrate that the award was inadequate. Separate benches of the Supreme Court were struck in March to hear these challenges, and the settlement was stayed pending the outcome.

To Do a Great Right

The Supreme Court began hearing arguments on the constitutional validity of the Bhopal Act on 9 March, and continued its hearings throughout April and May 1989. The constitutional bench included Justices S. Mukharji, K.N. Singh, M.H. Ranganathan, K.N. Saikia, and M.H. Ahmedi. Lawyer R.K. Garg, appearing on behalf of Charanlal Sahu, argued that the government's conflict of interest rendered it incapable of taking over the litigation on the victims' behalf and that the 'expropriation' of the victims' right to sue violated their right to life and to due process of law under the Code of Civil Procedure. Indira Jaising, appearing on behalf of Rajkumar Keswani and other individual victims, also focused on the government's conflict of interest. She referred to the articles that her client had written about the hazard in Bhopal and urged that the state of Madhya Pradesh should be held accountable for ignoring the danger. Shanti Bushan, appearing on behalf of the Bhopal Gas Peedit Mahila Udyog Sangathan, argued that the act and settlement violated the Bhopal victims' constitutional rights to access to justice and urged the Court to invalidate the act and scrap the settlement, even if that meant returning the money to Union Carbide.

Attorney General K. Parasaran and Gopal Subramanian argued the case for the government, urging the Court to uphold the constitutionality of the Bhopal Act. They defended the legislation and the final settlement on the basis that the governmental assumption of responsibility was the only way in which the mass of poor victims could ever hope to obtain compensation. Parasaran admitted that the act departed in some ways from the ordinary principles of 'natural justice' in that it did not provide for extensive victim participation in the litigation. But he also argued that the victims had been heard, both formally and informally, through their voluntary organizations and court interventions on their behalf at all levels. He further argued that it would have been impractical to consult the victims at each stage of the case. A requirement of more extensive consultation, he suggested, would have frustrated entirely the object of the act, which was to provide for an efficient and effective resolution of their claims.

Attorney General Parasaran also denied that the Government of India was, by reason of its alleged conflict of interest, incapable of fairly representing the victims. While Indian government financial institutions did own 22 per cent of UCIL, these institutions were independent from government, and the action was not, in any event, brought against the Indian company. Similarly, he denied that the government was using the Bhopal Act as a means of avoiding its own potential liability. He argued that the government could not be considered to have been negligent merely by reason of its licensing and regulatory responsibilities. Such liability, he urged, would ultimately be destructive of the government's effort to protect the welfare of the people in that it would drain the treasury and 'terrorize' the state from assuming any responsibility with respect to health and welfare. Finally, he pointed out, the government was, in any event, protected by the doctrine of sovereign immunity. Perhaps to bolster the attractiveness of upholding the settlement, Parasaran announced to the Court that the government would not be seeking any reimbursement for its own expenses out of the $470 million award.

The government lawyers concluded their argument by cautioning the Court that, if it were to strike down the act, it would be leaving a few privileged victims to enter into generous settlements with Union Carbide, while abandoning the majority of the poor victims to their own devices. The arguments concluded on 3 May 1989, and the Supreme Court reserved its decision.

The fifth anniversary of the disaster passed before the Supreme Court announced its decision. To mark the occasion, prayer meetings, marches, and demonstrations were held by the victims in Bhopal. Activist leaders continued calling for immediate compensation for the victims, while others insisted that the criminal charges be reinstated. Large crowds burned effigies representing Union Carbide and its officers and marched towards the factory. Police, waiting at the plant gates with bamboo *lathis*, prevented the crowd from entering the factory and arrested 800 persons who were detained in a make-shift jail at a local sports arena.

Two weeks later, on 22 December 1989, the Supreme Court announced its decision, dismissing the petition and upholding the validity of the Bhopal Act.[55] Speaking for the majority, Chief Justice Sabyaschi Mukharji accepted the attorney general's argument that the government's assumption of *parens patriae* on behalf of the victims was justified in the circumstances. While the victims were not *legally* incapable of protecting their own interests, the reality of the situation was such that they could never have pursued the claims on their own. As a welfare state, India was entitled, indeed obliged, to take some steps to protect the victims. As Justice Ranganathan added in a concurring opinion, 'in the stark reality of the situation, it cannot even be plausibly contended that the large number of victims of the gas leak disaster should have been left to fend for [themselves].'[56]

Justice Mukharji agreed with the petitioners that the act treated the victims differently from other victims of personal injury, but denied that this violated their right to equality before the law. The victims as a class were different and had to be treated differently. The urgency of their need, the presence of U.S. contingency lawyers, and the power of the foreign multinational were factors justifying governmental action. Nor did the Supreme Court accept that the government's conflict of interest rendered it incapable of representing the victims. Perhaps somewhat disingenuously in light of Judge Seth's decision to pierce Union Carbide's corporate veil, Justice Mukharji accepted the attorney general's proposition that UCIL was owned by independent financial institutions and not, therefore, by the Government of India. More important, as the Court pointed out, there was simply no non-governmental body that would have been capable of amassing the legal and financial resources that were required to pursue the victims' claims. While the act might have been improved, reliance upon some form of governmental agency was essential, given the enormity of the tragedy.

Justice Mukharji did feel that there was some force in the victims' argument that principles of natural justice must afford them some opportunity to have their views heard and taken into account by the government. Section 4 of the act required the government to have 'due regard' to the views of the victims and, the Court concluded, that meant that some kind of notice should have been given to them concerning the settlement. The Court concluded that such notice had not been given. But, then, in a pragmatic about-face, Justice Mukharji declined to hold the government strictly to this requirement because the consequences would be 'to put asunder what others have put together.'[57] He again expressed the Court's view that the settlement had been a fair and adequate one, and though settlement without notice was not quite proper, justice had been done. In 'view of the magnitude of the misery involved and the problems of this case,' setting aside the settlement 'would not be in the ultimate interest of justice.'[58] Justice Mukharji pointed out that the victims would still have the opportunity to present their views on the settlement in a separate review by the Supreme Court and concluded that 'to do a great right after all, it is permissible sometimes to do a little wrong.'[59]

The petitioners did win one small victory. They had argued that if the government was going to deprive them of their right to sue Union Carbide individually, it had a corresponding collective obligation towards them to provide interim compensation. They had urged the Court that, if the act was to be upheld on the basis of the state's obligation to protect the victims' welfare, it must be interpreted so as to impose a more complete responsibility on the government to care for the victims until the litigation was over. The chief justice accepted this argument (though several of his brethren disagreed). The act, he pointed out, eliminated the right of the victims to pursue litigation on their own or to settle their cases individually with the company. Thus, while it was enacted for their benefit, it also deprived them of the (remote) opportunity to take advantage of the law on their own. Justice Mukharji concluded that 'the provisions of the Act deprived the victims of that legal right and opportunity and that deprivation is substantial deprivation because upon immediate relief depends often the survival of these victims. In that background, it is just and proper that this deprivation is only to be justified if the Act is read with the obligation of granting interim relief or maintenance by the Central Government until the dues of the victims is realised from the Union Carbide after adjudication or settlement and then deducting therefrom the interim relief paid to the victims ... If it is only so read, it can only be held to be constitutionally valid.'[60]

The Court referred to this rather remarkably conclusion as an exercise in 'constructive intuition.' By searching for the spirit of the act, it was possible to 'perfect' its provisions by reading into it a substantial obligation on government. The Court also directed the timely and fair implementation of the relief scheme. It was necessary, said Mukharji, to reiterate that 'the promises made to the victims and the hopes raised in their hearts' could 'only be redeemed in some measure if attempts are made vigorously to distribute the amount realized.'[61] These conclusions represented one more small victory for the victims, but, as usual, they awaited with some scepticism to see if the promise would be fulfilled.

Settlement Review

The review of the settlement was to take an even more tortuous course than the challenges to the Bhopal Act. While arguments began shortly after the Court's settlement order, they were twice derailed. First, in the spring of 1990, after the case had been fully argued and the decision reserved, Chief Justice Mukharji died, and the case had to be entirely reheard. Then, in the meantime, just as the Supreme Court was taking steps to maintain the legitimacy of the settlement and its own reputation, politics in India underwent a dramatic transformation that threatened to undo everything that had been done. In late November 1989, the Rajiv Gandhi government lost the national election to a coalition led by V.P Singh, and the pleas from the social activists that the settlement be revoked were renewed. On 12 January 1990, the new law minister, Dinesh Goswami, announced that the government would support the demands of the victims for increased compensation and join in the effort to have the settlement overturned.[62] The prime minister confirmed that 'my government has decided in principle to review the settlement and to support petitions filed before the courts by voluntary groups for its review.' And, at a rally in Bhopal, attended by an estimated 100,000 people, he said, 'We believe there can be no deal over human corpses.' Then, after the case had been fully argued in the summer of 1990, Chief Justice Mukharji died, and the case had to be entirely reheard.

In the meantime, the combination of the change in government and the Supreme Court's earlier order did produce a small victory for the victims. During the first months of 1990, the new government met with representatives from the seven most prominent social-action groups. Admitting that the victims had not yet received any meaningful financial assistance, the government promised to pay interim compensation of 200 rupees per month ($13 U.S.) to approximately 500,000 residents of the thirty-six gas-affected wards.[63] The total estimated cost of these payments would be more than 3.5 billion rupees ($230 million).

At the final review hearing, the victims (through their lawyers Jaising, Garg, Bushan, and others) renewed their challenge to the Court's jurisdiction to transfer the case to itself and forge a settlement, and again attacked the government's failure to include them in the negotiations. They disputed the dismissal of the criminal charges, and sought to show that the settlement was inadequate because of the government's underestimation of existing and future injuries. Indeed, 12 July 1990, the Government of Madhya Pradesh had itself entered an affidavit indicating that the extent of the suffering may have been greater than that assumed in the settlement. Deaths had risen to 3,787 (as opposed to the earlier estimate of 3,000) and the number of injuries was now set at 202,672.[64] Yet, government authorities had downgraded many of the estimated injuries from 'permanent' to 'temporary' and from 'total' to 'partial.' This, of course, simply added to the petitioners' concern that the government was manipulating the figures to justify the settlement.

Attorney General Sorabjee, newly appointed and walking a fine (if not inconsistent) line, took no independent position, except that he 'supported' the petitioners, at the same time defending the right of the government under the act to enter into the settlement. Fali Nariman, acting for the company, sought to uphold the settlement in its entirety, arguing, among other things, that the risk of future injuries had been taken into account in the settlement and that, based on the government's new figures, the settlement, in fact, overcompensated the victims.

The Supreme Court finally announced its terminal decision in the Bhopal case on 3 October 1991, nearly seven years after the disaster.[65] In 199 pages of sometimes tortuous reasoning, the Court sought to mould a politico-legal compromise to put an end to the case. It rejected the argument that it had no power to transfer the case to itself, emphasizing (and probably expanding) its broad power under Article 142(1) of the Constitution, enabling it to 'pass any such decree or make such order as is necessary for doing complete justice in any cause.' In the primary judgment, Justice Venkatachaliah rejected the petitioners' jurisdictional argument as a 'hypertechnical' restriction on the Court's power to do justice.[66] He did, however, accept that there was merit in the claims that the criminal charges should not have been dismissed, and that the victims should have been consulted, or were at least entitled to be heard about the fairness of the settlement.

While of the view that the Court did, in appropriate cases, have the power to quash criminal proceedings, no reasons or justification had so far been forthcoming for this step in the Bhopal case. Moreover, the prohibition of all future proceedings, said Venkatachaliah, was essentially a legislative function, conferring a privileged immunity that might violate the principle of equality before the law. Reasoning that public policy in this case indicated the need for further investigation of the criminal allegations, he ordered that the quashing provision be deleted from the original order. Union Carbide's exposure to criminal charges was, in one fell swoop, renewed.

Would this alteration of the settlement undermine it entirely because it had been based on an illegality? This was the position taken by the petitioners, but not by the company. The answer given by Justice Venkatachaliah was no: agreements to stifle a criminal prosecution are only illegal when they are between private individuals and amount to an attempt to take criminal matters out of the hands of the court. In the present case, both the government and the court had been involved in the agreement to quash the criminal proceedings, and while the court had now reconsidered that element of the agreement, it was not at the time of the settlement 'illegal.' Moreover, he noted, this element of the settlement had not been the primary consideration for the agreement, but was rather merely a 'motive' for entering into it. The civil, as opposed to criminal, core of the settlement could therefore stand on its own.

Finally, Justice Venkatachaliah came to the core of the issue: the right of the victims to be heard, and the fairness of the settlement itself. He prefaced this portion of his judgment with the warning that, if the settlement was overturned, the entire amount of the funds would have to be returned to UCC (and UCC would, in turn, have to re-establish its undertaking to maintain $3 billion in security for future damages). 'A litigant,' he said, 'should not go back with the impression that the judicial process so operated as to weaken his position and whatever it did on the faith of the court's order operated to its disadvantage.'[67]

In its earlier consideration of the Bhopal Act, the Supreme Court had acknowledged that the failure to consult the victims was a potential violation of natural justice. This violation, it had suggested, could be redressed only by allowing the victims to be heard. Yet, Fali Nariman, acting for the company, had argued, with some force, that to provide a review in this court would be to treat the earlier settlement as a mere proposal. Venkatachaliah rejected this argument:

The whole issue, shorn of legal subtleties, is a moral and humanitarian one. What was transacted with the court's assistance between the Union of India on the one side and the UCC on the other is now sought to be made binding on the tens of thousands of innocent victims who, as the law has now declared, had a right to be heard before the settlement could be reached or approved. The implications of the settlement and its effect on the lakhs of citizens of this country are, indeed, crucial in their grim struggle to reshape and give meaning to their torn lives. Any paternalistic condescension that what has been done is after all for their own good is out of place. Either they should have been heard before a settlement was approved ... or, at least, must become demonstrable in a process in which they have a reasonable sense of participation that the settlement has been to their evident advantage or, at least, the adverse consequences are effectively neutralized.'[68]

In accordance with this decision, the Court then proceeded to develop a 'sui generis' review, noting that this was, perhaps, 'the last opportunity to verify our doubts and to undo injustice, if any, which may have occurred.'[69]

The petitioners argued, first, that too many claims had been excluded from the original claims process and that too few victims were in possession of documents to support their claims. Venkatachaliah rejected this argument on the basis that the claims agency had gone to extraordinary lengths to apprise the victims of their rights, and that even those who had not yet responded still had the opportunity to do so. As to documentation, the Court noted the liberal approach that had been taken by the commission to documentation (accepting, for example, prescription forms) and implicitly accepted the claims commissioner's argument regarding the need to protect against fraudulent claims and that it would 'be irrational and unscientific to admit all claims without reference to any documentary evidence as suggested by the petitioner.'[70] Justice Venkatachaliah also rejected the claim by the petitioners that the government had made an effort after the settlement to understate the damage figures.

Venkatachaliah then further bolstered his conclusion that the settlement was reasonable by referring to all the uncertainties of the litigation. At the time of the settlement, liability remained uncertain. UCC would continue to stand behind its corporate veil and also to demand proof of individualized causation. While, in the case of Bhopal, there might be strong epidemiological evidence of harm, Venkatachaliah emphasized the causal problems faced by the victims of toxic torts. Relying on U.S. authorities, he warned the petitioners that, if the litigation were to be revived, 'generalized proof of damages' might not be sufficient to prove 'individual damages.'[71] In a concurring judgment,

Chief Justice Ranganath Misra agreed that the settlement was vastly preferable to the prospect of another twenty years of litigation with an uncertain outcome, also pointing out that even if liability was established under the *Shriram* decision, there would be a real risk that U.S. courts would refuse to enforce the judgment.

Perhaps the strongest argument presented by the victims was that the settlement had not taken into account the likelihood of future injuries. At the least, they demanded, it should have included a 'reopener' clause in case future injuries should overwhelm and exhaust the settlement funds. Fali Nariman, acting for the company, argued that the settlement had taken into account future injuries and that a settlement must be final so that the defendant may proceed with its plans and activities. Justice Venkatachaliah acknowledged both positions, noting the tension between the desire for legal certainty (represented by the common law's insistence on the use of final lump sums) and the victims' legitimate fear that future events may show the settlement to have been vastly inadequate (represented by their request that he insert a reopener clause). He expressed his reluctance to 'sacrifice physically injured plaintiffs on the alter of the certainty principle,'[72] yet also held that the settlement should not have included a reopener clause. The compromise that he then develops is an ingenious gamble.

First, suggested the judge, the concerns, even of existing victims, that the settlement may be inadequate were valid, and some provision should be made to protect them against this possibility. He then proceeded to elaborate upon the concept of governmental responsibility hinted at in some of the Court's previous decisions. Given the way in which the settlement was reached, and the status of India as a welfare state, he ordered that the government stand ready to make up any shortfall (Justice Ahmadi vigorously dissented on this point, arguing that, in the absence of a finding of liability against the government, the Court had no authority to make such an order). Second, he also accepted that the concern expressed by the petitioners about possible future victims was also legitimate, and that some provision must be made for medical surveillance for those who may later develop symptoms. He thus ordered that an action plan be drawn up in this regard, including the 'establishment of a full-fledged hospital of at least 500 bed strength with the best of equipment for treatment of MIC related affliction' and medical surveillance. While acknowledging that it is 'not part of the function of this court to re-shape the settlement,'[73] he nevertheless ordered that the state of Madhya Pradesh provide free land for this facility and that UCIL and UCC jointly provide the capital outlay and operating expenses for a period of eight years. He estimated that this may amount to an additional outlay of 50 crore rupees (about $30 million). In support of this unusual order, he appealed to 'humanitarian considerations,' reminding the UCC of its offer many years earlier to provide such a facility. Finally, with respect to potential future victims, he ordered the Union of India to establish a group-insurance fund to cover currently asymptomatic individuals and children born after the disaster, again for a period of eight years. This fund would cover approximately one *lakh* (100,000) persons in the most seriously gas-affected wards. The premium, he said, may be paid out of the settlement funds.

Unfinished Business

This final decision did moderately improve the terms of the settlement and enhance its political acceptability. It was accepted by both the government and the company, though its good-faith implementation remained to be judged. Indeed, it would take nearly another year to finalize the claims process.

Following the Supreme Court's decision, the criminal charges against Warren Anderson and the local managers of UCIL were reinstated in the Bhopal criminal court. Company officials stated that this aspect of the judgment was 'unfortunate,' but were also confident that Anderson, at least, would never be extradited to India for trial. Nevertheless, in March 1992, Bhopal judge Gulab Sharma issued an arrest warrant for Anderson and gave UCC lawyers a month in which to appear and explain why the company's assets should not be seized. Then, in April 1992, Sharma blocked an effort by UCC to dispose of its $17 million share in UCIL,[74] and in May ordered the confiscation of $2.3 million that Union Carbide had earned from its stake in the Indian operation. Failing to secure Anderson's appearance, Sharma then severed the charges against nine Indian company officials, including Heshub Mindra and Vijay Ghokale, the chair and managing director of UCIL, and ordered that their manslaughter trial proceed in late July 1992. Once again, while dramatic, India's quest for ' justice' by pursuing the criminal charges could hardly be said to have materially advanced the victims' welfare.

Meanwhile, government authorities sought to deliver the compensation 'expeditiously,' as required by Justice Venkatachaliah. At the end of 1991, many of the victims had begun to receive the small pension (200 rupees per month) announced by the government in 1990. These payments would be terminated in 1993 (and the government intended to deduct the payments made so far from the settlement funds).[75] In his October 1991 judgment Justice Venkatachaliah had ordered the central and state governments to establish the necessary administrative machinery immediately, and to appoint forty claims adjudicators within four months. The central government took steps towards complying by establishing a special committee to work out the final compensation guidelines. Most of the files that had been documented had by then been tentatively categorized by type of injury.[76] Government doctors had pronounced 155,203 of the 639,793 claimants to be uninjured. Of the remaining claimants, 173,382 were categorized as having suffered only temporary injuries (economic losses and minor physical injuries). It was now accepted that more than 3,800 persons had died. About 22,000 victims had been classified as permanently injured or disabled (and, of these, only about 3,000 as seriously disabled), and an additional 8,500 were said to have been temporarily disabled. An outstanding quarter of a million claims remained unaccounted for.

Even those victims who had been tentatively verified would still have to present their cases to claims adjudicators. Yet, while a few of the claims courts were set up in the spring of 1992, they will had no compensation guidelines to go by, even after the February deadline set by the Supreme Court. Setting these guidelines was complicated by the necessity of working backwards from a fixed sum. Ironically, this required that the government, in advance of the final adjudication of claims, pre-estimate the final number of claims, the severity of the injuries, and the amounts that would be paid to individual victims. In other words, it became necessary to complete the process of quantification before the process was even begun in the tribunals. Even assuming that the department had accurate information on the requirements of the victims, this accounting task is a nightmare. Not surprisingly, the final compensation guidelines were not announced until July 1992, and, even then, were left so general as to provide little guidance to the adjudicators.

Prognosis: The Task Ahead

By the time the final compensation package was determined, increased numbers of victims, and the effects of inflation (and rupee deflation) had severely eroded the funds and, predictably, award levels were once again revised downwards. It was announced by Babulal Gaur, the minister for state relief, that the families of the victims would receive only 100,000 to 300,000 rupees ($3,700 to $11,000), while most injured individuals would receive a mere 50,000 to 100,000 rupees ($1,900 to $3,800). These sums would produce a stream of income for the families and survivors of between $120 and $720 a year for twenty years. The most catastrophically injured victims would receive more, perhaps as much as a lump sum of 400,000 rupees ($14,300). No amounts would be allocated to compensate for pain and suffering or business losses. Predictably, the scheme enraged all but a small and favoured minority of the victims.[77]

The special compensation courts would begin with claims from relatives of victims who had died and then claims of survivors. Traditional principles of compensation would require an individualized assessment of each victim's past loss and future need, adjusted by reference to the age of the victims, the severity of their injuries, their earning capacity, future medical needs, and so on. The use of so many discretionary variables, however, magnifies the problems of delay, uncertainty, error, and corruption. A system of checks and appeals, while therefore necessary, will further complicate and delay the process.

Thus, it will be years before the distribution effort is complete. Welfare commissioner Abdul Ghayoor Quereshi estimated that it would take three years. Previous experience teaches that it will likely be longer. Indeed, as of 3 December 1992, the eighth anniversary of the disaster, not one victim had received final compensation. Individual amounts will be siphoned away as the funds make their way down through the system. The adequacy of these very modest compensation packages will be further undermined by future events, especially the lack of knowledge about the long-term effects of exposure to MIC. Medical and social activists, backed by ICMR reports,[78] still insist that almost no attention has been paid to the more complex problems of chromosome damage, immune-deficiency, and mental-health problems in the gas-affected areas. Contemplating the problems of setting the levels of compensation, the head of the relief effort has always recognized that the primary problem is simply that 'we really don't know what the future has in store for us.'[79] Final awards may overcompensate some victims and will certainly undercompensate others.

Relief authorities are also concerned about the effect of a sudden injection of money into Bhopal. When the settlement was announced, touts, con artists, and criminals began to make their way to the city, hoping to reap some of the spoils. Loan sharks had advanced amounts to desperate families at exorbitant rates of interest. Most of the victims have no experience in managing large sums and, while the amounts awarded are intended to provide a stream of income as lifetime compensation, there is a real fear that the compensation awards will be quickly dissipated. Acknowledging these risks, the Supreme Court directed that mechanisms such as trust funds should be put in place to protect those who, owing to youth, 'illiteracy or ignorance' might be deprived of 'what may turn out to be the sole source of their living and sustenance.'[80] There could also be serious inflationary effects. When, shortly after the disaster, the government provided food and cash to some of the victims, the purchasing power of the rupee fell to an all-time low, and Bhopal became the most expensive city in India.[81] The inevitable economic disruption will exacerbate the social tension that already exists in Bhopal, increasing the amount of family breakdown and violence.

In addition to the problems that will be faced by those victims who do receive compensation is the plight of the many victims who simply disappeared from sight. Despite the relief department's efforts, more than 250,000 of the claims were never documented or classified. Of course, not all of these claims represent real victims. Many may have been duplicates – some fraudulently submitted and others inadvertently resubmitted by victims who did not understand the process, or who had gone for multiple treatments, thus completing the forms more than once. But a large number of real victims had simply fallen through the cracks during the agonizing eight years that now had gone by. Many of the victims had been slum dwellers or peripatetic workers who were simply unaware of the requirement that they appear at one of the documentation centres for examination. Others had died, and still others had simply given up in despair.

11

The Lessons of Bhopal

The Bhopal story is replete with ironies and contradictions. A plant producing an unneeded product virtually decimates a city. The sovereign state of India, proud of its hard-won independence from colonial rule, then resorts to the courts of a foreign nation to obtain justice for its citizens, pillorying its own legal system in the process. A major multinational corporation, whose policy is to maintain 'centralized integrated corporate strategic planning, direction and control,' argues that it had no responsibility for its subsidiary. The courts of the United States – a country that is among the 'foremost exporters of effective liberal legal ideologies for the ex-colonial nations of the Third World'[1] – refuse even to assert jurisdiction over a U.S.–based corporation. The Indian courts, earlier celebrated by Union Carbide for their innovativeness and integrity, attempt to live up to this assessment and are castigated by the company for their 'lawlessness.' The victims, to whom law gives its guarantees, are virtually excluded from legal view, and in the end are advised by the Supreme Court not to further pursue the 'uncertain promises of law.'[2]

In the end, the Bhopal saga is about those uncertain promises. It cannot be said that the law failed the victims entirely. An eventual settlement was achieved. But when measured against the goals specified in chapter 2, the final legal ledger cannot be viewed with any sense of satisfaction. The legal process proved itself incapable of preventing the tragedy and seriously defective in its effort to repair the human consequences once it had occurred. Indeed, for many of the victims, the litigation can itself be viewed as a second catastrophe; for, while they would in the end receive some compensation, it was achieved only at enormous further costs in human suffering.

Despite significant innovations, the Bhopal litigation remained trapped largely within a traditional model of tort compensation. The complex litigation was incredibly slow. It never reached trial, the final settlement took seven years, and the distribution of final compensation took even longer. Efforts were made to care for the victims in the interim, but those efforts were far from adequate. The lengthy delays compounded the already-difficult task of proving causation and fault. The adversarial approach to the dispute and the disparities in resources disempowered and revictimized the victims. The final level of compensation, assessed most optimistically, provides an average of only about $3,000 each to those victims who the government admits suffered injury and leaves many others out entirely. Because the long-term effects of the tragedy are still unknown, the requirement of finalizing a once-and-for-all lump sum for each of the victims means that the compensation figure is bound to be inaccurate, and likely inadequate to provide for their future needs. The litigation was enormously expensive compared with the amount of the final compensation. The legal costs to each party likely exceeded $100 million,[3] nearly half the total amount of the settlement. Nor would the final figure reimburse government authorities for the estimated $200 million lost by government instrumentalities and spent during the relief and documentation process.[4]

The award is unlikely to significantly alter industrial practices in the developing world, or to reduce environmental and health risks. The amount of Union Carbide's share was no more than what it had offered to settle the case many years earlier. The figures used understate the damage done and fail to reflect the full social costs of the Bhopal tragedy. They confirm to the victims that their lives are considered cheap, and license a continuing double standard of industrial safety.

Bhopal is also a vivid illustration of the way in which public participation and power is displaced by 'expertise' in a modern technological society. The location, regulation, and control of the Bhopal plant was entirely a function of élite decision making. No attempt was made to solicit public input or to disseminate public information. And, in the aftermath of the disaster, the section of the public most directly affected – the victims – was further disempowered. The entry of the state and of a cadre of professional lawyers, scientists, and engineers was legitimated and accelerated because of the widespread belief that the problem was a technical one and that its solution must lie with expert professionals. This one-dimensional interpretation of the problem excluded the victims' own understanding of the situation and further disempowered them. The state appropriated to itself the very definition of the 'problem' and, assisted by a host of lawyers and technocrats, designed a strategy that failed to respond to victims' own understanding of their dilemma. Scientific, medical, and legal experts competed among themselves for 'ownership' of knowledge about the causes and consequences of the tragedy and for custodianship of the victims' welfare. Again, the victims were neither consulted nor made privy to the information generated by these exercises. The non-experts who sought to come to the aid of the victims and to give voice to their interests and needs were characterized as political ideologues or greedy intervenors because they could make no claim to expertise. Their 'irrational' quest for vengeance has no place in modern scientific social discourse.

The story is not, however, entirely unredeemed. The victims did receive some compensation, and a multinational corporation was, ultimately forced to account (if only partially) for its operations in the developing world. The innovations forged by the courts, government agencies, and social activists during the litigation do point in promising directions, and even the failures serve to focus our attention more clearly on what is to be done.

Despite the unique characteristics and extraordinary dimensions of the Bhopal disaster, the lessons to be learned transcend this single tragedy. While Bhopal must be understood in the context of Indian law and society, its lessons should not be too sanguinely confined to that context, or entirely attributed to the deficiencies of the Indian legal system so thoroughly documented by the government in the U.S. courts. The obstacles faced by the victims, while magnified in India, are inherent in toxic harm, and therefore endemic to the legal systems of all countries. The more prominent of those obstacles included: (1) the disparity in the parties' resources and the enormous cost of the litigation; (2) the difficulty of satisfying the burden of proof of mechanical causation and fault, especially in the context of a systems accident; (3) the difficulty of locating a responsible defendant, especially in the context of complex business organization; (4) the difficulty of identifying the victims of toxic harms, especially in establishing medical causation and predicting long-term effects; and (5) the length of the litigation and the inability of the victims to sustain themselves without interim compensation.

These problems, while particularly acute in Bhopal, are faced by the victims of toxic harms wherever they occur. Indeed, many of the innovations attempted in the Bhopal litigation go beyond what might have been expected, even in the developed countries. These innovations include the consolidation of the claims and aggressive intervention by a government agency; the creation of a public body to document the claims; the involvement of public and private scientific agencies to conduct medical research; and robust judicial action on the issues of interim compensation, liability standards, and corporate responsibility.

Compensation Reform

The mechanisms for consolidating and processing the claims in Bhopal were innovative. The Bhopal Act, while defective in many ways, acknowledged the necessity of consolidating the claims in order to redress the strategic imbalance between the victims and Union Carbide and to ensure greater efficiency in the prosecution of the litigation. The scheme was designed to lend to the victims the expertise and resources of government and to eliminate the necessity of wasteful individualized litigation.

Yet, in several crucial respects, the Bhopal Act had the opposite effect from what was intended. The aggregation of the claims in an agency too closely related to the political arm of government, and the subsequent exclusion of the victims from the decision-making process, undermined its legitimacy, alienated the victims, and threw up unanticipated complications and obstacles to the resolution of the dispute. So long as the victims' compensation remains contingent upon the outcome of the case – that is, so long as they are left as stakeholders in the litigation – the agency must be seen to have legitimacy and the victims' voices must be allowed to be heard. Especially where there is a possibility of conflicting interest between government and the victims, the agency must have greater autonomy from the political arm of government and mechanisms must be set in place that ensure greater victim participation.

Enhancing participation is a difficult challenge. Any time that interests are aggregated, a balance must be struck between fairness and effectiveness. Individual interests must be adequately represented, but, in the end, collective decisions must be made that will not always satisfy all members of the group. It would, therefore, be impractical to require comprehensive consultation in and consent to all courses of action. Similar problems had been encountered in the Agent Orange settlement, in which numerous plaintiffs felt that they had been left out. As Judge Weinstein said in that case, securing full consent would be prohibitive and the enterprise 'quixotic'; the benefits of the class action can therefore be reaped only at some cost to individual rights.[5] Yet, in the case of Bhopal, the various victims' groups could have been far more satisfactorily included in the process. While no single non-government organization spoke for all the victims, several had very wide-based support. Representatives should have been part of a litigation-management committee. Such a committee would not always achieve unanimity, but the difference of views is no reason to exclude divergent voices. The fact that the victims' groups and public-interest lawyers achieved significant results *in spite* of government opposition to their participation demonstrates the desirability of including them from the outset.

The aggregation of claims does not, of course, solve all the problems. The substantive law too, threw up near-insurmountable barriers. India, like other countries, has placed its hope for the future on the development of science, industry, and technology. Yet, as Justice K.N. Singh of the Supreme Court pointed out, Indian law and social policy have developed unevenly, and at the time of Bhopal, remained 'bound by the shackles of conservative principles'[6] laid down in the nineteenth century. With the increasing prevalence of 'systems accidents,' the requirement that the victims prove exactly how the incident occurred, and that it was the 'fault' of an individual agent, is unrealistic and serves simply to deprive deserving victims of compensation. If private-law models of compensation are to be seriously defended in an era of increasing business and technological complexity, those models must acknowledge the realities of modern society. The most prevalent harms are not the result of simple traumatic collisions between isolated agents, but rather are the product of inevitably flawed networks of human action, organizational systems, and complicated technology. The concepts of absolute liability and enterprise responsibility, both mooted during the course of the Bhopal litigation, are ideas that must be taken seriously. These notions remove the requirement that the victim provide a detailed explanation of how the accident occurred, particularizing the negligent acts and omissions and demonstrating how it could (and should) have been prevented. The *Shriram* judgment provided the victims of Bhopal with an important bargaining endowment. The settlement would have been even less satisfactory without it. As such, the principle deserves to be nourished. At the very least, the burden of proof should be relaxed in the case of harm caused by complex and hazardous technologies. If fault must be retained as the basis of liability, there should be a presumption of fault in the case of harms caused by complex industrial processes. This presumption could be rebutted only by a clear demonstration by the enterprise that it had taken all steps to anticipate, design for, and prevent the specific hazard from materializing.[7]

Similarly, in order to ensure adequate funds for the victims, companies operating in hazardous sectors must provide satisfactory guarantees of financial responsibility through minimum capitalization and insurance requirements. Additionally, the notion of an 'all-purpose' corporate veil must be interrogated against the demand for public safety and environmental quality. Again, Bhopal teaches some important lessons in this regard. In the case of technology transfers, risk and liability issues should be addressed explicitly in any licensing, transfer, or operating agreement. In the case of multinationals, there should be a presumption of enterprise responsibility (which is addressed more fully in the context of the later discussion of international law).

In addition, a more sensible approach to rehabilitation and support must be developed to take the place of the antiquated lump-sum damage award. The law of tort does nothing for the victim in the weeks, months, and even years following an accident. Yet the failed effort of the Indian courts to secure interim compensation for the victims while the litigation dragged on demonstrates the problems that will be encountered. Where litigation is the chosen method of compensation, the requirement of 'due process' makes it extremely difficult to order the defendant to pay interim compensation prior to a finding of fault. Such orders might be made conditional upon the victims' undertaking to repay any funds received should the defendants be vindicated at trial, but this solution is entirely unworkable where the victims are likely to be impecunious. So long as tort litigation remains the primary mode of redress for victims, interim compensation and care will remain the province of charitable organizations or uncertain and ad hoc governmental programs. Because the decision to retain tort processes is a public one, the *public* should acknowledge its responsibility for the care of victims who are relegated to that system. The Supreme Court of India provided some support for this proposition when it accepted the argument that, because the government had taken over the victims' rights, it should also, as part of the social contract, provide for their welfare in the interim.

The method of providing final compensation must also be re-examined. Courts and legislatures must begin to develop remedial options to replace the antiquated lump-sum approach. Increasing medical knowledge has paradoxically taught us that we know much less than we think about the long-term effects of industrial and environmental illness. It is simply no longer defensible to suppose that we can estimate today the future life prospects, losses, and needs of a person who has been exposed to toxic substances. The inherently inaccurate once-and-for-all global sum should be replaced by a system that provides for periodic payments according to the actual and changing needs of the victim over time. Judgment funds must take into account these future contingencies and should also be backed by guarantees for additional minimum compensation should new injuries arise. Where the future is uncertain, as in the case of Bhopal, settlement funds could be insured to guarantee that they will meet unanticipated needs. The contingency insurance fund in the terminal Bhopal judgment shows one practical way in which future victims may be afforded some additional protection, while, at the same time, finally settling the dispute so that the defendant may plan its affairs with some certainty.

Finally, and perhaps most problematically, remains the difficulty faced by victims in establishing a causal link between their injuries and a specific source of danger. Modern toxic and environmental harm has blurred, if not obliterated, the line between 'injury' and 'illness.' Epidemiological knowledge has demonstrated that many modern diseases are clearly the result of industrial practices and hazardous substances, yet there is often no way for individual victims to demonstrate a direct causal link between their condition and a specific source. In the context of toxic torts it is therefore difficult to identify both defendants and plaintiffs. Defendants are difficult to identify because numerous firms may generate pollution or be manufacturers of a defective product, and it may be impossible therefore to distinguish which particular company 'caused' the harm suffered by the individual victim. Victims are difficult to identify because toxic injuries and illnesses are so difficult to trace unequivocally to a particular source or substance.

The documentation process in Bhopal went some way towards solving some of these problems. By enlisting public scientific agencies on behalf of the victims and allowing informal evidence of illness, the commission removed some of the obstacles that face the victims of toxic harms. Yet the burden still remained on the victims to establish injury and causation, and this onus gave rise to ferocious and sometimes violent confrontations between the victims and the government.

If the tort system is to cope with the consequences of modern technology, it must jettison the paradigm of mechanical causation and find some way to accommodate statistical and probabilistic evidence. The systemic undercompensation and underdeterrence that result from the victim's inability to establish causation could be alleviated by accepting rebuttable presumptions of causation. Additional assistance could be provided to adjudicators by experts or independent panels of scientists.[8] Once the victim demonstrates that he or she has been exposed to a particular substance, and has suffered a statistically associated harm, the onus would then shift to the defendant to disprove causation.[9] Such an approach, of course, risks the reverse problem: overcompensation and overdeterrence. A toxic substance may, for example, increase the incidence of cancer in the affected population by 30 per cent. But to compensate all cancer victims would charge too much of the harm to a single agent or activity. This problem could be mitigated by expanding the principle of 'lost chances' or 'proportional liability' whereby each individual receives compensation calculated on the basis of the statistical probability that his or her injury was caused by the agent in question. As David Rosenberg suggests in his article entitled 'The Causal Connection in Mass Exposure Cases,' victims would receive compensation 'in proportion to the probability of causation assigned to the excess disease risk in the exposed population ... despite the absence of individualized proof of the causal connection.'[10] So, in the example of a hazardous product or process that has increased the incidence of disease (e.g., the cancer rate) in the affected population by 30 per cent, every member of that population would receive 30 per cent compensation. Where numerous firms contributed to the risk, liability would be allocated among the defendant group according to their proportional contribution to the risk (for example, by reference to their production or market share).

Rosenberg's proposal contains intriguing and useful suggestions, but is flawed in several respects. While it relieves the victims of the burden of proving specific individualized causation, it by no means provides them with adequate compensation. As he readily admits, the idea of proportional liability is aimed principally at deterrence instead of compensation. It is designed to charge an industry with its share of social costs only. While this may be fair to industry, it means that the compensation funding will not be anywhere near adequate, except in extraordinary cases where the harms can be traced exclusively to the defendant group and the 'excess risk' is therefore 100 per cent.

Moreover, Rosenberg displays a tremendous faith in litigative mechanisms and the institutional competence of courts. While the aggregation of claims may increase the power of victims to prosecute their action, they must still do so within the confines of an adversarial system, with its attendent costs and delays. Large-scale litigation in which the stakes are very high will, of course, elicit the most vigorous defence. If past experience is anything to go by, class actions do not significantly expedite the trial process or dramatically lower the costs of litigation. Rosenberg seems satisfied that courts are well equipped to assess the technological, statistical, and medical evidence underlying a determination of proportional liability, but one might wonder whether different agencies staffed by experts might be better suited to deal with the problems of environmental harms.

The reforms that would be required to make tort law workable would render tort law almost unrecognizable. Consider the suggestions made to this point: (1) the elimination of fault; (2) the substitution of class actions for individualized litigation; (3) a supplementary public scheme of interim compensation; (4) the elimination of the necessity of proof of specific causation; (5) mandatory insurance requirements or alteration of the principle of limited liability; (6) the development of a concept of proportional liability; and (7) the elimination of lump-sum awards in favour of periodic and adjustable maintenance payments. Should such reforms succeed, virtually all that would be left of the tort system would be a skeletal institutional framework involving lawyers, courts, and litigation. Given the high costs of administering such a system, it must be asked whether the remaining light is worth the candle.

Non-Tort Models: Towards Public Responsibility

Not surprisingly, an innovative Indian judiciary, enormously disappointed by the uncertain promises of law, has already mooted various reform initiatives. Reflecting upon the tragic course of the litigation and the infirmities of the Bhopal Act, Chief Justice Mukharji suggested that a public fund should be created to ensure that victims of toxic incidents would receive more timely and adequate compensation. As a precondition to the granting of an industrial licence, he suggested, firms should be required to undertake to compensate any victims of their activities and to agree to abide by special judicial procedures guaranteeing compensation to victims without exposing them to the same lengthy and disempowering procedures exposed in the Bhopal case. Going even farther, Justice K.N. Singh called for the immediate creation of an 'industrial disaster fund' made up of contributions from government and industry, and administered by separate tribunals according to procedures designed to streamline cases and secure timely interim and final compensation to all victims of industrial accidents, whether caused by transnational or domestic industries, public or private.

These proposals are both constructive and realistic. Similar schemes are already in place in many countries, principally in the form of workers' compensation legislation, no-fault automobile-accident compensation schemes,[11] and environmental-damage funds. These models meet the requirement of public responsibility in so far as they guarantee compensation to all victims independently of the outcome of litigation. At least theoretically, these schemes can also fulfil the requirement of deterrence by assessing premiums from industry on the basis of their contribution to the overall risk, or by civil actions brought by the public authorities after the event.

One example of such a program is the American Comprehensive Environmental Response, Compensation and Liability Act (CERCLA). This legislation, enacted in 1980, authorizes government authorities to take remedial measures in respect of 'hazardous substances' and 'pollutants or contaminants.' The authorities may, for example, clean up toxic wastes and hazardous sites after a spill or before any damage occurs, so long as there is a hazardous risk. The act establishes a tax on industry to create a fund that can be used to fund clean-up operations, but ultimately places liability for these costs on the responsible parties. However, perhaps as a result of the cultural commitment of U.S. society to individualized litigation, combined with a fear of runaway costs, proposals to extend CERCLA to provide compensation for personal injuries have met with no success.[12]

A more instructive model is provided by the 1973 Japanese Law for the Compensation of Pollution-Related Health Damage.[13] This law grew out of the heightened awareness in Japan of the social costs of industrialization and, in particular, from the experience of serious toxic illnesses such as Minimata disease and the increasing frequency of respiratory illness from air pollution. The Japanese law creates an administrative mechanism for the compensation of environmental disease. Serious 'pollution zones' are identified by government authorities in which 'designated diseases' caused by toxic substances are demonstrated by epidemiological studies to be statistically high. The victim population is then ascertained according to the length of exposure and the symptoms exhibited. These victims are entitled to compensation on a 'no-fault' basis. In Class I areas (serious ambient air pollution), the compensation fund is financed from pollution and discharge levies imposed on local industries according to the amount of their emissions. In Class II areas (specific forms of toxic contamination), compensation is financed by a special charge against the individual polluter.

The advantages of such a regime are numerous. Once victims bring themselves within the class of the affected population, they have an absolute entitlement to compensation without being subject to the expense and agony of litigation. They need not prove specific causation so long as they live within the pollution zone and their illness is a designated disease. Difficult scientific questions concerning causation are taken over by an administrative authority with the necessary resources and expertise. Compensation may be secured much more rapidly and is administered more efficiently. The scheme incorporates the 'polluter pays' principle, forcing industry to internalize the costs of health-related damage and thus providing incentives to reduce the amount of pollution. Funding is regularized and predictable. It is fair to industry, and ensures the availability of compensation, which is no longer contingent upon locating a specific wrongdoer with sufficient assets or insurance.

Yet the Japanese regime is not without its problems. Victims are brought into the scheme only when they live in a designated 'pollution zone' and are able to demonstrate that they are suffering from a scheduled pollution-related disease. These determinations are made by administrative bodies. The question is whether individual victims of pollution disease and victims' groups will fare better in pressing their claims in this context than they will in court. The problem of administrative 'capture' is a well-known phenomenon referring to the relationship of interdependence between administrative bodies and regulated industries. Industries have a large degree of political power and, equally important, have control over information. They will, therefore, play a powerful, and restrictive, role in the designation of pollution zones and diseases. Finally, government departments are not immune from pressures to maintain the integrity of their budgets. There is, therefore, a danger that the designation of pollution zones, diseases, and victim populations made by an administrative body will be overly responsive to industrial interests or fiscally conservative pressures. Indeed, in 1987, under pressure from industry, the Japanese law was significantly amended to restrict compensation for health damage resulting from non-specific sources of air pollution.[14] And even today, more than three decades after the event, thousands of people who may have been affected by mercury poisoning at Minimata are still battling the Japanese government to be certified as 'official victims.'[15] As one commentator has concluded, at least for the time being, industry in Japan has effectively eliminated the core of the compensation system by insisting upon a return to older standards of causation and individualized liability.[16]

A further and related objection is that the level of compensation set by no-fault programs is usually modest compared with tort awards. They will provide medical care and income replacement, but the latter is usually set within modest limits. If compensation levels are set at too low a level, or victim populations are too narrowly defined, as in the case of Minimata, there is a danger that public programs may amount to little more than a cynical pact between government and industry, authorizing pollution at the expense of public health.

These are serious difficulties. However, they are not necessarily *structural* problems, and there is little reason to believe that litigative mechanisms provide a better alternative. At least formally, the administrative approach removes the burden from victims and acts on their behalf. It is equipped with scientific expertise and financial resources, and provides a central repository for information that would never be collected by individual victims' groups. Similarly, it may be true that compensation levels are modest in comparison with the occasionally generous tort award, but this is the price of a public scheme's *comprehensiveness*. So long as the victims are adequately cared for and compensated, such comprehensiveness seems vastly preferable to a situation in which a few individuals receive spectacular awards while most go uncompensated entirely. It must be remembered also that tort awards are significantly reduced by legal fees, and are vastly less efficient in delivering compensation than are non-tort plans. A recent Canadian study estimated that victims receive little more than 30 per cent of the money entering the tort system, compared with 80 or 90 per cent under alternative compensation programs.[17] To the extent that very-high-income earners do not receive full income replacement under a public compensation scheme, supplementary protection can be purchased.

It is true that the compensation benefits of public compensation schemes may succumb to conservative fiscal or political pressure; that benefit levels run the risk of erosion if they are not supported by political will. If compensation levels are too low, or classes are designated too narrowly, these schemes may lose their deterrent effect and, in fact, provide a licence to industry to pollute. This is a danger than can be avoided only by public vigilance. Yet there is no reason to believe that political leverage is less potent than legal leverage. Unlike tort litigation where problems are isolated and individualized, larger groups in society have an interest, if only potential, in the maintenance of public compensation programs. Litigation is a reactive process that responds to isolated occurrences and is therefore unlikely to spawn broad-based coalitions between different victim groups. In contrast, a public compensation scheme may be more proactive, and because it covers the problem of disease and injury more generally, quite disparate groups will have a common interest in its maintenance. And unlike litigation, where unevenly spread financial and legal resources significantly determine outcomes, the quality of public compensation schemes ultimately responds to political processes. One need not overemphasize the egalitarian qualities of democratic politics, or idealize the political process, in order to maintain that it at least provides a forum within which disempowered voices are more likely to be heard than in a court-room.

Irrational Distinctions?

Proposals to implement a 'disaster fund' or 'pollution compensation program' suggest promising models. Yet, as the Japanese experience reveals, even these schemes cannot fully solve the problem of causation. So long as entitlement to compensation remains limited to a class that has been exposed to a specific source of harm, causal problems will continue to plague the law. The notion of a 'disaster fund,' for example, harkens back to an older model of traumatic injury whereby victims can easily be distinguished from non-victims. It presupposes that disaster-related *injuries* can easily be distinguished from 'natural' *illnesses*. But, as Bhopal reveals, when confronted by problems of toxic exposure and environmental accidents, these distinctions are difficult to draw, defend, or apply. Two problems occur with compensation regimes that are limited to particular types of injury, caused by specific activities or sources. The first is that such a regime may reintroduce many of the causal problems associated with tort litigation. The second is that, once we abandon fault as the criterion of entitlement, it becomes difficult, if not impossible, to explain why one class of victims (for example, of a chemical disaster) should be treated differently from other individuals who suffer disability as a result of their exposure to some other socially generated risk.

The first problem may be illustrated by the Japanese law. To bring themselves within the specific programs, victims must demonstrate that they were exposed to a particular source of harm and that they suffer fromm a designated disease. In many cases, this may mean that the victims have a new burden: to litigate against a public agency to demonstrate that they are members of the class covered by the program or, even more problematically, that their form of injury should be included as a designated disease.

Throughout the world there are various 'no-fault' schemes, but all are limited to specific activities and arbitrarily designated victim groups defined by causal principles. Many jurisdictions have no-fault regimes with respect to industrial accidents (workers' compensation) and automobile accidents. In addition to its pollution compensation regime, Japan has a compensation system covering drug injuries. New South Wales even has a sporting-injuries compensation scheme.[18] In each case, victims must demonstrate a causal connection between their injuries and the activities covered by the scheme, and the population covered is treated better (or worse) than others who are injured by other causes.

Any compensation scheme that is confined to a class of injuries or a particular source of harm will necessarily have to draw 'irrational' distinctions between persons who suffer from disadvantages that are no fault of their own. So long as such schemes continue to draw distinctions between classes of victims, based on causal connections, individuals will continue to carry the burden of establishing that they are victims of a 'disaster' or of 'pollution' and that their injuries were caused by a specific incident or source. Essentially such schemes simply transfer the locus of dispute about causation from the courts to an administrative agency. Moreover, from the point of view of compensation, it is difficult to see why such 'victims' are more deserving than other individuals whose hurt, injury, or disease does not fall within the designated class. As Patrick Atiyah suggests, 'everywhere the present pattern of reform seems to be to institute limited no-fault schemes to deal with particular classes of injured persons whose claims are pressed by politically powerful groups, or whose light for some reason attracts public attention and sympathy.'[19]

The result of causal indeterminacy is that no-fault compensation schemes are under constant pressure to expand to cover disabilities incurred from increasingly disparate sources. There are, in turn, two responses to this pressure. The first is to conclude that such schemes are not feasible; that the pressure to expand will produce runaway costs and increase government expenditures beyond acceptable levels.[20] The second response is to accept and nourish the pressure to expand –

indeed, to abandon causal thinking entirely in developing compensation policies.

Into the latter camp fall those who argue that, if we take the compensation goal seriously, what is required is a public-responsibility model for all harms, whether catastrophic or creeping.[21] Under these proposals, compensation law ultimately merges into a comprehensive system of health care and income security. So, for example, Richard Gaskins, in his recent book, *Environmental Accidents*, has also entered a plea for a more comprehensive *public responsibility* model of compensation. After an exhaustive examination of environmental harm, and the bewildering array of compensation programs, Gaskins argues that the individualist orientation of existing schemes is 'built on a series of tacit assumptions that disguise the collective environment of personal injuries.'[22] Gaskins concludes that, once this orientation is abandoned, as it must be in the face of the socially complex nature of injury in modern society, we are led to a 'policy that would eliminate all distinctions in social entitlement based on causal categories.'[23] Accident compensation 'thus merges into general entitlement programs for disability.'[24] As Jane Stapleton argues in *Disease and the Compensation Debate*: 'Not only do the practical problems of proving disease causation suggest abandonment of tort in favour of a compensation fund, but this appears to be the more rational way to accommodate policy goals such as fairness, compensation and even deterrence.'[25] A comprehensive discussion of no-fault compensation is well beyond the scope of this book. But any work on toxic harm and compensation law would be radically incomplete if it did not at least address the policy options and canvass the contours of the debate.

The New Zealand accident-compensation system stands out as the most significant and far-reaching experiment in compensation reform. In 1974 New Zealand enacted its Accident Compensation Act, a comprehensive no-fault compensation scheme for all victims of accidental injury. The scheme abolished tort actions for personal injury and death and replaced them with a universal 'no-fault' entitlement to compensation administered by the Accident Compensation Commission. The scheme is financed by a levy on employers, an automobile charge, and general revenues, and provides scheduled payments for medical expenses, lost income, and pain and suffering to anyone incurring 'personal injury by accident.' The New Zealand system is not, of course, without its critics.[26] However, most observers, including the New Zealand Law Reform Commission in a recent assessment, have concluded that the scheme works well, providing timely and adequate compensation at a low administrative cost (only about 7 per cent of total expenditure).[27]

Even in New Zealand, however, victims must demonstrate that their injuries were caused by 'accident,' 'medical misadventure,' or some other specified risk as opposed, for example, to 'disease.' But epidemiological knowledge demonstrates that drawing the line between accident and illness, injury, and disease is scientifically problematic. It is equally problematic from the point of view of justice. Victims of illness find it difficult to understand why they should be treated differently from others. Indeed, the underlying 'accident preference' is one of the major political and ideological issues surrounding the scheme. Thus, like other limited schemes, there is constant pressure to expand coverage. In New Zealand, this has produced both of the responses suggested above. On the one hand, the Law Commission has recommended that the definition of 'injury' be expanded to include at least congenital disease.[28] On the other hand, critics have alleged that the costs of the program are getting out of control, giving rise to New Zealand's own 'insurance crisis.' This has prompted some to call for limits on benefit levels or even further restrictions upon entitlement. However, even the critics have admitted that, in comparison to levels in other countries, 'the new rates were not terribly high.'[29] The New Zealand scheme provides comprehensive cover to *all* accident victims. It thus provides compensation to a much larger injured population than does the tort system. Yet levies on employers (which are passed on to the consumer) do not significantly increase the cost of goods and services and are not greater than the insurance premiums paid by employers in other jurisdictions.[30] The total cost of the scheme amounts to about 1.2 per cent of GDP, which compares favourably with compensation costs in other countries.[31]

Public compensation schemes are also frequently attacked on the basis that the elimination of tort law will deprive law of its deterrent clout. If actors are not held accountable for the injuries they cause, they will have no incentive to reduce risks to human health and the environment. There are two things wrong with this argument. First, it vastly overstates the current importance of tort law and its ability to deter hazardous conduct. Second, it assumes that public-responsibility models ignore deterrence values. They do not. Instead, they simply separate the issue of victim compensation from the question of liability and deterrence.

There is little evidence that tort law plays a significant deterrent role in modern society, especially in the area of environmental safety and health.[32] There is, for example, no solid evidence that the abolition of tort liability in New Zealand has caused a decrease in safety. Indeed, a study of automobile accidents in the country found that such incidents have, in fact, declined since the introduction of the plan, a finding likely attributable to better regulatory and enforcement measures. The study concluded that, 'clearly, the removal of tort rights for personal injury cases did not produce the increase in accident-producing behavior predicted by the traditional theory of tort deterrence.'[33] Accident prevention can, no doubt, be improved, but the reintroduction of tort law has been firmly rejected as an unproven and wasteful method of accomplishing this goal.

Of vastly greater importance than tort law are regulatory and criminal regimes that set industrial standards for workplace safety, risk management, and pollution control, and provide effective sanctions and enforcement mechanisms. These deterrence measures can, indeed, be enhanced through public-responsibility models of compensation. Experience rating of premiums, as in the case of workers' compensation schemes, can play an important role.[34] Additionally, where the fund provides compensation following an industrial disaster, for example, there is no reason why the responsible actor could not be liable for the costs. Under many environmental-protection statutes, while government authorities may assume responsibility for clean-up and compensation following an environmental incident such as an oil spill, the responsible party is ultimately accountable for reimbursement of those expenses.

Of greater importance, unlike litigation, a public compensation system need not simply *react* to isolated events after they have occurred. Instead, it has the capacity to take *proactive* initiatives based on prior information. Contributions to the claim fund can be experience rated; or based on prior risk assessment; or gauged according to effluent levels, toxicity levels, health hazards, and so on. By calibrating contributions to *ex ante* risk, public responsibility models can, for example, promote Calabresi's market deterrence.

Finally, it is frequently argued that comprehensive disability and income security schemes are 'utopian,' that is, politically unfeasible or simply too expensive. The 'too expensive' argument can be partially met by reiterating the fact that the present tort system wastes enormous resources. Moreover, damage to human health and the environment is also expensive. The decision to compensate the victims does not increase costs – it simply redistributes those costs from individuals to other actors in society more generally. The question, therefore, is ultimately one not only of cost, but of distributive justice. There is no doubt that it would require major political mobilization to institute such a regime. Yet, while the regime's comprehensiveness makes it an enormously ambitious political project, that same feature might mobilize widespread support. As in the case of universal health-care systems, the breadth of coverage might promote links and coalitions between previously disparate groups. Workers, consumers, environmental groups, poverty organizations, and others might find common cause in supporting and maintaining such a system.

But this is not a complete response. The *logic* of a universal disability scheme may be inescapable: once we abandon fault as the basis of compensation there is no rational distinction between different victims on the basis of causal categories. But politics and policy are not driven by logic alone. As a matter of practical politics, it is simply a fact that, in all countries, some of the social costs of 'economic progress' are going to be discounted and left to be borne by the victims. Perennial debate in New Zealand over the cost of maintaining (or broadening) the scheme reveals that, especially in times of economic downturn, distributive justice will compete against a strongly ingrained social preference for capital accumulation and economic growth. This preference leads to a utilitarian trade-off in which individual victims are left to bear the burden of their harms as the price of 'social progress.'

Part of the problem is that the costs of a public compensation scheme are highly visible, whereas those of leaving victims privately to bear their own injuries are invisible. And there is no doubt that these visible costs are enormous. The political feasibility of a compensation scheme thus presupposes a sufficient level of wealth and an extraordinary social commitment to distribute that wealth to disabled persons. Some states, including Canada with its broad array of health, disability, and income security programs, are part-way there. But it would be naïve to suppose that such a regime is immediately in the cards in a country like India, despite its verbal commitment to democratic socialism and the general welfare.

However, it is possible that Bhopal, and the rising world concern with industrial and environmental harms, might prompt the development of more limited experiments and programs, such as the Supreme Court's proposed environmental or industrial compensation fund. Such schemes are more politically feasible and fiscally acceptable. Bhopal reveals how it is easier to focus public attention on a more specific social problem and to mobilize sympathy and support. The limited nature of the scheme means that its costs are less frightening. While its implementation might simply entrench an anomalous social preference for one class of the population, it might also begin a process of incremental reform.[35] Once on the path, an unavoidable tension might provide a degree of momentum. This tension arises from the fact that such schemes are based ultimately upon a social decision to relieve a class of persons from an undeserved disability. Yet, at the same time that one class is selected or recognized, others with equally undeserved disabilities will be left out. They will point out the arbitrary line that excludes them from the program and will demand that it be moved to include them.[36] Arbitrary lines, drawn on the basis of distinctions between different activities or different forms of disability, will have to be continually redrawn. Ultimately, we may come to realize that the only defensible distinctions between disabled persons are differences in their needs.

Local and International Lessons

While this book is primarily about repairing the wrong done to the victims of an industrial disaster, it would remain incomplete if it did not acknowledge the importance of preventing such a wrong in the first place, and of developing new systems for the mitigation of harm at both the local and the international level. After all, while I have argued that the compensation process failed the victims, it should not be forgotten that they were victimized originally by the interaction of political, legal, economic, and management systems that disregarded their welfare.

The risk mismanagement at Bhopal reveals the various failures that any response must address. These included (1) the failure to develop adequate information on the substances or processes that would be present; (2) the failure to assess the initial risks involved in the choice of technology; (3) the failure to manage those risks through proper siting of the facility; (4) the failure to communicate information to the community and to develop emergency response systems; (5) the failure to maintain the technology and operation in a safe state; (6) the failure to communicate new data as they became available; and (7) the failure of local administrators to respond to or reduce the risks associated with the operation. Each of these failures points to the need for a more effective regime of domestic and international risk management.

Developments in India

Following the Bhopal disaster, the Indian government enacted a new Environment Protection Act.[37] This statute, which borrowed heavily from the legislation of developed countries, incorporates a variety of useful reforms. Seeking to adapt the law to modern industrial conditions, the new legislation vests the central government with wide authority to take measures to reduce industrial and environmental risks. The statute authorizes the establishment of a central environmental authority with responsibility for coordinating environmental protection at all levels of government. It anticipates nation-wide environmental planning, and the articulation of environmental quality standards, pollution controls, and emissions standards. More specifically, the act provides for better zoning of industrial locations, a more intensive system of inspections, and the development of prevention guidelines and emergency response systems. It contemplates that entities which cause environmental harm will be financially responsible for clean-up costs. Penalties for offences have been increased to longer terms of imprisonment and larger fines, and the act provides that managers and directors will be held personally accountable for safety failures.

In addition to the Environment Protection Act, significant amendments were made to the Factories Act.[38] A new chapter was added on hazardous processes, authorizing the state to create site-appraisal committees to assess the location or expansion plans of hazardous facilities. Occupiers of hazardous installations are now required to make compulsory disclosure of all dangers, and to record and report incidents. They must develop policies on health and safety, and prepare emergency plans for approval by public authorities. In addition, facilities classified as hazardous must appoint qualified safety officers and strike safety committees with substantial worker participation. The statute also confers 'whistle blower protection' upon employees.

More generally, the statue creates a general duty upon occupiers of hazardous installations to ensure the health and safety of workers, ensuring adequate safety systems, equipment arrangements and maintenance, training and information, safe practices and processes. Significantly, 'occupiers' include anyone, including directors, with ultimate control over the affairs of the company. Reflecting India's status as an importer of hazardous technology, the amendments also impose a general duty on designers, manufacturers, importers, and suppliers to ensure (so far as practical) the safety of equipment and processes. Where a plant or machinery is manufactured outside India, the importer is obliged to ensure that it conforms at least to the required domestic safety standards and, where those standards in the country of origin are higher than in India, the equipment must meet those higher standards.

Although important developments, it remains to be seen how these new statutes will be implemented. While providing government with ample authority to set and enforce guidelines, at this point the statutes remain relatively general frameworks rather than detailed action plans. Both must be supplemented by detailed regulations and standards. This process has at least begun. In 1989, for example, rules were promulgated on the manufacture, storage, and transportation of hazardous chemicals.

More important, legal reforms must be backed by the devotion of sufficient resources so that they do not merely become further hollow legal promises. Both public and private resources must be devoted to environmental-impact and risk-assessment studies, and to maintaining adequate staffing levels and training of both employees and public inspectors. This process has begun in a modest way on the public side. For example, an International Labor Organization–aided project has identified nearly 600 major hazard installations that will be included in a developing control and inspection plan.

Industry must also be given incentives to devote greater resources to risk auditing and hazard control. The liability provisions of the Factories Act is a step in the right direction. The possibility of absolute liability, while still of uncertain status in domestic Indian law, may also have some impact. Recognizing the need to supplement formal responses, some Indian experts have suggested that, in the case of potentially hazardous industries, company officers and staff be required to live in close proximity to the plant. This would certainly enhance safety incentives.

Both industries and municipalities must engage in a continuous process of emergency-response planning. Such planning must include preparedness training and address communications systems, evacuation procedures, and medical responses. This process too has begun, with the new statutory obligation on facilities to prepare emergency plans, and a 'three tier' (central, state, and municipal) crisis-management plan for chemical emergencies, developed by the ministry of environment. A central databank should be maintained to provide readily accessible information on hazardous substances, health effects, and treatment in the event of an incident.

Any effective risk-management and environmental-protection program depends, first and foremost, upon the availability of comprehensive and accurate information. Standards setting, regulatory guidelines, emergency plans, disaster responses – all depend upon the acquisition and dissemination of reliable information. Information must flow freely between industry and government and among various government agencies.

Similarly, because health and environmental issues are ultimately questions of public choice, more open processes are required both to inform and to involve communities in decision making. Information must therefore flow to and from 'third parties,' including workers, researchers, public-interest groups, health professionals, and members of the general public. Public input should be enhanced at an early stage by encouraging and supporting the participation of public-interest and community groups in environmental-impact and risk-assessment studies. Affected communities should have a say in the location of dangerous industries and should be provided with complete information concerning risks and emergency responses.

However, as environmental experts in India and elsewhere have recognized, the law 'tends to privatise information or to secretize it ... The regime of privatisation operates through legitimate protection of patents, knowhow and trade-secrets. The secretisation process involves a spectrum of decisions by holders of public power on grounds of national integrity, development and quite often, and starkly, of unexamined bureaucratic culture which generates abundant confidentiality.'[39]

The protection of trade secrets and confidential business information is a legitimate concern of industry. However, such concerns must be balanced against the imperative of acquiring and disseminating accurate and comprehensive information for all purposes. Increasingly, environmental-protection legislation has been incorporating mandatory disclosure provisions and freedom of information.[40] Going even farther are regimes that recognize the community's 'right to know,' which require facilities to reveal the presence of hazardous substances to local communities.[41] Such legislation can play a useful role in empowering citizens to participate in decision-making processes that affect their lives, providing information that enhances the ability of non-governmental organizations to act as watch-dogs. Such public participation provides a channel of accountability and a check against corruption, political influence, and administrative 'capture' by the regulated industry. Surely it is one of the lessons of Bhopal that public education and consultation are more positive responses to risk than is secrecy.

The new Indian legislation is a welcome step forward. It signals a new recognition of environmental values and risk-management imperatives. It vests the government with enhanced authority and increased clout to deal with environmental problems and industrial offenders. Yet one should not become overly sanguine about the instrumental impact of formal legal guarantees. What is required is not necessarily more governmental *authority*, but more real *power* to ensure that the promises of law do not remain empty. Given the complexity of the problem of international transfers of hazardous technologies, that power must be sought not only on the domestic level, but also through international institutions.

International Initiatives: Problems and Possibilities

As Justice Singh of the Supreme Court pointed out, the problem of industrial and environmental risks in the Third World is international in scope. After the Second World War, direct colonial rule in the Third World rapidly began to shrink. But, at the same time that political domination came to an end, multinational businesses began to exercise greater power in the developing countries, in many cases exploiting their vulnerabilities, and in some cases influencing 'the political and economic policies of host countries which subverted the sovereignty of those countries.'[42] The developing world must, argued Singh, throw what power it has behind international efforts to develop codes of conduct for transnational enterprises and take steps to transform the formal guarantees of international law into concrete protections for the victims of international industry.

Developing countries urgently require the ability to participate in international trade and to import new technologies. But Bhopal is a vivid illustration of the fact that the technical and administrative infrastructure of importing states is often ill prepared to receive those new technologies. The importing state will usually have inadequate information about the risks associated with a new industrial venture and therefore be incapable of engaging in a full assessment of the environmental impact of the project. Even if it is initially fully informed about the associated hazards, its administrative regime may be ill equipped to manage the risk once the facility is operational.

As the International Law Commission of the United Nations reported in 1987, multinational corporations are at the forefront of industry in many developing countries. Because of their financial power and their control of technology and knowledge, these corporations often operate beyond effective state control. 'The developing countries were in a disadvantageous position. They needed the multinational corporations to operate within their territory in order to generate some economic development; at the same time, they lacked the expertise to appreciate the magnitude of the risk that the work of these corporations could cause and the power to compel the companies to disclose such risks. In this context these developing countries were also victims.'[43]

International institutions and their nation-states are acutely aware of these problems and have begun to respond to them. Indeed, since Bhopal, there has been a flurry of activity in the international arena, prompted in large measure by the world's horror at what had happened.[44] Yet it must be acknowledged that there are considerable obstacles in the way of multilateral initiatives in international law. The first of these is that traditional international law is about the relations between sovereign states. Individual citizens, non-governmental organizations, and corporations are not 'states' and are not, therefore, the subjects of international law. Treaties, conventions, and declarations may impose obligations on countries to control the conduct of industries, but international law-making and dispute-resolution bodies have no direct jurisdiction over non-governmental entities themselves.

Given that traditional international law applies only to the relations between states, the only way in which it might reach the activities of 'private' entities, such as transnational corporations, is if it imposes an obligation on states to control the activities of their corporate citizens abroad. But multinationals operating abroad are not generally subject to the law of their home state. The notion of sovereignty, upon which international law is built, makes it difficult, perhaps even undesirable, for one state to give its laws extraterritorial application.

Those initiatives that are under way to develop international regulation of multinational corporations and hazardous transfers are further hindered by notions of free trade and the unwillingness of the industrialized countries to forgo the competitive advantages offered to their companies by the less-developed world. By and large, international trade law is informed by the goal of encouraging rather than restricting the free flow of products and technologies, however hazardous.

Finally, even the developing world is suspicious of international regulation. These countries insist on asserting their sovereign right to determine what technologies they import and how they will be regulated. Ever mindful of their recent colonial past, the developing countries fear that international environmental and industrial law is simply a new form of imperialism. If formulated by the powerful and affluent nations of the world, these regulations would be insensitive to the needs and policies of Third World countries. They may reflect the higher priority that the affluent countries can now afford to place upon environmental safety and threaten to deprive the developing countries of the very capital and technology that they require in order to achieve even a fraction of that affluence. International regulation thus threatens to aggravate rather than reduce the inequality between nations.[45]

These, then, are the dynamics that characterize international negotiations and constrain the development of cooperative initiatives. The concluding section of this chapter, which canvasses some of these initiatives, illustrates the difficulties, but also points the way to more effective strategies.

Codes of Conduct

For years the international community has been considering the development of codes of conduct for multinational business and technology transfers. As Pedro Roffe, the chief of the Legal Policies Section for the United Nations Conference on Trade and Development (UNCTAD), explains, these initiatives originated in the 1960s in response to the recognition of the importance of technology transfers to the development of the industrializing countries of the world.[46] These countries were dependent upon the acquisition of technology, but also incompletely prepared for its reception because of their lesser-developed social, technical, and legal infrastructure.

The proposed U.N. International Code of Conduct on the Transfer of Technology[47] articulates the responsibilities of the contracting parties; specifies undesirable and forbidden practices; and contains useful sections pertaining to the provision of technical services and information, ongoing assistance, training, updated information, spare parts, and equipment. It seeks also to deal with the problematic issues of confidentiality and intellectual property rights.

Yet the code is not yet part of international law, and many obstacles lie in its way. As Roffe explains, the negotiations are characterized by a tension between the interests, perspectives, and policy goals of the different countries. The primary objectives of the industrialized countries and their multinational corporations are to gain entry to new markets, to protect their intellectual property, and, of course, to earn a profit. The interest of the developing countries, in contrast, is to generate wealth within their own geographical borders; to acquire indigenous skills, knowledge, and technology; and ultimately to gain a certain independence from the countries and firms upon whom they must currently rely for those resources. The parties have been unable to agree upon the definition of an 'international' technology transfer,[48] or on whether the code should be a legally binding document.

Other efforts to regulate multinational business are characterized by the same obstacles. These initiatives include the OECD Guidelines on Multinational Enterprises and the draft U.N. Code of Conduct on Transnational Corporations.[49] Both of these documents contain potentially valuable provisions. They urge multinational corporations to cooperate in the developmental goals of their host countries, to respect the policies of those countries, to refrain from anticompetitive practices, and to avoid improper political activities. They encourage companies to maintain good industrial relations, to maintain safe procedures, and to supply information on hazards to health and the environment to host governments and to their subsidiaries. Following Bhopal, the OECD 'clarified' its guidelines by indicating that multinationals should 'give due consideration to the member countries' aims and policies with regard to the protection of the environment and consumer interests.'[50]

Yet these codes are very limited measures. First, they are not binding on anyone and contain no sanctions or obligatory dispute-resolution mechanisms. The OECD guidelines are voluntary and the U.N. proposals are still in draft form after ten years, the negotiations characterized by the conflicting objectives of developing and developed countries. Second, because the proposals are compromises between such widely conflicting objectives, by and large they consist of general statements of intent and policy rather than specific requirements concerning operations and information. Third, both codes prohibit host states from treating multinationals differently from domestic corporations and mandate 'non-discriminatory' national treatment. Indeed, representatives of multinationals have been pressing for the inclusion of an even stronger provision mandating 'clarity and stability' of national laws and policies and requiring host states to take corporate interests into account when changing their laws. Nor do the codes deal with liability issues, apparently assuming that domestic legal systems with jurisdiction over subsidiaries are adequate to the task. Bhopal, however, teaches that they are not, and that the codes should deal with the potential responsibility of parent corporations for the defaults of their subsidiaries, and should address the problems of jurisdiction and dispute settlement.

Liability and Compensation

In addition to codes of conduct, various international bodies have been considering the question of liability for international environmental harms.[51] For example, since 1987 the International Law Commission of the United Nations has been debating: (a) the possibility of host-state liability for transfrontier consequences of an industrial accident; (b) the possibility of home-state liability for damages arising out of the operations of their multinationals abroad; and (c) the possibility of private liability of multinationals for their hazardous operations. Under one draft article, a state might be made liable for the transfrontier consequences of an industrial disaster in situations where the dangerous activity was carried out within territory under its control and where the activity was one in which there was 'an appreciable risk of causing transboundary injury.' Such a regime would have no application where, as in the case of Bhopal, the business was international but the physical consequences were confined within a single territory.

The commission is also considering the possibility that the home state of a multinational might be made liable for the injurious consequences caused by the operations of that company abroad. For example, under this proposal, the United States might be liable to India for the damage caused in a Bhopal scenario. Not surprisingly, many members of the commission objected to this approach. It is simply unacceptable to developed countries whose companies export technology. It might also be unacceptable to developing countries on the basis that it would likely encourage further foreign control over industrial practices in the host state. It would also reduce the transfer of potentially dangerous technologies with the consequent loss of development capital and jobs.[52]

Finally, the commission is considering the question of private liability of multinationals, the very issue raised by Bhopal. However, it has, for the time being, rejected this approach on the basis that international law concerns itself with the relations between states and that multinational corporations are not 'international legal persons' for the purposes of international law. As Professor McCaffrey, a member of the commission, concludes: 'it should not be forgotten that the particular province of the International Law Commission is, in the first instance at least, to formulate rules concerning the international obligation of states. For this reason ... the Commission should not become preoccupied with private law approaches to the liability problem.'[53]

But, as others have argued, the time is now past when the international community can be described solely in terms of an association of sovereign states. Multinational companies have become powerful actors in the international arena, and some way should be found to make them more accountable for their hazardous operations. As in the case of Union Carbide, their corporate structure can place them beyond the jurisdiction of the countries in which they operate. New technologies have given them 'virtually unrestricted power' to 'transfer within moments vast sums of capital between banks in different states, and to run industries and plants which pollute massively across international borders.'[54]

If the international community really cares to respond to Bhopal, it must address liability and compensation issues and deal with the reality of multinational business organizations. There is evidence that at least some U.S. courts are reconsidering the traditional hands-off approach to U.S. corporate conduct abroad. In 1990 the Supreme Court of Texas – clearly with Bhopal in mind – rejected the doctrine of *forum non conveniens* in an action brought by Costa Rican farm workers against Shell Oil and Dow Chemical. The farmers, who were employees of Standard Fruit (itself a subsidiary of the U.S. Dole Fruit Company), were suing for injuries resulting from their exposure to pesticides sold by the defendant to their employer. The court refused to dismiss the case. As Doggett J stated, the doctrine of *forum non conveniens*, which in the past often left the victims with no effective remedy at all, is not really about convenience, 'but connivance to avoid corporate accountability.'[55] He ended with a plea for 'comity,' which, he said, cannot be achieved 'when the United States allows its multinational corporations to adhere to a double standard when operating abroad and subsequently refuses to hold them accountable for those actions.'[56] This is a welcome development. So long as there is no oppression or abuse of process, it should be possible to secure jurisdiction over a multinational company in its home state.

Merely securing jurisdiction over the multinational, however, is not enough. The next question is the issue of when a multinational will be responsible for its subsidiary and against what standards its responsibility will be assessed. There are a variety of options. First, India's theory of strict multinational-enterprise liability should be taken seriously as one way to ensure that the entity best situated to control hazards and ensure compensation has the incentive to do so. But does this go too far? It might be objected that such a proposal is a form of environmental imperialism, imposing foreign standards of responsibility on industrial activities in the host country. There are two possible responses.

First, it can be said that strict liability does not interfere with host-country sovereignty or managerial discretion. All it does is give the victims the right to compensation. Government and industry may enter into whatever arrangement they wish regarding operating standards. The point of strict liability is simply that industry may not transfer the resulting risks to the local populace.

Nevertheless, such an approach may appear to some to go too far. If endorsed only by one or two of the developed countries, it will penalize their companies in comparison to multinationals operating out of other jurisdictions. If endorsed by only one or two host countries, it may affect their ability to attract foreign investment. These problems reveal again the need for widespread cooperation. If 'hazard ghettos' are to be avoided, a principle must be found that may be endorsed by as many countries as possible. A variety of more politically feasible compromises suggest themselves. In the area of nuclear damage and oil pollution, international instruments provide for strict, but limited liability.[57] These could be used as models for international conventions or contractual agreements with respect to hazardous installations. An alternative would be to adopt a *presumption* of multinational responsibility. According to this modified principle, the parent company would be liable *unless* it could adduce evidence that it was prevented by the host country from exercising control over its subsidiary, that the hazardous practices were mandated by the policies of the host country, or that its liability and responsibility had been expressly waived or limited in an agreement negotiated with the responsible authorities in the host country. Along the same lines, multinational responsibility could be measured against an 'international safety standard,' drawing upon the norms incorporated in emerging international instruments and promulgated by bodies such as the U.N., OECD, and ILO.[58] So, for example, a failure to communicate information, to undertake risk assessments and hazard audits, to maintain employee education and training, or to develop emergency response systems, might attract presumptive liability.

Such principles could be evolved by courts, but preferably would be enshrined in a uniform code. The code could itself include more detailed statements of internationally accepted practices and standards of responsible investment. To the extent that the strict provisions of the code were thought to be inappropriate to a particular project or technology transfer, they could be modified, though only through express contractual arrangements negotiated directly with the host countries. Such a regime would resolve, in part, the tension between the desirability of uniform industrial safety standards, and the unique needs, priorities, and policies of the host country. The code could also contain dispute-resolution mechanisms that recognized MNCs as legal entities. The International Court of Justice, for example, would have jurisdiction to rule on disputes between the MNC and the host country concerning the application of the code.

Preventive Measures: Informed Consent and Extraterritorial Initiatives

Developing countries confer upon multinationals a competitive advantage because they offer low-cost labour, access to markets, and lower operating expenses. Once there, companies have little incentive to minimize environmental and human risks. Lax environmental and safety regulation, inadequate capital investment in safety equipment, and poor communications between companies and governments compound the problem.

Many concerned observers argue that the more-developed countries have an obligation to assume a share of responsibility for health and environment in the Third World. The failure of these countries to take action, they argue, simply preserves and promotes an international economic regime that exploits the citizens of other countries. It confirms that the developed nations of the world are interested only in perpetuating double standards of safety, which devalues life in the Third World.[59] Yet, at present, home states play only a minimal role in the regulation of their industries abroad. They are reluctant to assume responsibility for enforcing international codes or to impose any requirements with respect to the overseas operations of companies under their jurisdiction.

Recently, however, the industrialized world has taken halting and modest steps to alter the double standard. Perhaps the most common approach is to require 'informed consent.'[60] What this means is that foreign-based multinationals have an unrestricted right to export to and operate in, the Third World, subject to the requirement that they provide information about the risks of these operations to the recipient country. Thus, the recipient country is able to make informed decisions about whether to accept the product or technology, where to locate it, and how to regulate it.

The informed-consent approach, which is expressed in many of the proposed codes of conduct[61] and enshrined in some domestic legislation of exporting countries, is a useful, but extremely limited measure. Its main advantage is that it does recognize the need to mediate between a concern for industrial safety and a respect for the sovereignty of the host state. But, because it is a compromise, it only superficially addresses the problem. In the first place, existing regimes apply primarily to hazardous products (pesticides, chemicals, and hazardous wastes) rather than processes. Moreover, because the developed world has little interest in impairing the ability of its industries to engage in international trade, the information that they require their companies to disclose is minimal. In the interests of protecting their intellectual property, multinationals limit their disclosure to the bare essentials, and refuse to provide information that might reveal trade secrets.

Perhaps more importantly, the informed-consent approach presupposes that the recipient country has adequate resources to evaluate properly the information that it receives and to develop appropriate regulations and operating conditions based on that information. Finally, it assumes that the recipient country possesses the political will and technical and legal resources to enforce compliance with its regulations and operating conditions once the technology is in place.[62] The Bhopal story reveals that these are all highly questionable assumptions.

Many argue that the developed world must go farther and that the export of industry and technology should be accompanied by the export of safety regulation. A common proposal is that the developed countries should ensure that their multinationals operating abroad conduct their operations in the developing world at the same level of safety required of their domestic operations.[63] One example of this approach is the 'Bhopal Resolution' of the European Parliament, which calls upon European firms to maintain levels of safety abroad that are comparable to those in place in their home operations.[64] The OECD is considering a similar proposal in its Conference on Accidents Involving Hazardous Substances: Hazardous Installations in Developing Countries.[65]

Such extraterritorial initiatives are promoted on the basis that developing nations may eagerly welcome hazardous operations even though they lack the necessary resources to regulate those hazards, to reduce the risks associated with them, or to repair the damage when it occurs.[66] Workers in the developing world, and local residents have almost no information about the hazards associated with imported technology. Nor are their governments always prepared or able to protect their welfare.

There are, however, several problems with home-state regulation. It is strenuously resisted by multinational corporations on the basis that it violates the 'non-discrimination' principle. It requires them to abide by higher standards than those imposed for domestic industries and deprives them of their competitive advantage (even though they already possess the necessary know-how and technology). A related objection, often offered by multinationals, is that absent almost unanimous agreement between the developed countries, home-state regulation will not improve the lot of the developing world, but will simply penalize those multinationals located in well-meaning countries. If only one country, the United States, for example, were to regulate the activities of its multinationals abroad, U.S. companies would be put at a comparative disadvantage against British, German, French, and Japanese companies. The result would be that only those firms operating from unregulated home countries would invest in the developing world. While some proponents of home-state regulation argue that the good reputation of the regulated industry might compensate for any competitive disadvantage, the problem could be thoroughly overcome only if the developed nations cooperated in regulating all multinationals, thus creating a level playing-field.

Nor does the developing world unequivocally welcome the idea of extraterritorial regulation, for it is arguably a form of environmental and legal 'imperialism.' The industrialized nations of the world have fashioned their industrial regulations over the course of time and in the context of considerable affluence. To impose these same regulations on the operation of industry in developing countries deprives those countries of the opportunity to formulate their own social policy on the basis of their own assessment of the costs and benefits of industrial development and better appreciation of local conditions and needs. Indeed, some developing nations have unequivocally rejected the 'same-standards' model on the basis that it would discourage foreign investment in their countries and deprive them of much needed jobs and technology.

Notwithstanding these objections, after Bhopal and Chernobyl, importing countries may have become somewhat less concerned about the potential loss of sovereignty that results from international regulation of hazardous business. And as one commentator points out, the loss of national autonomy that results from the international regulation of such industries 'pales by comparison to the social and economic decision-making powers which many third-world debtor countries now routinely surrender in exchange for loans by multilateral lending institutions.'[67] Indeed, international standards might, in fact, enhance the sovereignty of importing countries by reducing the ability of multinational businesses to demand concessions with respect to environmental and workplace safety requirements.

Gunther Handl and Robert Lutz suggest a compromise position on the same-standards model. Recognizing that state sovereignty must be balanced against risk reduction, they argue that international law should embrace a *presumption* of same standards: that the transfer of hazardous technology should be prohibited unless the recipient state can demonstrate that it will enforce equivalent standards of environmental and industrial safety. The presumption of equivalent standards could be rebutted if the importing country could demonstrate that lower standards are justified. As they conclude, 'This approach would not in itself assure adequate risk management in the recipient state. But it would force the receiving state to face squarely and publicly the risks involved and thereby could substantially contribute to risk reduction, perhaps even bringing about a reversal of the original decision to seek the transfer.'[68]

These proposals all contain valuable ideas. Yet a final problem with the 'same-standards' model – indeed, with all international and multilateral legal initiatives – is that it unrealistically relies upon formal legal mechanisms. It assumes that safety is a product of what is written in the books, rather than of political will backed by sufficient technical and administrative resources. Many developing countries have environmental and safety laws that are only somewhat less stringent than those in Canada or the United States. Indeed, India has now itself legislated a 'same standards' principle for hazardous imports. The problem in these countries has little to do with the applicable standards, but is one of compliance and enforcement. It is difficult to see how this problem is to be overcome simply by developing improved formal standards. The problem could be overcome only by the wholesale export of the technical and regulatory resources possessed by the enforcement agencies of the developed nations. Such a development seems unlikely, but it does focus attention on an important dimension of the problem and points the way towards more integrated and substantial strategies.

International Responsibility

The limitations of existing international regimes reveal new directions. Ultimately, what we learn is that most international initiatives fail to grapple with what the *Brundtland Report* has identified as the most serious obstacle to achieving a safer and cleaner world: 'the relative neglect of economic and social justice within and amongst nations.'[69] Just as it is necessary to adopt a model of public responsibility towards the individual victims of a disaster, so is it necessary for the world community to develop a model of public responsibility towards its less-developed members and towards the global environment more generally.

The suggestion that developing countries should import the type of environmental and safety laws currently in force in the developed world reveals a certain blindness to the vastly different needs and priorities of the developing world. It unrealistically assumes that *formal* legal equality between nations is the answer to the double standard of safety, and that the problem can be solved notwithstanding vast *substantive* inequalities in wealth, technical, and administrative resources. This, however, is simply not the case.

Formal legal responses are not the sole answer and may, indeed, exacerbate the problem. The blanket imposition of high industrial and environmental standards upon the domestic industrial operations in the Third World may be intended to make up for the inequalities between countries, but may, in fact, have the effect of increasing those inequalities by depriving the developing world of much-needed capital and technology. There is a certain hypocrisy, even in well-intentioned concern for the environments of developing countries, while at the same time requiring them to participate in the global economy on 'equal terms.'

The problems identified with existing international initiatives stem from the unilateral nature of well-meaning proposals to regulate multinationals, and their failure to address fully the problem of international inequality. So long as the genesis of such regulation is exclusively in the developed world, these proposals will seem paternalistic and, indeed, simply to be a new form of imperialism. They are not responsive to the local needs and aspirations of the recipient country and may have adverse social and economic consequences. If the developed world continues to export *hazards* to the Third World, it should also export *safety*, not only in the form of law, but also in concrete assistance. If the objective is to *empower* developing countries, the task is to develop a process whereby their technological, administrative, and managerial infrastructure acquires the capacity to manage risks more effectively.

Any such process must address the following 'deficits,' which Bhopal illustrates: (1) hazard information; (2) risk-assessment expertise; (3) regulatory infrastructure; (4) monitoring and compliance; and (5) emergency-response capability. All of these require that developing countries be endowed with enhanced information, expertise, and technical and material assistance. This process would begin with a much-expanded 'informed consent' model whereby both the multinational and the exporting state would share with the recipient country *all* of the industrial information required for domestic operation of the industry in the exporting state. This information would include technical data about the nature of the products and processes involved, comprehensive information about the nature of the risks associated with the industry and previous hazards, and risk-management techniques currently utilized by the firm and required by the law of the home state. The objective of this process would be to enable and assist the recipient country to do a full-scale environmental-impact assessment and risk analysis of the proposed installation, and to define the conditions under which the facility would operate.[70]

As Bhopal reveals, risk assessment, hazard auditing, and emergency planning are crucial components of this process and must be undertaken as early as possible, and renewed on an ongoing basis. In the case of international technology transfers, minimum assessment standards should be adopted and implemented. Such standards are now emerging in international codes, but only very tentatively.[71] They remain largely in draft form or as non-binding guidelines. Additional impetus might be provided if these provisions were, in turn, incorporated in the international-liability regime suggested above.

Any risk-assessment exercise must also be accompanied by emergency planning. Existing databanks on hazardous substances[72] should be enhanced to include information on the short- and long-term effects of those substances on health and environment, and must also develop mechanisms for the rapid transmission of necessary medical information.

As the Bhopal saga indicates, social-action and community groups can play a powerful role in the risk-management process. They are often best equipped to understand, articulate, and protect the interests of local communities. Along with workers, these groups may also be best situated to ensure governmental and corporate compliance with the safety regime. But they are too often disempowered, marginalized, and transformed into adversaries. Instead, non-governmental organizations should be brought into the process. As the OECD has recently recognized, the process must not simply be captured by 'experts.' In its Code on Accidents Involving Hazardous Substances, it emphasizes the imperative of providing citizens with full information and enhancing their role in the decision-making process.[73] It affirms that the public has a right to be informed about hazards to human health or to the environment arising from hazardous installations and that they should have an opportunity to be heard in the decision-making processes related to industrial location, risk assessment, accident prevention, and response. Hazard communication to local communities may also be the best way to mitigate the harmful effects of risks when they do materialize. Many lives in Bhopal would have been saved had the victims had even minimal information about the hazard.

The process should not end here. The Bhopal facility may have been a high-tech operation when it began. But the conditions under which it operated deteriorated over the years. The physical plant was improperly maintained, the level of training was reduced, new information was not communicated, and government authorities were unable to monitor the operation or detect the increasing risk. Thus, there must be some provision for providing continuing assistance to Third World countries after the decision has been made to import the technology. At a minimum, the parent corporation must agree to provide updated information to its subsidiary and to the host country, regardless of the degree of its day-to-day involvement in operations. In addition, as one of the import conditions provision must be made for periodic auditing of the installation. There is no single model for post-transfer auditing, but, once again non-government organizations can play a useful role, while the primary responsibility remains with the company. The International Labor Organization, has developed a Code of Safety, Health and Working Conditions in the Transfer of Technology to Developing Countries.[74] The code emphasizes the continuing responsibility of all parties in hazard management, specifying detailed procedures for the design, operation, and alteration of hazardous technologies. The ILO has also emphasized the 'basic responsibility of multinational companies' central management over the organization and control of the management of all their subsidiary units' with respect to health and safety.[75] The multinational should, as part of the transfer agreement, agree to provide financial and technical assistance for the purpose of post-transfer hazard management. Where the transfer is part of a development package, agency resources from the exporting country might also be enlisted periodically.

To be meaningful, all of these processes must be accompanied by technical and financial assistance from multinational companies and the exporting state. Such assistance should simply be considered as part of the cost of doing business, or as a crucial component of development assistance. Indeed, governmental assistance programs and international financial institutions should be vehicles to promote environmental and industrial safety as a part of development. Organizations such as the World Bank, the International Monetary Fund, and the U.S.–supported Multilateral Development Banks might, as a condition of financing industrial ventures, seek to ensure compliance with minimal environmental and industrial standards. As Thomas McGarity says with some understatement, 'These banks historically have not been among the more environmentally conscious of international institutions.'[76] Yet efforts to convince these organizations to take some initiative in this direction have been under way for some time and have met with some success.[77] A recent report on the Canadian International Development Agency, for example, recommended that development financing must be targeted to projects that are environmentally sustainable.[78] Financing should be aimed not only at economic growth but also at strengthening the capacity of public institutions in the developing world to cope with the human and environmental consequences of economic growth. Such financing must also be designed to ensure that information is made available to factor into development decisions the full costs of each project, including the depletion of stocks of natural resources, environmental degradation, and human health and safety. All sponsored development projects should be made subject to environmental-impact assessments to which the citizens of the recipient country have full access.

It would be unrealistic not to acknowledge that such changes will not come easily. What, after all, is in it for the developed countries? Why should they limit the profitability of their exports, limit the activities of their corporations abroad, or contribute significantly to environmental and industrial safety in developing countries? There may be several responses to these questions. The first is that existing development aid, which is aimed at improving the lot of less-advantaged countries, is often wasted or undermined by the adverse social impact of sponsored projects. At the very least, existing programs must be reoriented, better taking into account the social costs of such development. The social dislocation caused by environmental destruction is spawning a host of economic refugees and using up already-scarce foreign aid. Disasters like Bhopal, with potential intergenerational consequences, threaten to increase the dependency of developing countries upon that aid. Industrial and environmental safety must be acknowledged as themselves important forms of development assistance and should be valued as such.

Second, the ever-lengthening list of environmental and industrial disasters in all countries, but perpetuated most frequently in the Third World, has increased the social, moral, and political stakes. While the physical consequences of Bhopal were confined within the borders of India, its political and economic repercussions extended much farther. The developing countries *are* developing and will inevitably acquire greater political and economic power in the international arena. Perhaps now is the time to cultivate greater goodwill and cooperation.

Third, the export of hazards is gradually becoming more reciprocal. Hazardous products and processes exported to the Third World (such as pesticides) already return to the developed countries in a 'circle of poison.'[79] Other environmental issues are increasingly revealing the global consequences of hazardous industries and technologies. As the rest of the world begins to contemplate the transborder consequences of nuclear power and the atmospheric damage caused by carbon-dioxide emissions from fossil fuels, such countries as India and China are on the brink of massive increases in their production of energy from these sources. Investment capital from the industrialized world financed the 1,500-kilometre road into the Brazilian rain forest, opening the way for timber merchants, miners, and ranchers who are burning away the 'lungs of the planet' at an unimaginable pace. The internationalization of both business and environmental degradation is increasingly teaching the developed world that the provision of aid to poorer countries – in order better to manage the risks and effects of industrial develop-ment – may no longer be a matter of charity, but a self-interested imperative.

Industrial safety, environmental quality, and socio-economic develop-ment are inextricably linked. Any progress towards a solution must take this reality into account. A case in point is the 1987 Montreal Protocol on the Substances that Deplete the Ozone Layer.[80] Rushing to prevent the threat of global warming, the developing countries sought to formu-late a treaty that restricted international trade in, and use of, ozone-depleting substances. Yet many developing countries, poised on the brink of their own industrial revolutions, demanded and received more. If they were to forgo hazardous technologies in order to protect the global environment, they argued, there must be a quid pro quo in terms of development assistance. What these countries sought and received was the creation of a fund to finance the development of alternative technologies, and a commitment from the developed world to hasten the transfer of those technologies, to facilitate access to new information, and to provide technical information and assistance.

As this example illustrates, the growing awareness of the global dimension of many environmental problems has provided the impetus for enhanced international cooperation. Modern technology and business organization have thrown up problems that require multilateral responses and that acknowledge the problem of the inequality of wealth between countries. Such problems may prompt the development of unexpected models that empower developing countries to participate more effectively in both the definition of the problem and its solution.

As the Indian Supreme Court concluded, the horrendous mass disaster in Bhopal was 'unparalleled in its magnitude and devastation and remains a ghastly monument to the dehumanizing influence of inherently dangerous technologies.'[81] The suffering of the victims can be offset, if only in small measure, only if we acknowledge a common responsibility to ensure that such incidents never again happen.

Afterword

The third of December 1992 marked the eighth anniversary of the Bhopal disaster. At this time, the settlement was nearly four years old, and the Supreme Court's final review of the compensation arrangements had been completed more than a year earlier. Yet, at the time of writing (10 January 1993) not one of the victims of the gas leak has received final (as opposed to interim) compensation. Government guidelines on compensation were not announced until the summer of 1992, several months after the deadline set by the Supreme Court. And, when announced, they were left so vague as to provide little guidance either to the victims or to the claims commissioners. Other elements of the Supreme Court's final orders also remain unimplemented: the medical surveillance program that it had urged is not in place; the contingency insurance has not been purchased; and the new hospital is nowhere in sight. The Minister for Relief, Babulal Gaur, announced that the government would proceed with construction early in the new year, though, given events in Madhya Pradesh and Bhopal, this is unlikely to happen soon.

The continuing delay in delivering final compensation is explicable, if not excusable. First, the compensation process had been left in limbo during the challenges to the settlement. And, even after the litigation was conclusively over, authorities were still working to establish the infrastructure that would be required for the distribution of final compensation. Buildings had to be requisitioned or constructed to house the tribunals, and honest, experienced individuals had to be seconded from other posts or brought out of retirement to serve as claims adjudicators. Both of these tasks proved to be more difficult than expected. Indeed, even at the beginning of 1993, only seventeen of the promised forty courts have been established, though assurances have been made that the remainder will be in place 'imminently.'

Relations between the governments of India and the state of Madhya Pradesh had been strained throughout the litigation by bickering about financing the relief effort, and jurisdiction over the entire process. This friction had been further exacerbated during 1992 by reason of the fact that the centre and state governments were on opposite political sides of the worst sectarian conflict in India since independence – a conflict sparked by a dispute over a mosque in Ayodhya, fuelled by centuries-old communal antagonisms, and fanned by political opportunism. Indeed, in December, Bhopal itself had been the site of some of the most violent clashes between Hindus and Muslims, resulting in many deaths and the eventual suspension of ordinary government when the state was placed under 'president's rule.' Because of the conflict, the eighth anniversary of the disaster went virtually unnoticed even in India.

The victims' organizations and government are also still locked in an adversarial relationship. The government's failure to have the final compensation system in place by the end of the litigation has drawn the ire of the long-suffering victims. The relief action plan, now substantially downgraded – indeed, almost exhausted – also continues to be a source of irritation and frustration. The special industrial area, built at a cost of 80 million rupees and intended to house light industry and to provide training and employment for the victims, is now lying vacant, a casualty of continued intergovernmental disagreement over funding of the relief plan. The tailoring centres, which had once employed hundreds of women, are closed down. Enormously disappointed by the deterioration of the action plan, the victims' groups also charge that up to one quarter of the funds have been diverted to ordinary civic construction, and personal enrichment. The activists, in turn, are charged with personal aggrandizement and political opportunism, and their tactics are blamed for many of the delays.

However, the suffering caused by these delays is not entirely unmitigated, and the victims' organizations have continued to have positive influence both in and out of court. A year earlier, they had been effective in forcing government to reopen several health centres to document the claims of some of the individuals who had fallen through the cracks of the system earlier on. Even more substantially, in late 1992 the Bhopal Gas Peedit Mahila Udyog Sangathan successfully petitioned the court to add 100,000 more victims to the list of nearly a half-million people already receiving interim relief payments of 200 rupees per month. And when the welfare commissioner, Abdul Quereshi, applied to the court to have the compensation funds turned over to him by the Reserve Bank of India, these groups again intervened to secure a declaration that neither the government of India nor that of Madhya Pradesh could dip into those funds to reimburse their own administrative expenses, or to refund the amounts spent on interim relief so far. This left a sum that has now grown to 1482 crore rupees (nearly $520 million).

After the many delays, the process of final claims adjudication has at least begun. Even in advance of the announcement of final compensation guidelines, Welfare Commissioner Quereshi had instructed those courts that had been established to proceed, first, with the 10,000 claims involving death (of which the department had officially verified only about 4,000).

Although many of the victims have already been processed through the claims-documentation process and tentatively categorized by injury type, they must now re-prove their entitlements in front of claims commissioners. Survivors claiming compensation must establish that the death of a relation, or their own injury, was caused by the gas leak, and must then demonstrate the amount of their entitlement based on factors that include severity of injury, age, prior income or amount of the dependency upon a deceased breadwinner.

Proof of causation, of course, remains the most serious difficulty. The welfare commissioner has instructed the courts to take a 'lenient' approach. So, for example, where the death occurred within fifteen days of the gas leak, causation will be presumed. Otherwise, the victims must provide something more in the way of positive proof. In the death cases, preferred evidence is a post mortem report, or at least some documentation establishing that the death occurred shortly after the gas leak. Yet, as a survey by the Medico Friends Circle established, few families are likely to have obtained the necessary documents in the first place, or to have retained them through the long and traumatic years since the disaster. Already, after the initial 'easy cases' have been processed, the claims tribunals are denying about one out of every two claims because of inadequate proof. Social activists allege that the procedures are now so complex, and the burden of proof so high, that the victims will be forced to accept whatever amount they are offered.

Some form of proof is, of course, essential in order to identify the deserving victims. Total claims now amount to about eighty times the available funds. If the available funds are to be preserved to do some good where truly needed, quasi-scientific methods of victim identification must be preserved. The irony, of course, is that these same methods cause further delay, and also exclude many deserving victims altogether because too many survivors cannot satisfy even the modest evidentiary requirements to support their claims. To make matters worse, there is mounting concern for children born in the eight years since the disaster, many of whom are not included in the government's existing claim records.

In early November, Welfare Commissioner Quereshi announced that the first of the initial round of cases had been finally adjudicated. The claim was that of Bano Bibi, a widow of the disaster, with three sons and four daughters. The tribunal ordered that she receive total compensation of 200,000 rupees. This sum, which would be designed to care for herself and her children, was the equivalent of $7,140. It might produce a stream of income for her entire family of about $480 per year. By the end of the year, Bibi had still not received any funds, owing to the requirement that she wait sixty days until the expiry of the appeal period. She will soon receive compensation, though whether the amount will secure her welfare, and for how long, remain open, and very troubling questions.

On the eighth anniversary of the disaster, 740 death claims like Bibi's had been adjudicated. Welfare Commissioner Quereshi optimistically estimates that now that the process is in place and functioning, compensation will be complete within three years. Based on the experience to date, this seems unlikely. For example, even assuming that the cases could be disposed of in the anticipated forty courts as quickly as one per hour (which is very unlikely), it will still take more than five years to complete the process.

The legal system continues to enjoy an active, if ineffective, role in other respects. The criminal action against the Indian managers has still not come to trial. Sporadic procedures before Judge Majahit Ali Shah are continuing, though defence lawyers now argue that too much time has passed to allow for a fair trial of their clients. Beyond reiterating that UCIL had been negligent because the plant had been losing money, the Central Bureau of Investigation has still not advanced or disclosed the results of its investigation. Charges against the foreign defendants, including Warren Anderson, are still pending, but going nowhere. Anderson and UCC have been declared absconding debtors.

Despite a flurry of legislation, hazard-management practices, both public and private, remain depressingly ineffective. A National Safety Council survey of the previous year documented a reported 27 deaths and 256 injuries as a result of chemical leaks. Many other such incidents go unreported. An International Labor Organization report identified 6,000 hazardous installations that had to be covered by a mere 903 inspectors. Industrial fatalities in India continue to occur at four times the rate documented for North America and the United Kingdom.

The abundant promises of law are thus continually belied by the paucity of resources and the frequency of harm. While Bhopal has prompted significant political pronouncements, legislative initiatives, and judicial declarations, the only tests that ultimately matter are whether safety has been improved, and whether the innocent victims of industry are treated justly. On both counts, the story of Bhopal cannot yet be viewed with any satisfaction. Too little has been delivered so far to restore our faith in the uncertain promise of law.

Notes

1 *Sunday Magazine*, Calcutta, India, 16–22 Dec. 1984
2 From a study done by Dr Heeresh Chandra, head of the Department of Forensic Medicine, Gandhi Medical College, Bhopal (personal interview, 12 Dec. 1989)
3 Dr Heeresh Chandra, personal interview, 12 Dec. 1989
4 These are the figures entered into evidence before the Madhya Pradesh High Court in late 1987 in *Union of India v Union Carbide Corporation* (4 Apr. 1988), in Upendra Baxi and Amita Dhanda, eds., *Valiant Victims and Lethal Litigation: The Bhopal Case* (Bombay: N.M. Tripathi 1990), 338 at 381. These figures likely understate the damage done by the disaster.
5 'Bhopal: Five Years on the Nightmare Continues,' *Sunday Morning Post*, Hong Kong, 3 Dec. 1989, 3. See also S. Hearne, K. Cavey, E. Bainett, and A. Ahmed, 'The Health Effects of Methyl Isocyanate, Cyanide and Mono-methylamine Exposure,' in W. Morehouse and M.A. Subramaniam, eds., *The Bhopal Tragedy: What Really Happened and What It Means for American Workers at Risk* (New York: Council on International and Public Affairs 1986), 171.
6 'Memorandum in Support of Union Carbide's Motion to Dismiss the Actions on the Grounds of Forum Non Conveniens,' *In Re: Union Carbide Corporation Gas Plant Disaster at Bhopal, India, in December 1984*, in Upendra Baxi and Thomas Paul, eds., *Mass Disasters and Multinational Liability* (Bombay: N.M. Tripathi 1986), 27
7 The following account is generally accepted by most of the independent accounts of the disaster. See, for example, S. Hazarika, *Bhopal: Lessons of a Tragedy* (New York: Penguin 1987), 65–8; P. Shrivastava, *Managing Indus-*

trial Crises: Lessons of Bhopal (New Delhi: Vision Books 1987); L. Everest, *Behind the Poison Cloud: Union Carbide's Bhopal Massacre* (Chicago: Banner Press 1985), 22–8; A. De Grazia, *A Cloud over Bhopal* (Bombay: Kalos 1985), 67–75; Morehouse and Subramaniam, eds., *The Bhopal Tragedy*.

8 This is the theory introduced and urged by Morehouse and Subramaniam, eds., *The Bhopal Tragedy*, 7–8.

9 See 'Reply of Union of India to Union Carbide's Statement of Defence' in *Union of India* v *Union Carbide Corporation* (6 Jan. 1987), in Baxi and Dhanda, eds., *Valiant Victims*, 109 at 146–7.

10 Union Carbide Corporation, *Bhopal Methyl Isocyanate Incident Investigation Team Report* (Danbury, CT: Union Carbide Corporation, March 1985). The investigation and resulting report are fully described by Ashok Kalelkar, a member of the investigation team, in *The Investigation of Large-Magnitude Incidents: Bhopal as a Case Study* (Danbury, CT: Union Carbide Corporation 1988). The sabotage theory is fully elaborated in Union Carbide's Statement of Defence in *Union of India* v *Union Carbide Corporation* (10 Dec. 1986), in Baxi and Dhanda, eds., *Valiant Victims*, 33.

11 Kalelkar, *Case Study*, 26

12 *Investigation Team Report*

13 These are some of the criteria for risk assessment developed by Environment Canada in consultation with the chemical industry. See Environment Canada, *Bhopal Aftermath Review: An Assessment of the Canadian Situation* (Ottawa: Environment Canada 1986), 40–1.

14 Thomas N. Gladwin, 'A Case Study of the Bhopal Tragedy,' in Charles Pearson, ed., *Multinational Corporations, Environment, and the Third World* (Durham, NC: Duke University Press 1987), 223 at 232

15 Shrivastava, *Managing Industrial Crises*, 48; Everest, *The Poison Cloud*, 46

16 Union Carbide has denied this allegation and attacked Munoz's credibility. See 'Affidavit of Bud Holman in Support of Union Carbide's Motion to Dismiss on Grounds of Forum Non Conveniens,' in Upendra Baxi, *Inconvenient Forum and Convenient Catastrophe* (Bombay: N.M. Tripathi 1986), 84.

17 'EPA Calls for Curbs on Temik Insecticide,' *Times Colonist*, Victoria, 21 Mar. 1989

18 D. Dembo, W. Morehouse, and L. Wykle, *Abuse of Power: Social Performance of Multinational Corporations: The Case of Union Carbide* (New York: New Horizons Press 1990), 46–52

19 *Business Week*, 13 Jan. 1986, 37

20 H.C. Dhalakia, 'Air Pollution Control,' in S.L. Agarwal, ed., *Legal Control of Environmental Pollution* (Bombay: N.M. Tripathi 1977), 141

21 B. Bowonder, J. Kasperson, and R. Kasperson, 'Avoiding Future Bhopals' *Environment* 27/7 (1985), 7, 6, 13

22 *The Hindu*, 5 May 1989, 8. In this book, rupee amounts are sometimes given in lakhs (100,000) and sometimes in crores (10 million). Dollar figures provided are in U.S. currency, unless otherwise indicated. Over the course of writing this book the dollar value of the rupee has fluctuated considerably. Monetary equivalents cited reflect the exchange rate prevailing on the date referred to.

23 De Grazia, *A Cloud over Bhopal*, 16

24 Hazarika, *Lessons of a Tragedy*, 38–9

25 Dr Heeresh Chandra, personal interview, 12 Dec. 1989

26 *Union Carbide Corp.* v *Union of India* (4 May 1989, SC), in Baxi and Dhanda, eds., *Valiant Victims*, 539

27 See Ashok Bhargava, 'The Bhopal Incident and Union Carbide: Ramifications of an Industrial Accident,' *Bulletin of Concerned Asian Scholars* 18/4 (1986), 2.

28 Dr Heeresh Chandra, personal interview, 12 Dec. 1989

29 A study by the Indian Council of Medical Research (ICMR) did confirm that there were increased levels of thiocyanide in the urine of the victims, and they recommended the massive use of thiosulphate. Other authorities attacked the scientific veracity of this study; the Madhya Pradesh government refused to implement the ICMR recommendations and shut down the only clinic administering thiosulphate. On a petition from the victims and Dr Nisith Vohra, the Supreme Court ordered that the clinic be reopened and that an expert committee be struck to monitor the medical relief effort. See Anil Sadgopal and Sujit Das, 'Bhopal: The Continuing Toll,' *Economic and Political Weekly*, 28 Nov. 1987, 2041–3.

30 The notion that safety falls through the gaps in multinational negotiations is taken from Charles Pearson, ed., *Down to Business: Multinational Corporations, the Environment and Development* (Washington, DC: World Resources Institute 1985). For a more complete discussion, see chapter 2.

31 'Is Safer Safe Enough?' *Environment* 27 (Sept. 1985), 10

32 Hazarika, *Lessons of a Tragedy*, 53. This fine was settled in 1986 for $408,500. See Dembo, Morehouse, and Wykle, *Abuse of Power*, 84.

33 Ashok Bhargava, 'The Bhopal Incident and Union Carbide: Ramifications of an Industrial Accident,' *Bulletin of Concerned Asian Scholars* 18/4 (1986), 2; Shrivastava, *Managing Industrial Crises*

34 These allegations are taken from the work of various investigators as well as from the later pleadings in the subsequent litigation. The investigations are described in the following works: Everest, *The Poison Cloud*, 25–7; De

Grazia, *A Cloud over Bhopal*, 79–85; David Weir, *The Bhopal Syndrome* (Penang: International Organization of Consumers 1986), 19–20; Morehouse and Subramaniam, eds., *The Bhopal Tragedy*. Similar allegations later appeared in the pleadings filed by the Government of India. See 'UOI Memorandum in Opposition to Union Carbide's Motion to Dismiss,' in Baxi and Paul, eds., *Mass Disasters*; 'Reply of the Union of India to Union Carbide's Written Statement and Counterclaim' (6 Jan. 1987), in Baxi and Dhanda, eds., *Valiant Victims*, 109; 'Amended Plaint of UOI,' in Baxi and Dhanda, eds., *Valiant Victims*, 174.

35 Stuart Diamond, 'Warren Anderson: A Public Crisis, A Personal Ordeal,' *New York Times*, 19 May 1985; Weir, *The Bhopal Syndrome*, 31

36 Factories Act (1948) (Act no. 63 of 1948, 23 Sept. 1948) AIR 1948 Acts 179, s. 90

37 See affidavit of Raj Kumar Keswani in the Supreme Court of India, in *Rujkumar Keswani v Union of India*, writ petition no. 28 of 1989 (available from the author).

38 L.A. Kail, J.M. Poulson, C.S. Tyson, 'Operational Safety Survey, CO/MIC/Sevin Units, Union Carbide India Ltd. Bhopal Plant,' May 1982, UCC Document. See also Union of India (UOI) Memorandum, in Baxi and Paul, eds., *Mass Disasters*, 73.

39 UOI Memorandum, in Baxi and Paul, eds., *Mass Disasters*, 73

40 Thomas N. Gladwin, 'A Case Study of the Bhopal Tragedy,' in Pearson, ed., *Multinational Corporations*, 21

41 Shrivastava, *Managing Industrial Crises*, 57

42 UOI Memorandum, in Baxi and Paul, eds., *Mass Disasters*, 73

43 Weir, *The Bhopal Syndrome*, 15; Hazarika, *Lessons of a Tragedy*, 58–9

44 Everest, *The Poison Cloud*, 45

45 Ibid., 46

46 Ibid. Profits had been projected at $6 million. In 1984 the plant lost $4 million.

47 Pearson, ed., *Down to Business*, 61

48 See C.M. Abraham and A. Rosencranz, 'An Evaluation of Pollution Control Legislation in India,' *Columbia Journal of Environmental Law* 11 (1986), 101; see also Thomas N. Gladwin, 'A Case Study of the Bhopal Tragedy,' in Pearson, ed., *Multinational Corporations*, 223 at 235.

49 Factories Act (1948) (Act no. 63 of 1948, 23 Sept. 1948) AIR 1948 Acts 179. See also Insecticides Act (1968) (Act no. 46 of 1968, 2 Sept. 1968) AIR 1968 Acts 100; amended (Act no. 24 of 1977, 2 Aug. 1977) AIR 1977 Acts 71.

50 Air (Prevention and Control of Pollution) Act (Act 14 of 1981, 29 Mar. 1981) AIR 1981 Acts 197

51 The Environment Protection Act (Act no. 29 of 1986)

52 Shrivastava, *Managing Industrial Crises*, 39

53 Gladwin, 'A Case Study of the Bhopal Tragedy,' in Pearson, ed., *Multinational Corporations*, 236. See also Indian Law Institute, *Environmental Protection Act: Agenda for Implementation* (Bombay: N.M. Tripathi 1987), 42-4.

54 See Abraham and Rosencranz, 'An Evaluation of Pollution Control Legislation in India,' 101.

55 Indian Law Institute, *Environmental Protection Act*, 1

56 See Upendra Baxi, 'Taking Suffering Seriously: Social Action Litigation in the Supreme Court of India,' in R. Dhavan and R. Sudarshan, eds., *Judges and the Judicial Power* (London: Sweet and Maxwell 1985); P.N. Bhagwati, 'Judicial Activism and Public Interest Litigation,' *Columbia Journal of Transnational Law* 23 (1985), 561; J. Cassels, 'Judicial Activism and Public Interest Litigation in India: Attempting the Impossible?' *American Journal of Comparative Law* 37 (1989), 495.

57 *M.C. Mehta v Union of India* (1988) 1 SCALE 54

58 *M.C. Mehta v Union of India* (1986) 2 SCC 176, 1987 AIR SC 965; conditions modified (1986) 2 SCC 325, 1987 AIR SC 982

59 M. Galanter, 'Legal Torpor: Why So Little Has Happened in India after the Bhopal Tragedy,' *Texas International Law Journal* 20 (1985), 273 at 280. See generally S.C. Thanvi, 'Law of Torts,' in J. Minattur, ed., *The Indian Legal System* (Dobbs Ferry, NY: Oceana Publications 1978).

60 *Hindustan Times*, 11 May 1989; *Indian Post*, 17 Mar. 1988, reports on a leak of ammonia gas from a chemical plant near Bombay resulting in 100 injuries. At least four such leaks occurred over the past year in this state alone.

61 See V. Nanda and B. Bailey, 'Nature and Scope of the Problem,' in G. Handle and R. Lutz, eds., *Transferring Hazardous Technologies and Substances: The International Legal Challenge* (London: Graham and Trottman 1989); T. Whiteside, *The Pendulum and the Toxic Cloud: The Course of Dioxin Contamination* (New Haven: Yale University Press 1979).

62 P. Capel, W. Geiger, P. Reichert, and O. Wanner, 'Accidental Input of Pesticides into the Rhine River,' *Environmental Science and Technology* 22 (1988), 922; R. Deinenger, 'The Survival of Father Rhine,' *Journal of the American Waterworks Association* 79 (1987), 78

63 The study conducted for the U.S. EPA examined incidents involving toxic and radioactive materials: 'Acute Hazardous Data Base,' Washington, DC, noted in World Commission on Environment and Development, *Our Common Future* (Oxford: Oxford University Press 1987), 228 (hereafter cited as *The Brundtland Report*).

64 The chemical industry is the fifth-largest industrial sector in Canada: Environment Canada, *Canadian Situation*, 35.

65 See Charles Perrow, *Normal Accidents: Living with High-Risk Technologies* (New York: Basic Books 1984), 101–2.

66 See '200,000 in Mississauga and Oakville Moved from Homes as Chlorine Escapes,' *Globe and Mail*, 12 Nov. 1979; 'Losses Per Day Are Estimated at $25 Million,' *Globe and Mail*, 19 Nov. 1979, 1; 'Bill Promised on Dangerous Shipments,' *Globe and Mail*, 13 Nov. 1979, 11; *Globe and Mail*, 14 Nov. 1979, 2.

67 Environmental Protection Service, National Analysis of Trends in Emergency Systems, summarized in Environment Canada, *Summary of Spill Events in Canada, 1974–83* (Ottawa, 1987). The database recorded 21,587 spills in the relevant period. The most frequent source (in terms of tonnage) is industrial plants and non-oil chemicals, which accounted for 25 per cent of all spills in 1983.

68 Richard Gaskins, *Environmental Accidents: Personal Injury and Public Responsibility* (Philadelphia: Temple University Press, 1989), 231

69 M. Seltzer, 'Personal Injury Hazardous Waste Litigation: A Proposal for Tort Reform,' BC *Environmental Affairs Law Review* 10 (1982–3), 797, 798

70 '3000 Can't Go Home,' *Montreal Gazette*, 26 Aug. 1988, A1–2

71 *The Brundtland Report*, 224

72 Ibid.

73 In 1973 the World Health Organization estimated that there were 500,000 pesticide poisonings per year (excluding suicide attempts) resulting in hospitalization. See WHO, Technical Report Series no. 513, *Safe Use of Pesticides: Twentieth Report of the WHO Expert Committee on Insecticides* (1973). More recently WHO has put the figure for unintentional acute poisonings at one million. The data are discussed in J. Jeyaratnam, 'Acute Pesticide Poisoning: A Major Global Health Problem,' *World Health Statistics Quarterly* 43 (1990), 139. See also D. Weir and M. Shapiro, *Circle of Poison: Pesticides and People in a Hungry World* (San Francisco: Institute for Food and Development Policy 1981); Pearson, *Down to Business*, citing U.N. Economic and Social Commission for Asia and the Pacific, Committee on Industry, Technology, Human Settlements and the Environment, Seventh Session, 6–12 Sept. 1983, 2.

74 L.F. Duncan, 'Trends in Enforcement: Is Environment Canada Serious about Enforcing Its Laws?' in D. Tingley, ed., *Into the Future: Environmental Law and Policy for the 1990's* (Edmonton: Environmental Law Centre 1990), 55

75 T.F. Schrecker, *Political Economy of Environmental Hazards* (Ottawa: Law Reform Commission of Canada 1984)

76 K. Hawkins, *Environment and Enforcement* (Oxford: Clarendon Press 1984)

77 T. McMillan, Notes for a Statement (news conference announcing the proposed Environmental Protection Act, Ottawa, 18 Dec. 1986), cited in D. Chappell, 'From Sawdust to Toxic Blobs: A Consideration of Sanctioning Strategies to Combat Pollution in Canada,' *Studies in Regulation and Compliance* (Canada, Dept. of Justice, 1988)

78 See D. Saxe, *Environmental Offences: Corporate Responsibility and Executive Liability* (Aurora, ON: Canada Law Book 1990), 29–31

79 R. Brown and T.M. Rankin, 'Persuasion, Penalties and Prosecution: Administrative v. Criminal Sanctions,' in M. Friedland, ed., *Securing Compliance: Seven Case Studies* (Toronto: University of Toronto Press 1990), 348

80 D. Dewees and M. Trebilcock, 'The Efficacy of the Tort System and Its Alternatives: A Review of the Empirical Evidence,' University of Toronto Law and Economics Workshop Series, 21 Jan. 1991, 95–6

81 See, for example, the new Canadian Environmental Protection Act SC 1988, c. 22.

CHAPTER TWO

1 Among other sources, the following analysis draws upon World Commission on Environment and Development, *Our Common Future* (Oxford: Oxford University Press 1987; hereafter, *The Brundtland Report*); Charles Pearson, ed., *Down to Business: Multinational Corporations, the Environment, and Development* (Durham, NC: Duke University Press 1985); P. Shrivastava, *Managing Industrial Crises* (New Delhi: Vision Books 1987); R. Barnett and R. Muller, *Global Reach: The Power of Multinational Corporations* (New York: Simon and Schuster 1974); Robert Gilpin, *The Political Economy of International Relations* (Princeton: Princeton University Press 1987).

2 Gilpin, *International Relations*, 239

3 Ibid., 238

4 Union Carbide Statement of Defence in *Union of India* v *Union Carbide Corporation* (10 Dec. 1986), in Upendra Baxi and Amita Dhanda, eds., *Valiant Victims and Lethal Litigation: The Bhopal Case* (Bombay: N.M. Tripathi 1990), 103, and Amended Statement of Defence (8 Feb. 1988) in ibid., 198, 202

5 'Are Not Poverty and Need the Greatest Polluters?' Quoted in A.M. Sinjela, 'Developing Countries' Perceptions of Environmental Protection and Economic Development,' *Indian Journal of International Law* (1984), 493

6 J. Nehru, 'Tryst with Destiny,' speech given on the eve of independence, 14 Aug. 1947; reprinted in S. Gopal, ed., *Selected Works of Jawaharlal Nehru*, Vol. 3 (New Delhi: Oxford University Press 1985), 135

7 See Atul Kohli, *The State and Poverty in India: The Politics of Reform* (New York: Cambridge University Press 1987), 223.

8 *The Brundtland Report*, 106

9 Ibid., 69

10 Robert Dorfman, 'An Economist's View of Natural Resources and Environmental Problems,' in Pearson, ed., *Down to Business*, 8

11 Quoted in T. Howland, 'Can International Law Prevent Another Bhopal Tragedy?' *Denver Journal of International Law and Policy* 15 (1986–7), 301 at 312

12 U.S. Council on Environmental Quality, *Environmental Quality 1983* (Washington, DC: Council on Environmental Quality 1984), quoted in Pearson, ed., *Down to Business*, 11

13 *The Brundtland Report*, 83

14 Shrivastava, *Managing Industrial Crises*, 34

15 H.C. Dhalakia, 'Air Pollution Control,' in S.L. Agarwal, ed., *Legal Control of Environmental Pollution* (Bombay: N.M. Tripathi 1977), 142

16 *The Brundtland Report*, 77

17 See D. Weir and M. Schapiro, *Circle of Poison: Pesticides and People in a Hungry World* (San Francisco: Institute for Food and Development Policy 1981).

18 In 1973 the World Health Organization estimated that there were 500,000 pesticide poisonings per year (excluding suicide attempts) resulting in hospitalization. See WHO Technical Report Series no. 513, *Safe Use of Pesticides: Twentieth Report of the WHO Expert Committee on Insecticides* (1973). More recently, WHO has placed the figure for unintentional acute poisonings at one million. The data is discussed by J. Jeyaratnam, 'Acute Pesticide Poisonings: A Major Global Health Problem,' *World Health Statistics Quarterly* 43 (1990), 139. See also Pearson, ed., *Down to Business*, 2, citing U.N. Economic and Social Council, and Economic and Social Commission for Asia and the Pacific, Committee on Industry, Technology, Human Settlements and the Environment, Seventh Session, 6–12 Sept. 1983; and Informal Consultation on Planning and Strategy for the Prevention of Pesticide Poisoning, U.N. Doc. WHO/VBC/86.926 (1985).

19 Barnett and Muller, *Global Reach*, 136, 146

20 Weir and Schapiro, *Circle of Poison*, 8 (data from Research Department, Oil, Chemical and Atomic Workers International Union, 'Union Carbide – A Study in Corporate Power and the Case for Union Power' [June 1974]).

See also D. Dembo, W. Morehouse, and L. Wykle, *Abuse of Power: Social Performance of Multinational Corporations: The Case of Union Carbide* (New York: New Horizons Press 1990).

21 Socialist Eastern Europe owned the remaining 29 per cent. Data from *The Brundtland Report*, 87

22 See, for example, U.S. Congress, Senate Committee on Foreign Relations, Subcommittee on International Relations, *Multinational Corporations and United States Foreign Policy, Hearings on the International Telephone and Telegraph Company and Chile 1970–71*, pts. 1 and 2, 93d Cong., 1st sess., 1973; Barnet and Muller, *Global Reach*, 81–104.

23 See Mark Williams, 'Foreign Investment in India,' *Columbia Journal of Transnational Law* 26 (1988), 609.

24 Dembo, Morehouse, and Wykle, *Abuse of Power*

25 Whether or not perceptions about the mobility of capital are accurate is an open question. There is some evidence to suggest that large corporations cannot so easily relocate from one country to another. Protectionist laws in many countries, including tariffs, foreign-exchange regulations and other import barriers, mean that if multinationals desire access to local markets they must locate in that country. Nevertheless, international trade law, including the GATT, and 'free trade' pressures from industrial countries are increasingly eliminating such barriers and creating worldwide markets. While lax environmental laws are certainly not the only reason why a multinational company might choose to locate in a third-world country, they are certainly one factor. Some studies do indicate that, especially in hazardous industrial sectors (such as asbestos and benzedine production), the passage of stricter environmental and workplace regulations has caused industrial relocation. Pearson canvasses the available data on the problem of capital flight. He suggests that the problem may be overemphasized and discusses some studies which indicate that 'lax environmental controls are unlikely to attract much additional foreign capital and would lead to the needless sacrifice of local environmental quality' (*Down to Business*, 53). But he also concludes that hazardous industrial sectors *are* affected by the flight of capital problem: 'environmental and workplace regulations may have motivated relocation for industries producing highly toxic products (asbestos, benzedine dyes, and a few pesticides)' (ibid., 52, see also 60).

26 V.N. Kaul, secretary of Industry and Commerce, State of Madhya Pradesh, quoted in F. Bordewich, 'Lessons of the Bhopal Disaster,' *Atlantic*, Mar. 1987

27 For an analysis of the various forms of foreign participation in India, see

Mark Williams, 'Foreign Investment in India,' *Columbia Journal of Transnational Law* 26 (1988), 608.

28 Pearson, *Down to Business*, 33

29 Ibid., 33, 72

30 Allin Seward III (associate general counsel and secretary, Upjohn International Inc.), 'After Bhopal: Implications for Parent Company Liability,' *The International Lawyer* 21 (1987), 695 at 706

31 Ibid., 706–7

32 Pearson, *Down to Business*

33 Robert Lutz, 'The Export of Danger: A View from the Developed World,' in *International Journal of Law and Politics* 20 (1988), 629, 670

34 Principle 21 of the 1972 U.N. Declaration on the Human Environment, 16 Jun. 1972, 48/14 U.N. Doc. A/Conf 21 (1972). See T. Howland, 'Can International Law Prevent Another Bhopal Tragedy?' *Denver Journal of International Law and Policy* 15 (1986–7), 301 at 305

35 *Trail Smelter Arbitration* (*U.S.* v *Canada*), 3 R. Int'l Arb. Awards 1911 (1938)

36 See 'U.S. Pesticide Export Legislation Dies in Conference Committee,' *Panna Outlook Bulletin*, Oct. 1990, 1. See also, Lutz, 'The Export of Danger,' 629, 638.

37 See Lutz, 'The Export of Danger,' 641.

38 Second Revised Council Decision on Guidelines for Multinational Enterprises C (84) 90 (17 May, 1984), discussed in Lutz, 'The Export of Danger,' 629

39 For more detailed descriptions of the various regimes discussed here, and complete citations, see chapter 11.

40 Account from Phillipe J. Sands, 'Environment, Community and International Law,' *Harvard International Law Journal* 30 (1989), 393

41 Ibid.

42 Convention on Third Party Liability in the Field of Nuclear Energy, 29 July 1960, 956 UNTS 251 (Paris Convention); supplemented by OECD Brussels Convention, 31 Jan. 1963, 1041 UNTS 358; Vienna Convention on Civil Liability for Nuclear Damage, 21 May 1963, 1063 UNTS 265

43 Phillipe J. Sands, 'Environment, Community and International Law,' *Harvard International Law Journal* 30 (1989), 393, 409

44 Ibid., 411

45 For a suggestion along these lines, see Maureen Bent, 'Exporting Hazardous Industries: Should American Standards Apply?' *New York University Journal of International Law and Politics* 20 (1988), 777.

46 See B. Castleman, 'The Double Standard in Industrial Hazards,' in J. Ives,

ed., *The Export of Hazard* (New York: Methuen 1985), 60, 69; 'Double Standards: Asbestos in India,' *New Scientist* 89, (6 Feb. 1981), 522

47 Lutz, 'The Export of Danger,' 642–5

48 One example of the informed consent approach is the U.N. General Assembly Resolution on Products Harmful to Health and Environment. Various other codes and laws apply to pesticides, pharmaceuticals, hazardous wastes, and chemicals. For a description, see L. Gundling, 'Prior Notification and Consultation,' in G. Handl and R. Lutz, eds., *Transferring Hazardous Technologies and Substances: The International Legal Challenge* (London: Graham and Trottman 1989), 63.

49 See S. King, 'Hazardous Exports: A Consumer Perspective,' and A. Waldo, 'A Review of U.S. and International Restrictions on Exports of Hazardous Substances,' both in Ives, ed., *The Export of Hazard.*

50 R. Ruttenberg, 'Hazard Export: Ethical Problems, Policy Proposals and Prospects for Implementation,' in Ives, ed., *The Export of Hazard*

51 McWilliams, 'Tom Sawyer's Apology: A Reevaluation of United States Pesticide Export Policy,' *Hastings International and Comparative Law Review* 8 (1984), 61

52 Environment Canada, *Bhopal Aftermath Review: An Assessment of the Canadian Situation* (Ottawa: Minister of Supply and Services 1986), 35

53 Canadian Chemical Producers' Association, Position Paper on Confidentiality, quoted in T.F. Schrecker, *Political Economy of Environmental Hazards* (Ottawa: Law Reform Commission of Canada 1984), 69

CHAPTER THREE

1 Guido Calabresi and P. Bobbitt, *Tragic Choices* (New York: Norton 1978)

2 See, D. Rosenberg, 'The Causal Connection in Mass Exposure Cases: A "Public Law" Vision of the Tort System,' *Harvard Law Review* 97 (1984), 851; D. Rosenberg, 'Class Actions for Mass Torts: Doing Individual Justice by Collective Means,' *Indiana Law Journal* 62 (1986–7), 561; P. Campbell and H. Moore, 'Mass Tort Litigation in Tennessee,' *Tennessee Law Review* 53 (1985), 221; J. Weinstein, 'Preliminary Reflections on the Law's Reaction to Disasters,' *Columbia Journal of Environmental Law* 11 (1986); A. Rubin, 'Mass Torts and Litigation Disasters,' *Georgia Law Review* 20 (1986), 429; P. Huber, 'Environmental Hazards and Liability Law,' in R. Litan and C. Winston, *Liability: Perspectives and Policy* (Washington, DC: Brookings Institute 1988), 128.

3 See H.S. Cohn and D. Bollier, *The Great Hartford Circus Fire* (New Haven: Yale University Press 1991).

4 M. Mintz, *At Any Cost: Corporate Greed, Women and the Dalkon Shield* (New York: Pantheon 1985)

5 For a description, see chapter 4.

6 Paul Brodeur, *Outrageous Misconduct: The Asbestos Industry on Trial* (New York: Pantheon 1985)

7 P. Schuck, *Agent Orange on Trial: Mass Toxic Disasters in the Courts* (Cambridge, MA: Harvard University Press 1986)

8 D. Dembo, W. Morehouse, and L. Wykle, *Abuse of Power: Social Performance of Multinational Corporations: The Case of Union Carbide* (New York: New Horizons Press 1990), 46–52

9 See S.C. Thanvi, 'Law of Torts,' in J. Minattur, ed., *The Indian Legal System* (Dobbs Ferry, NY: Oceana Publications 1978), 589.

10 See J. Cassels, 'Judicial Activism and Public Interest Litigation in India,' *American Journal of Comparative Law* 27 (1989), 495; 'Bitter Knowledge, Vibrant Action: Reflections on Law and Society in Modern India,' *Wisconsin Law Review* (1991), 106. The innovativeness of the Indian legal system is discussed further in chapter 7.

11 See, for example, *Gobald Motor Services* v *R.N.K. Veluswami* AIR 1962 SC 1 (a fatal accident case relying on British and Canadian authority).

12 See Morton Horwitz, *The Transformation of American Law: 1780–1860* (Cambridge, MA: Harvard University Press 1977); J. Fleming, *The Law of Torts,* 7th ed. (Sydney: Law Book Co. 1987), 94.

13 See C. Backhouse, 'Married Women's Property Law in Nineteenth-Century Canada,' *Law and History Review* 6 (1988), 211; M. McCaughan, *Status of Married Women in Canada* (Toronto: Carswell 1977).

14 *Winterbottom* v *Wright* (1842), 10 M&W 109, 152 ER 402 at 405

15 *McPherson* v *Buick Motor Co.* (1916), 217 NY Supp. 382, 111 NE 1050

16 *Donoghue* v *Stevenson*, [1932] AC 562. Interestingly, the claim was never finally proved as the case did not ever go to trial.

17 *Donoghue* v *Stevenson* [1932], 580

18 An interesting example of a non-contractual obligation to warn of toxic risks, or to take precautions to prevent illness is the case of *Caldwell* v *Bechtel Inc.* 631 F 2d 989 (USCA, DC, 1980). The defendant engineering firm was hired to supervise safety compliance in the construction of a subway tunnel. It was held directly liable to an employee who had contracted silicosis from exposure to silica dust in the tunnel. Its assumption of responsibility created a direct duty to third parties to warn of the risks or take measures to mitigate them, notwithstanding that there was no privity between the parties.

19 See, for example, *Sterling* v *Velsicol Chemical Corporation* 647 F Supp. 603

(DC, Tenn. 1986). The plaintiffs were suing for damages resulting from water contamination from a toxic dump. Among other grounds of negligence were: (a) the defendant had failed to investigate the conditions at the dump site; (b) had not monitored the operation for leaks; (c) had not heeded warnings of the risk; (d) had failed to use state-of-the-art technology.

20 The issue of regulatory compliance as a defence to negligence is a complex one. On the one hand, safety regulations may be prima facie evidence of what constitutes reasonable care. On the other hand, the regulations may be inadequate or outdated and a regulatory-compliance defence may impede innovation. Generally, regulatory compliance is accepted as relevant, but not determinative, of the issue of standard of care. Compare the cases of *Solloway v Okanagan Builders Land Development Ltd* (1977) 71 DLR (3d) 102 (compliance with pollution-control permit a good defence) and *Bux v Slough Metals* [1974] 1 All ER 262 (CA) (formal compliance with safety regulations not a good defence).

21 Fleming, *The Law of Torts*, 94

22 (1866) 1 LR Ex. 265; aff'd (1868) LR 3 HL 330

23 Ibid., 279–80

24 *Smeaton v Ilford Corp.,* [1954] 1 Ch. 450

25 *Lohndorf v B.A. Oil Co. Ltd* (1958), 24 WWR 193

26 *Cairns v Canadian Refining & Smelting Co.* (1914), 6 OWN 562

27 *Mihalchuk v Ratke* (1966), 55 WWR 555 (Sask QB); *Cruise v Niessen,* [1977] 2 WWR 481

28 *Heard v Woodward* (1954), 12 WWR 312 (BCSC)

29 *Greenman v Yuba Power Products* (1963), 53 Cal. 2d 57, 377 P. 2d 897. See W.P. Keeton, ed., *Prosser and Keeton on the Law of Torts*, 5th ed. (St Paul, MN: West Publishing Co. 1984), 692–4.

30 *In Re Three Mile Island Litigation* 557 F Supp. 96 (1982)

31 See Huber, 'Environmental Hazards and Liability Law,' 133–4.

32 See Thanvi, 'Law of Torts,' 622.

33 *Read v J. Lyons and Co. Ltd,* [1947] AC 156

34 Fleming, *Law of Torts*, 303–5; *Prosser and Keeton on the Law of Torts*, 536–7

35 For judicial articulation of these arguments, see *Escola v Coca-Cola Bottling Co. of Fresno* 150 Pac. 436 (1944); *Hall v E.I. Dupont DeNemours & Co.* 345 F Supp. 353 (EDNY, 1972).

36 42 USC ss 9601–57 (1982 and Supp IV 1986)

37 RSO 1980, c. 141, as amended

38 As one judge commented in an older nuisance action against an electrical generating station, 'Very readily would I decide, if I felt at liberty to do

so, that the loss resulting to the plaintiff from the defendant's operation should without any qualification be borne by the corporation. That loss is truly just as much part of the cost of generating electrical energy as is, for example, the cost of the coal whose combustion is the original source of all the mischief': *Manchester v Farnworth*, [1930] AC 171 (HL).

39 Courts in Canada may be dispensing with the 'non-natural use' requirement and substituting a 'hazardous activity' or 'dangerous substance' test, for example, in cases involving pesticide spraying. See, for example, *Cruise v Niessen*, [1977] 2 WWR 481 (CA).

40 *Gertsen v Metropolitan Toronto* (1974), 2 OR (2d) 560 (Ont. HC). The municipality had accepted organic materials from another town and used it for landfill in a residential area. The decomposing material produced methane gas, which eventually exploded, injuring the plaintiff and his property. The court held both municipalities strictly liable on the basis that this was a non-natural and hazardous use of land. See also *State of New Jersey v Ventron Corp.* 468 A 2d 150 (1983) re toxic-waste disposal, and *Sterling v Velsicol Chemical Corp.* 647 F Supp. 303 (DC, Tenn., 1986) re contamination of wells from a chemical-disposal site.

41 146 NJ Super. 169 (1981)

42 Ibid., 175

43 *Lambert v Lastoplex Chemicals Ltd* (1971), 25 DLR (3d) 121 (SCC); *Hall v E.I. Dupont DeNemours & Co.* 345 F Supp. 353 (EDNY, 1972). For a discussion of the duty to warn in pharmaceutical cases, see P. Peppin, 'Drugs/Vaccine Risks: Patient Decision-Making and Harm Reduction in the Pharmaceutical Company Duty to Warn Action,' *Canadian Bar Review* 70 (1991), 473.

44 *Rivtow Marine Ltd v Washington Iron Works* (1973), 40 DLR (3d) 530 (SCC); *Cominco Ltd v Westinghouse Canada Ltd* (1982), 127 DLR (3d) 544, aff'd (1983), 45 BCLR 35

45 *Globe and Mail*, 19 Feb. 1990, A-9

46 *Caldwell v Bechtel Inc.* 631 F 2d 989 (USCA, DC, 1980)

47 See, for example, the U.S. Occupational Health and Safety *Hazard Communication Standard* 48 Fed. Reg. 53, 280 (1983); 29 CFR 1910.1200. For a general discussion, see N. Clare, 'Hazardous Chemicals in the Workplace: The Employer's Obligation to Inform Employees and the Community,' *St Mary's Law Journal* 20 (1989), 307.

48 See J. McLaren, 'The Common Law Nuisance Action and the Environmental Battle,' *Osgoode Hall Law Journal* 10 (1972), 505; R. Rychlak, 'Common Law Remedies for Environmental Wrongs: The Role of Private Nuisance,' *Mississippi Law Review* 59 (1989), 657; C. Tuohey, 'Toxic Torts as Absolute Nuisances,' *Western State University Law Review* 16 (1988–9), 5.

49 As the American Law Institute's *Restatement of Torts*, 2d ed. (St Paul, MN: The American Law Institute, 1979), explains: 'Life in organized society and especially in populous communities involves an unavoidable clash of individual interests. Practically all human activities, unless carried on in a wilderness, interfere to some extent with others or involve some risk of interference, and these interferences range from trifling annoyances to serious harms. It is an obvious truth that each individual in a community must put up with a certain amount of annoyance, inconvenience and interference, and must take a certain amount of risk in order that all may get on together. The very existence of organized society depends on the principle of "give and take, live and let live," so that the law of torts does not attempt to impose liability or shift the loss in every case where one person's conduct has some detrimental effect on another. Liability is imposed only in those cases where the harm or risk to one is greater than he ought to be required to bear under the circumstances' (112); see also *Bamford* v *Turnley* (1862) 3 B&S 66.

50 *R.* v *The Ship 'Sun Diamond'* (1983), 25 CCLT 19 (FCTD)

51 525 A 2d 287 (NJSC, 1987). See also *Sterling* v *Velsicol Chemical Corporation* 647 F Supp. 303 (DC, Tenn. 1986).

52 *Royal Anne Hotel Co.* v *Ashcroft*, [1979] 2 WWR 462, 95 DLR (3d) 756 (BCCA)

53 [1979] 2 WWR 462, 465

54 Ibid., 468

55 R. Posner, *Economic Analysis of Law*, 3d ed. (Toronto: Little, Brown 1986)

56 (1970), 257 NE 2d 870 (NYCA)

57 See also *Black* v *Canadian Copper Co.* (1917), 12 OWN 243; aff'd (1920), 17 OWN 399; and *Bottom* v *Ontario Leaf Tobacco Co. Ltd*, [1935] OR 205 (CA).

58 (1970), 257 NE 2d 870, at 876

59 *McKie* v *The K.V.P. Co. Ltd*, [1948] OR 398, 410–11; aff'd [1949] SCR 698

60 An Act Respecting the K.V.P. Company Ltd., SO 1950, c. 33

61 *Earl of Ripon* v *Hobart* (1834), 40 ER 65, 67

62 The old case of *Fletcher* v *Bealy* (1885), 28 Ch. D. 688 illustrates a rather conservative application by the courts of the logic of risk assessment. The defendant in this case was an alkalai manufacturer which stored a large amount of sulphuric 'vat waste' near the banks of a river. The plaintiff was a downstream paper manufacturer who used large quantities of river water in the production of fine paper. He brought evidence to show that the defendant was depositing 1,000 tons of waste per month in its dump and that there was a high risk that chemical run-off would find its way to the river, causing severe pollution. He sought an injunction. The court refused to grant the injunction. While it recognized the severity of the

consequences should the waste leak into the river, it denied that the risk was of sufficient magnitude to justify its immediate removal. It noted that the defendant had stated that it had no intention of allowing an accident to occur, that the risk would not be a serious one for several years, and that technological solutions to the problem might be found before any damage occurred.

63 159 F 2d 169 (1947), 173

64 M. Wheeler, 'A Proposal for Further Common Law Development of the Use of Punitive Damages in Modern Product Liability Litigation,' *Alabama Law Review* 40 (1989), 919; in Europe, see Council of European Communities, Council Directive on Liability for Defective Products 25/7/85, in *Official Journal of the European Communities* 7 (Aug. 1985), L210/29.

65 *Barker v Lull Engineering Co. Ltd* 573 P 2d 443 (1978), 456 and 455

CHAPTER FOUR

1 There is a large and growing literature on the problems of attempting to solve toxic- and mass-tort problems through traditional legal processes. See, for example, Richard Gaskins, *Environmental Accidents: Personal Injury and Public Responsibility* (Philadelphia: Temple University Press 1989); Peter Schuck, *Agent Orange on Trial: Mass Toxic Disasters in the Court* (Cambridge, MA: Harvard University Press 1987); D. Rosenberg, 'The Causal Connection in Mass Exposure Cases: A "Public Law" Vision of the Tort System,' *Harvard Law Review* 97 (1984), 851; D. Rosenberg, 'Class Actions for Mass Torts: Doing Individual Justice by Collective Means,' *Indiana Law Journal* 62 (1986–7), 561; P. Campbell and H. Moore, 'Mass Tort Litigation in Tennessee,' *Tennessee Law Review* 53 (1985), 221; J. Weinstein, 'Preliminary Reflections on the Law's Reaction to Disasters,' *Columbia Journal of Environmental Law* 11 (1986); A. Rubin, 'Mass Torts and Litigation Disasters,' *Georgia Law Review* 20 (1986), 429; Troyen Brennan, 'Causal Chains and Statistical Links: The Role of Scientific Uncertainty in Hazardous Substance Litigation,' *Cornell Law Review* 73 (1988), 469; Troyen Brennan, 'Helping Courts with Toxic Torts: Some Proposals Regarding Alternative Methods for Presenting and Assessing Scientific Evidence in Common Law Courts,' *University of Pittsburgh Law Review* 51 (1989), 1; Jane Stapleton, *Disease and the Compensation Debate* (London: Oxford University Press 1986); P. Huber, 'Environmental Hazards and Liability Law,' in R. Litan and C. Winston, eds., *Liability: Perspectives and Policy* (Washington, DC: Brookings Institute 1988), 128.

2 On the model of tort law as corrective justice, and the exclusion by this

model of other social goals, see E. Weinrib, 'Liberty, Community and Corrective Justice,' *Canadian Journal of Law and Jurisprudence* 1 (1988), 3; 'Understanding Tort Law,' *Valparaiso Law Review* 23 (1989), 485; 'Two Conceptions of Tort Law,' in R. Devlin, ed., *Canadian Perspectives on Legal Theory* (Toronto: Emond Montgomery 1991).

3 This thesis is elaborated by Gaskins, *Environmental Accidents*, and Stapleton, *Disease and the Compensation Debate*. Stapleton estimates that traumatic accidents account for only 10 per cent of all disability in England, pp. 5–6. She concludes that, because effective tort liability is confined to traumatic injury, the debate on law reform is distorted and biased away from the real problems of disability and compensation.

4 See the discussion below at pages 98–102.

5 An example of the problem is *Kaufman* v *T.T.C.*, [1960] SCR 251. In this case the plaintiff was injured when she was knocked over while ascending an escalator in the Toronto transit system. She alleged that her injuries were caused by the inadequate design of a round metal hand rail on the escalator. The Supreme Court of Canada held that she had not proved causation, since there was no evidence that she would have grasped a properly designed rubber, oval hand rail and thereby avoided her fall.

An even more striking example is the case of *Delaney* v *Cascade River Holidays* (1983), 44 BCLR 24 (BCCA), in which the plaintiff drowned when a river raft overturned. The plaintiff's estate urged that his death was caused by the fact that the rafting company provided life jackets with only a 21-pound buoyancy rating as opposed to the recommended 32-pound life jacket. The court refused to find in favour of the plaintiff. It noted that, while all of the passengers were wearing the smaller life jacket, only three of the eleven passengers drowned, and the court reasoned that there was no evidence that the plaintiff's life would have been saved by a better life jacket.

6 An example is the case of *Myers* v *Peel County Board of Education* (1981), 17 CCLT 269 (SCC). In this case a student was injured when he fell from rings on which he had been practising gymnastics. He alleged that he would not have been injured had the school provided more adequate matting on the floor. While it was, of course, impossible to say with certainty that he would not have been injured, the Supreme Court of Canada accepted that the provision of more adequate mats would have been a reasonable precaution, given the potential hazard. It concluded that the failure to provide more substantial mats had materially contributed to the risk and was willing to infer that it had 'caused' the plaintiff's injuries.

7 See Fleming, *The Law of Torts*, 7th ed. (Sydney: Law Book Co. 1987),

291–301. Essentially this inference arises only in situations where the accident is one that would not ordinarily occur but for carelessness, and in which the defendant is the only possible (or, at least, the most likely) wrongdoer, for example, having exclusive control of the hazard.

8 *Sindell* v *Abbott Laboratories* (1980) 26 Cal. 3d 588, 607 P 2d 924. Commentary upon this case and the problem of attributing responsibility to individuals or firms may be found in N. Sheiner, 'DES and a Proposed Theory of Enterprise Liability,' *Fordham Law Review* 46 (1978), 963. See also, J. Fleming, 'Probabilistic Causation in Tort Law,' *Canadian Bar Review* 68 (1989), 661; V. Schwartz and L. Mashigian, 'Failure to Identify the Defendant in Tort Law: Towards a Legislative Solution,' *California Law Review* 73 (1985), 941. Other cases in this area include, *Payton* v *Abbott Laboratories* 386 Mass 540, 437 NE 2d 171 (1982); *Hymowitz* v *Eli Lilly & Co.* 539 NE 2d 1069 (NYCA, 1989).

9 607 P 2d 924, 937

10 Alternative liability: The classic case is *Summers* v *Tice* in which two hunters fired in the direction of the plaintiff, but only one bullet struck him. The court held both hunters liable on the basis that they had both been negligent and, in fairness, should bear the burden of disproving their negligence: 33 Cal. 2d 80, 199 P. 2d 1 (1948); in Canada, see *Cook* v *Lewis* [1951] SCR 830.

   Concerted action: See, for example, *Abel* v *Eli Lilly & Co.*, 418 Mich. 311, 343 NM 2d 164 (1984), a DES case.

   Enterprise liability: See, for example, *Hall* v *E.I. Dupont DeNemours & Co.* 345 F Supp. 353 (EDNY 1972): multiple defendants manufacturing blasting caps.

11 607 P 2d, 943

12 C. Stone, 'Corporate Regulation: The Place of Social Responsibility,' in B. Fisse and P. French, eds., *Corrigible Corporations and Unruly Law* (San Antonio: Trinity University Press 1985), 13. See also C. Stone, 'The Place of Enterprise Liability in the Control of Corporate Conduct,' *Yale Law Journal* 90 (1980), 1.

13 Charles Perrow, *Normal Accidents: Living with High-Risk Technologies* (New York: Basic Books 1984). See also Gaskins, *Environmental Accidents*: 'Where complex events cannot plausibly be reduced to demonstrable causal relationships, knowledge which could be held by (or attributed to) discrete individuals, the courts have difficulty assigning both accountability and compensation' (62).

14 There is a large and growing literature on the problem of causation. In addition to the sources listed in note 1, see Fleming, 'Probabilistic Causa-

tion in Tort Law'; P. Peppin, 'Drug/Vaccine Risks: Patient Decision-Making and Harm Reduction in the Pharmaceutical Company Duty to Warn Action,' *Canadian Bar Review* 70 (1991), 473; E.D. Elliott, 'The Future of Toxic Torts: Of Chemophopia, Risk as a Compensable Injury and Hybrid Compensation Systems,' *Houston Law Review* 25 (1988), 781.

15 'Bhopal Fact Sheet,' Union Carbide Corporation, 30 Nov. 1989
16 Brennan, 'Causal Chains and Statistical Links,' 478
17 *Palmer v Nova Scotia Forest Industries* (1983), 60 NSR (2d), 350. For an account of this litigation, see Bruce Wildsmith, 'Of Herbicides and Humankind: Palmer's Common Law Lessons,' *Osgoode Hall Law Journal* 24 (1986), 161.
18 *Palmer v Nova Scotia Forest Industries* (1983), 348
19 Wildsmith, 'Of Herbicides and Humankind,' 177
20 Brennan, 'Causal Chains and Statistical Links,' 512
21 A concrete instance of such a scenario is provided by estimates that a single leak from the Windscale (Sellafield) nuclear plant in England in 1950 resulted in an additional 250 cases of thyroid cancer. See Stapleton, *Disease and the Compensation Debate*, 8.
22 *Hindustan Times*, 4 Sept. 1988. See also, S. Hearne, K. Carey, E. Barnett, and A. Ahmed, 'The Health Effects of Methyl Isocyanate, Cyanide and Monomethylamine Exposure,' W. Morehouse and M.A. Subramaniam, *The Bhopal Tragedy: What Really Happened and What It Means for American Workers at Risk* (New York: Council on International and Public Affairs 1986), 171.
23 Survey done by Drs Sootymala, Nishith Vora, and K. Satish, with technical help from the Centre for Community Health and Social Medicine, Jawaharlal Neru University, reported in *Indian Post*, 3 Dec. 1989, 3
24 See Peter Schuck, *Agent Orange on Trial: Mass Toxic Disasters in the Courts* (Cambridge, MA: Harvard University Press 1986).
25 The studies are discussed by Troyen Brennan, 'Helping Courts with Toxic Torts,' 48–57.
26 Schuck, *Agent Orange on Trial*, 140
27 *In Re Agent Orange Product Liability Litigation*, 597 F Supp 740 (NYDC, 1984)
28 See 'Weinstein Wraps Up Agent Orange Case,' *New York Law Journal* 200 (1988), 1, 3.
29 *In Re Agent Orange Product Liability Litigation*, 747
30 Steven Sugarman, 'Doing Away with Tort Law,' *California Law Review* 73 (1985), 555, 597–8
31 *In Re Agent Orange Product Liability Litigation*, 611 F Supp 1223 (EDNY, 1985)

32 [1972] 3 All ER 1008 (HL)

33 Ibid., 1010

34 As Lord Wilberforce said in the case: 'it is a sound principle that where a person has, by breach of a duty of care, created a risk, and injury occurs within that area of risk, the loss should be borne by him unless he shows that it had some other cause. Secondly, from the evidential point of view, one may ask why should a man who is able to show that his employer should have taken certain precautions, because without them there is a risk, or an added risk, of injury or disease, and who in fact sustains exactly that injury or disease, have to assume the burden of proving more: namely, that it was the addition to the risk, caused by the breach of duty, which caused or materially contributed to the injury? In many cases of which the present is typical, this is impossible to prove, just because honest medical opinion cannot segregate the causes of an illness between compound causes. And if one asks, which of the parties, the workman or the employers should suffer from this inherent evidential difficulty, the answer as a matter of policy or justice should be that it is the creator of the risk ... who should bear its consequences': ibid., 1012.

35 588 F Supp. 247 (1984)

36 Ibid., 411

37 816 F Supp. 1417

38 [1988] 2 WLR 557 (HL). The plaintiff, a child who had been born prematurely, suffered from oxygen deficiency. While the child was being observed in a special unit at the hospital, a catheter had been inserted into his body to monitor his oxygen level. By mistake, the catheter had been placed in a vein rather than an artery with the result that lower readings were recorded. As a consequence, the hospital administered more oxygen to the child than required. He was later found to be suffering from an incurable retinal condition. Medical evidence established that this condition could have been caused by excess oxygen, but also by a number of other problems that afflict premature babies.

39 [1988] 2 WLR 557 (HL), 561

40 Snell v Farrell, [1990] SCR 311, (1990) 72 DLR (4th) 289

41 See, for example, Gerald Robertson, 'Overcoming the Causation Hurdle in Informed Consent Cases: The Principle in McGhee v. N.C.B.,' University of Western Ontario Law Review 22 (1984), 75.

42 In the Canadian case of Seyfert v Burnaby Hospital Society (1986), 36 CCLT 224 (BCSC), the plaintiff was treated by the hospital for a stab wound and was discharged the next morning. Several days later it was discovered that the wound was much more serious than doctors had originally be-

lieved and required two more complicated operations. The plaintiff sued the doctors and the hospitals for negligence in discharging him early without adequate observation. The problem was that, even had the complications been discovered earlier, much of the additional surgery might still have been necessary. Nevertheless, McEachern CJ applied the *McGhee* case and held that the doctor's failure to observe the patient had at least contributed to the risk of complications. Taking into account the probability that the surgery might have been required anyway, the court awarded the plaintiff 25 per cent damages representing the loss of his chance to avoid the second operation and the longer period of convalescence.

43 In 1987 the English House of Lords reversed the trend towards a more liberal understanding of causation in *Hotson v East Berkshire Area Health Authority* [1987] 2 All ER 909 (HL). In this case, the plaintiff, a thirteen-year-old boy, had injured his hip in a fall. As a result of the fall, he had a 75 per cent chance of developing a deformed hip and a permanent disability. He was taken to a hospital, where his injury was incorrectly diagnosed, and sent home. Only five days later, after experiencing continued severe pain, was the boy returned to the hospital, where the nature of his injury was finally determined. By this time it was too late to prevent the permanent disability from resulting. The trial judge and the English Court of Appeal both held that, while the plaintiff stood a 75 per cent chance of developing the condition anyway, as a result of the hospital's negligence he had lost the remaining 25 per cent chance of recovery. They awarded him 25 per cent of his total loss. The House of Lords reversed this decision on the basis that the plaintiff had not established that his injury was 'caused' by the defendant's fault. It was more probable than not that he would have developed the condition anyway. While the Court did not unequivocally reject the idea of 'lost chances,' it did voice its distrust of statistics and reasserted the view that the plaintiff must establish *on the balance of probabilities* that his injury was, in fact, caused by the defendant's negligence and would not have occurred but for that negligence. See also *LaFerrière v Lawson*, [1991] 1 SCR 541, in which the Supreme Court of Canada rejected the doctrine of 'lost chances.'

44 This suggestion has been made by Rosenberg in 'The Causal Connection in Mass Exposure Cases,' 851, 859.

45 525 A 2d 287 (NJSC, 1987)

46 See *Sterling v Velsicol Chemical Corp.* 647 F Supp. 303 (1986): chemical contamination of wells – damages granted for enhanced risk where a 'reasonable probability' of future injury; *Jackson v Johns-Manville Sales Corp.* 781 F 2d 394: recovery allowed where greater than 50 per cent probability of cancer.

47 *In Re Three Mile Island Litigation* 557 F Supp. 96 (1982): $20 million award-ed for economic losses and $5 million for future medical study and emergency planning; *In Re Agent Orange Product Liability Litigation* 597 F Supp. 740 (1984, NYDC): A portion of the $180-million settlement was devoted to future medical testing.

48 *Anderson* v *W.R. Grace and Co.* (1986, D. Mass.) 628 F Supp 1219

49 Ibid., 1232

50 Osler J in *Rothwell* v *Raes* (1989) 66 OR (2d) 449, 514–55. See also Weinstein J in *In Re Agent Orange Product Liability Litigation* 597 F Supp. 740 (1984, NYDC); *Ayers* v *Jackson Township*, 525 A 2d 287 (NJSC, 1987), 297; Krever J in *Ferguson* v *Hamilton Civic Hospitals* (1983), 40 OR (2d) 577, 618–19.

51 In the case of *Naken* v *General Motors of Canada Ltd* (1984), 144 DLR (3d) 385 (SCC), the Supreme Court of Canada refused to allow a class action on behalf of nearly 5,000 owners of the Firenza automobile, which was al-leged to be defective. The Court reasoned that the various owners had bought their cars from different dealers and might have different rights against the dealers and the manufacturer. They might also have suffered different levels of damages. Because the individual circumstances of all the possible owners were different, a class action was not practical. Thus, eight years after it was begun, this apparently simple case was dismissed. The rules in Quebec are somewhat more liberal. In *Comité d'Environment de la Baie* v *Société d'Electrolyse et de Chime Alcan Ltée* [1990] RJQ 655, the court allowed 2,400 suits to be consolidated. The suits claimed $21 million for air pollution from the defendant's port operations.

52 *In Re Dalkon Shield I.U.D. Products Liability Litigation* 693 F 2d 847 (9th Cir. 1982)

53 For a discussion of these cases and a consideration of the class action in the context of environmental litigation, see S. Chester, 'Class Actions to Protect the Environment: A Real Weapon or Another Lawyer's Word Game,' in John Swaigen, ed., *Environmental Rights in Canada* (Toronto: Butterworths 1981), 60.

54 See the description in the fairness hearing in *In Re Agent Orange Product Liability Litigation* 597 F Supp. 740 (1984, NYDC).

55 This case is fully documented in Paul Brodeur, *Outrageous Misconduct: The Asbestos Industry on Trial* (New York: Pantheon 1985).

56 M. Trebilcock, 'The Social Insurance–Deterrence Dilemma of Modern North American Tort Law: A Canadian Perspective on the Liability In-surance Crisis,' *San Diego Law Review* 24 (1987), 929, 984. The same delays are typical in medical-malpractice cases. See D. Dewees and M. Trebil-cock, 'The Efficacy of the Tort System and Its Alternatives: A Review of

the Empirical Evidence,' University of Toronto Law and Economics Workshop Series, 21 Jan. 1991, 38.

57 'Manville Fund Gets $520 Million,' *Globe and Mail*, 8 Sept. 1990

58 See Martin Cherniak, *The Hawk's Nest Incident: America's Worst Industrial Disaster* (New Haven: Yale University Press 1986).

59 Ibid., 65

60 Brodeur, *Outrageous Misconduct*, 113–14

61 Walter Steele, 'Ethical Considerations for Catastrophe Litigators,' *Journal of Air Law and Commerce* 55 (1989), 123. Steele discusses *Shebay* v *Davis* 717 SW 2d 678 (Tex. Ct. Appeal 1986) in which such an agreement figured as part of a settlement against an oil refiner. See also American Bar Association, Committee on Ethics and Professional Responsibility, Informal Opinion 1039, in American Bar Association, *Informal Ethics Opinions* (1975), vol. 2.

62 The Dalkon Shield Litigation: Revised Annotated Reprimand by Chief Judge Miles Lord, *Hamline Law Review* 9 (1986), 7 footnote 7

63 For details on the companies' finances, see chapter 6.

64 The Canadian Supreme Court itself has criticized the irrationality of the system in a number of cases, including *Andrews* v *Grand and Toy Alberta Ltd*, [1978] 2 SCR 229.

65 S. Sathyam, Principal Secretary, Gas Tragedy Relief and Rehabilitation Department (personal interview, 13 Dec. 1989)

66 See J. O'Connell, *The Lawsuit Lottery: Only the Lawyers Win* (New York: Free Press 1979), 20–1: 'Many in the medical profession are understandably shocked by a system that, contrary to all medical wisdom, encourages accident victims to preserve, hug, and indeed nurture and memorialize every twinge and hurt from an accident.'

67 Ibid., 22

68 For an excellent critique of the failure of national accounting systems to take into account the economic value of unpaid labour (especially 'women's work'), see M. Waring, *If Women Counted: A New Feminist Economics* (San Francisco: Harper 1988).

69 For analyses of this problem, see K. Cooper-Stephenson and I. Saunders, *Personal Injury Damages in Canada* (Toronto: Carswell 1981); D. Reaume, 'Rethinking Personal Injury Damages: Compensation for Lost Capacities,' *Canadian Bar Review* 67 (1988), 82; J. Cassels, 'Lost Earning Capacity: Women and Children Last,' *Canadian Bar Review* 71 (1992), 445.

70 J. Kakalik, P. Ebner, W. Felsinger, and M. Shanley, *Costs of Asbestos Litigation* (Santa Monica: Rand Corporation 1983)

71 Ontario Task Force on Insurance (Pre-publication of the *Final Report* of the Ontario Task Force on Insurance, May 1986), 100–1

72 See J.A.G. Griffiths, *The Politics of the Judiciary*, 3d ed. (Atlantic Highlands, NJ: Humanities Press International 1985).

73 Developments discussed in P. Halpern and J. Carr, *Liability Rules and Insurance Markets* (Ottawa: Consumer and Corporate Affairs Canada 1981)

74 'The Product Liability Menace,' *Wall Street Journal*, 9 Dec. 1976. See also, 'A Life, and Industry, Who Pays?' *Globe and Mail*, 17 Apr. 1986, B21, and 'The Insurance Crisis,' *Maclean's*, 27 Jan. 1986, 26.

75 The following discussion of the insurance crisis draws on Kenneth Abraham, 'Environmental Liability and the Limits of Insurance,' *Columbia Law Review* 88 (1988), 942; Trebilcock, 'The Social Insurance–Deterrence Dilemma'; *Ontario Task Force on Insurance* (1986); J. Fleming, 'The Insurance Crisis,' *U.B.C. Law Review* 24 (1990), 1.

76 P. Huber, *Liability: The Legal Revolution and Its Consequences* (New York: Basic Books 1988). Readers who are tempted to accept these arguments at face value should see the critique by M. Hager, 'Civil Compensation and Its Discontents: A Response to Huber,' *Stanford Law Review* 42 (1990), 539.

7 See J. Cassels, 'Judicial Activism and Public Interest Litigation in India: Attempting the Impossible?' *American Journal of Comparative Law* 37 (1989), 495.

78 In a 1978 U.S. survey it was found that, even after large increases in insurance prices, those costs as a percentage of sales equalled only 0.115 per cent (insurance payments) and an additional 0.054 per cent for additional liability and legal expenses. See Sugarman, 'Doing Away with Tort Law,' 571.

79 Donald Harris, *Compensation and Support for Illness and Injury* (London: Oxford University Press, 1984), 46. For further discussion of this data and estimates regarding non-traumatic injury, see Stapleton, *Disease and the Compensation Debate*.

80 For an extended analysis of the problem of uncertainty, see Kenneth Abraham, 'Environmental Liability and the Limits of Insurance,' *Columbia Law Review* 88 (1988), 942. See also Trebilcock, 'The Social Insurance–Deterrence Dilemma.' These authors have identified a number of doctrinal sources of uncertainty, including: (a) expansion of strict liability (especially in the area of environmental harm); (b) expanded liability for latent harm and 'long-tail' risks; (c) unpredictable jury awards; (d) joint and several liability for harms regardless of the individual defendant's proportional contribution; and (e) relaxed causation rules.

81 R. Brown, 'Environmental Liability Insurance,' *Alternatives* 18 (1991), 18

82 Trebilcock, 'The Social Insurance–Deterrence Dilemma,' 985

83 This analysis is from M. Hager, 'Civil Compensation in and Its Discontents,' 566–72.

84 Huber, *Liability*, 149, 150

85 Trebilcock, 'The Social Insurance–Deterrence Dilemma,' 993

86 *Andrews* v *Grand and Toy Alberta Ltd*, [1978] 2 SCR 229

87 *Shackil* v *Lederle Laboratories*, 116 NJ 155, 561 A 2d 511 (NJSC, 1989), 533

88 Murphy J in *Todorovic* v *Waller* (1981), 150 CLR, 454

89 G. Calabresi, *The Costs of Accidents: A Legal and Economic Analysis* (New Ha-ven: Yale University Press 1970)

90 The 'polluter pays' principle has been adopted by the OECD as a guideline for policy; see OECD, *Recommendations of the Council on Guiding Principles Concerning International Economic Aspects of Environmental Policies* (Paris, 6 Jun. 1972).

91 On the economics of tort law, see R. Posner, *Economic Analysis of Law*, 3d ed. (Toronto: Little, Brown 1986), 147–77.

92 E.P. Belobaba, *Products Liability and Personal Injury Compensation in Canada: Towards Integration and Rationalization*, vol. 1 (Ottawa: Supply and Services Canada 1983), 86. The following critique of deterrence theory draws liber-ally upon this work.

93 See the excellent empirical studies on litigation rates in Harris, *Compensation and Support for Illness and Injury.*

94 J. Byrne and S. Hoffman, 'Efficient Corporate Harm: A Chicago Meta-phys-ic,' in B. Fisse and P. French, eds., *Corrigible Corporations and Unruly Law* (San Antonio: Trinity University Press 1985), esp. 120–1

95 Dewees and Trebilcock, 'The Efficacy of the Tort System,' 112

96 Information taken from T.F. Schrecker, *Political Economy of Environmental Hazards* (Ottawa: Law Reform Comm. of Canada 1984), 45–6, who refers to E. Grush and C. Saunby, 'Fatalities Associated with Crash-Induced Fuel Leakage and Fires,' Ford Motor Company report, reproduced in V. Kirsch, 'Ford Pinto and Mercury Bobcat Fires,' in M. Barzelay, ed., *Scientific Auto-mobile Accident Reconstruction*, vol. 3 (New York: Matthew Bender 1981).

97 *Grimshaw* v *Ford Motor Company* 119 Cal. App. 3d 757, 174 Cal. Rptr. 348 (1981)

98 Cal Rptr., 382, 384

99 It is arguable that the court was not objecting so much to the fact that Ford engaged in cost–benefit analysis, but to the numbers that it used in the anal-ysis. The figure placed on human life is probably too low. Moreover, the costs that Ford used were not those of a safer design, but of recalling defec-tive cars and retooling; i.e., the cost of correcting a mistake that should have been spotted had Ford done a correct cost–benefit analysis in the first place. See D. Luban, *Lawyers and Justice: An Ethical Study* (Princeton: Princeton University Press 1988), 212.

100 R. Posner, *Economic Analysis of Law*, 11–15

101 Ibid., 11–12

102 'Submissions of Intervenors with Regard to Interim Compensation,' in
    Union of India v *Union Carbide Corporation* (12 Dec. 1987), reproduced in
    Upendra Baxi and Amita Dhanda, eds., *Valiant Victims and Lethal Litigation:
    The Bhopal Case* (Bombay: N.M. Tripathi 1990), 268

CHAPTER FIVE

1 Daniel Magraw, 'The Bhopal Disaster: Structuring a Solution,' *University of
   Colorado Law Review* 57 (1985–6), 835

2 See Paul Brodeur, *Outrageous Misconduct: The Asbestos Industry on Trial*
   (New York: Pantheon 1985), 258–63.

3 This was the conclusion reached by a Rand study of the asbestos mediation effort. See D. Hensler, W. Felstiner, M. Selvin, and P. Ebener, *Asbestos
   in the Courts: The Challenge of Mass Toxic Torts* (Santa Monica: Rand Corp.
   1985). See also the discussion in R. Gaskins, *Environmental Accidents: Personal Injury and Public Responsibility* (Philadelphia: Temple University
   Press 1989), 175–8.

4 Indian Penal Code 304-A

5 See Brodeur, *Outrageous Misconduct*, and W. Morehouse and M.A. Subra-
   maniam, *The Bhopal Tragedy: What Really Happened and What It Means for
   American Workers at Risk* (New York: Council on International and Public
   Affairs 1986), 42.

6 M. Galanter, 'Legal Torpor: Why So Little Has Happened in India after
   the Bhopal Tragedy,' *Texas International Law Journal* 20 (1985), 282 – paying 10,000 rupees to survivors, 2,000 rupees to seriously injured, and
   smaller sums for minor victims.

7 Deborah Rhode, 'Solicitation,' *Journal of Legal Education* 36 (1986), 317, 323

8 Ibid.

9 Marc Galanter, 'When Legal Worlds Collide: Reflections on Bhopal, the
   Good Lawyer, and the American Law School,' *Journal of Legal Education* 36
   (1986), 292, 303

10 *In Re Union Carbide Corporation Gas Plant Disaster at Bhopal, India in December 1984* 634 F Supp. 842 (SDNY 1986), 844, n.1

11 Rhode, 'Solicitation,' 317. Rhode cites the example of a particularly 'indus-
   trious' lawyer who signed up 7,000 clients in one week, and two others
   who claimed, respectively, to represent 40,000 and 57,000 clients (p. 319),
   citing David Austern, 'Is Lawyer Solicitation of Bhopal Clients Ethical?'
   Legal Times, 21 Jan. 1985, 16; 'Bhopal Lawyer Disbarred,' *American Lawyer*

79 (May 1985); and J. Riley, 'Surprise Move Cancels First Bhopal Hearing,' *National Law Journal*, 18 Mar. 1985, 26
12 The following narrative is taken primarily from John Jenkins, *The Litigators* (New York: Doubleday 1989).
13 Galanter, 'When Legal Worlds Collide,' 307
14 Bhopal Gas Leak Disaster (Processing of Claims) Ordinance, No. 1, 1985; later the Bhopal Gas Leak Disaster (Processing of Claims) Act (29 Mar. 1985)
15 Preamble to the Bhopal Gas Leak Disaster (Processing of Claims) Act
16 See *Hawaii* v *Standard Oil of California* 405 U.S. 251 (1972); *Pfizer Inc.* v *Lord* 522 F 2d 612 (8 cir. 1975). For an in-depth analysis of the issue, see Lisa Butler, 'Parens Patriae Representation in Transnational Crises: The Bhopal Tragedy,' *California Western International Law Journal* 17 (1987), 175.
17 For a general account of class actions in mass tort litigation, see D. Rosenberg, 'The Causal Connection in Mass Exposure Cases: A "Public Law" Vision of the Tort System,' *Harvard Law Review* 97 (1984), 849; D. Rosenberg, 'Class Actions for Mass Torts: Doing Individual Justice by Collective Means,' *Indiana Law Journal* 62 (1986–7), 561; and S. Williams, 'Mass Tort Class Actions: Going, Going, Gone?' *Federal Rules Decisions* 98 (1983), 323.
18 Rosenberg, 'Class Actions for Mass Torts,' 565–6
19 Galanter, 'Torpor,' 290
20 *New York Times*, 23 Mar. 1986
21 Ibid., 25 Mar. 1986
22 Jenkins, *The Litigators*, 98–9
23 'Carbide has Upper Hand in Negotiations,' *Newstime*, Hyderabad, 30 Nov. 1988

CHAPTER SIX

1 In its 1983 annual report, UCIL reported net equity of only $26.7 million. It had issued a total of 32.58 million paid-up shares at an issue value of 10 rupees, and in 1983 reported accumulated reserves and surplus of 293.89 million rupees. Just prior to the accident, the shares were trading at 29.25 rupees per share (total value of approximately $60 million). Following the disaster, the price of shares fell to 15.8 rupees (total value of $32 million). See also the final judgment in which UCIL's assets are said to have been about Rs. 100 crore (about $60 million).
2 J. Stewart, 'Why Suits for Damages Such as Bhopal Claims Are Very Rare in India,' *Wall Street Journal*, 23 Jan. 1985
3 *Business Week*, 13 Jan. 1986, 37

4 *In Re Air Crash Disaster Near Bombay, India* (1982) 531 F Supp. 1175
5 From 'Union of India's Complaint,' filed in U.S. District Court, Southern District of New York, reproduced in Upendra Baxi and T. Paul, eds., *Mass Disasters and Multinational Liability: The Bhopal Base* (Bombay: N.M. Tripathi 1986), 1
6 Affidavit of N.A. Palkhivala in Support of Defendant's Motion for Dismissal, reprinted in Baxi and Paul, eds., *Mass Disasters*, 223.
7 Ibid., 227–8
8 Opinion and Order, *In Re: Union Carbide Corporation Gas Plant Disaster at Bhopal, India in December 1984*, 634 F Supp. 842 (SDNY 1986)
9 330 U.S. 518 (1947)
10 330 U.S. 501 (1947)
11 *Piper Aircraft Co.* v *Reyno* 454 U.S. 235, 102 S. Ct. 252, 70 L. Ed. 2d 419 (1981)
12 Opinion and Order, *In Re: Union Carbide Corporation Gas Plant Disaster*, 846
13 Ibid., 848
14 *M.C. Mehta* v *Union of India* (1986) 2 SCC 176
15 Opinion and Order, *In Re: Union Carbide Corporation Gas Plant Disaster*, 848
16 Ibid., 849
17 Ibid., 850
18 Ibid., 852
19 Ibid., 854
20 *Islamic Republic of Iran* v *Pahlevi*, 62 NY 2d 474 (1984), 483
21 Opinion and Order, *In Re: Union Carbide Corporation Gas Plant Disaster*, 863–4
22 *In Re Richardson-Merrell, Inc.* 545 F Supp. 1130, 1135 (SD Ohio 1982), modified, *Dowling* v *Richard-Merrell, Inc.* 727 F 2d 608 (6th Cir. 1984), 1135
23 Opinion and Order, *In Re: Union Carbide Corporation Gas Plant Disaster*, 846
24 Ibid., 865
25 Ibid., 867
26 Baxi and Paul, eds., *Mass Disasters*, iii
27 *Rakesh Shrouti* v *Union of India; Bi and Others* v *Union of India* (8 Apr. 1985). See also *In Re: Special Courts Bill, 1978* (1979) 1 SCC 380, which suggests the uncertain constitutional status of special tribunals in India.
28 For an analysis, see P.T. Muchlinski, 'The Bhopal Case: Controlling Ultrahazardous Industrial Activities Undertaken by Foreign Investors,' *Modern Law Review* 50 (1987), 545.
29 Upendra Baxi, *Inconvenient Forum and Convenient Catastrophe: The Bhopal Case* (Bombay: N.M. Tripathi 1986)
30 Opinion and Order, *In Re: Union Carbide Corporation Gas Plant Disaster*, 850

31 *In Re Air Crash Disaster Near Bombay* (1982) 531 F Supp. 1075
32 Union of India Memorandum in Opposition, in Baxi and Paul, eds., *Mass Disasters*, 85
33 *Dow Chemical* v *Castro Alfaro* 786 SW 2d 674 (1990, Texas SC), 686
34 Baxi, *Inconvenient Forum*, 29
35 'Union Carbide Fights for Its Life: Lawsuits Already Seek Damages Exceeding the Company's Net Worth,' *Business Week*, 24 Dec. 1984
36 Opinion and Order, *In Re: Union Carbide Corporation Gas Plant Disaster*, 856
37 Ibid., 865
38 Brief of *Amicus Curiae* on *Forum Non Conveniens* in ibid., reproduced in Baxi, *Inconvenient Forum*, 283, 284
39 S. King, 'Hazard Exports: A Consumer Perspective,' in J. Ives, ed., *Export of Hazard* (New York: Methuen 1985), 9. See also R. Ruttenberg, 'Hazard Export: Ethical Problems, Policy Proposals and Prospects for Implementation,' in ibid.
40 Opinion and Order, *In Re: Union Carbide Corporation Gas Plant Disaster*, 865
41 *Business Week*, 26 May 1986, 42
42 Chambers Hearing, *In Re: Union Carbide Corporation Gas Plant Disaster at Bhopal India in December 1984*, reproduced in Baxi, *Inconvenient Forum*, 309, 311
43 Ibid., 309, 312–13
44 Ibid., 322
45 Motion for Fairness Hearing, *In Re: Union Carbide Corporation Gas Plant Disaster*, reproduced in Baxi, *Inconvenient Forum*, 304, 305
46 *In Re: Union Carbide Corporation Gas Plant Disaster*, reproduced in Baxi, *Inconvenient Forum*, 326
47 *In Re: Union Carbide Corporation Gas Plant Disaster at Bhopal India in December 1984*, 809 F 2d 195 (2nd Cir., 1987), 200; certiorari denied 56 LW 3247
48 Ibid.
49 Ibid., 202
50 Ibid., 204
51 See Robert Lutz, 'The Export of Danger: A View from the Developed World,' *International Journal of Law and Politics* 20 (1988), 629; G. Handl, 'Environmental Protection and Development in Third World Countries: Common Destiny – Common Responsibility,' *International Law and Politics* 20 (1988), 603.
52 D. Robertson, 'Forum Non Conveniens in America and England: A Rather Fantastic Fiction,' *Law Quarterly Review* 103 (1987), 398, 405
53 Ibid.

54 Allin Seward III (Associate general counsel and secretary, Upjohn International Inc.), 'After Bhopal: Implications For Parent Company Liability,' *The International Lawyer* 21 (1987), 695, 706

55 'The analysis followed by Judge Keenan suggests a need for a clear delineation of responsibility between headquarters management and subsidiary personnel, with delegation to subsidiary management of as much autonomy as possible concerning operating matters and restriction of headquarters management to strategy and policy issues': Seward, 'After Bhopal,' 706–7.

56 *In Re: Union Carbide Corp. Gas Plant Disaster*, 809 F 2d 195 (2nd Cir. 1987), 204

CHAPTER SEVEN

1 *In Re: Union Carbide Corporation Gas Plant Disaster at Bhopal, India in December 1984* 634 F Supp. 842, 848

2 The following draws from J. Cassels, 'Bitter Knowledge, Vibrant Action: Reflections on Law and Society in Modern India,' *Wisconsin Law Review* (1991), 109, and 'Judicial Activism and Public Interest Litigation in India: Attempting the Impossible?' *American Journal of Comparative Law* 37 (1989), 495. See also J. Minattur, ed., *The Indian Legal System* (Dobbs Ferry, NY: Oceana Publications 1978); M. Galanter, *Law and Society in Modern India* (London: Oxford University Press, 1989), and R. Djavan, 'Borrowed Ideas: On the Impact of American Scholarship on Indian Law,' *American Journal of Comparative Law* 33 (1985), 505.

3 *Municipal Council, Ratlam v Vardichand* (1981) 1 SCR 97

4 Galanter Affidavit, in Union of India's Memorandum in Opposition to UCC Motion to Dismiss, reproduced in U. Baxi and Thomas Paul, eds., *Mass Disasters and Multinational Liability: The Bhopal Case* (Bombay: N.M. Tripathi 1986), 169–70

5 Ibid., 172

6 Ibid., 85; J. Stewart, 'Why Suits for Damages Such as Bhopal and Claims Are Very Rare in India,' *Wall Street Journal*, 23 Jan. 1985

7 A. Gledhill, 'The Expansion of the Judicial Process in Republican India, in Some Aspects of Indian Law Today,' *International and Comparative Law Quarterly* (1964) 4, 13, cited in Galanter Affidavit, in Baxi and Paul, eds., *Mass Disasters*, 174

8 S.D. Balsara, 'Law of Torts,' in *Annual Survey of Indian Law* 7 (1971), 310, 326, cited in Galanter Affidavit, in Baxi and Paul, eds., *Mass Disasters*, 177

9 Galanter Affidavit, in Baxi and Paul, eds., *Mass Disasters*, 178
10 The system permits some written pretrial interrogatories and requests for documents, but general wide-ranging oral and documentary discovery is not available. Discovery is limited to evidence that may be admitted at trial. It is not so broad as to allow discovery of any unprivileged material whatsoever that might reasonably lead to the discovery of admissible evidence. See M. Galanter, 'Legal Torpor: Why So Little has Happened in India after the Bhopal Tragedy,' *Texas International Law Journal* 20 (1985), 273, 277.
11 Ibid., and M. Galanter, 'When Legal Worlds Collide: Reflections on Bhopal, the Good Lawyer, and the American Law School,' *Journal of Legal Education* 36 (1986), 292
12 Constitution of India, art. 300. See Galanter Affidavit, in Baxi and Paul, eds., *Mass Disasters*, 180; and K.C. Joshi, 'Governmental Liability: An Avoidable Confusion,' *Journal of the Indian Law Institute* 15 (1973), 432.
13 Galanter Affidavit, in Baxi and Paul, eds., *Mass Disasters*, 180
14 *Charan Lal Sahu* v *Union of India* (SCI 22 Dec. 1989), reproduced in U. Baxi and A. Dhanda, eds., *Valiant Victims and Lethal Litigation; The Bhopal Case* (Bombay: N.M. Tripathi 1990), 550, 617
15 Discussed in Galanter, 'Legal Worlds,' 296; study taken from R. Ramamoorthy, 'Difficulties of Tort Litigants in India,' *Journal of the Indian Law Institute* 12 (1970), 313
16 Galanter, 'Legal Worlds'
17 See M. Galanter, 'New Patterns of Legal Services in India,' in his *Law and Society in Modern India* (Delhi: Oxford University Press, 1989), 279.
18 S.C. Thanvi, 'Law of Torts,' in Minattur, ed., *The Indian Legal System*, 630. See also Rajeev Dhavan, 'For Whom? And for What? Reflections on the Legal Aftermath of Bhopal,' *Texas International Law Journal* 20 (1985), 295, 302.
19 Galanter, 'Torpor,' 280. See, generally, Thanvi, 'Law of Torts.'
20 See Galanter, *Law and Society in Modern India*; R. Dhavan, 'Borrowed Ideas: The Impact of American Scholarship on Indian Law,' *American Journal of Comparative Law* 33 (1985), 505.
21 The following draws on J. Cassels, 'Judicial Activism and Public Interest Litigation in India: Attempting the Impossible?' *American Journal of Comparative Law* 37 (1989), 495.
22 See M. Galanter and U. Baxi, 'Panchayat Justice: An Indian Experiment in Legal Access,' in M. Cappelletti and B. Garths, eds., *Access to Justice*, vol. 3 (Milan: Sijthoff Giuffre 1979).
23 *Mumbia Kangar Sabha* v *Abdulbhia* AIR 1976 SC 1455

24 A. Agrawala, *Public Interest Litigation in India* (Bombay: N.M. Tripathi 1986), 20. Special Civil Application no. 2785/79, High Court of Gujarat; noted in M. Menon, 'Public Interest Litigation: A Major Breakthrough in the Delivery of Social Justice,' *Journal of the Bar Council of India* 9 (1982), 150. In *Mukesh Advani v State of Madhya Pradesh*, AIR 1985 SC 1368, the Court accepted a clipping of a newspaper story about bonded labour as the basis for a petition.

25 *M.C. Mehta v Union of India* (1987) 4 SCC 463

26 *Sheela Barse v Union of India* AIR 1983 SC 378

27 *Bandhua Mukti Morcha v Union of India* (1984) 3 SCC 161, 189; AIR 1984 SC 802, 815

28 Ibid.

29 Personal interview with S. Sathyam, principal secretary, Gas Tragedy Relief Department, 13 Dec. 1989

30 'Five Years After,' *Sunday*, 17–23 Dec. 1989, 67

31 Affidavit, Additional Director of Claims, in *Union Carbide Corp. v Union of India*, Civil Appeals O. 3187–8 of 1988 (SC, 3 Oct. 1991), 136

32 'Five Years After,' *Sunday*, 17–23 Dec. 1989, 68

33 Personal interview with S. Sathyam, principal secretary, Gas Tragedy Relief Department, 13 Dec. 1989

34 Plaint in *Union of India v Union Carbide Corporation* (5 Sept. 1986), in Baxi and Dhanda, eds., *Valiant Victims*, 3

35 Injunction Order in *Union of India v Union Carbide Corporation* (17 Nov. 1986), in Baxi and Dhanda, eds., *Valiant Victims*, 20

36 Temporary injunctions freezing a defendant's assets until trial are known as *Mareva* injunctions and are granted when the plaintiff can demonstrate a prima facie case against the defendant and a danger that a final judgment might not be satisfied. In the case of a multinational corporation, not resident within the country, with the capacity to salt away large amounts of funds in subsidiaries, such a danger may well exist.

37 Modification of Interim Injunction in *Union of India v Union Carbide Corporation* (30 Nov. 1986), in Baxi and Dhanda, eds., *Valiant Victims*, 31

38 Applications for Intervenor Status in *Union of India v Union Carbide Corporation* (27 Nov. 1986), in Baxi and Dhanda, eds., *Valiant Victims*, 25

39 Ibid., 26

CHAPTER EIGHT

1 Statement of Defence in *Union of India v Union Carbide Corporation* (10 Dec.1986), in Upendra Baxi and Amita Dhanda, eds., *Valiant Victims and Lethal Litigation: The Bhopal Case* (Bombay: N.M. Tripathi 1990), 33

2 Ibid., 64

3 For details, see chapter 1.

4 Statement of Defence, in Baxi and Dhanda, eds., *Valiant Victims*, 83

5 Reproduced in Memorandum in Opposition to Union Carbide's Motion to Dismiss, in U. Baxi and T. Paul, eds., *Mass Disasters and Multinational Liability: The Bhopal Case* (Bombay: N.M. Tripathi 1986), 66-7

6 UOI Memorandum in Opposition to Union Carbide's Motion to Dismiss, in Baxi and Paul, eds., *Mass Disasters*, 67. See also Reply of the Union of India to Union Carbide's Written Statement and Counterclaim (6 Jan. 1987), in *Union of India v Union Carbide Corporation*, in Baxi and Dhanda, eds., *Valiant Victims*, 109.

7 UOI Memorandum in Opposition to Union Carbide's Motion to Dismiss, in Baxi and Paul, eds., *Mass Disasters*, 68

8 Pursuant to Foreign Exchange Regulations Act, 1973, s. 29. The licence to manufacture pesticides was granted under the Industries (Development and Regulation) Act, 1951, and the Insecticides Act, 1968.

9 Details from UOI Memorandum in Opposition to Union Carbide's Motion to Dismiss, in Baxi and Paul, eds., *Mass Disasters*, 67. See also Reply of the Union of India to Union Carbide's Written Statement and Counterclaim (6 Jan. 1987), in *Union of India v Union Carbide Corporation*, in Baxi and Dhanda, eds., *Valiant Victims*, 109.

10 Details taken from UOI Memorandum in Opposition to Union Carbide's Motion to Dismiss, in Baxi and Paul, eds., *Mass Disasters*, 67. Plaint in *Union of India v Union Carbide Corporation* (5 Sept. 1986), in Baxi and Dhanda, eds., *Valiant Victims*, 7; Reply of the Union of India to Union Carbide's Written Statement and Counterclaim (6 Jan. 1987), in *Union of India v Union Carbide Corporation*, in Baxi and Dhanda, eds., *Valiant Victims*, 109; and Amended Plaint of UOI in *Union of India v Union Carbide Corporation*, in Baxi and Dhanda, eds., *Valiant Victims*, 174

11 Reply of the Union of India to Union Carbide's Written Statement and Counterclaim (6 Jan. 1987), in *Union of India v Union Carbide Corporation*, in Baxi and Dhanda, eds., *Valiant Victims*, 142

12 *Rylands v Fletcher* (1866) LR 1 Ex. 265, aff'd (1868) LR 3 HL 330

13 For a full analysis of the strict liability arguments, see P.T. Muchlinski, 'The Bhopal Case: Controlling Ultrahazardous Industrial Activities Undertaken by Foreign Investors,' *Modern Law Review* 50 (1987), 545.

14 Union Carbide Statement of Defence in *Union of India v Union Carbide Corporation* (10 Dec. 1986), in Baxi and Dhanda, eds., *Valiant Victims*, 72

15 Plaint in *Union of India v Union Carbide Corporation* (5 Sept. 1986), in Baxi and Dhanda, eds., *Valiant Victims*, 6-7

16 *Escola* v *Coca-Cola Bottling Co. of Fresno* (1944), 150 Pac. 2d 436
17 Ibid., 440–1
18 For an analysis of vicarious liability, see J. Swanton, 'Master's Liability for the Wilful Tortious Conduct of His Servant,' (1985–86) *University of Western Australia Law Review* 16 (1985–6), 1. One of the leading cases is *Canadian Pacific Railway Co.* v *Lockhart* [1942] AC 591 (PC).
19 J. Fleming, *The Law of Tort*, 7th ed. (London: Sweet and Maxwell 1987), 339–40
20 *Jennings* v *Canadian Northern Railway Co.*, [1925] 1 WWR 918 (BCCA); contra see *Keppel Bus Co.* v *Sa'ad bin Ahmad*, [1974] 2 All ER 700 (PC); *Barrett* v *The Arcadia*, [1977] 4 WWR 12 (BCSC).
21 [1978] 3 All ER 146; reversed [1980] 1 All ER 556
22 All ER, 150. This case was overruled by the House of Lords [1980] AC 27 on the grounds that the contract between the plaintiff and defendant contained an exclusion clause. Yet the House of Lords confirmed that, in the absence of such a clause, it would have held the defendant liable for the act of its employee.
23 Fleming, *The Law of Tort*, 340: 'a person who employs others to advance his own economic interest should in fairness be placed under a corresponding liability for losses incurred in the course of the enterprise; that the master is a more promising source of recompense than his servant who is apt to be a man of straw; and that the rule promotes wide distribution of tort losses ... deterrent pressures are most effectively brought to bear on large units like employers who are in a strategic position to reduce accidents by efficient organization and supervising their staff.'
24 *Hall* v *E.I. Dupont DeNemours & Co.* 345 F Supp. 353 (EDNY, 1972)
25 *Restatement 2d Torts*, s. 449 (1965)
26 See *R.* v *City of Quesnel* (1987) 4 FPR 393. For a general discussion of these principles in the context of environmental offences, see D. Saxe, *Environmental Offences: Corporate Responsibility and Executive Liability* (Aurora, ON: Canada Law Book 1990), 180.
27 Ashok Kalelkar, a member of the investigation team, in *The Investigation of Large-Magnitude Incidents: Bhopal as a Case Study* (Danbury, CT: Union Carbide Corporation 1988), 26
28 For a description of the companies' finances and assets, see chapter 6, p. 126, no. 1.
29 Statement of Defence, in Baxi and Dhanda, eds., *Valiant Victims* , 103
30 *Saloman* v *Saloman and Co.* [1897] AC 22 (HL)
31 L.C.B. Gower, *Gower's Principles of Modern Company Law*, 4th ed. (London: Stevens 1979), 128

32 *Walkovsky* v *Carlton* 276 NYS 2d 585, 223 NE 2d 6 (1966, NYCA)

33 Ibid., 9

34 Ibid., 11

35 For an excellent analysis of the history, advantages, and problems of limited liability, see P. Blumberg, 'Limited Liability and Corporate Groups' *Journal of Corporation Law* 11 (1985–6), 573.

36 See A. Ringleb and S. Wiggins, 'Liability and Large-Scale, Long-Term Hazards,' *Journal of Political Economy* 98 (1990), 574. See also C. Stone, 'The Place of Enterprise Liability in the Control of Corporate Conduct,' *Yale Law Journal* 90 (1980), 1. Discussing firms that handle toxic chemicals, Stone states that 'as long as limited liability is available as a protection, it is precisely in such areas of substantial risk that we can expect to find a disproportionate population of small, financially unaccountable companies,' (71).

37 As many commentators suggest, limited liability makes much more sense in the context of contractual debts than in the case of tort debts. A contractual creditor is aware that he or she is dealing with a limited-liability corporation and can investigate its credit and demand additional security or accept the risk of insolvency. A tort creditor is a stranger who has no such opportunity. See B. Welling, *Corporate Law in Canada: The Governing Principles* (Toronto: Butterworths 1984), 146–9; Henry Hansmann, 'The Uneasy Case for Limiting Shareholder Liability for Corporate Torts,' University of Toronto Law and Economics Workshop Series (1990), WS 1990-91-(7).

38 See, generally, T. Haddon, R. Forbes, and R. Simmonds, *Canadian Business Organizations Law* (Toronto: Butterworths 1984), 620–7.

39 *Wallersteiner* v *Moir* [1974] 3 All ER 217, 238. Per Lord Denning, the companies 'were just the *puppets* of Dr. Wallersteiner. He controlled their every movement. Each danced to his bidding. He pulled the strings. No one else got within reach of them. Transformed into legal language, they were his agents to do as he commanded.'

40 See J.L. Westbrook, 'Theories of Parent Company Liability and the Prospects for an International Settlement,' *Texas International Law Journal* 20 (1985), 321; D. Aronofsky, 'Piercing the Transnational Corporate Veil: Trends, Developments and the Need for Widespread Adoption of Enterprise Analysis,' *North Carolina Journal of International Law and Commercial Regulation* 10 (1985), 31; Haddon, Forbes, and Simmonds, *Canadian Business Organizations Law*, 639–52.

41 For a description, see Haddon, Forbes, and Simmonds, *Canadian Business Organizations Law*, 642–50.

42 370 U.S. 690 (1962). For an analysis of this case, see Aronofsky, 'Piercing the Transnational Corporate Veil,' 31.

43 *Union of India v Union Carbide Corporation*, Suit for Damages (5 Sep. 1986), in Baxi and Dhanda, eds., *Valiant Victims*, 5–6

44 Union Carbide Statement of Defence in *Union of India v Union Carbide Corporation* (10 Dec. 1986), in Baxi and Dhanda, eds., *Valiant Victims*, 61–2

45 From Indian government's Memorandum of Law in Opposition to Union Carbide Corporation's Motion to Dismiss, reproduced in Baxi and Paul, eds., *Mass Disasters*, 62

46 Ibid.

47 UOI Memorandum, in Baxi and Paul, eds., *Mass Disasters*, 63–4

48 'The Settlement Drama,' *India Today*, 15 Dec. 1987, 28

49 Union of India Reply, in Baxi and Dhanda, eds., *Valiant Victims*, 130

50 Rehfield deposition, quoted in Memorandum in Opposition to UCC's Motion to Dismiss, in Baxi and Paul, eds., *Mass Disasters*, 64; also in UOI Reply, in Baxi and Dhanda, eds., *Valiant Victims*, 130–1

51 UOI Reply, in Baxi and Dhanda, eds., *Valiant Victims*, 120–2

52 Fleming, *The Law of Tort*, 309–10

53 Ibid., 314–15; citing T.H. Tylor, 'The Restriction of Strict Liability,' *Modern Law Review* 10 (1947), 396; W.G. Friedman, 'Social Insurance and the Principles of Tort Liability,' *Harvard Law Review* 63 (1949), 241

54 *M.C. Mehta v Union of India* 1987 AIR SC 975; conditions modified 1987 AIR SC 982.

55 *M.C. Mehta v Union of India*, 1086

56 Ibid., 1099

57 Ibid.

58 Ibid.

59 Ibid., 1086

60 *Globe and Mail*, 26 Feb. 1987

61 Reported in 'The Costly Outcome of Bhopal,' *Washington Post*, 19 Feb. 1989

62 *Globe and Mail*, 3 Jul. 1987

63 Interlocutory Application no. 19 (3 Apr. 1987), *Union of India v Union Carbide Corporation*, reproduced in Baxi and Dhanda, eds., *Valiant Victims*, 156

CHAPTER NINE

1 The information in this chapter concerning the plight of the victims and the relief efforts pending trial is from my personal observations over the course of two visits to Bhopal, interviews with the principal secretary (S.

Sathyam) and other officers of the Bhopal Gas Disaster Relief Department and a variety of newspaper sources.

2 The information in this paragraph is taken from a variety of news sources including: 'The Settlement Drama,' *India Today*, 15 Dec. 1987; 'Bhopal's Unending Agony,' *Asiaweek*, 3 Jun. 1988, 67; 'Five Years After,' *Sunday*, 17–23 Dec. 1989, 66.

3 Indeed, after the final settlement of the case, some of these monies had still not been utilized and there was considerable dispute about their ownership. See *Union Carbide Corp.* v *Union of India, In the Matter of Indian Red Cross Society*, civil appeals nos. 3187 and 3188 of 1988 (SC, 3 Oct. 1991).

4 Personal interview, Bhopal, 13 Dec. 1989

5 See Anil Sadgopal and Sujit Das, 'Bhopal: The Continuing Toll,' *Economic and Political Weekly*, 28 Nov. 1987, 2041–3.

6 Affidavit of R.Y. Durve, additional director of claims, Claims Directorate, Bhopal Gas Leak Relief and Rehabilitation Department; presented in *Bhopal Gas Peedit Mahila Udyog Sangathan* v *Union of India*, writ petition no. 843 of 1988 (available from the author)

7 'Victimizing the Bhopal Gas Victims,' *Statesman*, New Delhi, 1988

8 Personal interview, Bhopal, 13 Dec. 1989

9 Application for Interim Compensation (Bhopal Dist Ct, 26 Nov. 1986), *Union of India* v *Union Carbide Corporation*, in Upendra Baxi and Amita Dhanda, eds., *Valiant Victims and Lethal Litigation: The Bhopal Case* (Bombay: N.M. Tripathi 1990), 235

10 Proposal for Interim Relief in *Union of India* v *Union Carbide Corporation* (Bhopal Dist Ct, 2 Apr. 1987), in Baxi and Dhanda, eds., *Valiant Victims*, 241

11 UCC Submission on Interim Compensation in *Union of India* v *Union Carbide Corporation* (Bhopal Dist Ct, 17 Aug. 1987), in Baxi and Dhanda, eds., *Valiant Victims*, 242

12 Quoted in 'The Settlement Drama,' *India Today*, 15 Dec. 1987

13 Submissions of Intervenors on Interim Compensation in *Union of India* v *Union Carbide Corporation* (Bhopal Dist. Ct, 12 Dec. 1987), in Baxi and Dhanda, eds., *Valiant Victims*, 261, 267

14 Order for Hearing regarding Interim Compensation in *Union of India* v *Union Carbide Corporation* (Bhopal Dist Ct, 27 Nov. 1987), in Baxi and Dhanda, eds., *Valiant Victims*, 253

15 An account of District Court proceedings leading to this petition can be found in *Union Carbide Corporation* v *Union of India* (1988) 6 AIR 206 (MPHC).

16 *Union Carbide Corporation* v *Union of India* (1988) 6 AIR 206 (MPHC).
17 Ibid., 210
18 Ibid.
19 Order for Interim Compensation in *Union of India* v *Union Carbide Corporation* (Bhopal Dist Ct, 17 Dec. 1987), in Baxi and Dhanda, eds., *Valiant Victims*, 283
20 Ibid., 286
21 Ibid., 288
22 Ibid., 287
23 Quoted in *Business India*, 6–19 Feb. 1989, 35
24 'Ruling without Trial Says Carbide,' *Statesman*, 18 Dec. 1987. See also *Financial Times*, 18 Dec. 1987.
25 Union Carbide Revision Application (Madhya Pradesh High Ct, 18 Jan. 1988) in *Union Carbide* v *Union of India*, in Baxi and Dhanda, eds., *Valiant Victims*, 309
26 Fatal Accidents Act, 1855, s. 3
27 Civil Revision on Interim Compensation in *Union of India* v *Union Carbide Corporation* (Madhya Pradesh High Ct, 4 Apr. 1988), reprinted in Baxi and Dhanda, eds., *Valiant Victims*, 338
28 Ibid., 355
29 *Padam Sen* v *State of Uttar Pradesh* AIR 1961 SC 218; *Manohar Lal* v *Seth Hirlal* AIR 1962 SC 527.
30 The attorney general had attempted to support a more expansive approach to the court's inherent jurisdiction by referring to certain dramatic developments in Indian constitutional law over the past decade, especially the courts' activism in public-interest litigation (PIL). However, Justice Seth pointed out that the court acquired its broad and novel jurisdiction and remedies in this area under article 32 of the constitution and not under the Code of Civil Procedure. Indeed, in PIL matters, the courts often refer to the inconsistency of the normal forms of procedure with the approach adopted in PIL. Seth thus concluded that, since the Bhopal matter is governed by the ordinary rules of civil law, PIL has no relevance.
31 *Vidya Devi* v *M.P.S.R.T. Corp.* AIR 1975 MP 89
32 Ibid.
33 See also *Secretary of State* v *Rukhminibai* AIR 1937 Nag. 354, in which the court departed from the traditional rule re common employment.
34 Civil Revision on Interim Compensation in *Union of India* v *Union Carbide Corporation*, in Baxi and Dhanda, eds., *Valiant Victims*, 338, 376–7
35 Ibid., 374
36 Ibid., 378

37 AIR 1965 SC 40

38 Civil Revision on Interim Compensation in *Union of India* v *Union Carbide Corporation*, in Baxi and Dhanda, eds., *Valiant Victims*, 338, 378

39 AIR 1986 SC 1370, cited in ibid., 378

40 One example is the English case of *D.H.N. Food Distributors Ltd* v *Tower Hamlets London Borough Council* [1976] 1 WLR 852 (Eng. CA). In that case a produce operation was run through a network of different corporations, each holding different assets. The technical issue was the level of compensation to be paid on expropriation, a lower level to be paid if the companies were treated as separate entities. The English Court of Appeal held that they should be treated as the same operation and so were entitled to the higher level of compensation.

41 *Workmen* v *Associated Industries, Ltd* AIR 1986 SC 1

42 Civil Revision on Interim Compensation in *Union of India* v *Union Carbide Corporation*, in Baxi and Dhanda, eds., *Valiant Victims*, 338, 379

43 Act no. 46 of 1973

44 Civil Revision on Interim Compensation in *Union of India* v *Union Carbide Corporation*, in Baxi and Dhanda, eds., *Valiant Victims*, 338, 379

45 Ibid., 381

46 Ibid., 383

47 Ibid.

48 Ibid., 341

49 See, for example, Henry Hansmann, 'The Uneasy Case for Limiting Shareholder Liability for Corporate Torts,' University of Toronto Law and Economics Workshop Series (1990–1), WS 1990-91-(7).

50 U.S. Supreme Court said, in *Bangor Operations Inc.* v *Bangor & Arrostrook*, 417 U.S. 703 (1974), 713, 'Although a corporation and its shareholders are deemed separate entities for most purposes, the corporate form may be disregarded in the interests of justice when it is used to defeat an overriding public policy.'

51 See Hansmann, 'The Uneasy Case for Limiting Shareholder Liability for Corporate Torts.'

52 A. Ringleb and S. Wiggins, 'Liability and Large-Scale, Long-Term Hazards,' *Journal of Political Economy* 98 (1990), 574. See also C. Stone, ' The Place of Enterprise Liability in the Control of Corporate Conduct,' *Yale Law Journal* 90 (1980), 71: 'As long as limited liability is available as a protection, it is precisely in these areas that we can expect to find a disproportionate population of small, financially unaccountable companies.'

53 J.L. Westbrook, 'Theories of Parent Company Liability and the Prospects

for an International Settlement,' *Texas International Law Journal* 20 (1985), 321, 324.

54 The example Westbrook provides is the case of *Container Corp. of America v Franchise Tax Board* 103 S. Ct 2933 (1983), in which the Court affirmed the 'unitary' treatment of a multinational for tax purposes.

55 D. Aronofsky, 'Piercing the Transnational Corporate Veil: Trends, Developments and the Need for Widespread Adoption of Enterprise Analysis,' *North Carolina Journal of International Law and Commercial Regulation* 10 (1985), 31, 32

56 Westbrook, 'Theories of Parent Company Liability and the Prospects for an International Settlement,' 321

57 Aronofsky, 'Piercing the Transnational Corporate Veil,' 31, 32

58 Mr S.S. Suri, joint secretary, Department of Chemicals and Petrochemicals, Ministry of the Environment (personal interview, 6 Dec. 1989)

59 Wallace Grubman, director of Unilever, reported in *Economic Times*, 27 Oct. 1989, 8

60 *National Law Journal*, 29 Feb. 1988, 42

61 *New York Times*, 9 May 1988, D4

62 Quoted in John Riley, 'Grass May Not Be Greener for Carbide,' *Nat. L.J.*, 2 Feb. 1987, 3

63 See the discussion of this point in *Pyton v Abbott Laboratories*, 386 Mass 540, 437 NE 2d 171 (1982), a DES case considering the application of the new theory of market-share liability.

64 *Mareva Compania Naviera S.A. v International Bulkcarriers Ltd* [1975] 2 Lloyd's Rep. 509 (CA)

65 *Anton Piller KG v Manufacturing Processes Ltd* [1976] Ch. 55 (CA)

66 'Bhopal's Unending Agony,' *Asiaweek*, 3 Jun. 1988, 66

67 The concept that legal language is open textured derives from H.L.A. Hart, *The Concept of Law* (London: Oxford University Press 1963). Hart also sought to emphasize that there is also a core of certainty in law that does not leave room for human choice. More recent jurisprudential work, however, has emphasized that the 'core' is much smaller and less determinate than Hart claimed; that all law application involves interpretation and that interpretation depends upon ideological, political, moral, and economic choices and perspectives. These claims are prominent in the work of the American Legal Realists and, more recently, the Critical Legal Studies movement. An accessible sampling of the work of the latter group may be found in D. Kairys, ed., *The Politics of Law* (New York: Pantheon 1982).

68 M. Galanter, *Law and Society in Modern India* (London: Oxford University Press 1989)

69 P.N. Bhagwati, 'Judicial Activism and Public Interest Litigation,' *Columbia Journal of Transnational Law* 23 (1985), 561

70 P.N. Bhagwati, 'Bureaucrats? Phonographers? Creators?' *The Times of India*, 21–23 Sept. 1986. Reproduced and discussed in A. Agarwala, 'The Legal Philosophy of P.N. Bhagwati,' *Indian Bar Review* 14 (1987), 136

71 See J. Cassels, 'Judicial Activism and Public Interest Litigation in India: Attempting the Impossible?' *American Journal of Comparative Law* 37 (1989), 495.

72 Intervenors' Submissions on Interim Compensation in *Union Carbide Corporation v Union of India* (Supreme Court of India, 3 Nov. 1988) reproduced in Baxi and Dhanda, eds., *Valiant Victims*, 516

73 Order on Recusal, in *Union of India v Union Carbide Corporation* (Bhopal District Ct, 16 Jun. 1988), in Baxi and Dhanda, eds., *Valiant Victims*, 231

CHAPTER TEN

1 Recusal Petition in *Union Carbide Corporation v Union of India* (Madhya Pradesh High Ct, 13 Oct. 1988), in Upendra Baxi and Amita Dhanda, eds., *Valiant Victims and Lethal Litigation: The Bhopal Case* (Bombay: N.M. Tripathi 1990), 384

2 *Indian Post*, 30 Jun. 1988

3 This particular letter was signed by Robert Borden. 'U.S. Lawyers Trying to Confuse Gas Victims?' *Madhya Pradesh Chronicle*, Nov. 1988

4 Union of India Petition on Interim Compensation in *Union of India v Union Carbide Corporation* (SC of India), in Baxi and Dhanda, eds., *Valiant Victims*, 479

5 *Hindustan Times*, 1 Feb. 1989

6 UCC Revision Petition on Interim Compensation in *Union Carbide Corporation v Union of India* (SC of India), in Baxi and Dhanda, eds., *Valiant Victims*, 405

7 *Hindustan Times*, 4 Feb. 1989, 12

8 UCC Revision Petition on Interim Compensation in *Union Carbide Corporation v Union of India*, in Baxi and Dhanda, eds., *Valiant Victims*, 436

9 *Hindustan Times*, 3 Nov. 1988

10 *Union Carbide Corporation v Union of India*, (1989) 1 SCC 674. 'Bhopal Payments Set at $470 Million for Union Carbide,' *New York Times*, 15 Feb. 1989, 1, 3

11 *Union Carbide Corporation* v *Union of India*, (1989) 1 SCC 674, 675

12 See, for example, *Union Carbide Corporation* v *Union of India*, Civil Appeals No. 3187–8 of 1988, 3 Oct. 1991, 26.

13 Rajkumar Keswani, 'Carbide Has Upper Hand in Negotiations,' *Newstime*, Hyderabad, 30 Nov. 1988

14 *Asian Wall Street Journal*, 15 Feb. 1989. Other news items describing the settlement and its fallout include 'The Settlement Drama,' *India Today*, 15 Dec. 1987, 28; 'Settling for Less,' *Far Eastern Economic Review*, 2 Mar. 1989, 27.

15 *The Patriot*, 20 Aug. 1989, 1

16 P.N. Bhagwati (former Chief Justice of India), 'Travesty of Justice,' *India Today*, 15 Mar. 1989

17 *The Hindu*, 6 May 1989

18 D.N. Dwivedi, 'How Not to Conduct a Debate,' *Hindustan Times*, 16 Mar. 1989

19 'The Horror Continues,' *India Today*, 15 Mar. 1989, 42

20 Personal interview with P. Motwani, chair, Consumer Guidance Society, Bombay, 16 Dec. 1989

21 Interview with S.S. Suri, joint secretary, Department of Chemicals and Petrochemicals, Ministry of Industry, New Delhi, 6 Dec. 1989

22 Upendra Baxi, 'Revictimizing the Bhopal Victims,' *Lex et Juris*, Mar. 1989, 34, 38

23 B. Mehta, *Indian Post*, 22 Nov. 1989, 8

24 Memorandum of Law in Support of Motion, *In Re: Union Carbide Gas Plant Disaster at Bhopal India in December 1984*, MDL no. 626, Misc. no. 21-38, 85 Civ. 2696, 9

25 *Hindustan Times*, 8 Mar. 1989, 10

26 *Indian Express*, 4 Mar. 1989, 2

27 *Union Carbide Corporation* v *Union of India et al.* (1989) 3 SCC 38

28 Ibid., 42

29 Ibid., 43

30 Ibid., 51

31 Ibid., 45

32 Ibid., 51

33 The calculations for the stream of income that the awards will produce assume a relatively generous real rate of return of 3 per cent, the figure used for such calculations in many Canadian jurisdictions. For comparison, the lump-sum ranges specified in the Workmen's Compensation Act, 1923 (Act no. 8 of 1923) are: disablement: Rs 24,000 ($1,500)–114,000 ($7,125); death: Rs 20,000 ($1,250)–90,000 ($5,625). The settlement compensation figures may also be contrasted with the following statistical data: (a) 1986 per-capita

income of factory workers: Rs 10,308 ($644); (b) 1991 per-capita GNP: Rs 6,380 ($398)–7,155 ($447); (c) per-capita net national product: Rs 5,670 ($364)–6,445 ($403); (d) 1990 per-capita consumption: Rs 4,084 ($255). From *Statistical Outline of India, 1992–93* (Bombay: B.S. Gupta 1992)

34 These estimates are taken from the 1988 Amended Plaint of the Union of India, in Baxi and Dhanda, eds., *Valiant Victims*, 197. By the end of 1991 the two governments estimated that they had spent approximately 185 crore rupees ($115 million) on relief and rehabilitation (including some monetary compensation).

35 'Five Years After,' *Sunday*, 17–23 Dec. 1989, 68

36 *Hindustan Times*, 25 Jul. 1989, 7

37 *Times of India*, 2 Dec. 1989; *Indian Post*, 3 Dec. 1989, 3

38 See Submissions of Intervenors on Revision of Interim Compensation in *Union Carbide Corporation* v *Union of India* (SC of India, 3 Nov. 1988), in Baxi and Dhanda, eds., *Valiant Victims*, 520.

39 *India Today*, 15 Mar. 1989, 43

40 '3 Bhopal Victims Freed on Bail,' *Indian Express*, Bombay, 1 May 1989

41 *Hindustan Times*, 18 May 1989, 13

42 'The Horror Continues,' *India Today*, 15 Mar. 1989

43 *The Week*, 10 Dec. 1989, 12

44 'The Long Haul Ahead,' *India Today*, 31 Mar. 1989, 96

45 Personal interview with S. Sathyam, principal secretary, Gas Tragedy Relief and Rehabilitation Department, 13 Dec. 1989

46 *Daily Mail*, Bombay, 14 Apr. 1989

47 *Nishith Vora* v *Union of India*, writ petition no. 11708 of 1985, and *Maman* v *Union of India*, writ petition no. 326 of 1989, 21 Apr. 1989, in Baxi and Dhanda, eds., *Valiant Victims*, 671. Accounts of the argument can be found in *Indian Post*, 22 Apr. 1989, and *Times of India*, 22 Apr. 1989.

48 *Nishith Vora* v *Union of India*, writ petition no. 11708 of 1985, and *Maman* v *Union of India*, writ petition no. 326 of 1989, 28 Apr. 1989, in Baxi and Dhanda, eds., *Valiant Victims*, 672. The accounts of the exchange between the lawyers and judges is from 'Relief for 773 Gas Victims,' *Times of India*, 29 Apr. 1989.

49 These payments, of 3,000 rupees were to begin on 7 May and to continue until next time court met on 15 Aug. The figures included 527 victims with temporary injury and disability; 83 with temporary disability and permanent injury; 163 with partial injury and permanent disability. The amounts were to be reimbursed by the central government.

50 *Bhopal Gas Peedit Mahila Udyog* v *Union of India*, petition no. 9012 of 1989, in Baxi and Dhanda, eds., *Valiant Victims*, 973

51 *The Week*, 10 Dec. 1989, 13

52 Personal interview with S. Sathyam, principal secretary, Gas Tragedy Relief and Rehabilitation Department, 13 Dec. 1989

53 'Faith in S.C. Partly Restored But Bhopal Victims Still Cynical,' *Sunday Observer*, 23 Apr. 1989

54 *Union Carbide Corporation* v *Union of India et al.* (1989) 3 SCC 38, 51–2

55 *Charan Lal Sahu et al.* v *Union of India* (SC of India, 22 Dec. 1989), in Baxi and Dhanda, eds., *Valiant Victims*, 550

56 Ibid., 623

57 Ibid., 611

58 Ibid., 613

59 Ibid.

60 Ibid., 601–2

61 Ibid., 615

62 *Globe and Mail*, 13 Jan. 1990, A-6

63 Affidavit of S.S. Gupta, in *In the Matter of Union Carbide Corporation* v *Union of India*, 12 Mar. 1990, (1990) 3 SCC 115

64. N.D. Jayaprakash, 'Perilous Litigation: The Leak Disaster Case,' *Economic and Political Weekly*, 22 Dec. 1990, 2761

65 *Union Carbide Corporation* v *Union of India*, Civil Appeals no. 3187–8 of 1988 (SC), 3 Oct. 1991, 26

66 Ibid., 34

67 Ibid., 105

68 Ibid., 123, para 59

69 Ibid., 127

70 Ibid., 134

71 Referring to *Sterling* v *Velsicol Chemical Corp.* 855 F 2d 118 (1988)

72 *Union Carbide Corporation* v *Union of India*, Civil Appeals no. 3187–8 of 1988 (SC), 3 Oct. 1991, 94

73 Ibid., 152

74 'Court Orders Union Carbide's Assets in India Confiscated to Block Their Sale,' *Times Colonist* , 1 May 1992. The confiscation applied to UCC's 50.9 per cent share in UCIL.

75 'Bhopal Victims Choke on Compensation Deal,' *The Times*, London, 5 Oct. 1991

76 *Union Carbide Corporation* v *Union of India*, Civil Appeals no. 3187-8 of 1988 (SC), 3 Oct. 1991, 87

77 'Blood Money: Bhopal Gas Victims Get a Raw Deal,' *India Today*, 31 Jul. 1992, 28

78 Indian Council of Medical Research, annual report on Health Effects of MIC, 1990

79 Personal interview with S. Sathyam, principal secretary, Gas Tragedy Relief Department, 13 Dec. 1989
80 *Union Carbide Corporation* v *Union of India*, Civil Appeals no. 3187-8 of 1988, 159
81 'The Long Haul Ahead,' *India Today*, 31 Mar. 1989, 96

CHAPTER ELEVEN

1 U. Baxi and T. Paul, eds., *Mass Disasters and Multinational Liability: The Bhopal Case* (Bombay: N.M. Tripathi 1986), iii
2 *Union Carbide Corporation* v *Union of India* (1989) 3 SCC 38, 51
3 As early as November 1988 it was reported that Union Carbide had spent $58 million on legal fees so far. See *Indian Post*, 27 Nov. 1988. By 1989 the state of Madhya Pradesh had spent $64 million on the litigation, excluding investigation and administrative costs. See 'Settling for Less,' *Far Eastern Economic Review*, 2 Mar. 1989, 27.
4 As of April 1988 the government of Madhya Pradesh claimed to have spent 526,600,000 rupees ($32.8 million) on relief: *Indian Express*, 6 Apr. 1988. As of March 1989 government officials estimated that 800 million to 900 million rupees ($60 million U.S.) had been spent: *Frontline*, 4–17 Mar. 1989, 19. In its amended complaint, filed in early 1988, the government claimed to have incurred expenditures and suffered losses of 2.5 billion rupees ($160 million). See Amended statement of complaint (29 Jan. 1988), in Upendra Baxi and Amita Dhanda, eds., *Valiant Victims and Lethal Litigation: The Bhopal Case* (Bombay: N.M. Tripathi 1990), 193. By the end of 1991, in addition to its own losses, the government claimed to have spent 1.85 million rupees ($115 million) on relief and rehabilitation.
5 *In Re Agent Orange Product Liability Litigation* 597 F Supp. 740 (1984), 761
6 *Charan Lal Sahu* v *Union of India* (Decision on the Validity of the Bhopal Act, Supreme Court, 22 Dec. 1989), in Baxi and Dhanda, eds., *Valiant Victims*, 617
7 Such a principle resembles the regulatory offence of strict liability in environmental law where an actor is strictly liable for harm, subject to a 'due diligence' defence. For a discussion, see D. Saxe, *Environmental Offences: Corporate Responsibility and Executive Liability* (Aurora, ON: Canada Law Book 1990).
8 This is the suggestion of Troyen Brennan, in 'Helping Courts with Toxic Torts: Some Proposals Regarding Alternative Methods for Presenting and Assessing Scientific Evidence in Common Law Courts,' *University of Pittsburgh Law Review* 51 (1989), 1.

9 See, for example, the suggestion of W. Wagner, in 'Trans-Science in Torts' *Yale Law Journal* 96 (1986), 428. Wagner suggests that courts should accept 'qualitative' evidence of causation where quantitative evidence is unavailable. The burden of proof would shift when the plaintiff is able to demonstrate exposure to substantial concentrations of a hazardous substance and suffers an injury consistent with that exposure. Wagner suggests that in order not to overdeter, this principle should apply only in the case of 'abnormally dangerous substances,' where (a) the manufacturer should have known of the hazard, and (b) the costs of the hazard outweighed the benefits at the time of making. The difficulty with this suggestion is that the cost–benefit analysis required by the rule seems to presuppose the very type of quantitative evidence that is unavailable.

10 David Rosenberg, 'The Casual Connection in Mass Exposure Cases: A "Public Law" Vision of the Tort System,' *Harvard Law Review* 97 (1984), 859. See also D. Rosenberg, 'Class Actions for Mass Torts: Doing Individual Justice by Collective Means,' *Indiana Law Journal* 65 (1987), 561.

11 In Canada, the most comprehensive of such schemes is the Quebec automobile compensation system. For a description, see J. O'Connell and C. Tenser, 'North America's Most Ambitious No-Fault Law: Quebec's Auto Insurance Act,' *San Diego Law Review* 24 (1987), 917.

12 See R. Gaskins, *Environmental Accidents: Personal Injury and Public Responsibility* (Philadelphia: Temple University Press 1989), 272–8. See also the model statute drafted by the Environmental Law Institute, in J. Trauberman, 'Statutory Reform of "Toxic Torts": Relieving Legal, Scientific and Economic Burdens on the Chemical Victim,' *Harvard Environmental Law Review* 7 (1983), 177.

13 Law no. 111, 1973. See J. Gresser, 'The 1973 Japanese Law for the Compensation of Pollution-Related Health Damage: An Introductory Assessment,' *Law in Japan* 8 (1975), 91; J. Gresser, K. Fujikura, and A. Morishima, *Environmental Law in Japan* (Cambridge, MA: MIT Press, 1981); Alice Stewart, 'Japan's 1987 Amendment to the 1973 Pollution-Related Health Damage Compensation Law: Tort Reform and Administrative Compensation in Comparative Perspective,' *Harvard International Law Journal* 29 (1988), 475.

14 Stewart, 'Japan's 1987 Amendment to the 1973 Pollution-Related Health Damage Compensation Law,' 475

15 B. Aronson, 'Review Essay: Environmental Law in Japan,' *Harvard Environmental Law Review* 7 (1983), 135; E. Terry, 'Tragic aftermath in Japan's Sea of Death,' *Globe and Mail*, 5 Jan. 1991, D3

16 Stewart, 'Japan's 1987 Amendment to the 1973 Pollution-Related Health Damage Compensation Law,' 475
17 Ontario Task Force on Insurance, pre-publication of the *Final Report* of the Ontario Task Force on Insurance, May 1986), 101
18 Sporting Injuries Insurance Act, 1978 (NSW). See B. Kercher and M. Noone, *Remedies*, 2nd ed. (Sydney: The Law Book Co. 1990), 528.
19 P. Crane, *Atiyah's Accidents, Compensation and the Law*, 4th ed. (London: Weidenfeld and Nicolson 1987), 549–50
20 See P. Huber, 'Environmental Hazards and Liability Law,' in R. Litan and C. Winston, eds., *Liability: Perspectives and Policy* (Washington, DC: Brookings Institute 1988), 128.
21 See, for example, D. Harris, M. McLean, H. Genn, S. Lloyd-Bostock, P. Fenn, P. Colfield, and Y. Blittan, *Compensation and Support for Illness and Injury* (London: Oxford University Press 1984); Jane Stapleton, *Disease and the Compensation Debate* (Oxford: Oxford University Press, 1986); S. Sugarman, 'Doing Away with Tort Law,' *California Law Review* 73 (1985), 555, and 'Serious Tort Reform,' *San Diego Law Review* 24 (1987), 795. Another energetic proponent of such a system is Terrence Ison. His proposal is that the current system of tort law be scrapped altogether in favour of an integrated scheme of disability insurance: 'The theme of it is that the fragmented array of categorized systems of disability compensation that now exist should be replaced entirely by an advanced system of social insurance, together with the retention of voluntary life insurance.
  'All causes of action in tort for damages for personal injury or death would be abolished. Workers' compensation, automobile insurance benefits, compensation for victims of crime, the sickness benefits under the Unemployment Insurance Act, and other government systems involving the categorized treatment of disability would also be abolished as separate systems of compensation. They would merge into the new plan, and the revenues of those systems would be channelled into the new plan.
  'The plan would provide basic income security need in the event of disability or death, and beyond that would provide income insurance for disability.' The revenues of the insurance fund would be derived from: a charge on motor vehicles (replacing automobile insurance); a charge on employment (replacing the workers' compensation assessments levelled at present); taxes on certain categories of hazardous consumption activity (such as cigarettes); income tax. See T. Ison, 'The Politics of Reform in Personal Injury Compensation,' *University of Toronto Law Journal* 27 (1977), 385, 389.

22 Gaskins, *Environmental Accidents*, 292
23 Ibid., 298
24 Ibid., 299
25 Stapleton, *Disease and the Compensation Debate*, 49
26 See, for example, L. Klar, 'New Zealand's Accident Compensation Scheme: A Tort Lawyer's Perspective,' *University of Toronto Law Journal* 33 (1983), 80; R.S. Miller, 'The Future of New Zealand's Accident Compensation Scheme,' *University of Hawaii Law Review* 11 (1989), 1.
27 For assessments, see T. Ison, *Accident Compensation: A Commentary on the New Zealand Scheme* (London: Croom Helm 1980); New Zealand Law Commission, *Personal Injury: Prevention and Recovery, Report on the Accident Compensation Scheme*, Report No. 4 (Wellington, NZ, 1988); C. Brown and J. Smillie, 'The Future of Accident Compensation,' *New Zealand Law Journal* (1991), 249.
28 New Zealand Law Commission, *Personal Injury*, para 172
29 Miller, 'The Future of New Zealand's Accident Compensation Scheme,' 23
30 Brown and Smillie, 'The Future of Accident Compensation,' 251. One problem with the funding arrangements, however, is that they are highly regressive. While benefits are income related, consumers pay equally (regardless of income) as a part of the price of goods and services.
31 B. Dunlop, 'Personal Injury, Tort Law, and Compensation,' *University of Toronto Law Review* 41 (1991), 431, 440
32 At the conclusion of their detailed review of the empirical literature on the deterrent effect of tort law, D. Dewees and M. Trebilcock are led to a 'relatively bleak judgment about the properties of the tort system as a deterrent mechanism': Dewees and Trebilcock, 'The Efficacy of the Tort System and Its Alternatives: A Review of the Empirical Evidence,' University of Toronto Law and Economics Workshop Series, 21 Jan. 1991, 112. Yet the authors also advise against a general disability compensation plan such as the one endorsed here on the basis of 'widely differential severity of the moral hazard problem [referring to the disincentive to avoid the insured risk].' The authors imply that any reform towards no-fault compensation should therefore be developed more on a sectoral basis.
33 Craig Brown, 'Deterrence in Tort and No-Fault: The New Zealand Experience,' *California Law Review* 73 (1985), 1002. There is contradictory evidence in Canada. One study has suggested that the introduction of no-fault in Quebec is related to an increase in the rate of automobile accidents. See, M. Gaudry, 'The Effects on Road Safety of the Compulsory Insurance, Flat Premium Rating and No-Fault Features of the 1978 Quebec Automobile

Act,' in *Report of Inquiry into Motor Vehicle Accident Compensation in Ontario* (Osborne Report, 1988), vol. 2. Gaudry's data, however, do not suggest that the no-fault element was a significant problem or that tort law is a deterrent (even in tort regimes, drivers are insured). Instead, he concludes that the increase was due more to the compulsory insurance of previously uninsured vehicles and that differential risk-rating of insurance is a deterrent. For Australian evidence criticizing no-fault on deterrence grounds, see R. McEwin, 'No-Fault and Road Accidents: Some Australasian Evidence,' *International Review of Law and Economics* 9 (1989), 13. For an exhaustive review of the deterrence literature generally, see Dewees and Trebilcock, 'The Efficacy of the Tort System.'

34 Dewees and Trebilcock, 'The Efficacy of the Tort System,' 98

35 Stapleton warns of the danger of incrementalism – that a limited scheme will simply entrench anomalous preferences for particular classes. This has arguably occurred in common-law countries in terms of the preference for a very limited class of tort victims who are generously treated relative to all other accident victims. It has also occurred, at least so far, in New Zealand in the preference for accident over illness. The problem is that the more generous treatment of one class creates strong vested interests and may block moves to divert funds in order to broaden the class. Stapleton suggests that it might be strategically more sensible to begin with a complete comprehensive system, or indeed, to work backwards by beginning with a scheme that covers only those who are, at this point, not covered at all by the tort system (i.e., disease): Stapleton, *Disease and the Compensation Debate*, 142–55.

36 This tension is one that India is already familiar with in administering affirmative-action programs for caste and tribal groups. As some groups are selected for preferential treatment, others demand also to be included. The process may ultimately transform preferential programs for specific groups into programs targeted simply at need or disadvantage. For a discussion of this phenomenon, see M. Galanter, 'Pursuing Equality in the Land of Hierarchy,' in his *Law and Society in Modern India* (London: Oxford University Press 1989), 185. Another example of this tendency is workers' compensation. Originally based on the traumatic-injury model, most programs, under tremendous pressure, are gradually moving to include occupational illness of uncertain origin.

37 The Environment (Protection) Act, Act no. 29 of 1986 (23 May 1986)

38 Act no. 58 of 1948, as amended by Act no. 20 of 1987

39 Indian Law Institute, *Environment Protection Act: An Agenda for Implementation* (Bombay: N.M. Tripathi 1987), 32

40 See T.M. Rankin, 'Information and the Environment: The Struggle for Access,' in J. Swaigen, ed., *Environmental Rights in Canada* (Toronto: Butterworths 1981), 285.

41 See, for example, the U.S. Emergency Planning and Community Right to Know Act (1986) 42 USC, ss. 11001–50, Supp. IV 1986; enacted as part of Superfund Amendments and Reauthorization Act (SARA Title III).

42 *Charan Lal Sahu* v *Union of India* (Decision on the Validity of the Bhopal Act, Supreme Court, 22 Dec. 1989), in Baxi and Dhanda, eds., *Valiant Victims*, 550, 619

43 Report of the International Law Commission on the Work of its Thirty-Ninth Session, 42 UN. GAOR Supp (no. 10) 1987, 101

44 For a comprehensive description of initiatives prompted by Bhopal, Seveso, Chernobyl, and other such disasters, see G. Handl and R. Lutz, eds., *Transferring Hazardous Technologies and Substances: The International Legal Challenge* (London: Graham and Trotman 1989).

45 As the Sri Lankan ambassador and president of the U.N. General Assembly said, 'developing countries have of late been warned of the price that has to be paid in the form of environmental pollution for industrial development. All developing countries are aware of the risks, but they would be quite prepared to accept from the developed countries even 100 per cent of their gross national pollution if thereby they could diversify their economies': in A.M. Sinjela, 'Developing Countries Perceptions of Environmental Protection and Economic Development,' *Indian Journal of International Law* 24 (1984), 493–4, n. 29.

46 P. Roffe, 'Transfer of Technology: UNCTAD's Draft International Code of Conduct,' *International Law* 19 (1985), 689

47 Draft International Code of Conduct on the Transfer of Technology, TD/CODE/TOT/41 (1983)

48 The developed countries insist that transfers should be considered 'international' only if the technology is transferred across national borders. Developing countries assert that even local transfers may be international if one of the parties is controlled by a foreign entity, for example, a local affiliate of a multinational. While this would appear to be a more realistic assessment of the economics of multinational business, the developed countries object that the application of the code to local affiliates of a foreign corporation is discriminatory and unfairly holds their operations to a higher standard than those to which other local companies are held.

49 OECD, *Declaration on International Investment and Multilateral Enterprises*, OECD Press Release A(76)20, 21 Jun. 1976, reprinted 15 *International Legal Materials* 967 (1976); U.N. Commission on Transnational Corporations,

Draft U.N. Code of Conduct on Transnational Corporations, U.N. Doc.
E/C.10/1982/6 (1982), reprinted 23 *International Legal Materials* 626 (1984)
50 *International Environmental Reporter, Current Report* 392 (1986)
51 See D. Magraw, ' International Legal Remedies,' in Handl and Lutz, eds.,
Transferring Hazardous Technologies and Substances, 240; S. McCaffrey, 'The
Work of the International Law Commission Relating to Transfrontier
Environmental Harm,' *New York Journal of International Law and Politics* 20
(1988), 715.
52 See McCaffrey, 'Transfrontier Environmental Harm,' 715, 723–5.
53 Ibid., 730
54 Phillipe J. Sands, 'Environment, Community and International Law,' *Harvard International Law Journal* 30 (1989), 393, 400
55 *Dow Chemical v Castro Alfaro* 786 SW 2d 674 (1990, Texas SC), cert. denied
111 S. Ct. 671 (1991).
56 Ibid., 687
57 See, for example, the Brussels Convention on the Liability of Nuclear
Ships, Convention on Civil Liability for Oil Pollution Damage, Convention
on the Establishment of an International Fund for Compensation for Oil
Pollution Damage. These are discussed by S. McCaffrey, who suggests
that similar model contracts, or model laws, could be developed that
provide for strict, but limited liability for industrial hazards. See S. Mc-
Caffrey, 'Expediting the Provision of Compensation to Accident Victims,'
in Handl and Lutz, *Transferring Hazardous Technologies and Substances*, 199.
See also Magraw, 'International Legal Remedies,' in Handl and Lutz,
Transferring Hazardous Technologies and Substances, 240.
58 This suggestion is made by J.L. Westbrook in 'Theories of Parent Company Liability and the Prospects for an International Settlement,' *Texas International Law Journal* 20 (1985), 321. Westbrook suggests a compromise
principle of liability, which he calls 'multinational management responsibility,' that measures corporate conduct against acceptable standards of
international investment and management, as evidenced in existing codes
of conduct and investment contracts.
59 As Maureen Bent argues, the failure of the United States to take action
reveals that it is interested only in 'protecting the profits of its corporations at the expense of people living in developing countries': M. Bent,
'Exporting Hazardous Industries: Should American Standards Apply?'
Journal of International Law and Politics 20 (1988), 782–3. On extraterritorial
initiatives, generally, see M. Bothe, 'The Responsibility of Exporting
States,' in Handl and Lutz, eds., *Transferring Hazardous Technologies and
Substances*, 158.

60 See L. Gundlin, 'Prior Notification and Consulting,' in Handl and Lutz, eds., *Transferring Hazardous Technologies and Substances*, 63; R. Lutz, 'The Export of Danger: A View from the Developed World,' *New York University Journal of International Law and Politics* 20 (1988), 629; J. Ives, ed., *The Export of Hazard* (Boston: Routledge and Kegan Paul, 1985).

61 See, for example, OECD Guidelines on Multinational Enterprises; United Nations Code of Conduct on Transnational Corporations; United Nations General Assembly resolution, *Protection against products harmful to health and the environment* (Resolution 3/137, 17 Dec. 1982); OECD, *Decision-Recommendation on Exports of Hazardous Wastes* (OECD Doc C (86)64, reprinted in 142 OECD *Observer* 28 [1986]).

62 See, for example, Bent, 'Exporting Hazardous Industries,' 777; Lutz, 'The Export of Danger,' 629.

63 Bent, 'Exporting Hazardous Industries,' 777

64 Resolution on the Poison Gas Catastrophe in India, 28 O. J. Eur. Comm. (no. C 12) 84 (1985), cited in G. Handl, 'Environmental Protection and Development in Third World Countries: Common Destiny – Common Responsibility,' *Journal of International Law and Politics* 20 (1988), 620

65 OECD Conference on Accidents Involving Hazardous Substances: Hazardous Installations in Developing Countries, OECD Doc. Env/Conf/Acc/88.4 (1987), cited in Handl, 'Environmental Protection and Development in Third World Countries,' 620

66 See, for example, Bent, 'Exporting Hazardous Industries,' 777.

67 Handl, 'Environmental Protection and Development in Third World Countries,' 613

68 G. Handl and R. Lutz, 'An International Policy Perspective on the Trade of Hazardous Materials and Technologies,' *Harvard International Law Journal* 30 (1989), 366

69 World Commission on Environment and Development, *Our Common Future* (London: Oxford University Press 1987), 49

70 These information requirements would involve some sacrifice by multinationals of technical and business secrets. This sacrifice could be reduced by both international and private agreements (contained in the technology transfer itself) regarding the (limited) confidentiality of certain forms of information. Models for such agreements can be found in the information provisions contained in environmental protection legislation of most developed countries.

71 See, for example, the OECD non-binding guidelines on environmental impact assessment, OECD Doc. C(85) 104, and later modification OECD Doc.

c(86) 26; World Health Organization, 'Report on Environmental Pollution Control in Relation to Development,' (1985) *International Environmental Reporter, Current Report* 237 (1987); ILO Draft Code of Practice on Safety, Health and Working Conditions in the Transfer of Technology to Developing Countries. For comprehensive descriptions of these initiatives, see D. Wirth, 'International Technology Transfer and Environmental Impact Assessment,' and R. Lutz and G. Aron, 'Codes of Conduct and Other International Instruments,' both in Handl and Lutz, eds., *Transferring Hazardous Technologies and Substances.*

72 Registries, databases, and information banks on hazardous substances have been developed by both the OECD's Group on the Unintended Occurrence of Chemicals in the Environment and the United Nations Environment Program (International Registry of Potentially Toxic Chemicals). For a description, see V. Nanda and B. Bailey, 'Nature and Scope of the Problem,' in Handl and Lutz, eds., *Transferring Hazardous Technologies and Substances*, 3. For a description of possible hazard-management regimes along the lines suggested here, see G. Handl, 'Internationalization of Hazard Management in Recipient Countries: Accident Preparedness and Response,' in Handl and Lutz, eds., *Transferring Hazardous Technologies and Substances*, 106.

73 OECD, 'Decision-Recommendation Concerning the Provision of Information to the Public and Public Participation in Decision-Making Processes Related to the Prevention of, and Response to, Accidents Involving Hazardous Substances,' 277. See also, United Nations Environment Program, Awareness and Preparedness for Emergencies at the Local Level, described in G. Handl, 'Internationalization of Hazard Management in Recipient Countries: Accident Preparedness and Response,' in Handl and Lutz, eds., *Transferring Hazardous Technologies and Substances*, 114.

74 Described in Lutz and Aron, 'Codes of Conduct and Other International Instruments,' in Handl and Lutz, eds., *Transferring Hazardous Technologies and Substances*, 147–9

75 International Labour Conference, 71st Session, Provisional Record no. 34 (Geneva, 1985), 49–51

76 Thomas McGarity, 'Bhopal and the Export of Hazardous Technologies,' *Texas International Law Journal* 20 (1985), 333, 337

77 See, for example, World Bank Department of Environment, Guidelines for Identifying, Analyzing and Controlling Major Hazard Installations in Developing Countries (1985). For discussions of these initiatives, see McGarity, 'Bhopal and the Export of Hazardous Technologies'; Lutz, 'The

Export of Danger'; and D. Wirth, 'International Technology Transfer and Environmental Impact Assessment,' in Handl and Lutz, eds., *Transferring Hazardous Technologies and Substances*, 83.

78 Jim MacNeill, John Cox, and David Runnalls, CIDA *and Sustainable Development* (Halifax: Institute for Research on Public Policy 1989)

79 D. Weir and M. Schapiro, *Circle of Poison: Pesticides and People in a Hungry World* (San Francisco: Institute for Food and Development Policy 1981)

80 16 Sep. 1987 (1987) 26 *International Legal Materials* 1541

81 *Union Carbide Corporation* v *Union of India* (SCC 4 May 1989) in Baxi and Dhanda, eds., *Valiant Victims*, 539

Index

Page references for names of cases, and material in the notes, are cited in the index only in instances of substantial discussion.